W9-CDI-274

America's
TEST KITCHEN

ALSO BY THE EDITORS AT AMERICA'S TEST KITCHEN

The Cook's Illustrated Cookbook
Slow Cooker Revolution
The Best Simple Recipes
The America's Test Kitchen Menu Cookbook
The America's Test Kitchen Healthy Family Cookbook
The America's Test Kitchen Family Baking Book
The America's Test Kitchen Family Cookbook

AMERICA'S TEST KITCHEN ANNUALS:
The Complete America's Test Kitchen TV Show Cookbook
The Best of America's Test Kitchen (2007–2012 Editions)
Cooking for Two (2010 and 2011 Editions)
Light and Healthy (2010 and 2011 Editions)

THE TV COMPANION SERIES:
America's Test Kitchen: The TV Companion Cookbook (2009 and 2011 Editions)
Behind the Scenes with America's Test Kitchen
Test Kitchen Favorites
Cooking at Home with America's Test Kitchen
America's Test Kitchen Live!
Inside America's Test Kitchen
Here in America's Test Kitchen

THE COOK'S COUNTRY SERIES:
From Our Grandmothers' Kitchens
Cook's Country Blue Ribbon Desserts
Cook's Country Best Potluck Recipes
Cook's Country Best Lost Suppers
Cook's Country Best Grilling Recipes
The Cook's Country Cookbook
America's Best Lost Recipes

THE BEST RECIPE SERIES:
The Best One-Dish Suppers
Soups, Stews & Chilis
More Best Recipes
The New Best Recipe
The Best Skillet Recipes
The Best Slow & Easy Recipes
The Best Chicken Recipes
The Best International Recipe
The Best Make-Ahead Recipe
The Best 30-Minute Recipe
The Best Light Recipe
The Cook's Illustrated Guide to Grilling & Barbecue
Best American Side Dishes
Cover & Bake
Steaks, Chops, Roasts & Ribs
Baking Illustrated
The Best Italian Classics
The Best American Classics
Perfect Vegetables

For a full listing of all our books or to order titles:
http://www.cooksillustrated.com
http://www.americastestkitchen.com
or call 800-611-0759

PRAISE FOR AMERICA'S TEST KITCHEN TITLES

"Further proof that practice makes perfect, if not transcendent. . . . If an intermediate cook follows the directions exactly, the results will be better than takeout or Mom's."

NEW YORK TIMES ON *THE NEW BEST RECIPE*

"Expert bakers and novices scared of baking's requisite exactitude can all learn something from this hefty, all-purpose home baking volume."

PUBLISHERS WEEKLY ON *THE AMERICA'S TEST KITCHEN FAMILY BAKING BOOK*

"Scrupulously tested regional and heirloom recipes."

NEW YORK TIMES ON *THE COOK'S COUNTRY COOKBOOK*

"An instant classic."

CHICAGO SUN-TIMES ON *AMERICA'S BEST LOST RECIPES*

"This tome definitely raises the bar for all-in-one, basic, must-have cookbooks. . . . Kimball and his company have scored another hit."

PORTLAND OREGONIAN ON *THE AMERICA'S TEST KITCHEN FAMILY COOKBOOK*

"A foolproof, go-to resource for everyday cooking."

PUBLISHERS WEEKLY ON *THE AMERICA'S TEST KITCHEN FAMILY COOKBOOK*

"The strength of the Best Recipe Series lies in the sheer thoughtfulness and details of the recipes."

PUBLISHERS WEEKLY ON *THE BEST RECIPE SERIES*

"One of the best books of the year."

MINNEAPOLIS STAR-TRIBUNE ON *THE BEST INTERNATIONAL RECIPE*

"These dishes taste as luxurious as their full-fat siblings. Even desserts are terrific."

PUBLISHERS WEEKLY ON *THE BEST LIGHT RECIPE*

"Like a mini-cooking school, the detailed instructions and illustrations ensure that even the most inexperienced cook can follow these recipes with success."

PUBLISHERS WEEKLY ON *BEST AMERICAN SIDE DISHES*

"Makes one-dish dinners a reality for average cooks, with honest ingredients and detailed make-ahead instructions."

NEW YORK TIMES ON *COVER & BAKE*

"[*Steaks, Chops, Roasts & Ribs*] conquers every question one could have about all things meat."

SAN FRANCISCO CHRONICLE ON *STEAKS, CHOPS, ROASTS & RIBS*

"The best instructional book on baking this reviewer has seen."

LIBRARY JOURNAL (STARRED REVIEW) ON *BAKING ILLUSTRATED*

"A must-have for anyone into our nation's cooking traditions—and a good reference, too."

LOS ANGELES DAILY NEWS ON *THE BEST AMERICAN CLASSICS*

America's TEST KITCHEN

THE TV COMPANION COOKBOOK

2012

America's TEST KITCHEN

THE TV COMPANION COOKBOOK 2012

BY THE EDITORS AT
AMERICA'S TEST KITCHEN

PHOTOGRAPHY BY
DANIEL J. VAN ACKERE
CARL TREMBLAY
STEVE KLISE

AMERICA'S TEST KITCHEN
BROOKLINE, MASSACHUSETTS

AMERICA'S TEST KITCHEN
17 Station Street, Brookline, MA 02445

AMERICA'S TEST KITCHEN: THE TV COMPANION COOKBOOK 2012
1st Edition

ISBN-13: 978-1-933615-95-0 ISBN-10: 1-933615-95-8
ISSN 2161-6671
Hardcover: $34.95 US

Manufactured in the United States of America

10 9 8 7 6 5 4 3 2 1

Distributed by America's Test Kitchen
17 Station Street, Brookline, MA 02445

EDITORIAL DIRECTOR: Jack Bishop
EXECUTIVE EDITOR: Elizabeth Carduff
SENIOR EDITOR: Lori Galvin
CONTRIBUTING EDITOR: Elizabeth Emery
EDITORIAL ASSISTANT: Alyssa King
DESIGN DIRECTOR: Amy Klee
ART DIRECTOR: Greg Galvan
DESIGNER: Sarah Horwitch Dailey
ASSOCIATE ART DIRECTOR: Matthew Warnick
STAFF PHOTOGRAPHERS: Steve Klise and Daniel J. van Ackere
ILLUSTRATOR: Jay Layman
FOOD STYLISTS: Marie Piraino and Mary Jane Sawyer
PRODUCTION DIRECTOR: Guy Rochford
SENIOR PRODUCTION MANAGER: Jessica Lindheimer Quirk
SENIOR PROJECT MANAGER: Alice Carpenter
TRAFFIC AND PRODUCTION COORDINATOR: Kate Hux
COLOR AND IMAGING SPECIALIST: Andrew Mannone
PRODUCTION AND IMAGING SPECIALISTS: Judy Blomquist and Lauren Pettapiece
COPYEDITOR: Cheryl Redmond
PROOFREADER: Debra Hudak
INDEXER: Elizabeth Parson

CONTENTS

America's
TEST KITCHEN

PREFACE

WRITING THE ANNUAL CHRISTMAS LETTER IS A GOOD way of reminding ourselves of what went right, and what went wrong, during the last 12 months. This year, our 21-year-old, Caroline, came back from California and returned to college, a nice surprise. Our 13-year-old, Emily, had a good year in school and was rewarded with our family's first puppy, a whip-smart black-and-white spaniel. Our oldest, Whitney, graduated in high style from the Rhode Island School of Design. Hurricane Irene left us mostly unscathed. It was a banner year for apples. Yes, it was a terrible year for rabbit hunting (snow too deep) but I didn't fall off my horse, get a cold, or lose my mind.

In my business life, however, I think of the last year in terms of our public television show *America's Test Kitchen*. My first thought is, Did we come up with any real game-changers? Well, actually, yes. A few of my favorite recipes are Perfect Scrambled Eggs, an elegant solution for a recipe that everyone thinks they make well but few actually can. (The eggs are finished over low heat for the perfect consistency.) Our Best Simple Roast Chicken sounds pedestrian but is, in point of fact, a true watershed moment in the kitchen. No brining or salting; a preheated skillet was the first magic trick and then the oven was turned off halfway through roasting. Superb and simple. Our Thin-Crust Pizza recipe from Di Fara Pizza on Avenue J in Brooklyn is equally transformative. The dough is left to rest in the refrigerator for up to three days, making a crust that was easy to roll out and packed with flavor. (I liked it so much that I actually went to Di Fara and met the owner, who opened the store back in 1964. He still shows up every day to make pizza.) I also ate bowls and bowls of our Creamy Chocolate Pudding (real chocolate flavor plus a creamy consistency), made the Classic Spaghetti and Meatballs for a Crowd recipe a half-dozen times (no frying; the meatballs are oven-roasted), taste-tested our Braised Turkey recipe that makes its own gravy and solves the problem of evenly cooked white and dark meat, and tucked into our Vegetable Lasagna, which is truly worth the effort (they rarely are).

All of these recipes and every recipe, taste test, and equipment test from the 2012 season of *America's Test Kitchen* are included in this volume for both quick and long-term reference. I think that, as a body of work, they do answer the question, Is there really something new in the kitchen? with a resounding "Yes!" Through sheer luck or, from time to time, by virtue of a truly creative moment, our test cooks do surprise our collective palates while appealing to our sense of deep culinary curiosity. The power goes out, the ovens go dark, and shazam! We discover a whole new way to roast a chicken.

If any of you have spent time on a farm, you will be familiar with the notion that praise is rare and, when actually given, is no more than a nod. You are expected to always do your best so no words of encouragement are necessary. A similar sensibility is expected among our test cooks—we assume that the recipes will turn out well. If praise is to be had, they know that they have to look to you, our readers, for a pat on the back or a kind word. From their colleagues they are more likely to receive a "Did you test..." even after they thought they were long done.

So there you have it. Here is a full season of *America's Test Kitchen* and, I hope, a collection of recipes that will change your home cooking forever. We think that it's good work but you're the only one who can say for sure whether we have had a good year or a great one. Enjoy!

Christopher Kimball
Founder and Editor, *Cook's Illustrated* and *Cook's Country*
Host, *America's Test Kitchen* and
Cook's Country from America's Test Kitchen

America's

TEST KITCHEN

WELCOME TO AMERICA'S TEST KITCHEN

THIS BOOK HAS BEEN TESTED, WRITTEN, AND EDITED by the folks at America's Test Kitchen, a very real 2,500-square-foot kitchen located just outside of Boston. It is the home of *Cook's Illustrated* and *Cook's Country* magazines and is the Monday-through-Friday destination for more than three dozen test cooks, editors, food scientists, tasters, and cookware specialists. Our mission is to test recipes over and over again until we understand how and why they work and until we arrive at the "best" version.

Our television show highlights the best recipes developed in the test kitchen during the past year—those recipes that our test kitchen staff makes at home time and time again. These recipes are accompanied by our most exhaustive equipment tests and our most interesting food tastings.

Christopher Kimball, the founder and editor of *Cook's Illustrated* magazine, is host of the show and asks the questions you might ask. It's the job of our chefs, Julia Collin Davison, Bridget Lancaster, Rebecca Hays, Yvonne Ruperti, and Bryan Roof, to demonstrate our recipes. The chefs show Chris what works and what doesn't, and they explain why. In the process, they discuss (and show you) the best examples from our development process as well as the worst.

Adam Ried, our equipment expert, and Lisa McManus, our gadget guru, share the highlights from our detailed testing process in equipment corner segments. They bring with them our favorite (and least favorite) gadgets and tools. Jack Bishop is our ingredient expert. He has Chris taste our favorite (and least favorite) brands of common food products. Chris may not always enjoy these exercises (red wine vinegar isn't exactly as fun to taste as chocolate or peanut butter), but he usually learns something as Jack explains what makes one brand superior to another.

Although just nine cooks and editors appear on the television show, another 50 people worked to make the show a reality. Executive Producer Melissa Baldino conceived and developed each episode along with Associate Producer Stephanie Stender. Meg Ragland and Debbie Paddock assisted with all the historical recipe research. Guy Crosby, our science expert on the show, researched the science behind the recipes. Along with the on-air crew, executive chefs Erin McMurrer and Keith Dresser helped plan and organize the 26 television episodes shot in May 2011 and ran the "back kitchen," where all the food that appeared on camera originated. Taizeth Sierra, Hannah Crowley, and Amy Graves organized the tasting and equipment segments.

During filming, chefs Daniel Cellucci, Andrea Geary, Andrew Janjigian, Rebeccah Marsters, Suzannah McFerran, Rebecca Morris, Chris O'Connor, Alexandra Pournaras, Kelly Price, Dan Souza, and interns LaShara Darkenwald, Matthew Lawless, Stephanie Pixley, and Alyssa Reppucci cooked all the food needed on set. Cooks Lynn Clark, Lan Lam, Carolynn Purpura, Diane Unger, and Sarah Wilson worked on-set developing recipes for our magazines and books. Assistant Test Kitchen Director Gina Nistico and Senior Kitchen Assistants Leah Rovner and Meryl MacCormack were charged with making sure all the ingredients we needed were on

hand. Kitchen assistants Maria Elena Delgado, Ena Gudiel, and Andrew Straaberg Finfrock also worked long hours. Chefs Danielle DeSiato-Hallman, Sarah Gabriel, Christie Morrison, Adelaide Parker, Kate Williams, and Dan Zuccarello helped coordinate the efforts of the kitchen with the television set by readying props, equipment, and food. Mary Brunco led all tours of the test kitchen during filming.

Special thanks to director and editor Herb Sevush and director of photography Jan Maliszewski.

We also appreciate the hard work of the video production team, including Stephen Hussar, Michael McEachern, Peter Dingle, Roger Macie, Gilles Morin, Brenda Coffey, Ken Fraser, Joe Christofori, Brian Doyle, Aaron Frutman, Bob Hirsch, Griff Nash, Mark Scheffler, James Hirsch, Joseph Battista, Eric Joslin, Atalia Krohmal, and Andrew Morse. Thanks also to Peter Tannenbaum, Nick Dakoulas, and Jesse Prent, the second unit videographers.

We also would like to thank Nancy Bocchino, Bara Levin, and Victoria Yuen at WGBH Station Relations, and the team at American Public Television that presents the show: Cynthia Fenneman, Chris Funkhouser, Judy Barlow, and Tom Davison. Thanks also for production support from Elena Battista and DGA Productions, Boston, and Zebra Productions, New York.

DCS by Fisher & Paykel, Kohler Company, Diamond Crystal Kosher Salt, Cooking.com, Miracle-Gro, and Sunsweet helped underwrite the show and we thank them for their support. We also thank Marcy McCreary, Ann Naya, and Bailey Snyder for handling underwriter relations and Deborah Broide for managing publicity.

Meat was provided by Ronnie Savenor at Savenor's Market of Boston, Massachusetts. Fish was supplied by Ian Davison of Constitution Seafoods of Boston, Massachusetts. Live plants and garden items for the show were furnished by Mahoney's Garden Center of Brighton, Massachusetts. Aprons for Christopher Kimball were made by Nicole Romano and staff aprons were made by Crooked Brook. Props were designed and developed by Jay Layman, Christine Vo, and Erica Lee and Foam Props of Woburn, Massachusetts.

AMERICA'S TEST KITCHEN

THE TV COMPANION COOKBOOK 2012

SOUP AND BREAD *from Scratch*

CHAPTER 1

Loaf pans are piled high in preparation for making Best Whole Wheat Sandwich Bread.

WHAT COULD BE MORE SATISFYING ON A CHILLY DAY THAN A RICH and cheesy vegetable soup accompanied by a hearty, nutty-tasting bread? Two of our favorites are broccoli-cheese soup and whole wheat bread. And although a meal of soup and bread should be an unfussy, straightforward affair, it is often anything but. For one, broccoli-cheese soup is often so sorely lacking in actual vegetable flavor one might be led to ask, "Where's the broccoli?" Cheese and cream tend to dominate this soup to the point that we may as well drop "broccoli" from its name. We wanted to reclaim the star ingredient's rightful place in this soup, so when simply adding more broccoli didn't generate enough vegetable flavor, we did some research—and started by throwing out the rule book on vegetable cookery.

Whole wheat bread often suffers a similar fate: the hallmark of this loaf, a hearty, nutty wheat flavor, is all but undetectable in most recipes. We wanted a hearty yet light-textured sandwich loaf that really tasted like wheat—one that would be perfect simply toasted with butter or as the base for a satisfying sandwich. Join us as we discover how to make these hearty favorites.

WHOLE WHEAT SANDWICH BREAD

WHY THIS RECIPE WORKS: Most whole wheat bread recipes turn out either squat bricks or white bread in disguise. We wanted a nutty, hearty, light-textured sandwich loaf that really tasted like wheat. We started with a good white-flour recipe and worked our way backward to "unrefine" it. We made a series of loaves, replacing different amounts of all-purpose flour with whole wheat to find the highest percentage of whole wheat flour that we could use before the texture suffered. To bump the amount of whole wheat up even more, we substituted protein-rich bread flour for the all-purpose flour. Next, we soaked the flour overnight in milk, with some wheat germ for added flavor. This softened the grain's fiber, kept the dough moist, and coaxed out sweet flavor. Finally, to give our bread well-developed flavor, we turned to a biga (or pre-ferment), a mixture of flour, water, and yeast left to sit overnight to develop a full range of unique flavors.

MOST RECIPES FOR WHOLE WHEAT SANDWICH BREAD lead to one of two pitfalls. They either pay lip service to being "whole wheat," yielding loaves containing so little of the whole grain stuff that they resemble the fluffy, squishy bread you find at the supermarket, or they call for so much whole wheat that the loaves bake up coarse and dense. We wanted to create sandwich bread with a full-blown nutty—but not bitter—taste and a hearty yet soft crumb that sliced neatly.

The cornerstone of any good bread is gluten—the network of proteins that forms when the flour is kneaded with water and provides structure for the loaf. The challenge when making whole wheat bread is that the very thing that gives it character and distinguishes it from white bread—the presence of bran, the outer layer of the cereal grain that's stripped away in refined flour—is also an impediment to gluten development. The fiber in bran has sharp edges that tend to cut the gluten strands, weakening their bonds and making the dough less able to contain gases during proofing and baking. When there's too much whole wheat in the mix, the upshot is a heavy, crumbly loaf. Bran is also what makes whole wheat bitter.

Since baking with whole wheat flour leads to a minefield of issues, we decided to start with a known quantity—a good white flour recipe—and then work our way backward to "unrefine" it. We consulted Richard Miscovich, a baking instructor at Johnson & Wales University, in Providence, R.I., who gave us his trusted recipe for a white flour *pain de mie,* the French equivalent of our sandwich bread.

To see firsthand the effects of swapping in whole wheat flour, we made a series of loaves, replacing a portion of the 3 cups of all-purpose white flour in Miscovich's recipe with whole wheat in amounts from 25 to 100 percent. Because whole wheat flour absorbs more liquid than its refined counterpart, we incrementally increased the amount of water as well to keep the dough pliant and workable. Per Miscovich's method, we mixed the dough, turned it midway through the first rise to remove large gas bubbles and promote even fermentation, and shaped it into loaves. Before putting the bread in the oven, we poured boiling water into an empty loaf pan that we'd positioned on the bottom rack. The water would supply steam—a common bread baker's technique that prevents the crust from drying out. We then placed the loaves in the oven on a preheated baking stone (its heat would help ensure a maximum amount of rise before the crumb set, locking in volume).

Once the loaves' crusts turned a burnished mahogany color, we pulled them from the oven and let them cool. The loaves ranged from tall, airy beauties to compact bricks. In fact, the results followed our expectations exactly: The higher the percentage of whole wheat flour, the squatter the loaf and the denser the crumb.

After sampling slices from each loaf, we concluded that 40 percent whole wheat flour was as high as we could go before the texture began to take a turn for the worse. But we were facing a Catch-22: The flavor contributed by this amount of whole wheat—while decent—was still far from the full-fledged wheat taste we were after, but if we added any more whole wheat flour, the lack of gluten would interfere with the bread's structure.

There was one immediate thing we could try to get the proportion of whole wheat up a notch without impacting the height of the bread or its texture: Substitute bread flour for all purpose flour. Thanks to the boost in gluten development from its extra protein, we were able to bump up the amount of whole wheat flour to 50 percent. But if we wanted to up the count even further, we'd need another approach.

Delving into more bread research, we uncovered a crucial piece of information: Many whole grain bread recipes require soaking the grains in some of the water or other liquid from the recipe before incorporating them into the dough. A prolonged soak—most sources recommended overnight—accomplishes three things: First and foremost, it softens the grain's fiber, thereby preventing the sharp edges from puncturing and deflating the dough. Second, the hydrating effect also prevents the grains from robbing moisture from the dough, which would toughen the crumb. Third, steeping the grains activates the wheat's enzymes, converting some starches into sugars and, in turn, reducing bitterness and coaxing out a sweet flavor.

A soaker dough might be just the thing that would allow us to ramp up the percentage of whole wheat flour. We made another series of breads, incrementally increasing the whole wheat as far as we dared beyond 40 percent. This time we mixed the wheat flour in each batch with the milk we were already using until it formed a rough dough. We kneaded it briefly, then covered the bowl and let it rest on the counter overnight. The next morning, we broke each soaker dough into small pieces that would be easier to knead with the remaining ingredients (white flour, water, yeast, sugar, butter, and salt) and baked the loaves. The results were even better than we had hoped: We were able to bring the total proportion of wheat flour up to 60 percent with no decrease in loaf volume. Even better, the flavor of this bread was considerably more wheaty than any loaf we'd baked so far.

To add even more wheat flavor to the bread, we made another batch, mixing a small amount of wheat germ into the soaker. The germ, which is removed along with the bran during the milling process, is a significant source of not only the whole grain's nutrition but also its sweet flavor. Just as we'd hoped, it strengthened the bread's wheat taste even further, and everyone agreed that we'd taken that flavor as far as it could go. But our work was not yet done. We wanted this loaf to be the best it could be.

SCIENCE DESK

SOAKING WHEAT FOR BETTER BREAD

When developing the recipe for whole wheat bread, our goal was to cram as much whole wheat into the dough as possible to create a seriously wheaty sandwich loaf. Fifty percent whole wheat wasn't enough to get us to this goal—but any more and the bread got too heavy and developed off-flavors. Would giving the whole wheat flour a long soak before creating the final dough allow us to bump up its amount?

THE EXPERIMENT

We baked two loaves, each with a 60:40 ratio of whole wheat to refined bread flour. For the first loaf, we soaked the whole wheat flour overnight in the milk from our recipe before combining it with the other ingredients. For the second loaf, we didn't give the whole wheat flour any special treatment and proceeded with the recipe as usual.

THE RESULTS

The texture and flavor of the bread made with the soaked flour was markedly better than that of the loaf in which we didn't soak the whole wheat.

THE EXPLANATION

Soaking has a twofold effect on the final loaf. First, it dulls the flour's hard, fibrous bran, blunting its ability to disrupt gluten development and produce a denser crumb. Soaking also activates enzymes in the flour that convert some of the starches into sugars, thereby sweetening the bran's natural bitterness. The technique allowed us to pack our bread with roughly 50 percent more whole wheat than most recipes call for and still create a loaf with earthy-sweet flavor and a soft yet hearty crumb.

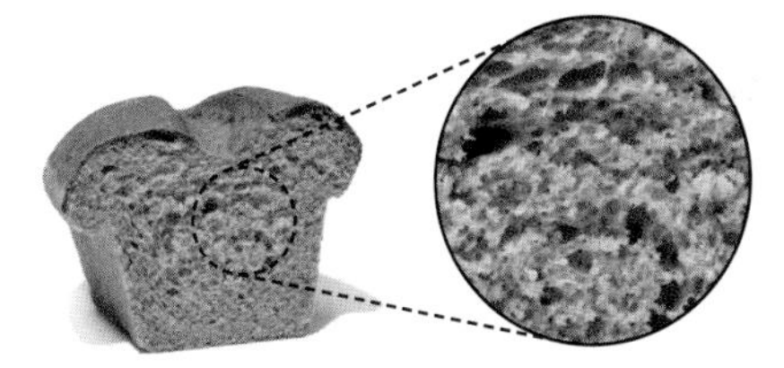

SOAKED FLOUR

Lighter texture, no bitterness

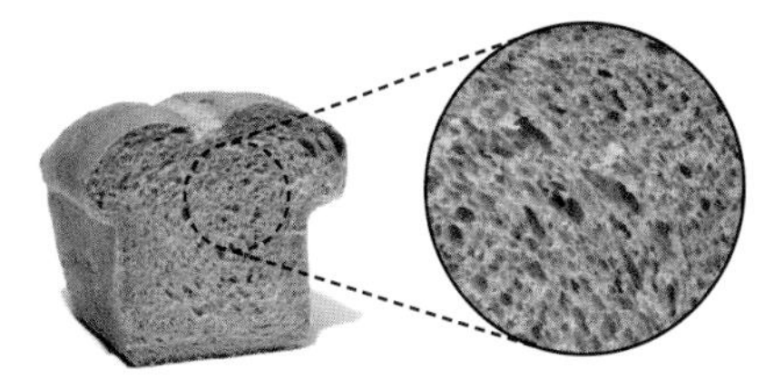

UNSOAKED FLOUR

Dense texture, bitter flavor

We'd baked enough bread over the years to know that the difference between a good-tasting loaf and one that offers the most robust, well-developed flavor can boil down to the use of a biga (also known as a starter or pre-ferment). When left to sit overnight, this mixture of flour, water, and yeast develops a full range of unique flavors that give bread even more character.

Our recipe was already an overnight process, so just before making the soaker we mixed the bread flour and water with a small amount of yeast and left the two bowls to sit at room temperature. But then we thought of something: The biga had used up all the remaining liquid in our dough.

Usually when we make bread, we use cold water to help keep the dough cool during the kneading process—the friction causes the dough's temperature to rise and can lead to an overproofed product whose flavor and texture both suffer. But all the liquid in our recipe was now incorporated into either the biga or the soaker—and after their overnight rest, both would be at room temperature.

There was nothing to do about the biga—it needed to rest at around 75 degrees to properly ferment. But we wondered if we could get away with refrigerating the soaker as it sat overnight and then using it to keep the final dough's temperature cool.

Fortunately, the refrigerator did not inhibit the soaking process one bit, and when we kneaded the chilled soaker with the room-temperature biga the next morning, the finished dough came out of the mixer at an ideal 75 degrees. We then proofed, shaped, and baked the dough as before. The result? A unanimous thumbs up from our tasters, all of whom appreciated the bread's newfound complexity.

Now that we had our basic recipe figured out, there were just two minor tests to sort through. White sugar had been working fine, but when we experimented with brown sugar, molasses, and honey, our tasters voted for the honey, citing superior flavor and complexity. And then there was the fat. Butter was making the bread just a tad too tender and rich. No problem: Cutting back on the fat by more than half was a good start, and then swapping out even more of the butter for vegetable oil was an easy fix.

That was the last batch we pulled out of the oven—a hearty yet soft-textured loaf that sliced cleanly and offered up an earthy, faintly sweet flavor. Admittedly, making this bread was not a speedy process, but the results were worth the wait.

RATING WHOLE WHEAT FLOUR

Whole wheat flour boasts a brown color and more pronounced wheat flavor than the refined white stuff derived from just the grain's stripped-down inner layer, or endosperm. To find the best bag of whole wheat flour for our whole wheat sandwich bread, we tasted five brands in our bread and in pancakes. The flours were milled in a range of grain sizes, from coarse to fine. Their textures in bread corresponded, with coarse flour giving us coarse and crumbly loaves, and more finely milled flour producing a finer crumb. In pancakes, the coarsely ground flours won favor for their bold wheat taste. In the end, only one brand had it all, earning praise for a "sweet," "full" wheat flavor; tender, airy pancakes; and bread with just the right soft yet hearty crumb. Brands are listed in order of preference. See www.americastestkitchen.com for updates to this testing.

RECOMMENDED

KING ARTHUR Premium 100% Whole Wheat Flour

PRICE: $4.49 for 5 lb
WHEAT TYPE: Hard red wheat
GRIND: Steel-rolled
COMMENTS: Sandwich bread made with this flour boasted "sweet, full, pleasing wheat flavor" and a crumb that was "hearty without being too dense." Pancakes earned similar praise; as one taster put it, "this one isn't trying to hide its whole wheat taste."

BOB'S RED MILL Organic Whole Wheat Flour

PRICE: $3.99 for 3 lb
WHEAT TYPE: Hard red wheat
GRIND: Stone-ground
COMMENTS: This flour's "nutty," "sweet," "earthy" flavor worked well for both whole wheat bread and pancakes, but tasters felt that its "soft, downy" texture made it "too light" for whole wheat sandwich bread.

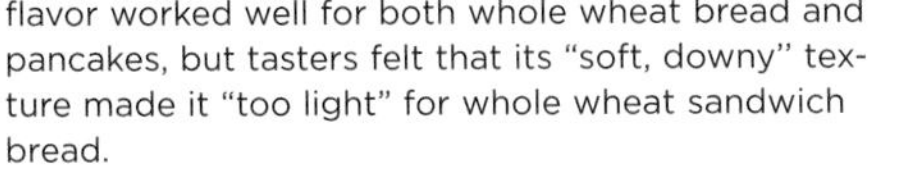

RECOMMENDED WITH RESERVATIONS

HODGSON MILL Old Fashioned Whole Wheat Flour

PRICE: $4.69 for 5 lb
WHEAT TYPE: A combination of hard and soft red wheat
GRIND: Graham
COMMENTS: As the only graham flour in the bunch (this is the coarsest type of flour available), this product carried out a split performance. Its coarse grind interfered with gluten development and rendered the sandwich loaf dense and crumbly. On the other hand, this flour made tender pancakes that, like the bread it created, stood out for their "bold" whole wheat flavor.

GOLD MEDAL Whole Wheat Flour

PRICE: $3.29 for 5 lb
WHEAT TYPE: Hard red wheat
GRIND: Steel-rolled
COMMENTS: "Blindfolded, I would have mistaken it for white," said one taster about this whole wheat sandwich loaf with "muted" flavor. The same theme played out in the pancakes, with tasters noting that their flavor was "nice and clean [but] not overly wheaty."

PILLSBURY Best Whole Wheat Flour

PRICE: $4.99 for 5 lb
WHEAT TYPE: Hard red wheat
GRIND: Steel-rolled
COMMENTS: Bread baked with this last-place flour had an "almost too-fine" texture that made it "soft" and "almost commercial-tasting." That lack of wheaty flavor sank it to the bottom of the rankings in pancakes, too, with one taster advising, "If you want to hide whole wheat flour, use this one."

Best Whole Wheat Sandwich Bread

MAKES TWO 8-INCH LOAVES

The test kitchen's preferred loaf pan measures 8½ by 4½ inches; if you use a 9 by 5-inch loaf pan, start checking for doneness 5 minutes earlier than advised in the recipe. If you don't have a baking stone, bake the bread on an overturned and preheated rimmed baking sheet set on the lowest oven rack. If you don't have a stand mixer, you can mix the dough by hand: Stir the wet and dry ingredients together, along with the biga, with a stiff rubber spatula until the dough comes together and looks shaggy. Transfer the dough to a clean counter and knead by hand to form a smooth, round ball, 15 to 25 minutes, adding additional flour, if necessary, to prevent the dough from sticking to the counter.

BIGA

- **2 cups (11 ounces) bread flour**
- **1 cup water, heated to 110 degrees**
- **½ teaspoon instant or rapid-rise yeast**

SOAKER

- **3 cups (16½ ounces) whole wheat flour**
- **½ cup (2⅞ ounces) wheat germ**
- **2 cups whole milk**

DOUGH

- **6 tablespoons unsalted butter, softened**
- **¼ cup honey**
- **2 tablespoons instant or rapid-rise yeast**
- **2 tablespoons vegetable oil**
- **4 teaspoons salt**

1. FOR THE BIGA: Combine flour, water, and yeast in large bowl and stir with wooden spoon until uniform mass forms and no dry flour remains, about 1 minute. Cover bowl tightly with plastic wrap and let sit at room temperature for at least 8 hours or up to 24 hours.

2. FOR THE SOAKER: Combine flour, wheat germ, and milk in separate large bowl and stir with wooden spoon until shaggy mass forms, about 1 minute. Transfer dough to lightly floured counter and knead by hand until smooth, 2 to 3 minutes. Return soaker to bowl, cover tightly with plastic, and refrigerate for at least 8 hours or up to 24 hours.

3. FOR THE DOUGH: Tear soaker apart into 1-inch pieces and place in bowl of stand mixer fitted with dough hook. Add biga, butter, honey, yeast, oil, and salt and mix on low speed until cohesive mass starts to form, about 2 minutes. Increase speed to medium and knead until dough is smooth and elastic, 8 to 10 minutes. Transfer dough to lightly floured counter and knead by hand to form smooth, round ball, about 1 minute. Place dough in large, lightly greased bowl. Cover tightly with plastic and let rise at room temperature for 45 minutes.

4. Gently press down on center of dough to deflate. Spray rubber spatula or bowl scraper with vegetable oil spray; fold partially risen dough over itself by gently lifting and folding edge of dough toward middle. Turn bowl 90 degrees; fold again. Turn bowl and fold dough 6 more times (total of 8 folds). Cover tightly with plastic and allow to rise at room temperature until doubled in size, about 45 minutes.

5. Grease two 8½ by 4½-inch loaf pans. Transfer dough to well-floured counter and divide in half. Press 1 piece of dough into 17 by 8-inch rectangle, with short side facing you. Roll dough toward you into firm cylinder, keeping roll taut by tucking it under itself as you go. Turn

SECRETS TO SERIOUSLY WHEATY SANDWICH BREAD

1. MAKE BIGA: Combine bread flour, water, and yeast and let mixture rest overnight to create bubbly, aromatic starter dough.

2. MAKE SOAKER: Steep whole wheat flour and wheat germ in milk to hydrate bran and help reduce its bitterness.

3. KNEAD SOAKER: Briefly knead soaker, then chill overnight to ensure that final dough reaches proper temperature.

4. COMBINE BIGA AND SOAKER: Tear soaker into 1-inch pieces and mix with biga (and remaining ingredients). Knead, then let rise for 45 minutes.

5. FOLD AND TURN: Deflate center of dough, then fold it in on itself. Turn bowl 90 degrees; fold again. Repeat for total of 8 folds. Let rise for 45 minutes.

6. DIVIDE AND PRESS: Halve dough and pat each portion into 17 by 8-inch rectangle, with short side facing you.

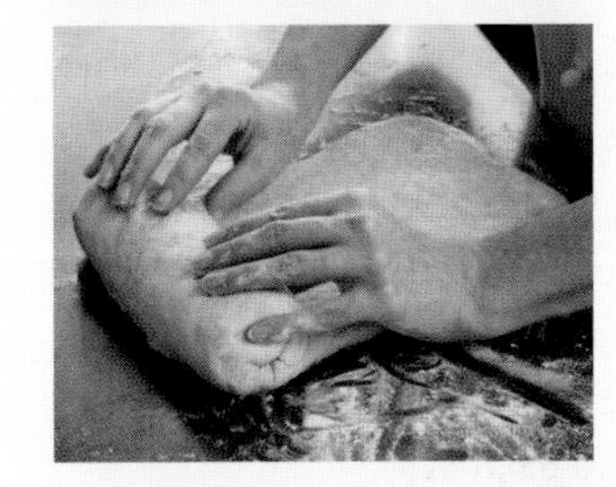

7. ROLL: Roll each sheet toward you into tight cylinder. Keep roll taut by tucking it under itself as you go. Pinch seams to seal.

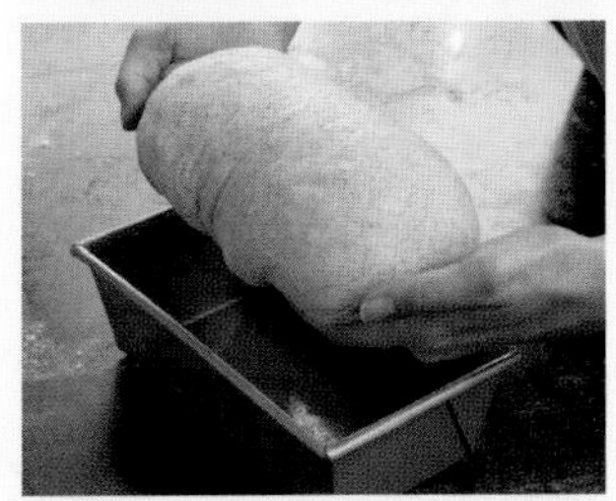

8. PLACE AND RISE: Place each loaf seam side down in prepared loaf pans. Let dough rise until almost doubled in size, 1 to 1½ hours.

9. ADD STEAM: Place empty loaf pan on lower oven rack and fill with boiling water. Steam prevents crust from drying out before loaves expand.

10. SLASH TOPS: Using serrated knife blade, make shallow slash down center of each loaf to stop bread from tearing randomly when it rises. Bake 40 to 50 minutes.

loaf seam side up and pinch it closed. Place loaf seam side down in prepared pan, pressing gently into corners. Repeat with second piece of dough. Cover loaves loosely with greased plastic and let rise at room temperature until nearly doubled in size, 1 to 1½ hours (top of loaves should rise about 1 inch over lip of pan).

6. One hour before baking, adjust oven racks to middle and lowest positions, place baking stone on middle rack, place empty loaf pan or other heatproof pan on bottom rack, and heat oven to 400 degrees. Bring 2 cups water to boil on stovetop. Using sharp serrated knife or single-edge razor blade, make one ¼-inch-deep slash lengthwise down center of each loaf. Working quickly, pour boiling water into empty loaf pan in oven and set loaves on baking stone. Reduce oven temperature to 350 degrees. Bake until crust is dark brown and loaves register 200 degrees, 40 to 50 minutes, rotating loaves front to back and side to side halfway through baking. Transfer pans to wire rack and let cool for 5 minutes. Remove loaves from pans, return to rack, and let cool to room temperature, about 2 hours, before slicing and serving. (Bread can be wrapped in double layer of plastic wrap and stored at room temperature for up to 3 days. Wrapped with additional layer of aluminum foil, bread can be frozen for up to 1 month.)

NOTES FROM THE TEST KITCHEN

WHOLE WHEAT EXTREMES

Whole wheat sandwich breads typically fall into one of two categories: squishy, Wonder Bread–like loaves or rock-solid specimens that are dense enough to support a brick.

LIGHTWEIGHT

HEAVYWEIGHT

RATING PULLMAN LOAF PANS

A Pullman loaf pan is a bread pan with a slide-on lid; it produces a squared-off loaf with a compact crumb that's perfect for sandwiches. The pans are commonly associated with the cramped kitchens of 19th-century Pullman railcars, where the flat-topped breads the pans produced were easier to stack than domed loaves baked in traditional pans. We baked sandwich bread in three models to see how each pan performed. We can't recommend two of the pans—both made from uncoated steel—at all. Both reacted with the canola oil-based cooking spray we used, discoloring and giving off a fishy odor. Fortunately, the nonstick aluminized steel model in our lineup produced perfectly baked bread that released easily, with no fishy odor, plus it cleaned up in a snap. Brands are listed in order of preference. See www.americastestkitchen.com for updates to this testing.

HIGHLY RECOMMENDED

USA PAN 13 by 4-inch Pullman Loaf Pan and Cover
(model #1160PM)
PRICE: $33.95
COMMENTS: The bread from this pan emerged with the proper tight crumb and golden-brown crust. The lid slid on and off easily, and the nonstick coating released perfectly, making the pan a snap to clean. Created with lightweight material, it was simple to maneuver in and out of the oven.

NOT RECOMMENDED

MATFER BOURGEAT 15¾ by 4-inch Bread Pan with Cover
(model #340841)
PRICE: $71.95
COMMENTS: This French-made professional-quality pan was slightly longer than its American counterparts and required extra dough. Its dark surface baked the bread faster and darker than our winner, though it was still acceptable. The canola spray reacted with the iron in the steel, giving off a slight fishy smell. Furthermore, the pan became mottled after one use. While this pricey pan did not come with instructions, we later learned that it requires extensive seasoning and careful handling to prevent discoloration and rust.

PADERNO World Cuisine Blue Steel Bread Pan with Cover
(model #41778-35)
PRICE: $48.88
COMMENTS: The moment we opened the oven door to remove this pan, we were hit by the strong smell of fish. Despite a coating of nonstick spray on the pan, the bread stuck in some places, making it difficult to remove, and the stuck bits of bread that were jammed into the sharp corners were nearly impossible to extract. The pan came with no care instructions, but we later learned that blue steel requires seasoning and extensive care for best performance.

BROCCOLI-CHEESE SOUP

✓ WHY THIS RECIPE WORKS: We were after a soup with pure broccoli flavor that wasn't hiding behind the cream or the cheese. Overcooked broccoli has a sulfurous flavor, but we discovered when we cooked our broccoli beyond the point of just overcooked—for a full hour—those sulfur-containing compounds broke down, leaving behind intense, nutty broccoli. Its texture was fairly soft, but that was perfect for use in a soup. Adding baking soda to the pot sped up the process, shortening the broccoli's cooking time to a mere 20 minutes. A little spinach lent bright green color to the soup without taking over the flavor. After adding cheddar and Parmesan, we had a soup so full of flavor and richness that it didn't even need the cream.

IF TRUTH-IN-ADVERTISING RULES APPLIED TO RECIPE titles, broccoli-cheese soup would be called "Cheesy Cream of Cheese Soup Garnished with Broccoli." Giving the broccoli top billing might lure you into thinking the dish will be full of this nutrient-rich vegetable, but most times you can barely detect its presence. We were determined to create a soup in which the cheese enhanced, rather than camouflaged, one of our favorite vegetables.

In most cases, the amount of broccoli called for is paltry—usually a mere pound hidden beneath 2 to 3 cups of sharp cheddar and a glut of cream. The most obvious first step to try, then, was to reverse the proportions of broccoli and cheese. Following the typical approach but upping the broccoli to a full 2 pounds, we blanched the broccoli while sweating onions and other aromatics in another pot. We combined these ingredients with chicken broth and some of the broccoli cooking water, pureed them, returned the liquid to the pot, and stirred in a cup of shredded cheese and ¼ cup of cream. But to our chagrin, tasters frowned as they took their first bites. Despite the soup's lovely bright green color, its broccoli flavor hadn't much improved.

Roasting the broccoli until browned before combining it with the other ingredients would be a surefire way to bump up its flavor—but it would also muddy the soup's color. Plus, we were reluctant to take the trouble. So it was back to the books. Eventually we came across something completely different and almost comically counterintuitive: Cook the ever-living daylights out of the broccoli. We'd always thought overcooking intensified broccoli's off-putting sulfur flavors, so we probably would have dismissed this method had it not been for the source: Alice Waters. The renowned California chef is famous for getting the best out of fresh produce. Following her technique, we briefly sautéed the chopped florets and stalks in a little butter, added about a cup of water, covered the pot, and let it simmer for a full hour. The results looked like olive-drab mush (so much for not muddying the appearance), but the flavor was remarkably improved—complex, with no trace of sulfur.

Curious, we queried our science editor for an explanation. It turns out that when moist heat breaks down the vegetable's cell walls, it triggers the formation of sulfur-containing compounds called isothiocyanates. The longer the broccoli is cooked, the more these compounds are produced and the more pungent the broccoli's taste—but only up to a point. With really prolonged heating, the isothiocyanates break down into less pungent compounds, the most volatile of which eventually evaporate, leaving only nutty, sweet flavors behind.

This was unquestionably a breakthrough. When we incorporated the super-overcooked broccoli into our soup, its flavor stood up nicely against the rich, sharp cheddar. But all wasn't perfect: The soup now had an unappealing gray cast, and we weren't keen on minding the pot for an hour. Our science editor had a suggestion: Add baking soda to the cooking water. He predicted just a pinch would accelerate the breakdown of the broccoli's cell walls and more quickly transform the sulfurous compounds into more pleasant ones. When we tried his suggestion, the results were striking. After 20 minutes of braising, the broccoli was fully softened—and just as sweet and nutty as the long-cooked batch. Only one problem remained: the soup's drab color.

This time the inspiration for our solution came not from Alice Waters but from Popeye. Just 2 ounces of fresh baby spinach added right before we pureed the soup ensured a bright color and also enhanced the vegetable flavor.

BROCCOLI-CHEESE SOUP

As for the cheese, we found that incorporating just 3 ounces of cheddar, along with half that amount of Parmesan, gave the soup enough cheesy flavor without making it heavy. And the cream? Everyone agreed that the soup was plenty rich without it. Once we floated a few crisp croutons on top of each portion, we knew our broccoli soup makeover was complete.

Broccoli-Cheese Soup

SERVES 6 TO 8

To make a vegetarian version of this soup, substitute vegetable broth for the chicken broth.

- **2 tablespoons unsalted butter**
- **2 pounds broccoli, florets chopped into 1-inch pieces, stalks peeled and sliced ¼ inch thick**
- **1 onion, chopped coarse**
- **2 garlic cloves, minced**
- **1½ teaspoons dry mustard**
- **Pinch cayenne pepper**
- **Salt and pepper**
- **3–4 cups water**
- **¼ teaspoon baking soda**
- **2 cups low-sodium chicken broth**
- **2 ounces (2 cups) baby spinach**
- **3 ounces sharp cheddar cheese, shredded (¾ cup)**
- **1½ ounces Parmesan cheese, grated (¾ cup), plus extra for serving**
- **1 recipe Buttery Croutons (page 42)**

1. Melt butter in Dutch oven over medium-high heat. Add broccoli, onion, garlic, mustard, cayenne, and 1 teaspoon salt and cook, stirring frequently, until fragrant, about 6 minutes. Add 1 cup water and baking soda. Bring to simmer, cover, and cook until broccoli is very soft, about 20 minutes, stirring once during cooking.

2. Add broth and 2 cups water. When mixture begins to simmer, stir in spinach and cook until wilted, about 1 minute. Transfer half of soup to blender, add cheddar and Parmesan, and process until smooth, about 1 minute. Transfer soup to bowl and repeat with remaining soup. Return soup to Dutch oven, place over medium heat and bring to simmer. Adjust consistency of soup with up to 1 cup water. Season with salt and pepper to taste. Serve, passing extra Parmesan separately.

SIMPLY *Chicken*

CHAPTER 2

In making Quick Chicken Fricassee, Julia explains how an egg yolk whisked into sour cream gives the sauce a tangy, silky-smooth finish.

TODAY'S CHICKEN DISHES ARE MEANT TO BE QUICK AND EASY, A WAY to get dinner on the table with a minimum amount of time and fuss. But convenience often comes at the expense of flavor. Traditional chicken dishes, the sort our grandmothers used to make, tend to be rich, flavorful, and satisfying—but they can also take all day to prepare, which is probably why they took center stage at Sunday dinner. Take chicken fricassee, the classic French dish of poached chicken in a rich cream sauce; many recipes brown the chicken prior to braising it, a time-consuming addition to an already lengthy preparation requiring poaching the chicken pieces, mushrooms, and onions, and reducing the cooking liquid to make a sauce. We wanted to find a way to streamline this recipe and punch up the flavors while we were at it.

Roast chicken is another old-fashioned favorite that's better suited to Sunday supper than Tuesday night dinner. From years of experience we know that salting or brining the bird is the most reliable way to ensure juicy, well-seasoned meat. Great, if you can plan ahead and have the time. But we wanted dinner on the table in an hour, so we set out to find a faster way to get juicy, tender chicken.

CHICKEN FRICASSEE

✓ WHY THIS RECIPE WORKS: In search of a streamlined technique that would give this classic French braise weeknight potential and a brighter, more complex sauce, we replaced the bone-in chicken parts with convenient boneless, skinless breasts and thighs. We found two ways to add back the richness that we'd lost when we opted for boneless chicken: We browned the meat in a combination of butter and oil, and we browned the vegetables until they developed their own fond to serve as the base of the sauce. Increasing the amount of glutamate-rich mushrooms boosted the fricassee's meaty flavor. As a final step, we finished the sauce with sour cream, which added body and a pleasant tang. Whisking an egg yolk into the sour cream thickened the sauce and made it incredibly silky.

THERE'S A REASON LEGENDARY CHEFS FROM AUGUSTE Escoffier to Fannie Farmer to Julia Child and James Beard published recipes for chicken fricassee. Made the classic French way by poaching chicken pieces, mushrooms, and pearl onions in stock and saucing them with a cream-enriched reduction of the cooking liquid, the dish captures both richness and clean chicken flavor all on one platter. There's also a reason the dish has fallen out of favor: It's a bit bland for modern tastes, and many versions feel fussy and time-consuming. Still, we were intrigued and had ideas for a few refinements—namely, a streamlined technique that would give the dish weeknight potential, and a brighter, more complex sauce.

First up: The thick bone-in chicken parts would have to go. They took up too much room to brown in a single batch and required nearly 30 minutes of poaching. Instead, we decided to try the busy cook's favorite timesaver: boneless, skinless breasts and thighs. These thinner pieces of meat not only fit nicely into our 12-inch skillet, but they were mostly cooked through after the initial sear.

That was the good news. The bad news was that doing without skin and bones meant losing the chicken's two primary sources of flavor. Browning the meat in a combination of butter and oil added back some richness. But predictably, sautéing the skinless meat left very few browned bits (called fond) in the pan for creating a flavorful sauce.

In the past we've built up savory flavor by thoroughly browning vegetables until they develop their own fond. We took the same tack here, but made two key changes to the traditional fricassee components: First, we swapped the pearl onions for a regular chopped onion, which would provide more surface area for browning and caramelization. Second, because mushrooms are an excellent source of glutamates—compounds that significantly boost meaty umami flavor in food—we upped their amount from 12 ounces to a full pound.

Sure enough, sautéing these ingredients for eight to 10 minutes with a splash of white wine coated the pan with a layer of dark, browned bits. Just before deglazing with chicken broth, we stirred in a little minced garlic as well as a tablespoon of flour to help gently thicken the sauce. Finally, we slid the chicken back into the skillet to finish cooking. Within 10 minutes, the breast meat was up to temperature and the poaching liquid had reduced to savory gravy.

The final step was to finish the sauce with dairy. Our tasters found that the traditional choice of heavy cream muted the flavors we had so carefully built up. Sour cream was the best choice, adding body and pleasant tang. To create a satiny smooth consistency, we decided to try a technique popular in many early fricassee recipes: whisking an egg yolk into the sauce. Yolks contain the powerful emulsifier lecithin, and we were guessing it would have the same impact on our gravy as it does in mayonnaise—keeping fat (in this case from the sour cream) suspended in water. We whisked a single yolk into the sour cream before incorporating the mixture into the thickened broth, and were pleased to find that it turned the sauce incredibly silky. All that was left was to add a squeeze of lemon juice, ground nutmeg, and minced tarragon to lend a little more complexity.

Earlier generations might not consider our streamlined approach a true "fricassee," but they couldn't take issue with this quick dish's deep, rich chicken flavor and smooth, creamy sauce.

QUICK CHICKEN FRICASSEE

Quick Chicken Fricassee

SERVES 4 TO 6

Two tablespoons of chopped fresh parsley may be substituted for the tarragon in this recipe.

- **2 pounds boneless, skinless chicken breasts and/or thighs, trimmed**
- **Salt and pepper**
- **1 tablespoon unsalted butter**
- **1 tablespoon olive oil**
- **1 pound cremini mushrooms, trimmed and sliced ¼ inch thick**
- **1 onion, chopped fine**
- **¼ cup dry white wine**
- **1 tablespoon all-purpose flour**
- **1 garlic clove, minced**
- **1½ cups low-sodium chicken broth**
- **⅓ cup sour cream**
- **1 large egg yolk**
- **½ teaspoon ground nutmeg**
- **2 teaspoons lemon juice**
- **2 teaspoons minced fresh tarragon**

1. Pat chicken dry with paper towels and season with 1 teaspoon salt and ½ teaspoon pepper. Heat butter and oil in 12-inch skillet over medium-high heat until butter is melted. Place chicken in skillet and cook until browned, about 4 minutes. Using tongs, flip chicken and cook until browned on second side, about 4 minutes longer. Transfer chicken to plate.

2. Add mushrooms, onion, and wine to now-empty skillet and cook, stirring occasionally, until liquid has evaporated and mushrooms are browned, 8 to 10 minutes. Add flour and garlic; cook, stirring constantly, 1 minute. Add broth and bring mixture to boil, scraping up any browned bits. Add chicken and any accumulated juices to skillet. Reduce heat to medium-low, cover, and simmer until breasts register 160 degrees and thighs register 175 degrees, 5 to 10 minutes.

3. Transfer chicken to clean platter and tent loosely with aluminum foil. Whisk sour cream and egg yolk together in bowl. Whisking constantly, slowly stir ½ cup hot sauce into sour cream mixture to temper. Stirring constantly, slowly pour sour cream mixture into simmering sauce. Stir in nutmeg, lemon juice, and tarragon; return to simmer. Season with salt and pepper to taste, pour sauce over chicken, and serve.

RATING CUTTING BOARDS

To find the best cutting board, we had our test cooks try out eight boards—wood, bamboo, plastic, and composite models priced from $22 to nearly $150—over a three-month period. Wood and bamboo boards excelled when it came to their "grip" of knives; their soft, subtly textured surfaces offered just enough give for the knife's edge to stick lightly as we diced onions and chiles. When it came to the wood and bamboo boards' performance, construction proved key, with end-grain boards (in which blocks of wood are glued together with exposed grain facing up) warping more easily than edge-grain boards (in which the grain runs parallel to the surface). For wood boards, we also considered maintenance; wood and bamboo need to be oiled regularly, but we found a teak winner that retained its soft, smooth, flat surface even after a few weeks of use with no oiling. Brands are listed in order of preference. See www.americastestkitchen.com for updates to this testing.

HIGHLY RECOMMENDED

PROTEAK Edge Grain Teak Cutting Board (model #107)
PRICE: $84.99 **MATERIAL:** Mexican teak
DIMENSIONS: 18 by 24 in **DISHWASHER-SAFE:** No
CUTTING: ★★★ **DURABILITY:** ★★★ **USER-FRIENDLINESS:** ★★★
COMMENTS: Roomy, knife-friendly, and durable, this teak slab was worth every penny. It resisted warping and cracking, showed only minor scratches, and was easy to lift and clean, thanks to handholds on each end.

RECOMMENDED

OXO Good Grips Carving & Cutting Board (model #1063789)
PRICE: $21.95 BEST BUY **MATERIAL:** Polyproplene (plastic)
DIMENSIONS: 14.5 by 21 in **DISHWASHER-SAFE:** Yes
CUTTING: ★★★ **DURABILITY:** ★★ **USER-FRIENDLINESS:** ★★★
COMMENTS: Our favorite bargain board sports rubber strips on both sides that keep its lightweight frame anchored to the counter. It did suffer deep scratches and gouges but never split or warped, and it cleaned up stain-free.

JOHN BOOS Chop-N-Slice Reversible Cutting Board (model #214)
PRICE: $44.99 **MATERIAL:** Maple
DIMENSIONS: 15 by 20 in **DISHWASHER-SAFE:** No
CUTTING: ★★★ **DURABILITY:** ★★ **USER-FRIENDLINESS:** ★★★
COMMENTS: This reversible edge-grain board's slightly rough surface offered a secure hold on the counter and it gently gripped the knives. Though it absorbed stains and developed hair-line cracks, it never warped.

NOT RECOMMENDED

SAGE Non-Skid Chop Board (model #SNS-14169S)
PRICE: $46.95 **MATERIAL:** Wood-laminate composite
DIMENSIONS: 16 by 19 in **DISHWASHER-SAFE:** Yes
CUTTING: ★ **DURABILITY:** ★★ **USER-FRIENDLINESS:** ★★★
COMMENTS: This model is thin and lightweight; dishwasher-safe; and stayed put thanks to its nonskid feet. Unfortunately, it warped after several commercial dishwasher runs and was the only model to commit the ultimate cutting board no-no: It dulled a knife.

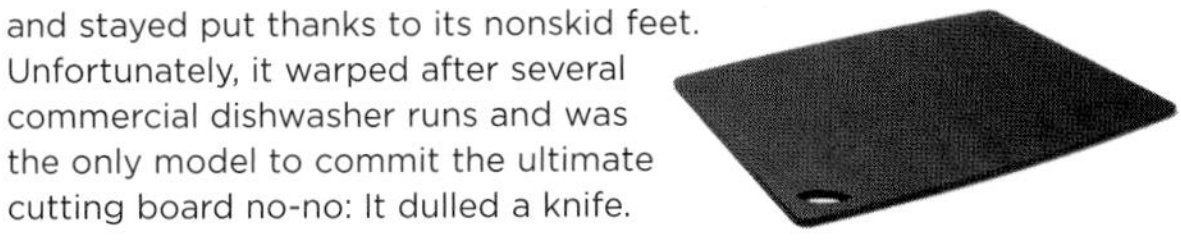

NOT RECOMMENDED *(cont.)*

THE CUTTING BOARD FACTORY Industrial Grade Polymer Cutting Board (model #CG-18024)
PRICE: $27.93 **MATERIAL:** High-density polyethylene (plastic)
DIMENSIONS: 18 by 25.25 in **DISHWASHER-SAFE:** Yes
CUTTING: ★★ **DURABILITY:** ★ **USER-FRIENDLINESS:** ★★
COMMENTS: This plastic board is reversible and can be custom-cut to any size. It never warped, even in the commercial dishwasher. But chef's knives couldn't grip its slick surface, and the cleaver left cuts so deep that it pulled up strips of plastic.

CATSKILL CRAFTSMEN End Grain Chopping Block (model #1822)
PRICE: $79 **MATERIAL:** Yellow birch
DIMENSIONS: 17 by 20.75 in **DISHWASHER-SAFE:** No
CUTTING: ★★ **DURABILITY:** ★ **USER-FRIENDLINESS:** ★
COMMENTS: What this hefty end-grain block offered in knife-friendliness (a cushiony, grippy surface for controlled cutting) it utterly lacked in durability. And this board cracked after a few rinses and eventually warped.

TOTALLY BAMBOO CONGO Large Prep Board (model #20-3476)
PRICE: $140 **MATERIAL:** Butcher block-style bamboo
DIMENSIONS: 16.5 by 21.75 in **DISHWASHER-SAFE:** No
CUTTING: ★★ **DURABILITY:** ★ **USER-FRIENDLINESS:** ★
COMMENTS: Both copies of this end-grain board arrived slightly distorted, and the warping worsened somewhat over time. Though its feet kept it steady, the rubber pads peeled off.

THINK BAMBOO Heavy Duty Cutting Board (model #TB002)
PRICE: $89.95 **MATERIAL:** End-grain bamboo encased by edge-grain bamboo
DIMENSIONS: 17.5 by 23.5 in **DISHWASHER-SAFE:** No
CUTTING: ★ **DURABILITY:** ★ **USER-FRIENDLINESS:** ★
COMMENTS: Small cracks visible on arrival in this hybrid-grain board widened after the first wash. Scratches visibly marred the surface and the cleaver left deep scores.

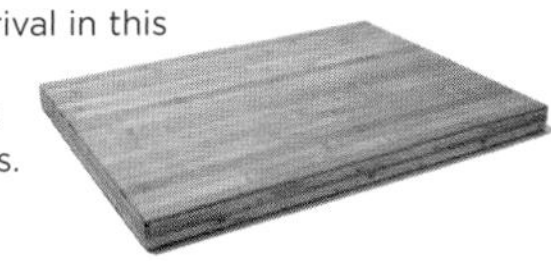

BEST SIMPLE ROAST CHICKEN

WHY THIS RECIPE WORKS: Roast chicken is often described as a simple dish, and it is, at least in terms of flavor—when done properly, the rich flavor and juicy meat of the chicken need little adornment. But the actual process of preparing and roasting chicken is anything but simple: Recipes often call for complicated trussing techniques and rotating the bird multiple times during the course of cooking. The most time-consuming part is salting or brining the bird, a step that ensures juiciness and well-seasoned meat. We wanted to find a way to skip this step—without sacrificing flavor—and get roast chicken on the table in just an hour. After systematically testing the various components and steps of a typical recipe, we discovered we could ditch both the V-rack and flipping the chicken by using a preheated skillet; preheating the pan and placing the chicken breast side up gave the thighs a jump start on cooking. Starting the chicken in a 450-degree oven and then turning the oven off while the chicken finished cooking slowed the evaporation of juices, ensuring moist, tender meat.

IF THERE'S ONE THING WE'VE LEARNED FROM YEARS OF experience in the test kitchen, it's that the best way to guarantee a juicy, well-seasoned roast chicken is to brine or salt the bird (at least 30 minutes for brining and up to 24 hours for salting) before it hits the oven. We've found that such pretreatment reliably solves the classic roast-poultry predicament: how to keep the lean, delicate breast meat from overcooking by the time the fattier leg quarters come up to temperature. The salt in both methods buffers the meat against overcooking by restructuring its proteins, enabling it to retain more of its natural juices.

While we stand by these methods, we realize that on a weeknight, many cooks just don't have time to salt or brine. We got to thinking: Wouldn't it be great if we could come up with a foolproof way to roast chicken that didn't call for any preroasting treatment?

The best approach, it seemed to us, was to modify our standard method for roasting chicken, which calls for submerging the bird in a salt-sugar brine (sugar encourages good browning) for an hour; brushing it with melted butter; and roasting it in a 375-degree oven in a V-rack, starting wing side up. The bird is turned twice (once to expose the other wing and the second time to expose the breast) and pulled from the oven when the breast and thigh meat hit around 160 and 170 degrees, respectively. We would take that recipe, skip the brine, and then put every other step under the microscope—from the roasting pan, to the V-rack, to the oven temperature, to whether or not to flip.

We started with the V-rack. This piece of equipment keeps the bird elevated so the oven's heat can circulate evenly around the roast and the skin avoids sitting in juices that prevent it from crisping up. We definitely wanted crisp skin, but we also knew that we could use the pan's surface to our advantage. If we preheated the pan, then placed the chicken in it breast side up, the thighs would get a jump start on cooking, much as they would if we seared them first in a skillet. This change would mean the flipping would also go, since that would entail placing the breast directly against the pan's hot surface for part of the cooking time, which would dry it out even faster.

We compared a pan-seared bird against one roasted in the traditional rack setup and found the results surprisingly decent. The skin was still pale, but tasters agreed that the breast meat was better now that the thigh meat had a head start in the pan and we could shave a few minutes off the cooking time. The V-rack and flipping were out; preheating the roasting pan was in.

Now what about oven temperature? Since the 375-degree oven wasn't really doing the breast meat any favors, we reasoned our next move should be lowering the heat to cook that delicate meat more gently. We readied a few more birds and experimented with dropping the temperature down to 300 degrees, but the results were disappointing: Though the white meat became marginally juicier, there was an obvious—and unacceptable—trade-off: The skin had gone from patchily browned to pale. Cranking up the heat above 375 degrees improved the skin but, not surprisingly, reversed the slight gains we'd made with juicier breast meat.

Without any clear idea of how to proceed, we decided to roast a chicken according to a recipe developed by

celebrated French chef Joël Robuchon, which is widely regarded as one of the best. He places the bird in a buttered baking dish and rubs it with softened butter—and then does something totally unexpected: He puts it in a cold oven and promptly cranks the heat to 410 degrees. We found that while the hotter temperature did color the skin a deeper shade of bronze, it didn't produce meat any juicier than chickens we'd roasted in preheated ovens. And with this method, we were back to constant flipping.

But could there be something to the idea of a dramatic shift in oven temperature? What if we reversed Robuchon's method by starting the chicken at a relatively hot temperature to brown the skin, but then turned off the oven midway through cooking? We'll admit that we wouldn't be the first in the test kitchen to try something like this. A few years back, a colleague shut off the heat partway through cooking a notoriously tough eye-round roast as a way to make the meat tender and keep it juicy.

We decided to give this radical approach a shot, but to go back to using a preheated roasting pan and no rack. We set the dial to Robuchon's recommended 410 degrees, brushed the chicken with melted butter, seasoned it aggressively with salt and pepper, and lowered it into the hot skillet breast side up so that the thighs would start cooking immediately. Then after about 30 minutes, we cut off the heat, let the bird idle in the oven until the breast and thigh meat hit their target temperatures about 30 minutes later, and let it sit on the counter for its requisite 20-minute rest, during which juices would be released and then drawn back into the meat.

We're not exaggerating when we say that this latest bird was a huge success: Beneath the layer of nicely tanned skin was white meat so tender and moist that even the dark meat loyalists among us were reaching for second helpings. A quick conversation with our science editor helped us understand why the approach was so effective: In meat with a lot of surface area like chicken, most of the moisture loss that occurs during cooking is through surface evaporation. Shutting off the oven will cool the chicken's exterior relatively rapidly, in turn slowing the evaporation of juices. In the meantime, heat that's already inside the chicken will continue beaming deeper into the interior, eventually bringing it to the desired safe temperature (the same carryover cooking that occurs when meat is resting). The net result is a juicier chicken with virtually no chance of overcooking.

We were very happy with the progress we'd made with the meat, but we wondered if we could darken the skin on the breast another shade by increasing the oven's heat. We tested temperatures all the way up to 500 degrees and found the ceiling when the hottest ovens filled with smoke midway through cooking as the rendered fat burned in the roasting pan. The finest of the flock emerged from a 450-degree oven: beautifully dark amber skin encasing tender, juicy meat.

Still, all was not well. The higher heat forced more of the juices to evaporate, leaving us with less for a pan sauce. We reasoned that if we replaced the roasting pan with a skillet, the juices would pool in the smaller space and not evaporate as quickly. Plus, its long handle and less cumbersome shape would make shuffling the chicken in and out of the oven easier. When we made the switch, we found the only minor downside was that the skin on the back of the chicken sat in the juices, which turned it soggy. But since this skin is rarely eaten anyway—and the rest of the skin was so gorgeous—we weren't too bothered.

We made two other small adjustments: We swapped the melted butter for olive oil, which gave us equally good results with even less work. We also broke with our older recipe by trussing the legs, making it easier for us to temp the thighs since it brought the leg quarters closer to the breast. We weren't worried that tying the legs together would slow down the cooking of the inner thigh (the main reason we avoided this technique in the past); in fact, now that we were relying on carryover cooking, it might even help keep the heat in.

The only item left on our checklist? Making good use of the pan drippings. We spooned out and discarded all but 1 tablespoon of the fat, making sure to leave the flavorful browned bits in the pan, and worked up a simple sauce with mustard, tarragon, and lemon juice.

We looked at the clock. We had started cooking only an hour beforehand, but thanks to our new foolproof, dead-simple technique, we were already sitting down to the best roast chicken we'd ever made without brining or salting. This was definitely going to be our standard method for weeknight roast chicken.

Best Simple Roast Chicken

SERVES 4

We prefer to use a 3½- to 4-pound chicken for this recipe; however, this method can be used to cook a larger chicken. If roasting a larger bird, increase the cooking time in step 2 to 35 to 40 minutes. Cooking the chicken in a preheated skillet will ensure the breast meat and thigh meat finish cooking at the same time.

- **1 tablespoon kosher salt**
- **½ teaspoon pepper**
- **1 (3½- to 4-pound) whole chicken, giblets discarded**
- **1 tablespoon olive oil**
- **1 recipe pan sauce (optional; recipes follow)**

1. Adjust oven rack to middle position, place 12-inch ovensafe skillet on rack, and heat oven to 450 degrees. Combine salt and pepper in bowl. Pat chicken dry with paper towels. Rub entire surface with oil. Sprinkle evenly all over with salt mixture and rub in mixture with hands to coat evenly. Tie legs together with twine and tuck wing tips behind back.

2. Transfer chicken, breast side up, to preheated skillet in oven. Roast chicken until breast registers 120 degrees and thighs register 135 degrees, 25 to 35 minutes. Turn off oven and leave chicken in oven until breast registers 160 degrees and thighs register 175 degrees, 25 to 35 minutes.

3. Transfer chicken to carving board and let rest, uncovered, for 20 minutes. While chicken rests, prepare pan sauce, if making. Carve chicken and serve.

Tarragon-Lemon Pan Sauce

MAKES ABOUT ¾ CUP; ENOUGH FOR 1 RECIPE SIMPLE ROAST CHICKEN

- **1 shallot, minced**
- **1 cup low-sodium chicken broth**
- **2 teaspoons Dijon mustard**
- **2 tablespoons unsalted butter**
- **2 teaspoons chopped fresh tarragon**
- **2 teaspoons lemon juice**
- **Pepper**

While chicken rests, remove all but 1 tablespoon of fat from now-empty skillet using large kitchen spoon, leaving any fond and jus in skillet. Place skillet over medium-high heat and add shallot; cook until softened, about 2 minutes. Stir in chicken broth and mustard, scraping up any browned bits. Cook until reduced to ¾ cup, about 3 minutes. Off heat, whisk in butter, tarragon and lemon juice. Season with pepper to taste; cover and keep warm. Serve with chicken.

Thyme-Sherry Vinegar Pan Sauce

MAKES ABOUT ¾ CUP; ENOUGH FOR 1 RECIPE SIMPLE ROAST CHICKEN

- **1 shallot, minced**
- **2 garlic cloves, minced**
- **2 teaspoons chopped fresh thyme**
- **1 cup low-sodium chicken broth**
- **2 teaspoons Dijon mustard**
- **2 tablespoons unsalted butter**
- **2 teaspoons sherry vinegar**
- **Pepper**

While chicken rests, remove all but 1 tablespoon of fat from now-empty skillet using large kitchen spoon, leaving any fond and jus in skillet. Place skillet over medium-high heat and add shallot, garlic, and thyme; cook until softened, about 2 minutes. Stir in chicken broth and mustard, scraping up any browned bits. Cook until reduced to ¾ cup, about 3 minutes. Off heat, whisk in butter and vinegar. Season with pepper to taste; cover and keep warm. Serve with chicken.

NOTES FROM THE TEST KITCHEN

PROPER TEMPING

Inserting the thermometer too far or not far enough, or at the wrong angle, can give you an inaccurate reading. Here's our method:

WHITE MEAT: Insert probe low into thickest part of breast, just above bone (typically coolest spot, as bone conducts heat poorly). Withdraw probe slowly, checking for lowest registered temperature.

DARK MEAT: Insert probe down into space between tip of breast and thigh. Angle probe outward ever so slightly so it pierces meat in lower part of thigh.

HERE'S THE *Beef*

CHAPTER 3

THE RECIPES

EQUIPMENT CORNER

WHEN A CRAVING FOR BEEF STRIKES, WE TAKE IT SERIOUSLY—ONLY hearty, stick-to-your-ribs fare will do. Chili and thick, juicy burgers typically come to mind as meals that will satisfy most any meat lover in our test kitchen. But while chili is essentially just meat cooked with chiles and spices, determining what makes a great pot of chili is anything but simple; debate about which ingredients belong—or have no place—in chili can be passionate (and loud). We set out to create our own favorite chili, with our own rules. We started by building the best basic chili from the ground up, and then entered the strange world of secret ingredients to determine what's legit and what's just laughable.

And when it's a burger we want, a thin patty hidden in an enormous bun won't do. But bigger burgers often disappoint with their bland flavor and dense texture. We wanted to create the ultimate thick and juicy pub-style burger, one with a crusty exterior and juicy interior that's evenly rosy from center to edge. And we wanted a rich, meaty flavor that could stand up to a variety of bold toppings for a truly satisfying burger that would please even the most ardent carnivore.

One variation on our Juicy Pub-Style Burgers includes a rich topping of crispy shallots and blue cheese.

OUR FAVORITE CHILI

OUR FAVORITE CHILI

WHY THIS RECIPE WORKS: Our goal in creating an ultimate beef chili was to determine which of the "secret ingredients" recommended by chili experts around the world were spot-on—and which were expendable. We started with the beef—most recipes call for ground beef, but we preferred meaty blade steaks, which don't require much trimming and stayed in big chunks in our finished chili. For complex chile flavor, we traded in the commercial chile powder in favor of ground dried ancho and de árbol chiles; for a grassy heat, we added fresh jalapeños. Dried beans, brined before cooking, stayed creamy for the duration of cooking. Beer and chicken broth outperformed red wine, coffee, and beef broth as the liquid component. To balance the sweetness of our pot, light molasses beat out other offbeat ingredients (including prunes and Coca-Cola). For the right level of thickness, flour and peanut butter didn't perform as promised; instead, a small amount of ordinary cornmeal sealed the deal, providing just the right consistency in our ultimate beef chili.

CHILI DEVOTEES (OR "CHILIHEADS," AS THEY ARE known) are an opinionated, even cheerily belligerent bunch. Each cook will swear that the only chili worth eating is his or her own: rich with slow-cooked meat and redolent with chile peppers and spices, all bound in an unctuous sauce. But chili is basically just meat cooked with ground chiles; how could one be so much better than another? The key, any chilihead will tell you, lies in the all-powerful "secret ingredients."

We lost count of the references unearthed in our research to the intriguing additions that could magically improve a humble pot of chili, but the specifics were hard to nail down. (Chiliheads are as secretive as they are argumentative.) It took a lot of digging to compile a list. The Internet yielded fascinating new leads, like prunes floated atop the simmering chili (removed before serving), and obscure cookbooks revealed a couple of others (chocolate, beer). Chiliheads were reluctant to reveal the key to their own success; luckily, they could occasionally be coaxed to divulge the details of other cooks' recipes, including one chili that was thickened with "just a touch of peanut butter."

Inspired by these inventive (some might say wacky) cooks, we were determined to make our own ultimate chili. Before we began developing our recipe, we looked one more place for ideas: chili cook-offs. Who, we reasoned, would know more about producing the ultimate chili than these die-hard cooks who labor 40 weekends per year to defend their bragging rights? It turns out that the chili cook-off circuit is a fascinating world unto itself, but our sleuthing yielded little in the way of practical instruction.

Enticing as our ever-increasing list of secret ingredients was, it was getting us nowhere until we developed a basic recipe that these strange additions could embellish. Adopting the opinionated swagger of a veteran chili cook, we brashly laid down our own ground rules: To live up to our high expectations, our chili would have to be all beef (diced, not ground), and it would have pinto beans, tomatoes, onions, and garlic. These last four ingredients are actually highly controversial in some parts of the United States, but: Our recipe, our rules. It's the chilihead way.

We began by testing five different cuts of beef: flap meat, brisket, chuck-eye roast, skirt steak, and short ribs, all in ¾-inch dice, and all browned before going into the pot with sautéed onions, jalapeños, and garlic, diced tomatoes, beef broth, and quick-brined pinto beans. For the sake of simplicity, we seasoned each pot with ⅓ cup of chili powder.

Though the short ribs were extremely tender, some tasters felt that they tasted too much like pot roast. (Not to mention that it took $40 worth of them to make just one pot of chili.) The brisket was wonderfully beefy but lean and a bit tough. The clear winner was chuck-eye roast, favored for its tenderness and rich flavor. The beans were praised for their soft, creamy texture (attributed to the hour-long brine), and tasters embraced the addition of the tomatoes and aromatics. But we were far from home free: Our tasters also complained that the chili powder gave the dish a gritty, dusty texture, and the flavor was "less than vibrant."

NOTES FROM THE TEST KITCHEN

SECRET WEAPONS... OR WEIRD EXTRAS?

When chili cook-offs proved a bust, we combed the Internet for claims of "secret" ingredients to see if any would actually improve our recipe. Most were better left on the shelf.

THEY'RE IN!

Cornmeal brought great body to the sauce, while beer, molasses, and unsweetened cocoa added depth and complexity.

DIDN'T CUT IT

We'll pass on ingredients like peanut butter, red wine, cola, prunes, and coffee. "Umami bombs" such as anchovies and shiitake mushrooms are also off our list.

Making our own chili powder seemed the best way to solve both of those problems, so we decided to give it a try. Of all the dried chiles that are available in most supermarkets, we chose anchos for their earthiness and de árbols for their smooth heat. We removed the stems and seeds from six dried ancho chiles and four dried de árbol chiles, then toasted the anchos in a dry skillet until they were fragrant (the very thin de árbols burned when we tried to toast them). After cooling the anchos, we ground them in a spice grinder along with the de árbols and 2 teaspoons each of cumin and oregano, both common seasonings in commercial chili powder blends. The sauce in chili made with our own spice blend was not only much more deeply flavored but also remarkably smooth. Why was the batch made with the supermarket chili powder so gritty in comparison?

Research revealed that at many processing plants dried chiles are ground whole—stems, seeds, and all. The stems and seeds never break down completely, and that's what gives some commercial powders that sandy texture. Making chili powder is undeniably a time-consuming step, but for our ultimate chili it was worth it.

Nevertheless, before venturing into the world of secret ingredients, we wondered if we could streamline our recipe a bit. Finding we were spending far too much time trimming the chuck-eye roast of fat and sinew, we switched to blade steak, which also comes from the chuck and was simpler to break down into ¾-inch chunks; it took half the time and our tasters were none the wiser. Rather than grind the chiles in successive batches in a tiny spice grinder, we pulverized them all at once in the food processor, adding a bit of stock to encourage the chile pieces to engage with the blade rather than simply fly around the bowl. The puree still wasn't quite as fine as we wanted it to be, but we'd address that later. We also used the food processor to chop the onions and jalapeños. Since stovetop cooking required occasional stirring to prevent scorching, we moved the bulk of the cooking to the gentler heat of the oven, where it could simmer unattended for an hour and a half.

Happy with our basic recipe, we were ready to spring a series of unlikely ingredients on our colleagues. Our research had indicated that chili cooks' secret weapons tended to fall into five categories: cooking liquids, complexity builders, sweeteners, meat enhancers, and thickeners. In a series of blind tastings, we set out to separate the wonderful from the simply weird.

At this point, the only liquid in our recipe was the predictable beef broth. In our next four pots of chili we added Guinness, red wine, coffee, and lager to the mix. The stout gave the chili a bitter edge and flattened out the bright notes of the jalapeños and tomatoes, and the wine was too tangy. Tasted just 30 minutes into the cooking time, the coffee seemed promising, but it did not end well, becoming as bitter and acidic as the dregs in the office urn. The lightly hoppy flavor of the lager, however, complemented the tomatoes, onions, and jalapeños beautifully—not so surprising, perhaps, since chili and beer pair well by tradition. Lager was in.

Next up: the chili complexity builders, ingredients that add depth without being readily discernible. Cloves and cinnamon were deemed too identifiable and sweet, but members of the chocolate family—unsweetened chocolate, unsweetened cocoa, and bittersweet chocolate—performed well, with tasters appreciating the complexity that each provided. Since we would be sweetening the pot in the next test, we named the unsweetened cocoa the winner in this round and added it to our recipe.

The aim of adding a sweet ingredient to chili is to smooth out any sharp or acidic flavors without making the dish noticeably sweet. We had high hopes for the two prunes left to float on the top of the simmering chili, but that technique was too subtle for our tasters. Four ounces of Coca-Cola added to the pot had the surprising effect of enhancing the tomato flavor too much, and brown sugar was deemed "OK but kind of boring." The winner in this round? Molasses, which lent the chili an "earthy, smoky depth" that tasters loved.

The next category, meat enhancers, yielded the most surprising results. Many cooks swear by the practice of augmenting their chili with "umami bombs" in the form of anchovies, soy sauce, mushrooms, or even Marmite (and competitive cooks tend to go straight for the monosodium glutamate in the form of stock cubes or Sazón Goya). We found that adding such ingredients dramatically increased the meaty flavor of the chili, but in doing so they threw the balance of chiles, aromatics, and spices out of whack. It was just too meaty, or as one taster observed, "like chewing on a bouillon cube." Tasters even persuaded us to switch from beef broth to chicken broth, citing better balance. Good-quality meat was meaty enough, thanks.

NOTES FROM THE TEST KITCHEN

THE TRUTH ABOUT CHAMPIONSHIP CHILI

The Terlingua International Chili Championship is, according to 2006 champion Dana Plocheck, "the Masters of chili," so we were delighted when our research turned up the winning recipes from the past 20 years. That delight turned to disbelief, however, as we pored over each recipe: Not one champ from this West Texas competition included so much as a diced onion or bell pepper to flavor the pot, and the chile flavor was supplied not by fresh or dried chiles, but exclusively by supermarket (or mail-order) chili powder. Nor did any of the recipes boast any novel yet promising "secret" ingredients that might be fun to try in our own chili. (Who could get inspired by dried chicken granules or packets of Sazón Goya?) In fact, all of the winning recipes looked astonishingly similar.

Turns out that cook-off chili can be disqualified for having any distinguishing features—including obvious bits of chopped tomatoes or onions. Therefore, cooks strive to make their chili look just like their competitors'. In fact, the only way to make a chili taste distinctive is to apply layer after layer of seasoning and spice. And that is precisely what participants do, adding successive "dumps" (the word competitors use for their custom-mixed spice packets) to the chili pot over the course of the cooking time. Secrets like these might just be better off remaining secret.

NOTES FROM THE TEST KITCHEN

GETTING THE FUNDAMENTALS RIGHT

No secret ingredient can make up for a dish that takes too many shortcuts. Here's how we laid the groundwork for a top-notch bowl of chili.

TYPICAL STARTING POINTS	UPPING THE ANTE

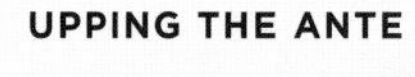

GROUND BEEF

Ground chuck can't help but turn dry and nubbly after hours of cooking in the chili pot.

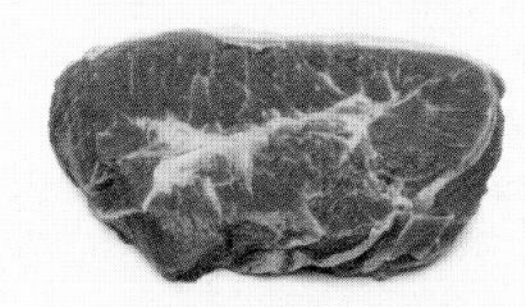

WHOLE BLADE STEAK

Starting with whole steak allows us to cut the meat into beefy chunks that stay moist and tender.

BOTTLED CHILI POWDER

Commercial chili powders lack depth, and the ground seeds and stems they often contain will turn the stew gritty.

THREE KINDS OF CHILES

For complex chile flavor, we grind dried ancho and de árbol chiles into a paste. Fresh jalapeños bring grassy heat.

CANNED BEANS

They're certainly convenient, but canned beans can also be bland and mushy.

BRINED DRIED BEANS

Soaking dried beans in brine before cooking seasons them throughout and contributes to creamier texture.

On to the most eagerly anticipated ingredient test of them all: peanut butter. Intended to thicken the chili, it's not as bizarre as you might think. Mexican cooks often add ground seeds and nuts to mole to give it richness, texture, and depth, so why not add peanut butter to chili? We tested more prosaic thickeners as well: flour and the traditional masa (dough made with limed corn, then dried and ground). The flour subtly thickened the chili, but it didn't offer anything in terms of flavor. The peanut butter, on the other hand, lent a "big roasted flavor" to the chili, but it also left a strange aftertaste that had tasters simply saying "yuck." The masa was well received for its thickening properties and the subtle corn flavor it contributed, but even for the ultimate chili we balked at buying a 4-pound bag of masa just to use 3 tablespoons. This is where we introduced our own quirky ingredient to the pantheon of secret ingredients. We found that when we added 3 tablespoons of cornmeal to our food processor chile paste, its bulk helped us achieve a finer grind, and it accomplished the thickening goal admirably.

Other cooks might accuse us of being full of beans, but this chili, with its tender beef and complex sauce, plus its own secret ingredients, is one we will defend with the vigor of the most seasoned chilihead.

Our Favorite Chili

SERVES 6 TO 8

A 4-pound chuck-eye roast, well trimmed of fat, can be substituted for the steak. Because much of the chili flavor is held in the fat of this dish, refrain from skimming fat from the surface. Dried New Mexican or guajillo chiles make a good substitute for the anchos; each dried de árbol may be replaced with ⅛ teaspoon cayenne. If you prefer not to work with any whole dried chiles, the anchos and de árbols can be replaced with ½ cup commercial chili powder and ¼ to ½ teaspoon cayenne pepper, though the texture of the chili will be slightly compromised. Good choices for condiments include diced avocado, finely chopped red onion, chopped cilantro, lime wedges, sour cream, and shredded Monterey Jack or cheddar cheese.

- Salt
- 8 ounces (1¼ cups) dried pinto beans, picked over and rinsed
- 6 dried ancho chiles, stemmed, seeded, and torn into 1-inch pieces
- 2–4 dried de árbol chiles, stemmed, seeded, and split in 2 pieces
- 3 tablespoons cornmeal
- 2 teaspoons dried oregano
- 2 teaspoons ground cumin
- 2 teaspoons cocoa
- 2½ cups low-sodium chicken broth
- 2 onions, cut into ¾-inch pieces
- 3 small jalapeño chiles, stemmed, seeded, and cut into ½-inch pieces
- 3 tablespoons vegetable oil
- 4 garlic cloves, minced
- 1 (14.5-ounce) can diced tomatoes
- 2 teaspoons molasses
- 3½ pounds blade steak, ¾ inch thick, trimmed and cut into ¾-inch pieces
- 1 (12-ounce) bottle mild lager, such as Budweiser

1. Combine 3 tablespoons salt, 4 quarts water, and beans in Dutch oven and bring to boil over high heat. Remove pot from heat, cover, and let stand 1 hour. Drain and rinse well.

2. Adjust oven rack to lower-middle position and heat oven to 300 degrees. Place ancho chiles in 12-inch skillet set over medium-high heat; toast, stirring frequently, until flesh is fragrant, 4 to 6 minutes, reducing heat if chiles begin to smoke. Transfer to food processor and let cool. Do not wash out skillet.

3. Add de árbol chiles, cornmeal, oregano, cumin, cocoa, and ½ teaspoon salt to food processor with toasted ancho chiles; process until finely ground, about 2 minutes. With processor running, slowly add ½ cup broth until smooth paste forms, about 45 seconds, scraping down sides of bowl as necessary. Transfer paste to bowl. Place onions in now-empty processor and pulse until roughly chopped, about 4 pulses. Add jalapeños and pulse until consistency of chunky salsa, about 4 pulses, scraping down bowl as necessary.

4. Heat 1 tablespoon oil in Dutch oven over medium-high heat. Add onion mixture and cook, stirring occasionally, until moisture has evaporated and vegetables are softened, 7 to 9 minutes. Add garlic and cook until fragrant, about 1 minute. Add chile paste, tomatoes, and molasses; stir until chile paste is thoroughly combined. Add remaining 2 cups broth and drained beans; bring to boil, then reduce heat to simmer.

5. Meanwhile, heat 1 tablespoon oil in now-empty skillet over medium-high heat until shimmering. Pat beef dry with paper towels and season with 1 teaspoon salt. Add half of beef and cook until browned on all sides, about 10 minutes. Transfer meat to Dutch oven. Add half of beer to skillet, scraping up any browned bits, and bring to simmer. Transfer beer to Dutch oven. Repeat with remaining 1 tablespoon oil, remaining steak, and remaining beer. Stir to combine and return mixture to simmer.

6. Cover pot and transfer to oven. Cook until meat and beans are fully tender, 1½ to 2 hours. Let chili stand, uncovered, for 10 minutes. Stir well, season with salt to taste, and serve. (Chili can be refrigerated for up to 3 days.)

JUICY PUB-STYLE BURGERS

WHY THIS RECIPE WORKS: Few things are as satisfying as a thick, juicy pub-style burger. But avoiding the usual gray band of overcooked meat is a challenge. We wanted a patty that was well-seared, juicy, and evenly rosy from center to edge. Grinding our own meat in the food processor was a must, and sirloin steak tips were the right cut for the job. Cutting the meat into small ½-inch chunks before grinding and lightly packing the meat to form patties gave the burgers just enough structure to hold their shape in the skillet. A little melted butter improved their flavor and juiciness, but our biggest discovery came when we transferred the burgers from the stovetop to the oven to finish cooking—the stovetop provided intense heat for searing, while the oven's gentle ambient heat allowed for even cooking, thus eliminating the overcooked gray zone.

MAKING HAMBURGERS FROM PREGROUND BEEF SURE gets dinner on the table in a hurry. But when our goal is a memorably thick, juicy burger full of big beefy flavor—the kind served in the best high-end pubs—we wouldn't dream of using the preground stuff. The fact is, supermarket ground beef is mediocre. Because it's typically purchased in bulk from beef processing plants, supplemented with meat scraps, and then reground, the flavor and texture vary from package to package. More often than not, we find that the beef has literally been ground to a pulp that cooks up dry and pebbly, no matter how much care we take. And it never has the rich meaty flavor we crave.

So when we decided to create a thick, pub-style burger, we knew that grinding our own beef was a given. What we didn't yet know was which cut of beef we would use, how coarsely or finely we would process the meat, or what cooking method would produce a well-seared, thickly crusted burger that was juicy and evenly medium-rare within.

Standing at the meat counter, we were first inclined to reach for a chuck roast. This popular burger cut boasts a robust amount of fat that lubricates and flavors the meat as it cooks. But it also contains a fair amount of sinew—no problem for a dedicated meat grinder, but more work than our food processor (the test kitchen's go-to alternative to a meat grinder) could handle. Instead, we settled on sirloin steak tips. While not quite as rich as chuck, this cut offers supremely beefy flavor without gristly sinew.

As for the grinding process itself, we found that cutting the meat into ½-inch chunks, freezing it until just firm, and then pulsing it in the food processor in batches into rough 1⁄16-inch bits worked well. This relatively coarse grind, coupled with a light touch when packing the meat into disks, is the key to a tender burger, and cutting the meat into relatively small chunks helped create a more even grind that stuck together better. We first formed the beef into loosely packed meatballs, which we then flattened into patties. Both measures gave the burgers just enough structure to hold their shape when flipped.

On to the next issue: More than a few tasters hinted that they missed the richness of well-marbled chuck. Supplementing the steak tips with another, fattier cut of beef—a common restaurant trick—would be one way to boost flavor, but we weren't wild about adding more butchering work to the process. Instead, we experimented with adding straight fat. First we tried olive oil, which was a total flop; it seeped out as soon as the burger started to cook and did little to flavor the meat. But melted butter, which solidified as it hit the cold meat, created pinhead-size particles of fat strewn throughout the patties, which improved the burgers' flavor and juiciness. Even better, the extra fat boosted the browning on its exterior.

But good browning was about the only thing the exterior had going for it. Between their crisp, craggy shells and deep pink centers, the patties were marred by a thick band of gray meat and no amount of extra fat was going to help. Clearly, we needed to rethink our cooking method. Up to now, we had been following a pretty standard approach for pan-fried burgers: preheating a skillet over high heat until it was good and hot, then cooking the patties to medium-rare for about four minutes per side.

JUICY PUB-STYLE BURGERS WITH CRISPY SHALLOTS AND BLUE CHEESE

But we had an alternative method in mind—one we developed for cooking thick-cut steaks. In that recipe, we used a combination stove-oven technique, in which the intense heat of the burner produced a great crust and the gentler, more ambient heat of the oven prevented the gray band of meat from forming beneath it. We followed suit here, quickly searing the burgers in a skillet and then transferring them (in the pan) to a 350-degree oven. But the results were only marginally better. The problem was that the portion of the burgers in direct contact with the skillet continued to cook faster than the top half. Lowering the oven temperature to 300 degrees helped, but only a little. That's when we decided to transfer the burgers from the skillet after searing to a cool baking sheet for finishing in the oven. That did it. After about 5 minutes, the burgers emerged with perfect interiors—juicy and rosy throughout.

This being a premium pub-style burger, it needed a few premium (yet simple) toppings. We threw together a quick tangy-sweet sauce to smear on each toasted and buttered bun and then created a few flavorful topping combinations: crispy shallots and blue cheese; sautéed onions and smoked cheddar; aged cheddar and peppercorn-crusted bacon; and pan-roasted mushrooms and Gruyère.

Admittedly, this burger required more time and effort than your average patty fashioned from supermarket ground beef. But it took only one bite to confirm that the fresh, deeply beefy-tasting, insanely juicy results were well worth the extra trouble.

NOTES FROM THE TEST KITCHEN

TO DIMPLE OR NOT TO DIMPLE

To prevent hamburgers from puffing up during cooking, many sources recommend making a slight depression in the center of the raw patty before placing it on the heat. But we find the need for a dimple depends entirely on how the burger is cooked. Meat inflates upon cooking when its connective tissue, or collagen, shrinks at temperatures higher than 140 degrees. If burgers are cooked on a grill or under a broiler, a dimple is in order. Cooked with these methods, the meat is exposed to direct heat not only from below or above but also on its sides; as a result, the edges of the patty shrink, cinching the hamburger like a belt, compressing its interior up and out. But when the patty is cooked in a skillet, as in our recipe for Juicy Pub-Style Burgers, only the part of the patty in direct contact with the pan gets hot enough to shrink the collagen. Because the edges of the burger never directly touch the heat, the collagen it contains doesn't shrink much at all, and the burger doesn't puff.

DIMPLED FOR GRILL AND BROILER

NOT DIMPLED FOR SKILLET

Don't bother "dimpling" burgers cooked in a skillet. Unlike burgers cooked on a grill or under a broiler, their edges never get hot enough to shrink, pushing the interior up and out and resulting in a puffy patty.

THICK, JUICY, PERFECTLY COOKED BURGERS

1. FREEZE AND GRIND: Chilling the beef chunks until firm and then processing them into 1/16-inch pieces ensures a coarse grind that stays loosely packed.

2. ADD BUTTER: Coating the raw ground beef with melted butter not only ensures that the burgers cook up super-juicy, but also encourages flavorful browning.

3. SEAR, THEN BAKE: Searing on the stove and then finishing in a low-heat oven trades the usual overcooked exterior for a well-browned crust and juicy center.

Juicy Pub-Style Burgers

SERVES 4

Sirloin steak tips are also sold as flap meat. When stirring the butter and pepper into the ground meat and shaping the patties, take care not to overwork the meat or the burgers will become dense. For the best flavor, season the burgers aggressively just before cooking. The burgers can be topped as desired or with one of the test kitchen's favorite combinations (recipes follow).

- **2 pounds sirloin steak tips or boneless beef short ribs, trimmed and cut into ½-inch chunks**
- **4 tablespoons unsalted butter, melted and cooled slightly**
- **Salt and pepper**
- **1 teaspoon vegetable oil**
- **4 large hamburger rolls, toasted and buttered**

1. Place beef chunks on baking sheet in single layer. Freeze meat until very firm and starting to harden around edges but still pliable, 15 to 25 minutes.

2. Place one-quarter of meat in food processor and pulse until finely ground into 1/16-inch pieces, about 35 pulses, stopping and redistributing meat around bowl as necessary to ensure beef is evenly ground. Transfer meat to baking sheet, overturning processor bowl and without directly touching meat. Repeat grinding with remaining 3 batches of meat. Spread meat over baking sheet and inspect carefully, discarding any long strands of gristle or large chunks of hard meat or fat.

3. Adjust oven rack to middle position and heat oven to 300 degrees. Drizzle melted butter over ground meat and add 1 teaspoon pepper. Gently toss with fork to combine. Divide meat into 4 lightly packed balls. Gently flatten into patties ¾ inch thick and about 4½ inches in diameter. Refrigerate patties until ready to cook. (Patties can be refrigerated for up to 1 day.)

4. Season 1 side of patties with salt and pepper. Using spatula, flip patties and season other side. Heat oil in 12-inch skillet over high heat until just smoking. Using spatula, transfer burgers to skillet and cook without moving for 2 minutes. Using spatula, flip burgers over and cook for 2 minutes longer. Transfer patties to rimmed baking sheet and bake until burgers register 120 to 125 degrees (for medium-rare), 3 to 5 minutes.

5. Transfer burgers to plate and let rest for 5 minutes. Transfer to rolls, add desired toppings, and serve.

Pub-Style Burger Sauce

MAKES ABOUT 1 CUP; ENOUGH FOR 1 RECIPE JUICY PUB-STYLE BURGERS

- **¾ cup mayonnaise**
- **2 tablespoons soy sauce**
- **1 tablespoon packed dark brown sugar**
- **1 tablespoon Worcestershire sauce**
- **1 tablespoon minced chives**
- **1 garlic clove, minced**
- **¾ teaspoon pepper**

Whisk all ingredients together in bowl.

VARIATIONS

Juicy Pub-Style Burgers with Sautéed Onions and Smoked Cheddar

Heat 2 tablespoons vegetable oil in 12-inch skillet over medium-high heat until just smoking. Add 1 thinly sliced onion and ¼ teaspoon salt; cook, stirring frequently, until softened and lightly browned, 5 to 7 minutes. Top each burger with 1 ounce shredded smoked cheddar cheese before transferring to oven. Top with onions just before serving.

Juicy Pub-Style Burgers with Peppered Bacon and Aged Cheddar

Adjust oven rack to middle position and heat oven to 375 degrees. Arrange 6 bacon slices on rimmed baking sheet and sprinkle with 2 teaspoons coarsely ground pepper. Place second rimmed baking sheet on top of bacon and bake until bacon is crisp, 15 to 20 minutes. Transfer bacon to paper towel–lined plate and cool. Cut bacon in half crosswise. Reduce oven temperature to 300 degrees. Proceed with recipe, topping each burger with 1 ounce grated aged cheddar cheese before transferring to oven. Top with bacon just before serving.

Juicy Pub-Style Burgers with Crispy Shallots and Blue Cheese

Heat ½ cup vegetable oil and 3 thinly sliced shallots in medium saucepan over high heat; cook, stirring frequently, until shallots are golden, about 8 minutes. Using slotted spoon, transfer shallots to paper towel–lined plate, season with salt, and let drain until crisp, about 5 minutes. (Cooled shallots can be stored at room temperature for up to 3 days.) Top each burger with 1 ounce crumbled blue cheese before transferring to oven. Top with crispy shallots just before serving.

Juicy Pub-Style Burgers with Pan-Roasted Mushrooms and Gruyère

Heat 2 tablespoons vegetable oil in 12-inch skillet over medium-high heat until just smoking. Add 10 ounces thinly sliced cremini mushrooms, ¼ teaspoon salt, and ¼ teaspoon pepper; cook, stirring frequently, until browned, 5 to 7 minutes. Add 1 minced shallot and 2 teaspoons minced thyme and cook until fragrant. Remove skillet from heat and stir in 2 tablespoons dry sherry. Top each burger with 1 ounce grated Gruyère cheese before transferring to oven. Top with mushrooms just before serving.

RATING MEAT GRINDERS

Meat lovers who appreciate not just a good burger, but a great one, know that grinding your own meat is worth the effort—provided you're using a well-made machine. Hoping to single out a worthwhile contender, we processed 1-inch chunks of sirloin steak tips and pork butt using four models. The lone hand-cranked apparatus performed the worst, becoming jammed with stringy, fatty wads of meat. The other three models, all motorized, ground both cuts of meat faster than our favorite food processor (our usual go-to for grinding meat) and no fat or sinew got stuck around the grinder plate. Our winner quickly pulverized pounds of meat with its powerful motor, but at about $200, it's a pricey purchase. However, if you already own a KitchenAid stand mixer, its affordable grinder attachment performed admirably. Brands are listed in order of preference. See www.americastestkitchen.com for updates to this testing.

HIGHLY RECOMMENDED

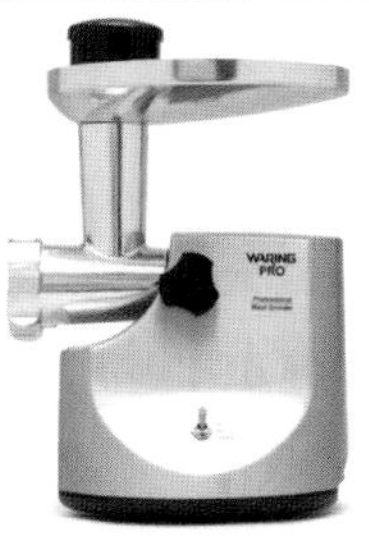

WARING PRO Professional Meat Grinder (model #MG-800)
PRICE: $199.99
COMMENTS: This all-metal machine doesn't come cheap, but it quickly ground through pounds of meat with ease and won't scuff up like its plastic counterparts. Its powerful (albeit loud) motor offers a reverse mode to help unclog any stuck pieces—but we never had to use it.

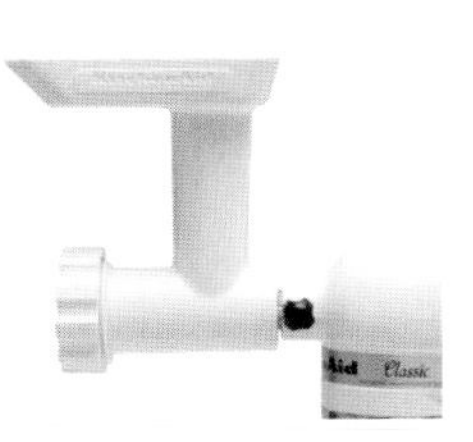

KITCHENAID Food Grinder Attachment (model #108716)
PRICE: $48.74
COMMENTS: The go-to choice for anyone who already owns a KitchenAid stand mixer, this accessory rivaled the brawnier Waring Pro, and was the only model with (mostly) dishwasher-safe parts. The only downsides: It has just two grinding plates, coarse and medium (no fine), and a plastic hopper and auger (we'd prefer all metal).

RECOMMENDED

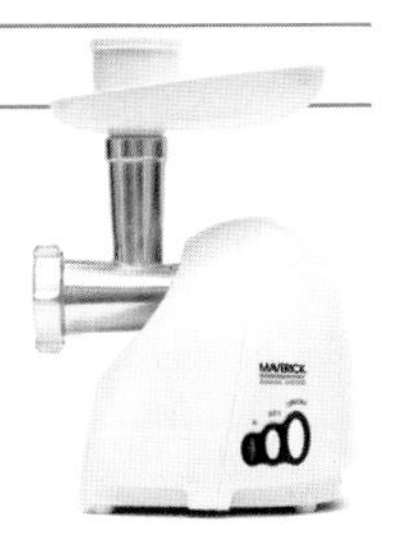

MAVERICK Mince Master 575-Watt Meat Grinder (model #MM-5501)
PRICE: $89.95
COMMENTS: After a fussy assembly process, this machine made short work of both steak tips and pork butt, thanks to its powerful motor, though we would have preferred an all-metal design.

KITCHENAID 12-Cup Food Processor (model #KFP750)
PRICE: $199.99
COMMENTS: As long as you don't mind reloading the bowl of the processor three times to chop 1 pound of sirloin cubes to a texture resembling ground meat, our favorite food processor is a viable alternative to a dedicated grinder.

NOT RECOMMENDED

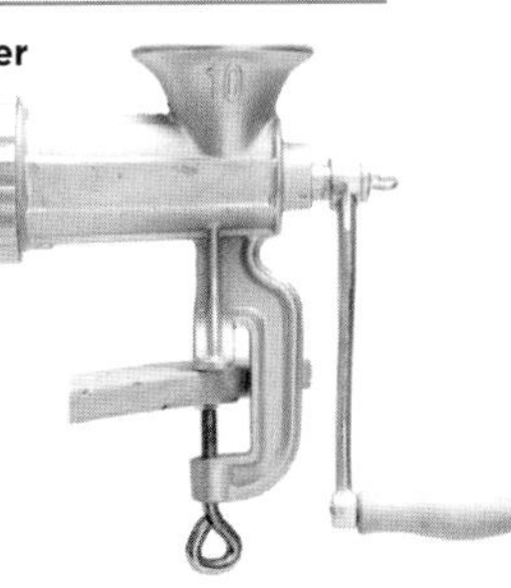

WESTON Deluxe Heavy-Duty Meat Grinder (model #361001W)
PRICE: $40.49
COMMENTS: This manual model clogged easily, forcing us to stop and restart the grinding several times, and lost about half of the meat in the process. Plus, it required babying: Twist the nut that attaches the grinding plate one shade too hard, and the crank won't budge.

COLD-WEATHER *Comfort*

CHAPTER 4

THE RECIPES

Split Pea and Ham Soup

Buttery Croutons

Easy Caramel Cake

Test cook Andrea Geary carefully spreads frosting on one layer of our Easy Caramel Cake.

WHEN COLD WEATHER SETS IN AND THE BEACH IS BEHIND US FOR THE time being, it's comfort food we crave. And nothing says comfort to us quite like a hot, stick-to-your-ribs soup or a layer cake slathered in sweet frosting. Split pea and ham soup combines meaty chunks of ham with the earthy creaminess of peas. This soup used to be a frugal way to stretch a meal, with a leftover ham shank providing the backbone of flavor as the fat from the ham melted into the broth. But nowadays people rarely roast a ham—perhaps once a year for the holidays—so using a leftover bone to flavor the soup is not an option. We wanted to find a way to get that rich, meaty flavor into our split pea soup using an equally flavorful (but more accessible) substitute.

Caramel cake is a true Southern delicacy, and if you're not familiar with it, you should be. Layers of tender-yet-sturdy yellow cake are topped with a rich, toffee-flavored caramel frosting—a treat that's guaranteed to satisfy any sweet tooth. But caramel frosting is notoriously tricky to get right, typically requiring a candy thermometer and precise timing to achieve the ideal consistency. We wanted an easier, foolproof frosting for our cake—one that would brighten even the bleakest day.

SPLIT PEA AND HAM SOUP

SPLIT PEA AND HAM SOUP

WHY THIS RECIPE WORKS: We wanted a spoon-coating, richly flavorful broth studded with tender shreds of sweet-smoky meat, all without requiring the old-fashioned ham bone traditionally used to infuse the soup with flavor. Substituting ham hocks made the soup greasy and was skimpy on the meat. Ham steak, however, was plenty meaty and infused the soup with a fuller pork flavor. Without the bone, our soup needed richness and smokiness, and adding a few strips of raw bacon to the pot did the job. Unsoaked peas broke down just as well as soaked and were better at absorbing the flavor of the soup.

SPLIT PEA SOUP USED TO BE THE THING TO MAKE AFTER serving a roast ham for Sunday supper. Once you were done frying ham and eggs for breakfast and shaving off meaty slabs for ham sandwiches at lunch, you would drop the bone (with hunks of meat still clinging to it) into a big soup pot with a bag of split peas and cover it with water. After hours of simmering, the meat would fall off the bone, the fat would melt into the broth, and the peas would disintegrate and thicken the rib-sticking potage. That was the idea, anyway. But in our experience, this thrifty dish has never amounted to anything greater than the sum of its parts. Too often it turns into an overly thick—dare we say sludgy—green mash with one-note flavor. Plus, these days, we rarely serve roast ham, so procuring a leftover bone is not as simple as reaching into our refrigerator. But the thought of what this dish is meant to be—a spoon-coating, richly flavorful broth studded with tender shreds of sweet-smoky meat—was enough to send us back to the kitchen.

Without a ham bone, we had to find an equally flavorful replacement. Most of the recipes we came across swapped in ham hocks, but these fatty, sinewy knuckle pieces (we tried both fresh and smoked) only rendered our soup greasy. Plus, unless you find a particularly substantial specimen, hocks tend to be skimpy on meat, making a supplemental form of pork necessary.

Our tasters wanted plenty of ham strewn throughout the pot, so we made a point of shopping for meatier alternatives and returned to the test kitchen with Canadian bacon and ham steak. The former was disappointing. Unlike regular American strip bacon made from fat-streaked (read: flavorful) pork belly, the Canadian version comes from the lean loin region of the pig, and its meek flavor barely broke through the thick fog of peas. Ham steak, however, was a welcome addition to the pot; after quartering the slab and letting it simmer in the broth (a classic base of water fortified with sautéed onion and garlic, carrots and celery added midway through cooking to preserve their texture, bay leaves, and a pair of thyme sprigs) for about 45 minutes, the liquid had taken on significantly fuller pork flavor, and the ham itself was tender enough to pull into meaty shreds with a pair of forks.

But as our tasters rightly pointed out, the ham steak was hardly an equal substitute for bone. We all agreed that the soup was still lacking richness and could use more smokiness—a perfect job for American bacon, we figured. (Apparently, two forms of pork were going to be necessary after all.) But the quick fix we were hoping for proved elusive. We crisped a few strips and added them to the pot only to find that they overwhelmed the ham and peas. Instead, we slid raw bacon into the soup along with the ham steak, which offered subtler flavor, and the slices could be fished out right before serving.

As for the peas, we knew from experience that the presoaking step in many recipes was not only unnecessary, but also undesirable. Unsoaked peas break down just as readily as soaked peas, and the resulting soup is actually more flavorful, since they absorb the pork-enriched broth.

All that was left to do was work up a few garnishes. A handful of fresh peas seemed appropriate; their sweetness popped against the hearty, smoky broth. Fresh chopped mint leaves and a drizzle of good balsamic vinegar added freshness and sweetness, respectively, and punched up the flavors even more. Finally, we floated gently fried croutons on the surface. As our tasters ladled out second (and even third) helpings, we knew that we'd reworked this stodgy supper into an updated classic.

Split Pea and Ham Soup

SERVES 6 TO 8

Four slices of regular sliced bacon can be used, but the thinner slices are a little harder to remove from the soup. Depending on the age and brand of split peas, the consistency of the soup may vary slightly. If the soup is too thin at the end of step 3, increase the heat and simmer, uncovered, until the desired consistency is reached. If it is too thick, thin it with a little water. In addition to sprinkling the soup with Buttery Croutons, we also like to garnish it with fresh peas, chopped mint, and a drizzle of aged balsamic vinegar.

- **2 tablespoons unsalted butter**
- **1 large onion, chopped fine**
- **Salt and pepper**
- **2 garlic cloves, minced**
- **7 cups water**
- **1 pound ham steak, skin removed, cut into quarters**
- **3 slices thick-cut bacon**
- **1 pound (2 cups) green split peas, picked over and rinsed**
- **2 sprigs fresh thyme**
- **2 bay leaves**
- **2 carrots, peeled and cut into ½ inch pieces**
- **1 celery rib, cut into ½ inch pieces**
- **1 recipe Buttery Croutons (recipe follows)**

1. Melt butter in Dutch oven over medium-high heat. Add onion and ½ teaspoon salt and cook, stirring frequently, until onion is softened, 3 to 4 minutes. Add garlic and cook until fragrant, about 30 seconds. Add water, ham steak, bacon, peas, thyme, and bay leaves. Increase heat to high and bring to simmer, stirring frequently to keep peas from sticking to bottom. Reduce heat to low, cover, and simmer until peas are tender but not falling apart, about 45 minutes.

2. Remove ham steak, cover with aluminum foil or plastic wrap to prevent drying out, and set aside. Stir in carrots and celery and continue to simmer, covered, until vegetables are tender and peas have almost completely broken down, about 30 minutes longer.

3. When cool enough to handle, shred ham into bite-size pieces. Remove and discard thyme, bay leaves, and bacon slices. Stir ham back into soup and return to simmer. Season with salt and pepper to taste and serve. (Soup can be refrigerated for up to 3 days. If necessary, thin it with water when reheating.)

Buttery Croutons

MAKES ABOUT 2 CUPS

- **3 tablespoons unsalted butter**
- **1 tablespoon olive oil**
- **3 slices hearty sandwich bread, cut into ½-inch cubes**
- **Salt**

Heat butter and oil in 12-inch skillet over medium heat. When butter is melted, add bread cubes and cook, stirring frequently, until golden brown, about 10 minutes. Transfer croutons to paper towel–lined plate and season with salt to taste.

EASY CARAMEL CAKE

WHY THIS RECIPE WORKS: A Southern favorite, caramel cake boasts a rich toffee-flavored frosting spread over yellow cake layers, but the best part—the caramel frosting that develops a thin, crystalline crust on its exterior—is notoriously troublesome to make. We wanted an easier, even foolproof caramel icing that would stay creamy long enough to frost a two-layer cake. But first, we needed a cake that would be sturdy enough to support the thick frosting. Using the reverse creaming method—beating the butter into the dry ingredients—and switching from cake flour to all-purpose flour gave us a tender, fine-crumbed cake with enough structure to handle the heavy frosting. For a truly easy caramel frosting, we simply simmered the brown sugar and butter before adding cream, and rather than use a candy thermometer we relied on visual cues to know when to add the cream and when to remove the mixture from the heat. To ensure that the icing wouldn't stiffen before we frosted the cake, we beat a little softened butter into the finished frosting. The fat from the butter kept the frosting soft and spreadable for a few precious extra minutes. After about 30 minutes, the crystalline crust formed, while the icing closest to the cake remained silky and smooth.

WE LOVE THE RICH, TOFFEE-FLAVORED FROSTING ON A caramel cake. Spread over yellow cake layers, this unique frosting starts out creamy but quickly firms up to a fudge-like consistency. The exterior of the frosting develops a thin, crystalline crust while the frosting closest to the cake remains silky and smooth.

While the appeal of this Southern specialty is clear, it's easy to understand why few bakers make it, even in the South. Caramel frosting is notoriously tricky. Traditional recipes call for cooking granulated sugar (sometimes with water) in a saucepan until dark amber, carefully adding cream while it violently sputters, then beating in butter and confectioners' sugar. Some recipes shortcut the process by starting with brown sugar, but you generally still need a candy thermometer to recognize when the caramel has reached the "soft ball" stage. If these challenges aren't enough, the frosting can harden at lightning speed. Our goal was a foolproof caramel icing that would stay creamy long enough to frost a two-layer cake—without racing the clock.

We first needed a sturdy cake with enough flavor to stand up to the sweet frosting. We started with the test kitchen's recipe for classic yellow cake, which relies on the reverse creaming mixing method. Standard creaming beats butter and sugar until fluffy, then alternately adds the wet and dry ingredients. The result is a tender, fluffy cake. Reverse creaming beats the butter and then the liquid into the dry ingredients. Less air is beaten into the batter, and the crumb is finer and less fluffy.

Tests confirmed that reverse creaming produced a somewhat sturdier cake better suited to caramel frosting. Switching from cake flour to higher-protein all-purpose flour gave the cake yet more structure to handle the heavy frosting. To temper the cake's sweetness, we tried cutting back on the 1½ cups of sugar, but even a slight reduction made the cake dry. We had better luck replacing the milk with tangy buttermilk.

We researched "easy" caramel frostings made with brown sugar. The most promising recipe cooked 2 cups of brown sugar, 12 tablespoons of butter, and ½ cup of heavy cream over medium heat; when bubbles formed around the perimeter of the saucepan, the mixture was transferred to a mixer to beat in confectioners' sugar. This method was easy, but because the brown sugar was cooking in so much liquid, it never developed enough caramelized flavor. For our next test we simmered just the sugar and butter before adding the cream; now the flavor of caramel was unmistakable.

But the icing still stiffened before we finished frosting the cake. Upping the amount of butter kept the mixture soft for longer, but it also made the frosting greasy. Thinking of how creamy buttercream frostings whip softened butter with confectioners' sugar, we tried beating a little softened butter into the finished frosting. This frosting was rich and silky, and the fat from the butter kept the frosting soft and spreadable for a few precious extra minutes. The best part? The signature of a Southern caramel cake, the crystalline crust, formed in about 30 minutes.

EASY CARAMEL CAKE

Easy Caramel Cake

SERVES 8

In step 5, the cooled frosting stays soft and spreadable longer than other recipes, but it will harden over time. If the frosting does begin to stiffen, you can microwave it for about 10 seconds (or until it returns to a spreadable consistency).

CAKE

- **½ cup buttermilk, room temperature**
- **4 large eggs, room temperature**
- **2 teaspoons vanilla extract**
- **2¼ cups (11¼ ounces) all-purpose flour**
- **1½ cups (10½ ounces) granulated sugar**
- **1½ teaspoons baking powder**
- **½ teaspoon baking soda**
- **¾ teaspoon salt**
- **16 tablespoons unsalted butter, cut into 16 pieces and softened**

FROSTING

- **12 tablespoons unsalted butter, cut into 12 pieces and softened**
- **2 cups packed (14 ounces) dark brown sugar**
- **½ teaspoon salt**
- **½ cup heavy cream**
- **1 teaspoon vanilla extract**
- **2½ cups (10 ounces) confectioners' sugar, sifted**

1. FOR THE CAKE: Adjust oven rack to middle position and heat oven to 350 degrees. Grease two 9-inch round cake pans, line with parchment paper, grease parchment, then flour pans. Whisk buttermilk, eggs, and vanilla in 2-cup liquid measuring cup. Using stand mixer fitted with paddle, mix flour, sugar, baking powder, baking soda, and salt on low speed until combined. Beat in butter, 1 piece at a time, until only pea-size pieces remain. Pour in half of buttermilk mixture, increase speed to medium-high, and beat until light and fluffy, about 1 minute. Slowly add remaining buttermilk mixture to bowl and beat until incorporated, about 15 seconds.

2. Divide batter evenly between prepared pans and smooth top with rubber spatula. Bake cakes until golden and toothpick inserted in center comes out clean, 20 to 25 minutes. Let cakes cool in pans on wire rack for 10 minutes, then turn out onto wire racks. discard parchment, and let cool completely, at least 1 hour. Clean mixer bowl and paddle and set aside.

3. FOR THE FROSTING: Heat 8 tablespoons butter, brown sugar, and salt in large saucepan over medium heat until small bubbles appear around perimeter of pan, 4 to 8 minutes. Whisk in cream and cook until ring of bubbles reappears, about 1 minute. Off heat, whisk in vanilla.

4. Transfer hot frosting mixture to dry, clean bowl of stand mixer fitted with paddle and beat on low speed, gradually mixing in confectioners' sugar until incorporated. Increase speed to medium and beat until frosting is pale brown and just warm, about 5 minutes. Add remaining butter, 1 piece at a time, and beat until light and fluffy, about 2 minutes.

5. TO ASSEMBLE: Place 1 cake round on serving platter. Spread ¾ cup frosting over cake, then top with second cake round. Spread remaining frosting evenly over top and sides of cake. Serve.

SHAKE AND BAKE *Reinvented*

CHAPTER 5

THE RECIPES

EQUIPMENT CORNER

Bridget and Chris get ready to enjoy Nut-Crusted Chicken Breasts with a squeeze of lemon.

ADDING A BREADING OR NUT-BASED COATING TO CHICKEN OR PORK is a great way to add flavor to these lean cuts—without the mess and grease of deep-frying. Fortunately, things have come a long way from the days of packaged bread crumb–style coatings, which, while simple, leave a lot to be desired in terms of flavor and texture. But that's not to say that homemade coatings are without fault. Take nut-crusted chicken breasts for example; lean, mild chicken breasts need a serious flavor boost, and rich, crunchy nuts would seem to be the ideal solution. But on their own, they form a dense, heavy coating that has a tendency to slide right off the chicken as soon as you cut into it. For a nut crust that was light yet crunchy, we'd need to think beyond just nuts.

A breaded coating can be just the thing to give lean, bland pork chops a flavor boost. A bound breading (a triple layer of flour, eggs, and bread crumbs) is a common approach, but it frequently turns gummy and flakes off the meat. We wanted a light, flavorful coating that would be guaranteed to stay put. And while we were at it, we wanted to develop a coating with some serious crunch, one that would provide a satisfying contrast to the moist, tender meat beneath.

NUT-CRUSTED CHICKEN BREASTS

WHY THIS RECIPE WORKS: Adding chopped nuts to a coating is a great way to add robust flavor to otherwise lean and mild boneless, skinless chicken breasts. But nut coatings are often dense and leaden, and the rich flavor of the nuts rarely comes through. Using a combination of chopped almonds and panko bread crumbs—rather than all nuts—kept the coating light and crunchy, and the bread crumbs helped the coating adhere. Instead of frying the breaded chicken breasts, we found that baking them in the oven was not only easier, but also helped the meat stay juicy and ensured an even golden crust. But it wasn't until we cooked the coating in browned butter prior to breading the chicken that we finally achieved the deep nutty flavor we sought.

INCORPORATING CHOPPED NUTS INTO THE COATING of a boneless, skinless chicken breast not only adds a new, more robust flavor element, but also boosts the crust's crunch factor. But in our experience this technique comes with some problems: The crust becomes dense and leaden, and the rich flavor of the nuts rarely comes through. Plus it's all too easy to dry out a lean boneless breast.

Ensuring juicy, flavorful meat was a simple fix: We salted the breasts (poking them with a fork first to help the salt penetrate) and rested them briefly before dredging and frying. For the crust, we wondered if a simple "breading" of nuts would help, but when we dredged the breasts in flour, dipped them in beaten eggs, and dragged them through chopped almonds, the crushed pieces barely adhered to the meat. Using bread crumbs in the final dredge, which would absorb liquid from the eggs to help act as glue, was definitely going to be necessary. A mixture of half nuts and half Japanese panko—coarser and crunchier than conventional bread crumbs—gave us just the light, crisp texture we wanted. To improve flavor, we added Dijon mustard to the egg wash and lemon zest, fresh thyme, and a dash of cayenne to the nut-crumb mixture.

But the crust still wasn't particularly nutty—and batch-frying the breasts was a hassle. Reviewing our research recipes, we noticed a few that baked the breaded breasts. No question: "oven-frying" would be easier. And maybe the circulating oven heat would also toast the nuts and deepen their flavor. We breaded the next batch, arranged the breasts on a wire rack set in a sheet pan, and baked them until they were cooked through. The chicken emerged juicy and shrouded in an even, golden crust but—infuriatingly—no more nutty-tasting than before.

Adding more almonds only robbed the crust of the panko's crispness. But how could we add more nuttiness without adding more nuts? Then it hit us. We've achieved exactly this result in other recipes by calling on a powerhouse ingredient: browned butter. We gave it a shot, swirling a large butter knob in a skillet for about five minutes and then cooking the panko, ground nuts, and a minced shallot in the browned butter until fragrant and russet-colored. Our tasters reached for second helpings of this latest batch. The technique worked equally well with pecans, pistachios, hazelnuts, and peanuts, making this an easy weeknight dish we could turn to again and again.

Nut-Crusted Chicken Breasts with Lemon and Thyme

SERVES 4

This recipe is best with almonds, but works well with any type of nut. We prefer kosher salt in this recipe. If using table salt, reduce salt amounts by half.

- **4 (6- to 8-ounce) boneless, skinless chicken breasts, tenderloins removed, trimmed**
- **Kosher salt**
- **1 cup whole almonds, chopped coarse**
- **4 tablespoons unsalted butter**
- **1 shallot, minced**
- **1 cup panko bread crumbs**
- **2 teaspoons grated lemon zest, zested lemon cut into wedges**
- **1 teaspoon minced fresh thyme**
- **⅛ teaspoon cayenne pepper**
- **1 cup all-purpose flour**
- **3 large eggs**
- **2 teaspoons Dijon mustard**
- **¼ teaspoon pepper**

NUT-CRUSTED CHICKEN BREASTS WITH LEMON AND THYME

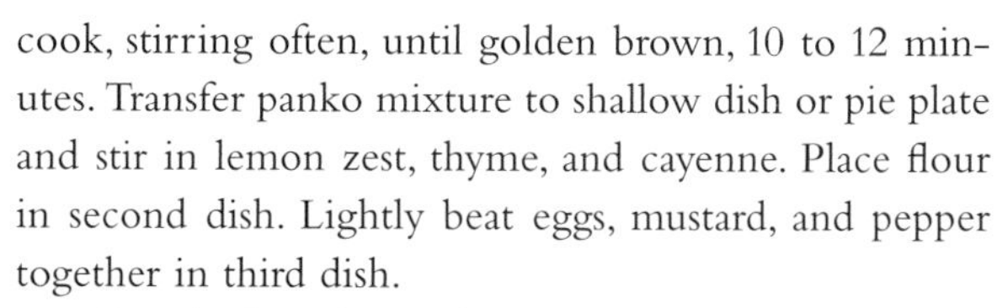

1. Adjust oven rack to lower-middle position and heat oven to 350 degrees. Set wire rack in rimmed baking sheet. Pat chicken dry with paper towels. Using fork, poke thickest half of breasts 5 to 6 times and sprinkle with ½ teaspoon salt. Transfer breasts to prepared wire rack and refrigerate, uncovered, while preparing coating.

2. Pulse almonds in food processor until they resemble coarse meal, about 20 pulses. Melt butter in 12-inch skillet over medium heat, swirling occasionally, until butter is browned and releases nutty aroma, 4 to 5 minutes. Add shallot and ½ teaspoon salt and cook, stirring constantly, until just beginning to brown, about 3 minutes. Reduce heat to medium-low, add panko and ground almonds and cook, stirring often, until golden brown, 10 to 12 minutes. Transfer panko mixture to shallow dish or pie plate and stir in lemon zest, thyme, and cayenne. Place flour in second dish. Lightly beat eggs, mustard, and pepper together in third dish.

3. Pat chicken dry with paper towels. Working with 1 breast at a time, dredge in flour, shaking off excess, then coat with egg mixture, allowing excess to drip off. Coat all sides of breast with panko mixture, pressing gently so that crumbs adhere. Return breaded breasts to wire rack.

4. Bake until chicken registers 160 degrees, 20 to 25 minutes. Let chicken rest for 5 minutes before serving with lemon wedges.

VARIATIONS

Nut-Crusted Chicken Breasts with Orange and Oregano

This version works particularly well with pistachios or hazelnuts.

Substitute 1 teaspoon grated orange zest for lemon zest (cutting zested orange into wedges) and 1 teaspoon minced fresh oregano for thyme.

Nut-Crusted Chicken Breasts with Lime and Chipotle

This version works particularly well with peanuts.

Substitute 1 teaspoon grated lime zest for lemon zest (cutting zested lime into wedges). Omit thyme and add 1 teaspoon chipotle chile powder, ½ teaspoon ground cumin, and ½ teaspoon ground coriander to toasted panko along with lime zest.

Pecan-Crusted Chicken Breasts with Bacon

Substitute 1 cup pecans, chopped coarse, for almonds. Cook 2 finely chopped slices bacon in 12-inch skillet over medium heat until crisp, 5 to 7 minutes. Remove bacon from skillet with slotted spoon and transfer to paper towel–lined plate. Pour off all but 2 tablespoons fat left in skillet. Reduce butter to 2 tablespoons and melt in fat left in skillet over medium heat before adding shallot. Increase shallots to 2. Omit lemon zest and lemon wedges and substitute 1 tablespoon minced fresh parsley for thyme. Add crisp bacon to toasted panko along with parsley.

CRISPY PAN-FRIED PORK CHOPS

WHY THIS RECIPE WORKS: A breaded coating can be just the thing to give lean, bland pork chops a flavor boost—but not when it turns gummy and flakes off the meat. Using boneless chops was fast and easy. Cornstarch formed an ultra-crisp sheath. Buttermilk brought a lighter texture and tangy flavor to the breading, and minced garlic and mustard perked up the breading's flavor. Crushed cornflakes added a craggy texture to the pork chops, especially once we added cornstarch to them before dredging the meat. Finally, to ensure our breading adhered to the chops, we gave the meat a short rest and we lightly scored the pork chops before adding them to the pan.

BACK WHEN PORK WAS FAT-STREAKED AND FLAVORFUL, great pan-fried pork chops came together from nothing more than a coating of seasoned flour and a quick turn in shimmering oil. The finished product—succulent meat encased in a delicate, crisp crust—was utterly simple and on the table in a matter of minutes, making this dish an ideal candidate for a weeknight supper.

But now that the fat, and the flavor, have been all but bred out of pigs, a fried pork chop needs more than a scant, spiced-up shell to give it appeal. Most recipes address that problem by simply packing on a more substantial crust—usually a triple layer of flour, eggs, and bread crumbs called a bound breading. It's a technique that works well enough, though we often find the coating a tad leathery and marred by gummy spots. Plus, this thick type of breading almost never clings tightly to the chop; it tends to flake off with the prick of a fork. Our goal? A bound-breading makeover that would result in a lighter, crispier, more flavorful sheath that stayed where it was put.

We had one decision made before we even pulled out our frying pan: To keep this dish fast and easy, we'd forget bone-in chops and go with boneless center-cut loin chops. Shallow-frying these thin, tender chops takes just two to five minutes per side. Plus, four of them fit snugly in a large skillet, so we'd need to fry only two batches to feed four people.

As for the coating, we would put each component under the microscope and see what we learned. First up: the flour. A light dusting is meant to absorb moisture from both the meat and the eggs, creating a tacky base coat that acts as glue for the breading. But flour contains 10 to 12 percent protein—and when these proteins mix with the water (from the meat and the egg wash), they build structure that ultimately contributes to a heavier, tougher coating. In addition, pork exudes far more liquid than, say, chicken, and this can create gummy spots in the flour. If our goals were to lighten up the breading and get rid of any gumminess, this ingredient would have to go.

Fortunately, the only other option we could think of was a good bet: cornstarch. When cornstarch absorbs water, its starch granules swell and release sticky starch that forms an ultra-crisp sheath when exposed to heat and fat, and we've used this powder to create just such a delicate, brittle layer on everything from oven fries to roast chicken. When we swapped the two ingredients, the chops boasted a casing that was indeed lighter and crispier.

But to our chagrin, we now had a new problem—the breading was barely holding on to the meat at all, with shards falling away like chipped paint as soon as we cut into it. After some research, we understood why: When it comes to creating sticky glue, cornstarch and egg wash are not the best pairing. First, cornstarch absorbs liquid less readily than flour. Second, the moisture in raw egg is bound up in its proteins, making it less available to be soaked up—an effect that not even the juicy pork could compensate for. Clearly, a wetter type of wash was in order. We tried heavy cream and buttermilk and noticed an immediate improvement in how the crust stuck to the chops. Tasters liked the subtle tang that buttermilk brought to the breading, so we settled on it, adding a dollop of mustard and a little minced garlic to perk up its flavor even more.

This wasn't the only good news to come out of switching liquids: The coating was now markedly lighter. When we thought about it, this effect made sense. Even a small amount of egg coagulates and puffs up when it cooks, so of course it would lead to a heavier coating than a dip in buttermilk.

CRISPY PAN-FRIED PORK CHOPS

Up to this point, we'd been using bread crumbs as the final coat. But with buttermilk as our wash, they were absorbing too much liquid and weren't staying as crunchy. Fortunately, breading choices abound. We rolled the chops in Ritz crackers (too tender), Melba toast (too bland), cornmeal (too gritty), and Cream of Wheat (too fine). The best option turned out to be crushed cornflakes. These crisp flakes are a popular way to add craggy texture to oven-fried chicken, so we weren't surprised when they worked here, too. On a whim, we added cornstarch to them before dredging the meat. Once swollen, the starch granules again worked their magic, turning the flakes even crispier in the hot fat.

With all three elements of our breading recalibrated, we prepped one last batch to fry. But just as we were about to put the chops in the pan, we were called away from the kitchen. When we returned about 10 minutes later, we threw them into a hot skillet as usual. To our surprise, the breading on these chops seemed practically soldered to the meat. Could the stronger grip have something to do with the resting period? To check, we fried up two batches of chops: one fried immediately after coating, and the other rested for 10 minutes first. Sure enough, the coating on the rested chops had a noticeably firmer grasp on the meat. Why? According to our science editor, the brief rest gave the cornstarch layer extra time to absorb moisture to form an even stickier paste. He also suggested a final step to ensure that the crust stayed put: lightly scoring the chops. Etching a shallow crosshatch pattern onto the meat's surface released moisture and tacky proteins that gave the coating an exceptionally solid footing.

With a crispy, flavorful coating that stayed glued to the meat, our pan-fried pork chops were just about perfect. The only problem? We needed a way to add a little variety, so we could turn to this dish at least a couple of times a month. A Latin-influenced spice rub with cumin, chili powder, and coriander applied to the meat before dredging did the trick, as did a bold three-pepper rub. With or without a spice rub, this approach has banished bland pork chops from our table for good.

NOTES FROM THE TEST KITCHEN

WHERE BREADED COATINGS GO WRONG

The components of a traditional breading—flour, beaten egg, and bread crumbs—present special challenges when applied to juicy pork chops. Here's how we ensured a crust that stays put and packs plenty of crunch.

1. PROBLEM: Gummy patches under the coating

SOLUTION: We swap flour—the usual breading base coat—for cornstarch. Unlike flour, cornstarch contains no protein, so it cooks up lighter and crispier.

2. PROBLEM: Breading pulls away

SOLUTION: We trade in a typical egg wash for buttermilk. It makes for a lighter shell that clings nicely to the chops.

3. PROBLEM: Soggy bread-crumb crust

SOLUTION: For an ultra-crunchy exterior, we ditch porous bread crumbs for cornflakes (engineered to retain their crunch in liquid) with cornstarch, which forms a brittle sheath when heated.

Crispy Pan-Fried Pork Chops

SERVES 4

We prefer natural to enhanced pork (pork that has been injected with a salt solution to increase moistness and flavor) for this recipe. Don't let the chops drain on the paper towels for longer than 30 seconds, or the heat will steam the crust and make it soggy. You can substitute ¾ cup store-bought cornflake crumbs for the whole cornflakes. If using crumbs, omit the processing step and mix the crumbs with the cornstarch, salt, and pepper.

- **⅔ cup cornstarch**
- **1 cup buttermilk**
- **2 tablespoons Dijon mustard**
- **1 garlic clove, minced**
- **3 cups cornflakes**
- **Salt and pepper**
- **8 (3- to 4-ounce) boneless pork chops, ½ to ¾ inch thick, trimmed**
- **⅔ cup vegetable oil**
- **Lemon wedges**

1. Place ⅓ cup cornstarch in shallow dish or pie plate. In second shallow dish, whisk buttermilk, mustard, and garlic until combined. Process cornflakes, ½ teaspoon salt, ½ teaspoon pepper, and remaining ⅓ cup cornstarch in food processor until cornflakes are finely ground, about 10 seconds. Transfer cornflake mixture to third shallow dish.

2. Adjust oven rack to middle position and heat oven to 200 degrees. Set wire rack in rimmed baking sheet. With sharp knife, cut ⅟₁₆ inch-deep slits on both sides of chops, spaced ½ inch apart, in crosshatch pattern. Season chops with salt and pepper. Dredge 1 chop in cornstarch; shake off excess. Using tongs, coat with buttermilk mixture; let excess drip off. Coat with cornflake mixture; gently pat off excess. Transfer coated chop to prepared wire rack and repeat with remaining chops. Let coated chops stand for 10 minutes.

3. Heat ⅓ cup oil in 12-inch nonstick skillet over medium-high heat until shimmering. Set clean wire rack in rimmed baking sheet. Place 4 chops in skillet and cook until golden brown and crisp, 2 to 5 minutes. Carefully flip chops and continue to cook until second side is golden brown, crisp, and chops register 145 degrees, 2 to 5 minutes longer. Transfer chops to paper towel–lined plate and let drain 30 seconds on each side. Transfer to prepared wire rack, then transfer to oven to keep warm. Discard oil in skillet and wipe clean with paper towels. Repeat process with remaining ⅓ cup oil and pork chops. Serve with lemon wedges.

VARIATIONS

Crispy Pan-Fried Pork Chops with Latin Spice Rub

Combine 1½ teaspoons ground cumin, 1½ teaspoons chili powder, ¾ teaspoon ground coriander, ⅛ teaspoon ground cinnamon, and ⅛ teaspoon red pepper flakes in bowl. Omit pepper and coat chops with spice rub after seasoning with salt in step 2.

Crispy Pan-Fried Pork Chops with Three-Pepper Rub

Combine 1½ teaspoons pepper, 1½ teaspoons white pepper, ¾ teaspoon coriander, ¾ teaspoon ground cumin, ¼ teaspoon red pepper flakes, and ¼ teaspoon ground cinnamon in bowl. Omit pepper and coat chops with spice rub after seasoning with salt in step 2.

NOTES FROM THE TEST KITCHEN

GETTING OUR CRUNCHY COATING TO STICK

Besides rethinking the ingredients in our coating, we came up with two other quick tricks to make sure the breading stays glued to the chop.

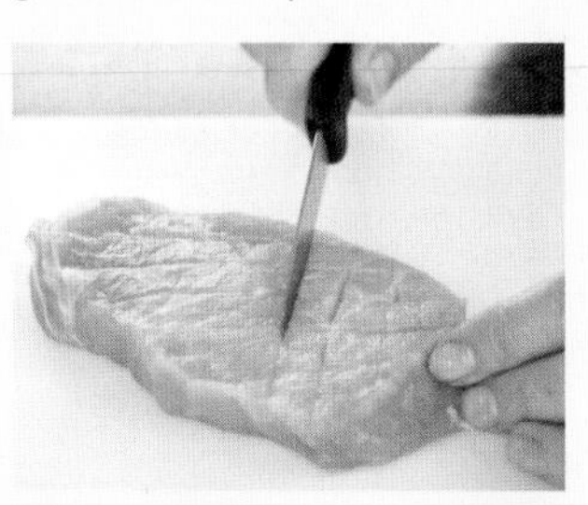

1. SCORE: Making shallow cuts in the chops' surface releases juices and sticky meat proteins that dampen the cornstarch and help the coating adhere.

2. REST: Letting the chops sit for 10 minutes after coating gives the cornstarch more time to absorb liquid and turn into an adhesive paste.

RATING FOOD PROCESSORS

We've gladly paid top dollar for our favorite food processor, the KitchenAid 12-Cup Food Processor, which costs $199. It slices and chops evenly, cleanly, and quickly and boasts a compact, intuitive design. To find out if any new contenders could beat our favorite, we tested five models alongside the KitchenAid. A good food processor should have a razor-sharp blade and perform certain core tasks—shredding, chopping, slicing, and grinding—with ease. The ideal machine should also be able to whip up batches of dough—both pastry and pizza—and mayonnaise. After putting each machine through its paces, we came back to our established winner as the one to beat. Brands are listed in order of preference. See www.americastestkitchen.com for updates to this testing.

HIGHLY RECOMMENDED

KITCHENAID 12-Cup Food Processor (model #KFP750)
PRICE: $199 **BOWL CAPACITIES:** 12 and 4 cups
GRATING/SLICING: ★★★ **CHOPPING:** ★★★
GRINDING: ★★★ **PASTRY:** ★★★
PIZZA DOUGH: ★★ **MAYONNAISE:** ★★★
EASE OF USE: ★★★ **CLEANUP:** ★★★
COMMENTS: Still the one to beat. It's simple to operate, powerful, moderately priced, and offers ample capacity in an intuitive, compact design. The 4-cup mini bowl is essential for small jobs like whipping mayonnaise and mincing herbs. We disliked the dough blade, finding the regular metal blade far more effective.

RECOMMENDED

VIKING Food Processor, 12-Cup (model #VFP12BR)
PRICE: $334.95 **BOWL CAPACITIES:** 12 and 3 cups
GRATING/SLICING: ★★ **CHOPPING:** ★★★
GRINDING: ★★ **PASTRY:** ★★★
PIZZA DOUGH: ★★★ **MAYONNAISE:** ★★★
EASE OF USE: ★★★ **CLEANUP:** ★★
COMMENTS: Quiet and powerful, this model rivaled the KitchenAid almost across the board (and bested it in the pizza dough test). But its steep price was a deterrent, as was the manufacturer's recommendation to hand-wash each component. (Note: The bowls and blades emerged unscathed from one dishwasher cycle.) Wheels on the rear of the base are a nice plus for moving it around.

CUISINART Custom 14-Cup Food Processor (model #DFP-14BCN)
PRICE: $199 **BOWL CAPACITY:** 14 cups
GRATING/SLICING: ★★ **CHOPPING:** ★★
GRINDING: ★★ **PASTRY:** ★★★
PIZZA DOUGH: ★★★ **MAYONNAISE:** ★★★
EASE OF USE: ★★★ **CLEANUP:** ★★★
COMMENTS: We developed a real appreciation for this user-friendly classic, but came away with a couple of quibbles. First, precutting vegetables into 1-inch chunks (per the manufacturer's recommendation) was tedious, and even then the results were uneven. Second, its feed tube was short—too short for a russet potato, which had to be trimmed extensively to fit into the chute (though once trimmed, the potato sliced perfectly).

RECOMMENDED WITH RESERVATIONS

CUISINART Elite Collection 14-Cup Food Processor (model #FP-14DC)
PRICE: $235.37 **BOWL CAPACITIES:** 14, 11, and 4 cups
GRATING/SLICING: ★★ **CHOPPING:** ★★
GRINDING: ★★ **PASTRY:** ★★★
PIZZA DOUGH: ★★★ **MAYONNAISE:** ★★
EASE OF USE: ★★ **CLEANUP:** ★★
COMMENTS: Cuisinart's much-anticipated new release may pack power (good for pizza dough), heft, and plenty of extra bowls, but it didn't do anything better than the cheaper, simpler, more compact KitchenAid. Mayonnaise never came out perfectly emulsified, and chopped carrots emerged accompanied by wasted end pieces. The leakproof rubber gasket "SealTight" lid constantly trapped food bits.

HAMILTON BEACH Big Mouth Deluxe 14-Cup (model #70575)
PRICE: $99.99 **BOWL CAPACITY:** 14 cups
GRATING/SLICING: ★★ **CHOPPING:** ★★
GRINDING: ★★ **PASTRY:** ★★★
PIZZA DOUGH: ★★ **MAYONNAISE:** ★★★
EASE OF USE: ★★ **CLEANUP:** ★★
COMMENTS: On the one hand, this machine's well-labeled blades and lock/unlock indications made it easy to use. (Other brands constantly left us guessing.) On the other, its wide-mouth feed tube was overcomplicated with pop-up lids and double-barreled inserts that were somewhat hard to clean. Performance-wise, it was generally fair across the board.

OMEGA Professional Food Processor, 11-Cup (model #O660)
PRICE: $179.95 **BOWL CAPACITIES:** 11 and 4 cups
GRATING/SLICING: ★★ **CHOPPING:** ★★
GRINDING: ★★★ **PASTRY:** ★★
PIZZA DOUGH: ★ **MAYONNAISE:** ★★★
EASE OF USE: ★★ **CLEANUP:** ★★★
COMMENTS: This model almost cloned the KitchenAid in looks and price—but not performance. Though it turned out perfect bread crumbs, nuts, and mayonnaise, it strained with a double batch of pizza dough. Plus, the curve of its kidney-shaped feed tube was so subtle that we mistakenly put the pusher in backward more than once.

Salmon AND SOLE

CHAPTER 6

THE RECIPES

Glazed Salmon

- Asian Barbecue Glaze
- Pomegranate-Balsamic Glaze
- Orange-Miso Glaze
- Soy-Mustard Glaze

Baked Sole Fillets with Herbs and Bread Crumbs

SCIENCE DESK

White, Out

TASTING LAB

Canned and Ventresca Tuna

For Glazed Salmon, the test kitchen uses a few tricks to ensure that once the glaze is spooned over the fillets it doesn't slide off.

FISH FILLETS COOK IN A FLASH, MAKING THEM AN IDEAL CENTERPIECE to a weeknight meal. And with a little extra effort, they can easily be dressed up for company. But because they cook so quickly, there's little margin for error, and the fish can go from just right to overcooked in the blink of an eye. Glazed salmon can be particularly troublesome; most recipes broil the fish to help the sticky glaze form into a substantial sweet-tart coating, but a successful glaze typically is achieved at the expense of the salmon, which falls victim to the harsh heat of the broiler and inevitably develops a thick band of dried-out flesh on the exterior.

Baking is one of the gentler methods for preparing sole fillets, which require precise timing and a gentle touch, but it's by no means a foolproof technique. If you've ever attempted to transfer sole fillets from baking sheet to serving platter, you know what we mean: This delicate fish inevitably falls apart when handled after cooking. We wanted to find a foolproof approach to preparing sole that would allow us to make the transfer in one piece—and while we were at it, we hoped to dress it up a bit to create a quick, versatile dish we could serve for any occasion.

GLAZED SALMON

WHY THIS RECIPE WORKS: The traditional method for glazed salmon calls for broiling, but reaching into a broiling-hot oven every minute to baste the fish is a hassle and, even worse, the fillets often burn if your timing isn't spot-on. We wanted a foolproof method for producing glazed salmon that was succulent and pink throughout while keeping the slightly crusty, flavorful browned exterior commonly associated with broiling. Reducing the temperature and gently baking the fish cooked the salmon perfectly. To rapidly caramelize the fillets before their exteriors had a chance to toughen, we sprinkled the fillets with sugar and quickly pan-seared each side before transferring them to the oven. To ensure the glaze stayed put, we rubbed the fish with a mixture of cornstarch, brown sugar, and salt before searing.

THERE ARE FEW BETTER WAYS TO HIGHLIGHT THE rich, silky flesh of salmon than by offsetting it with a sweet-tart glaze. Most recipes brush the fish with a sticky mixture and then place it a few inches from the broiler element, basting it every minute or so to ensure a substantial coating. Of course, we didn't relish the idea of repeatedly reaching into a hot oven, but the method seemed viable enough. When we tried it, however, the sugary glaze charred and, as can happen with thick cuts of meat, a band of leathery overcooked flesh developed on the outside, with only the very center of the salmon exhibiting the translucent, buttery texture we were looking for.

The problem was the broiler. It was simply too hard to pinpoint the proper doneness using such extreme heat, and repeatedly opening and closing the oven door to apply the glaze only complicated matters. But we had another idea: So-called slow-cooked salmon is a popular restaurant dish these days, and the approach reverses the tactic we'd been trying. The fish bakes in a low-temperature oven, rendering its flesh terrifically moist and tender. The likely trade-off would be a well-lacquered exterior, but we thought it was worth a shot. We switched the oven to "bake," moved the rack to the middle position, and gently cooked the fish plain (we'd address the glaze later). After 10 minutes at 300 degrees, the salmon was cooked perfectly.

Now that our salmon was succulent and pink throughout, we had only one problem: Tasters missed the slightly crusty, flavorful browned exterior of the broiled fish. Cranking the heat back up was out of the question. Instead, we briefly seared each side of the fish in a hot skillet before transferring it to the low oven. But while the crust was nicely browned, one bite revealed that we had virtually negated the benefits of our slow-cooked technique. The outer layer of the fish was tough and dry—reminiscent of the broiled recipes we'd tried.

What we needed to do was more rapidly caramelize the fillets before their exteriors had a chance to turn tough and leathery—and that's when we remembered a favorite test kitchen technique: To expedite browning on everything from pork tenderloin to tuna, we lightly sprinkle the flesh with sugar. Here, we tried brown sugar (for its subtle molasses flavor), and it took only a minute for a delicate, flavorful crust to form. We then seared the skin side of the fish for another minute to promote even cooking and transferred the skillet to the oven. Seven minutes later, we had just what we wanted: a golden brown exterior and a pink, wonderfully moist interior.

That just left us with the glaze. We combined more brown sugar with vinegar, then added mirin, soy sauce, and mustard to create a teriyaki-inspired glaze that would serve as a perfect foil to the rich, fatty salmon. We brought the mixture to a boil in a saucepan; reduced it for five minutes, until it was thick enough to coat the back of a spoon; then brushed it over the seared salmon fillets. But even before we got the fish into the oven, much of the glaze slid off and pooled in the bottom of the pan. Basting the salmon every couple of minutes would certainly help, but we hated to go that tedious route.

Another obvious remedy would be to further thicken the glaze, so we tried adding a small amount of cornstarch to the mixture. The result? Better, but too much of the sauce still dribbled down the sides of the fish. Adding more cornstarch was not an option; any more than a teaspoon rendered the mixture gummy and gloppy. We were running out of ideas when an altogether different approach occurred to us: What if instead of trying to create a tackier glaze, we worked on getting the salmon itself to have more "stickability"? We had a hunch that rubbing cornstarch on the surface of the fish would add texture, essentially creating tiny nooks and crannies to trap the glaze.

Fingers crossed, we combined ¼ teaspoon of cornstarch with the brown sugar we were already rubbing on the fish, plus ½ teaspoon of kosher salt for seasoning, and then seared the fillets. As we'd hoped, the surface was now quite coarse, mottled all over with tiny peaks and valleys. We proceeded with the recipe, spooning the glossy glaze over the salmon and then transferring it to the low oven. This time the mixture stuck, resulting in a glistening, well-lacquered exterior.

With our glaze holding fast to the fillets, we whipped up three more variations: a fruity pomegranate version spiked with balsamic vinegar, an Asian barbecue mixture drawing sweetness from hoisin sauce and tartness from rice vinegar, and a salty, citrusy orange-miso version.

Not only was this adapted restaurant technique easier and more foolproof than the frequent basting method in other recipes, but we had dinner on the table in about 20 minutes.

Glazed Salmon

SERVES 4

To ensure uniform pieces of fish that cook at the same rate, buy a whole center-cut fillet and cut it into 4 pieces. Prepare the glaze before you cook the salmon. You will need a 12-inch ovensafe nonstick skillet for this recipe. If your nonstick skillet isn't ovensafe, sear the salmon as directed in step 2, then transfer it to a rimmed baking sheet, glaze it, and bake as directed in step 3.

- **1 teaspoon packed light brown sugar**
- **½ teaspoon kosher salt**
- **¼ teaspoon cornstarch**
- **1 (1½- to 2-pound) skin-on salmon fillet, about 1½ inches thick**
- **Pepper**
- **1 teaspoon vegetable oil**
- **1 recipe glaze (recipes follow)**

1. Adjust oven rack to middle position and heat oven to 300 degrees. Combine brown sugar, salt, and cornstarch in small bowl. Use sharp knife to remove any whitish fat from belly of salmon and cut fillet into 4 equal pieces. Pat fillets dry with paper towels and season with pepper. Sprinkle brown sugar mixture evenly over top of flesh side of salmon, rubbing to distribute.

2. Heat oil in 12-inch ovensafe nonstick skillet over medium-high heat until just smoking. Place salmon, flesh side down, in skillet and cook until well browned, about 1 minute. Using tongs, carefully flip salmon and cook on skin side for 1 minute.

3. Remove skillet from heat and spoon glaze evenly over salmon fillets. Transfer skillet to oven and cook until fillets are still translucent when cut into with paring knife and register 125 degrees (for medium-rare), 7 to 10 minutes. Serve.

SCIENCE DESK

WHITE, OUT

What's the white stuff that sometimes mysteriously forms on salmon and sometimes doesn't? This film is a protein called albumin. When the muscle fibers in the fish are heated, they contract, pushing the moisture-filled albumin to the surface of the flesh. Once this protein reaches temperatures between 140 and 150 degrees, its moisture is squeezed out, and it congeals and turns white. Not only does the white albumin detract from the salmon's appearance, but its formation indicates a loss of moisture in the fish.

Cooking salmon at a low temperature can mitigate albumin coagulation. Gentle cooking results in less-intense muscle contractions, so that less of the albumin moves to the surface of the fish and more of it stays trapped in the flesh. The fish not only stays more moist, but it looks better, too.

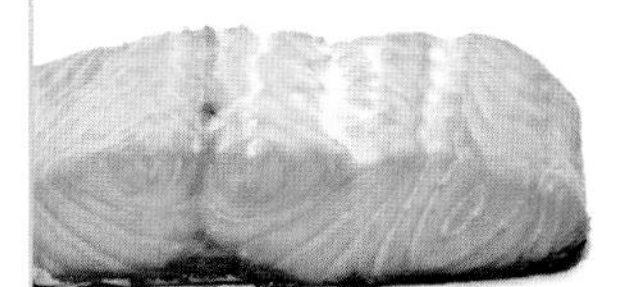

HIGH HEAT = MORE WHITE STUFF

LOW HEAT = LESS WHITE STUFF

Asian Barbecue Glaze

MAKES ABOUT ½ CUP, ENOUGH FOR 1 RECIPE GLAZED SALMON

Toasted sesame oil gives this teriyaki-like glaze rich flavor.

- **2 tablespoons ketchup**
- **2 tablespoons hoisin sauce**
- **2 tablespoons rice vinegar**
- **2 tablespoons packed light brown sugar**
- **1 tablespoon soy sauce**
- **1 tablespoon toasted sesame oil**
- **2 teaspoons Asian chili-garlic sauce**
- **1 teaspoon grated fresh ginger**

Whisk ingredients together in small saucepan. Bring to boil over medium-high heat; simmer until thickened, about 3 minutes. Remove from heat and cover to keep warm.

Pomegranate-Balsamic Glaze

MAKES ABOUT ½ CUP, ENOUGH FOR 1 RECIPE GLAZED SALMON

This fruity, tangy glaze is a perfect match for rich salmon.

- **3 tablespoons packed light brown sugar**
- **3 tablespoons pomegranate juice**
- **2 tablespoons balsamic vinegar**
- **1 tablespoon whole grain mustard**
- **1 teaspoon cornstarch**
- **Pinch cayenne pepper**

Whisk ingredients together in small saucepan. Bring to boil over medium-high heat; simmer until thickened, about 1 minute. Remove from heat and cover to keep warm.

Orange-Miso Glaze

MAKES ABOUT ½ CUP, ENOUGH FOR 1 RECIPE GLAZED SALMON

Miso is a fermented soy bean paste that adds deep flavor to foods. We prefer milder white miso here, rather than the strong-flavored red miso.

- **1 teaspoon grated orange zest plus ¼ cup juice**
- **2 tablespoons white miso**
- **1 tablespoon packed light brown sugar**
- **1 tablespoon rice vinegar**
- **1 tablespoon whole grain mustard**
- **¾ teaspoon cornstarch**
- **Pinch cayenne pepper**

Whisk ingredients together in small saucepan. Bring to boil over medium-high heat; simmer until thickened, about 1 minute. Remove from heat and cover to keep warm.

Soy-Mustard Glaze

MAKES ABOUT ½ CUP, ENOUGH FOR 1 RECIPE GLAZED SALMON

Mirin, a sweet Japanese rice wine, can be found in Asian markets and the international section of most supermarkets.

- **3 tablespoons packed light brown sugar**
- **2 tablespoons soy sauce**
- **2 tablespoons mirin**
- **1 tablespoon sherry vinegar**
- **1 tablespoon whole grain mustard**
- **1 tablespoon water**
- **1 teaspoon cornstarch**
- **⅛ teaspoon red pepper flakes**

Whisk ingredients together in small saucepan. Bring to boil over medium-high heat; simmer until thickened, about 1 minute. Remove from heat and cover to keep warm.

BAKED SOLE FILLETS WITH HERBS AND BREAD CRUMBS

WHY THIS RECIPE WORKS: We wanted a fuss-free, foolproof sole preparation that was suitable for a weeknight dinner yet impressive and elegant enough to serve to company. We found that rolling the fillets into compact bundles eased the transport from baking dish to plate and covering the baking dish with foil protected the delicate fish from the drying heat of the oven. To ramp up the fillets' mild flavor, we brushed them with Dijon mustard; seasoned them with salt, pepper, fresh herbs, and lemon zest; and drizzled them with melted butter and garlic. Then we rolled them up, drizzled them with more butter, and baked them. For texture, we added a mixture of herbs, butter, and panko bread crumbs to the sole at two intervals. We removed the foil before the fish was done cooking, basted the fillets with pan juices, topped them with most of the bread-crumb mixture, and then returned them to the oven uncovered. Just before serving, we sprinkled the remaining crumbs over the fillets.

WE LOVE THE SUBTLE FLAVOR AND FINE TEXTURE OF sole, but it's nearly impossible to translate this fish into a simple, foolproof weeknight meal. For starters, every cooking method has its drawbacks. Both sautéing and pan-frying yield nice golden color, but a hot skillet can overcook the thin fillets in a flash. Plus, sole's footprint is wide, meaning the fillets must be cooked in batches. Poaching, meanwhile, is gentler—but also downright bland without a flavorful poaching liquid and sauce for serving.

Baking, however, struck us as both forgiving and convenient, though the technique was not without fault. Of the recipes we turned up, most were uninspired (coated with plain bread crumbs), overwrought (wrapped artfully around blanched asparagus), or both (en papillote with zucchini), so we selected a few of the more sensible options and gave them a go.

Simply laying the fillets flat on a baking sheet seemed promising—until they broke into pieces when we transferred them to dinner plates. Rolling them into compact bundles eased the transport from baking dish to plate, but the trade-off was a thicker piece of fish that cooked unevenly.

But the technique itself—baking rolled fillets—showed promise, so we experimented with oven temperatures (300 to 450 degrees) to even out the cooking. After 30 minutes at 325 degrees, the fillets were nicely done from edge to center. Covering the baking dish with aluminum foil offered the delicate fish further protection from the drying heat of the oven.

With the cooking method settled, we set out to ramp up the still-flat flavor: We sprinkled the fillets with salt and pepper and minced fresh herbs and lemon zest, drizzled them with melted butter, rolled them, drizzled more butter, and put them in the oven. The flavor? Better, but still mild. Once we worked a clove of minced garlic into the butter and a slather of Dijon mustard over each fillet, the flavor popped.

All we had left to address? The baked fillets' one-dimensional texture and unappetizing pallor. A topping of panko (Japanese-style bread crumbs) toasted in butter along with garlic offered a possible solution to both problems, but adding a measure of herbs to the crumbs once they were cooled made it even better. As for when to add the crumbs, they absorbed moisture and lost their lovely crispness when added at the outset, but lacked cohesion with the fish when sprinkled on after cooking. We compromised with a hybrid technique, removing the foil with five to 10 minutes remaining, basting the fillets with pan juices, topping them with most of the toasted crumbs, and then returning them to the oven uncovered. Just before serving, we sprinkled on the remaining crumbs. This way, most of the crumbs fused to the fish and the final showering offered delicate crispness.

Fuss-free and foolproof, these crumb-topped, herb-filled fillets were exactly what we had hoped to create: fish suitable for a weeknight dinner, yet impressive and elegant enough to serve to company.

BAKED SOLE FILLETS WITH HERBS AND BREAD CRUMBS

Baked Sole Fillets with Herbs and Bread Crumbs

SERVES 6

Try to purchase fillets of similar size. If using smaller fillets (about 3 ounces each), serve 2 fillets per person and reduce the baking time in step 3 to 20 minutes. We strongly advise against using frozen fish in this recipe. Freezing can undermine the texture of the fish, making it hard to roll. Fresh basil or dill can be used in place of the tarragon.

- **3 tablespoons minced fresh parsley**
- **3 tablespoons minced fresh chives**
- **1 tablespoon minced fresh tarragon**
- **1 teaspoon grated lemon zest**
- **5 tablespoons unsalted butter, cut into pieces**
- **2 garlic cloves, minced**
- **6 (6-ounce) boneless, skinless sole or flounder fillets**
- **Salt and pepper**
- **1 tablespoon Dijon mustard**
- **⅔ cup panko bread crumbs**
- **Lemon wedges**

1. Adjust oven rack to middle position and heat oven to 325 degrees. Combine parsley, chives, and tarragon in bowl. Reserve 1 tablespoon herb mixture; stir lemon zest into remaining herb mixture.

2. Melt 4 tablespoons butter in 8-inch skillet over medium heat. Add half of garlic and cook, stirring frequently, until fragrant, 1 to 2 minutes. Remove from heat and set aside.

3. Pat fillets dry with paper towels and season both sides with salt and pepper. Place fillets on cutting board, skinned side up, with tail end pointing away from you. Spread ½ teaspoon mustard on each fillet, sprinkle each evenly with about 1 tablespoon herb–lemon zest mixture, and drizzle each with about 1½ teaspoons garlic butter. Tightly roll fillets from thick end to form cylinders. Set fillets seam side down in 13 by 9-inch baking dish. Drizzle remaining garlic butter over fillets, cover baking dish with aluminum foil, and bake 25 minutes. Wipe out skillet but do not wash.

4. While fillets are baking, melt remaining 1 tablespoon butter in now-empty skillet over medium heat. Add panko and cook, stirring frequently, until crumbs are deep golden brown, 5 to 8 minutes. Reduce heat to low, add remaining garlic, and cook, stirring constantly, until garlic is fragrant and evenly distributed in crumbs, about 1 minute. Transfer to bowl, stir in ¼ teaspoon salt, and season with pepper to taste. Let cool, then stir in reserved 1 tablespoon herb mixture.

5. After fillets have baked 25 minutes, remove baking dish from oven. Baste fillets with melted garlic butter from baking dish, sprinkle with all but 3 tablespoons bread crumbs, and continue to bake, uncovered, until fillets register 135 degrees, 6 to 10 minutes longer. Using thin metal spatula, transfer fillets to plates, sprinkle with remaining bread crumbs, and serve with lemon wedges.

RATING SUPERMARKET CANNED TUNA

Canned tuna has never been high-class fare, but nowadays some manufacturers are promising top-quality fish and processing methods that preserve fresh flavor. We wanted to find out if there had been a revolution in the tuna aisle, so we gathered eight brands of canned solid white albacore tuna, most packed in water, and sampled them in tuna salad sandwiches to find the best one. Though three brands dominate the market, none of these came out on top; instead, tasters preferred two smaller industry newcomers. Most large seafood producers cook their fish twice: once before it's canned, then again after being sealed in the can to kill harmful bacteria. Our two recommended brands, however, pack raw fish into the cans by hand and cook the meat only once, for tuna with a fresher flavor and firmer, heartier texture. They also don't pack their tuna in any liquid, thus preventing its flavor from becoming diluted. Brands are listed in order of preference. See www.americastestkitchen.com for updates to this testing.

RECOMMENDED

WILD PLANET Wild Albacore Tuna
PRICE: $3.39 for 5-oz can (85 cents per oz)
INGREDIENTS: Albacore tuna and sea salt
SODIUM: 250mg per 2-oz serving
COMMENTS: "Rich and flavorful, but not fishy," this hand-packed tuna containing no extra liquid held its own in the mayonnaise-y salad and was praised for its "hearty" yet "tender" bite.

AMERICAN TUNA Pole Caught Wild Albacore
PRICE: $4.99 for 6-oz can ($1.00 per oz)
INGREDIENTS: Albacore tuna
SODIUM: 20mg per 2-oz serving
COMMENTS: This product stood out to tasters because it "actually tastes like tuna." The "distinct chunks" boasted fish flavor that was "pronounced" but not overpowering.

RECOMMENDED WITH RESERVATIONS

STARKIST Selects Solid White Albacore Tuna in Water
PRICE: $1.69 for 4.5-oz can (47 cents per oz)
INGREDIENTS: White tuna, water, salt, pyrophosphate
SODIUM: 170mg per 2-oz serving
COMMENTS: Most tasters appreciated that this supposedly higher quality tuna's "solid chunks", but flavorwise it was a mixed bag: To some the meat had "decent" tuna flavor, while others thought the fish fell flat in tuna salad. Since our tasting, StarKist has slightly changed the formulation of this product; tasters felt the new version was comparable in taste and texture.

BUMBLE BEE Prime Fillet Solid White Albacore Tuna in Water
PRICE: $1.99 for 5-oz can (54 cents per oz)
INGREDIENTS: White tuna, water, salt, pyrophosphate added
SODIUM: 140mg per 2-oz serving
COMMENTS: The general consensus about this product whose manufacturer claims comes from a superior grade tuna? Ambivalence. Tasters described the meat's "very fine" texture as "shredded without being squished," and though its flavor was "rather bland" and "mild," it was "moist and pretty tasty" and made a "good, basic tuna sandwich."

RECOMMENDED WITH RESERVATIONS *(cont.)*

CHICKEN OF THE SEA Solid White Albacore Tuna in Water
PRICE: $1.99 for 5-oz can (57 cents per oz)
INGREDIENTS: Solid white tuna, water, vegetable broth (contains soy), salt, pyrophosphate
SODIUM: 180mg per 2-oz serving
COMMENTS: The favorite non-gourmet offering of the "big three" brands, this tuna tasted familiar to many of us. Almost everyone found the meat "decent" but "watery." Others complained that it reminded them "why I never wanted this in my lunchbox as a kid."

CROWN PRINCE Natural Solid White Albacore Tuna in Water
PRICE: $2.99 for 6-oz can (70 cents per oz)
INGREDIENTS: Albacore tuna, spring water, sea salt
SODIUM: 105mg per 2-oz serving
COMMENTS: Though this tuna consistently racked up points for its "hearty" texture, tasters' votes were split when it came to flavor. Some said the fish tasted "meaty" and "pleasant," or was "very, very fishy" and "fermented tasting."

STARKIST Solid White Albacore Tuna in Water
PRICE: $1.67 for 5-oz can (51 cents per oz)
INGREDIENTS: White tuna, water, vegetable broth, salt, pyrophosphate; contains soy
SODIUM: 190mg per 2-oz serving
COMMENTS: Without much tuna flavor to speak of, this conventional StarKist sample was more of a "family-friendly protein delivery system" than its premium sibling. That said, a few tasters picked up on a big hit of salt—presumably a result of the meat soaking in vegetable broth, which seemed to affect this brand more than others.

BUMBLE BEE Solid White Albacore Tuna in Water
PRICE: $1.69 for 5-oz can (46 cents per oz)
INGREDIENTS: White tuna, water, vegetable broth, salt, pyrophosphate added; contains soy
SODIUM: 140mg per 2-oz serving
COMMENTS: Though the tuna's "mild" flavor didn't offend anyone, it didn't impress either. Where this lesser Bumble Bee sample really lost points was in the texture department, where it elicited censure for tasting "soupy" and "watery."

RATING VENTRESCA TUNA IN OLIVE OIL

There's canned tuna—and then there's ultra-premium ventresca tuna packed in olive oil. The imported European equivalent of sushi-grade toro, ventresca tuna is cut from the fatty belly of either the bonito del norte or yellowfin species, and the buttery, tender, olive oil-packed slices make a luxe addition to any niçoise salad or Spanish tapas spread. We tasted six brands, priced from $1.20 to $4.72 per ounce, plus shipping, to find the best one (most brands listed are mail-order only). One in particular, our top-rated ventresca tuna, left tasters swooning over its "creamy, delicate" meat boasting "full, rich tuna flavor." We think it's worth the occasional splurge, but since it fetches $35 for 8.5 ounces before shipping, we also elected a more frugal alternative that cost one-quarter the price and can be found in some supermarkets. The "firm-fleshed," "briny" ventresca yellowfin fillets from our Best Buy scored almost as high with our tasters, who appreciated its "very moist and tender" texture. Brands are listed in order of preference. See www.americastestkitchen.com for updates to this testing.

HIGHLY RECOMMENDED

NARDIN Bonito Del Norte Ventresca Fillets

PRICE: $35 for 8.5 oz ($4.12 per oz)
COMMENTS: This Spanish import's "tender" yet "firm" fillets garnered raves from tasters, who enjoyed its "rich," "fresh," "intensely tuna-y" flavor so much that it was deemed good enough to eat "as-is without any accoutrements."

RECOMMENDED

TONNINO Tuna Ventresca Yellowfin in Olive Oil

PRICE: $7.99 for 6.7 oz ($1.20 per oz) **BEST BUY**
COMMENTS: At one-quarter the price of our favorite ventresca tuna, this yellowfin sample was a relative bargain—but no slouch. Its "large, dark pink flakes" were "firm-fleshed" yet "very moist and tender," with "assertive," "briny" flavor that tasted "like the sea." A perfect addition to any appetizer platter, according to one taster.

ORTIZ Yellowfin Ventresca Tuna

PRICE: $15.95 for 110g (about 3.8 oz) ($4.20 per oz)
COMMENTS: Impressed by this sample's "great meatiness," "richness," and "concentrated," "pronounced flavor," tasters likened this tuna to "dark-meat chicken." To most, the "nice big flakes" offered "good chew," though a few tasters found them slightly dry.

RECOMMENDED *(cont.)*

ORTIZ Bonito Del Norte Ventresca

PRICE: $17.95 for 110g (about 3.8 oz) ($4.72 per oz)
COMMENTS: At a whopping $4.72 per ounce, this was the most expensive sample we tried—and it made a convert of one self-proclaimed canned tuna-hater, who declared, "This stuff is fantastic!" The "moist," "supple" chunks were so large that they dwarfed one taster's fork, and were "tender" enough to "melt in your mouth," though a few tasters found their flavor "way fishy."

CONSORZIO Ventresca de Atun

PRICE: $8.99 for 112g (about 3.9 oz) ($2.31 per oz)
COMMENTS: Most tasters found this tuna's "firm," "toothsome" flakes "appealing" and praised its "richness," "assertive tuna flavor," and "lemony finish." However, there were more than a few comments that the fish was distractingly salty.

A'S Do Mar Ventresca

PRICE: $9.99 for 125g (about 4.4 oz) ($2.27 per oz)
COMMENTS: These "firm tan-pink rectangles" were "salty and a little dry"—almost "cured," according to a few tasters—with a texture that some tasters deemed no better than "generic canned tuna." Still, others found the chunks pleasantly "firm" with a flavor that was "sweet, meaty, and rich."

FALL *Classics*

CHAPTER 7

THE RECIPES

French-Style Pot-Roasted Pork Loin

- French-Style Pot-Roasted Pork Loin with Port and Figs
- French-Style Pot-Roasted Pork Loin with Marsala and Mushrooms

Classic Gingerbread Cake

TASTING LAB

Premium Pork

Yvonne demonstrates that with a whisk and a little elbow grease, the batter for Classic Gingerbread Cake comes together in a flash—no stand mixer required.

WHEN THE HEAT OF SUMMER DIES DOWN AND THE CRISP, COOL AIR of fall breezes in, our thoughts turn to slow-cooked roasts. Pot roast almost always starts with a fatty, flavorful cut that's virtually guaranteed to turn tender and juicy after hours of cooking. But sometimes we crave something different than the usual beef pot roast, so we wondered: Could we cook a lean (some might even say bland) pork loin in a covered pot in the oven and get the same juicy results? We wouldn't be satisfied unless we could produce a slow-roasted loin every bit as tender, moist, and flavorful as its fattier (and more forgiving) counterparts.

Of course, a warm, inviting fall meal wouldn't be complete without dessert, and we think gingerbread cake fills the bill perfectly. But this simple snack cake's moist, tender crumb typically comes at a price: a gummy, sunken center—not to mention a glut of extraneous spices. We were determined to find a way to keep gingerbread cake from collapsing. We also wanted to uncover the secret to striking the right balance of spice, with plenty of ginger to make this cake worthy of its name and just enough supporting players to provide a subtle but welcome spicy background heat.

POT-ROASTED PORK LOIN

WHY THIS RECIPE WORKS: *Enchaud Perigordine* is a fancy name for what's actually a relatively simple French dish: slow-cooked pork loin. Cooked in the oven in a covered casserole dish with a trotter (pig's foot) for body and flavor, the roast turns out incredibly moist and flavorful, with a rich jus to accompany it. At least it does when it's prepared in France. But while pigs in France are bred to have plenty of fat, their American counterparts are lean, which translates to a bland and stringy roast. To improve the flavor and texture of our center-cut loin, we lowered the oven temperature (to 225 degrees) and removed the roast from the oven when it was medium-rare. Searing just three sides of the roast—rather than all four—prevented the bottom of the roast from overcooking due to direct contact with the pot. Butterflying the pork allowed us to salt a maximum amount of surface area for a roast that was thoroughly seasoned throughout. And while we eliminated the hard-to-find trotter, we added butter for richness and a sprinkling of gelatin to lend body to the sauce.

FRENCH CUISINE IS WELL KNOWN FOR ITS MANY DISHES that feature a lackluster cut of meat turned sumptuous and flavorful by surprisingly simple methods, but the one that impresses us most is enchaud Perigordine. A specialty in the southwest Perigord region of France, it throws the loin—one of the least-promising cuts for slow-cooking—into a covered casserole with garlic and a trotter (or pig's foot) to bake for several hours. You'd expect that a roast with so little fat or collagen to protect it would emerge from the pot dried out and tasteless. Instead, the finished meat is astonishingly moist and flavorful, with plenty of rich-tasting, viscous jus to drizzle on top. Unfortunately, our attempts to make this dish at home have always turned out exactly as we had expected: bland and stringy, with barely any juices in the pot to speak of. We're never sure what gets lost in translation but the promise of a dish that produced juicy, tender, savory results from this bland (but widely available) roast was motivation enough for us to find an approach of our own. We had just one stipulation: The trotter had to go. Though it imparts body and flavor to the sauce, hunting one down would complicate this genuinely simple dish.

The basic method for preparing enchaud Perigordine is simple: Season a loin with salt and pepper, tie it with kitchen twine so it cooks evenly, and sear it in a Dutch oven. Then remove the roast, sauté garlic (and a little onion) in the rendered fat, add seasonings (and a trotter or two), bake in a covered casserole, and, finally, let it rest briefly before serving to allow the juices to redistribute. We gave a few new recipes a try, and when not one of the roasts—cooked at both high heat and more moderate temperatures—turned out like the juicy, rich-tasting pot-roasted loins we've enjoyed, we realized we had a very fundamental problem to deal with: the pork itself.

While French pigs are bred to have plenty of fat, American pork boasts far less marbling, and the center-cut roast that we were using is perhaps the leanest cut of all. The blade-end roast, the part of the loin closest to the shoulder, has more fat and flavor, but it's not nearly as readily available. We were stuck with the center-cut loin and wondered if we could improve the results by lowering the oven temperature further than we'd tried before and pulling out the roast when it hit the medium-rare mark (140 degrees). Sure enough, this test proved that the lower the oven temperature, the more succulent the roast. Our tasters clearly favored the pork cooked in the 225-degree oven for about an hour and 10 minutes. Not only was it far juicier than any of our previous attempts, but a small pool of concentrated jus had accumulated at the bottom of the pot. In this very low oven, the outer layers of the loin absorbed less heat (and consequently squeezed out less moisture) during the time it took the center to climb to 140 degrees. There was just one texture-related setback: The bottom of the roast, which was in direct contact with the pot, cooked more quickly than the top. We easily solved this problem by searing just the top and sides of the roast while leaving the bottom raw. But we still had work to do. Engineering juicier meat hadn't improved its bland flavor. Plus, without the trotter, the sauce lacked body.

FRENCH-STYLE POT-ROASTED PORK LOIN

Salting and brining are our go-to methods when we want to draw seasoning into large cuts of pork and help the meat retain moisture during cooking. Brining wouldn't be helpful here, because soaking in a salt solution adds extra water to the meat, which would simply leach out and dilute the jus. Salting was the better option. The downside was that it took at least six hours (with superior results after 24 hours) for the salt to penetrate deep into the thick roast. We wondered if we couldn't find a faster way. Splitting the loin lengthwise into two smaller pieces and liberally seasoning each one with salt seemed like it might hasten the seasoning process, but when we gave it a shot tasters complained that the interior of each mini loin was still bland. Slicing a pocket into the top of the loin and sprinkling the interior with salt was strike two. Though the center of the roast was well seasoned, it was just as easy to get an unseasoned bite. After some further experimentation we landed on an effective technique: "double-butterflying." By making two sweeping cuts—the first a half-inch from the bottom of the roast and another into the thicker portion that we created with the first cut—we were able to open up the loin like a tri-fold book and expose a vast amount of surface area. Then we rubbed each side with 1½ teaspoons of kosher salt, rolled the roast back up, and secured it with kitchen twine. While this method required a bit more knifework, it produced perfectly seasoned meat. Even better, butterflying made it possible to add fat and flavor directly to the meat, bringing us closer to the French original. For "fattening up" the roast, bacon fat, rendered salt-pork fat, and butter all seemed like viable options, and though each produced richly flavorful, supremely juicy roasts, tasters particularly enjoyed the subtly sweet flavor imparted by butter. In fact, we pushed that sweetness one step further and added 1 teaspoon of sugar to the salt rub. To round out the roast's savory depth, we then sliced a few garlic cloves and caramelized them in the butter before using the mixture to coat the meat. Finally, we sprinkled the rolled roast with herbes de Provence, a heady combination that includes dried basil, fennel, lavender, marjoram, rosemary, sage, and thyme. That left just the flavorful-but-thin jus to attend to.

We knew one way to bulk up the jus would be to put bones in the pot. Not only do the bones themselves contain gelatin, but the connective tissue surrounding them also turns into gelatin over the course of long cooking. We wanted to see what would happen if we started with a bone-in loin, removed the bones and then used them to make a quick stock to add to the pork as it roasted. This worked beautifully. When we opened the pot about an hour later, the jus was as glossy and thickened as the trotter-enhanced liquid. The only problem was that making the stock added 30 minutes to an already lengthy cooking time. We wondered if adding powdered gelatin, which we've used in the past to mimic slow-cooked stocks, would do the trick here, and found that 1 tablespoon bloomed in ¼ cup chicken broth lent just the right viscosity. But bones also contribute flavor, and we still had to make up for that loss. Reducing ⅓ cup of white wine (after sautéing the onions) and whisking in 1 tablespoon of butter along with the gelatin rendered the sauce rich and balanced but not remarkable. It was only our final inspiration—a diced apple cooked along with the onions—that really brought the sauce together. Enchaud is traditionally served with pickles as a counterpoint to its rich flavors, and tasters raved that the softened bits of sweet-tart fruit worked in the same way. A variation with port and figs was equally satisfying. The French method had started us off, but it was kitchen testing that made slow-cooking a super-lean cut something truly great.

French-Style Pot-Roasted Pork Loin

SERVES 4 TO 6

We strongly prefer the flavor of natural pork in this recipe, but if enhanced pork (injected with a salt solution) is used, reduce the salt to 2 teaspoons (1 teaspoon per side) in step 2. The pork can be prepared through step 2, wrapped in plastic wrap, and refrigerated for up to 2 days.

- **2 tablespoons unsalted butter, cut into 2 pieces**
- **6 garlic cloves, sliced thin**
- **1 (2½-pound) boneless center-cut pork loin roast, trimmed**
- **Kosher salt and pepper**
- **1 teaspoon sugar**
- **2 teaspoons herbes de Provence**
- **2 tablespoons vegetable oil**
- **1 Granny Smith apple, peeled, cored, and cut into ¼-inch pieces**
- **1 onion, chopped fine**
- **⅓ cup dry white wine**
- **2 sprigs fresh thyme**
- **1 bay leaf**
- **1 tablespoon unflavored gelatin**
- **¼–¾ cup low-sodium chicken broth**
- **1 tablespoon chopped fresh parsley**

1. Adjust oven rack to lower-middle position and heat oven to 225 degrees. Melt 1 tablespoon butter in 8-inch skillet over medium-low heat. Add half of garlic and cook, stirring frequently, until golden, 5 to 7 minutes. Transfer mixture to bowl and refrigerate while preparing pork.

2. Position roast fat side up. Insert knife ½ inch from bottom of roast along 1 long side and cut horizontally, stopping ½ inch before edge. Open up flap. Keeping knife parallel to cutting board, cut through thicker half of roast about ½ inch from bottom of roast, stopping about ½ inch before edge. Open this flap up. If uneven, cover with plastic wrap and use meat pounder to even out. Sprinkle 1 tablespoon salt evenly over both sides of loin (½ tablespoon per side) and thoroughly rub into pork until slightly tacky. Sprinkle sugar evenly over inside of loin, then spread with cooled toasted garlic mixture. Starting from short side, roll roast tightly and tie with kitchen twine at 1-inch intervals. Sprinkle tied roast

NOTES FROM THE TEST KITCHEN

SECRETS TO JUICY, RICH-TASTING POT-ROASTED PORK LOIN

1. BUTTERFLY AND SALT: Opening up the roast like a book creates more surface area for seasoning, ensuring that the salt thoroughly penetrates the meat.

2. ADD FAT AND TIE: Spreading butter over the surface enriches this lean cut, bringing it closer in flavor and juiciness to well-marbled French pork. The roast is then rolled up and tied.

3. SEAR TIED ROAST ON 3 SIDES: Browning only the sides of the roast not in contact with the pan prevents the bottom of the meat from overcooking.

4. COOK IN LOW OVEN: Baking the pork in a gentle 225-degree oven until medium-rare guarantees that the meat will cook up tender and juicy, not chalky and dry.

5. ADD GELATIN: Adding gelatin to the exuded meat juices replaces the body and richness lost by omitting the hard-to-find pig's trotter used in the French original.

evenly with herbs de Provence and season with pepper.

3. Heat 1 tablespoon oil in Dutch oven over medium heat until just smoking. Add roast, fat side down, and brown on top and sides (do not brown bottom of roast), 5 to 8 minutes. Transfer to plate. Add remaining 1 tablespoon oil, apple, and onion; cook, stirring frequently, until onion is softened and browned, 5 to 7 minutes. Stir in remaining sliced garlic and cook until fragrant, about 30 seconds. Stir in wine, thyme, and bay leaf and cook for 30 seconds. Return roast, fat side up, to pot; place large sheet of aluminum foil over pot and cover tightly with lid. Transfer pot to oven and cook until pork registers 140 degrees, 50 minutes to 1½ hours.

4. Transfer roast to carving board, tent loosely with foil, and let rest for 20 minutes. While pork rests, sprinkle gelatin over ¼ cup chicken broth and let sit until gelatin softens, about 5 minutes. Remove thyme sprigs and bay leaf from jus. Pour jus into 2-cup liquid measuring cup and, if necessary, add chicken broth to measure 1¼ cups. Return jus to pot and bring to simmer over medium heat. Whisk softened gelatin mixture, remaining 1 tablespoon butter, and parsley into jus and season with salt and pepper to taste; remove from heat and cover to keep warm. Slice pork into ½-inch-thick slices, adding any accumulated juices to sauce. Serve pork, passing sauce at table.

VARIATIONS

French-Style Pot-Roasted Pork Loin with Port and Figs

Substitute ¾ cup chopped dried figs for apple and port for white wine. Add 1 tablespoon balsamic vinegar to sauce with butter in step 4.

French-Style Pot-Roasted Pork Loin with Marsala and Mushrooms

Microwave ½ cup chicken broth and ½ ounce dried porcini mushrooms, rinsed, in covered bowl until steaming, about 1 minute. Let stand until softened, about 5 minutes. Drain mushrooms through fine-mesh strainer lined with coffee filter, reserve liquid, and chop mushrooms. Proceed with recipe, substituting 4 ounces trimmed and chopped cremini mushrooms and chopped porcini for apple. Substitute Marsala wine for white wine, and use porcini soaking liquid to soften gelatin in step 4. Add 2 teaspoons lemon juice to sauce with butter in step 4.

RATING PREMIUM PORK

Everything seems to be going upscale nowadays. We wanted to know if pedigreed pork, such as Berkshire (known as Kurobuta in Japan) and Duroc, was worth its premium price tag. We mail-ordered bone-in chops and a roast we cut into chops from five different specialty producers and compared them with supermarket chops. Three mail-order chops were 100 percent Berkshire pork; one was a Berkshire blend; and the last was a Duroc blend. There were startling differences in their color: The pure Berkshire meat was crimson, while the blends were not quite as dark but had more color than the pale supermarket chops. Once pan-seared, the Berkshire meat won us over with its tender texture and intense pork taste. As it turns out, there is a connection between rich flavor and deep color. Color reflects the meat's pH level; the higher the pH, the darker the meat—and the better its flavor and texture. So if you can't splurge, try to pick out the reddest supermarket chops. Brands are listed in order of preference. See www.americastestkitchen.com for updates to this testing.

HIGHLY RECOMMENDED

SNAKE RIVER FARMS American Kurobuta (Berkshire) Pork

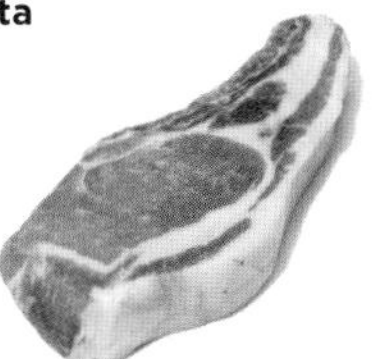

PRICE: $10 per lb
COMMENTS: Tasters raved about these reddish-pink chops' extremely juicy, tender texture and "intense pork-y flavor," which some likened to "smoked bacon." The same meat is sold as Kurobuta in Japan.

D'ARTAGNAN Berkshire Pork Chops, Milanese-Style Cut

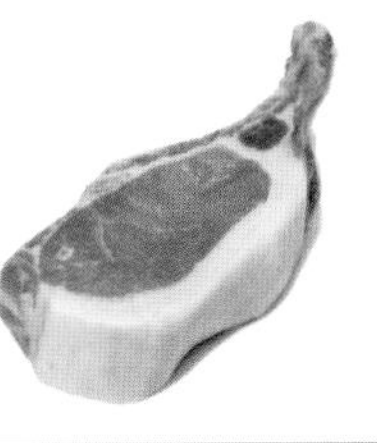

PRICE: $10.99 per lb
COMMENTS: Just as crimson-colored as our winner, these Berkshire chops (butchered from either end of the loin, Milanese-style) were "rich, nutty, tender, and juicy" with "tasty caramelized fat on the exterior."

RECOMMENDED

EDEN FARMS French-Cut Kurobuta Pork
PRICE: $17.50 per lb
COMMENTS: French-cut with the top of the bone stripped of meat, these 100-percent Berkshire chops were "exceptionally moist" and tender, with a flavor "reminiscent of bacon." A few tasters found the color, which had a slightly less red hue than that of our winner, had a somewhat less-rich flavor.

RECOMMENDED *(cont.)*

HERITAGE ACRES Berkshire and Berkshire-blend Pork
PRICE: $8.95 per lb
COMMENTS: Tasters were split on these chops: Some praised their "moist, juicy" texture and "mild, clean," "sweet" flavor, and others found nothing remarkable in the flavor, noting that it was "like corn," and "not super pork-y." Their color lacked the deep ruddiness of the 100-percent Berkshire pork.

VERMONT QUALITY MEATS Duroc and Duroc-blend Pork

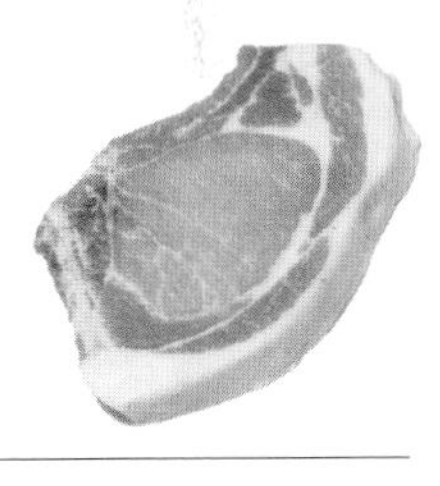

PRICE: $7.60 per lb
COMMENTS: As one taster summed up, the flavor of these faintly pink heritage-blend chops was "not amazing—just decent." Others noted that their texture was "somewhat coarse and dry."

SUPERMARKET PORK CHOPS

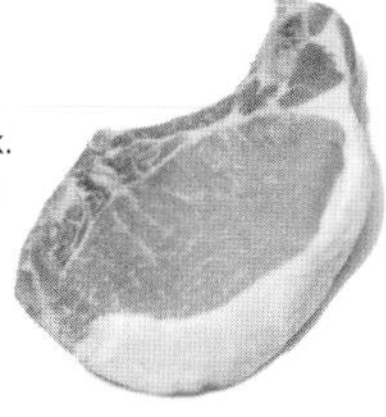

PRICE: $4.29 per lb
COMMENTS: These last-place chops dulled in comparison to the 100-percent Berkshire pork. Their off-white meat was "moist enough," but "chalky," "coarsely grained," and "relatively bland."

CLASSIC GINGERBREAD CAKE

CLASSIC GINGERBREAD CAKE

WHY THIS RECIPE WORKS: Most gingerbread recipes that are moist also suffer from a dense, sunken center, and flavors range from barely gingery to spice overload. Focusing on flavor first, we bumped up the ginger flavor by using ground ginger and grated fresh ginger and accented the ginger with cinnamon and fresh-ground pepper. As for the liquid components, dark stout had a bittersweet flavor that brought out the caramel undertones of the molasses. Finally, swapping out the butter for vegetable oil and replacing some of the brown sugar with granulated let the spice flavors come through. To prevent a sunken center, we incorporated the baking soda with the wet ingredients instead of the other dry ones, which helped to neutralize those acidic ingredients before they were incorporated into the batter and allowed the baking powder to do a better job. And vigorous stirring gave our bread the structure necessary to further ensure the center didn't collapse.

AS WE STEPPED THROUGH THE FAUX-VINTAGE GATES OF the "living museum" at Plimoth Plantation, we were hoping for salvation. Or at least insight into a cake that dates back to the Colonial era. After a week of baking countless batches of uninspired gingerbread cake, we still lacked a workable baseline recipe. The cake we had in mind was moist through and through and utterly simple—a snack cake that would bake in a square pan. But without exception, every recipe we tried that had the moistness we wanted also suffered from a dense, sunken center. Equally disappointing, flavors ran the gamut from barely gingery to addled with enough spices to make a curry fan cry for mercy. So much for simple: This cake had us flummoxed.

Hoping to glean some Colonial wisdom that might help our cake bake up both moist and even, we came to spend a day at this circa-1627 Pilgrim village in Plymouth, Massachusetts. When the museum's culinarian showed up bearing a stack of weathered cookbooks, we were sure we'd come to the right place. But as we prepared these vintage recipes, our optimism faded. Apparently, early Americans liked their gingerbread dry and dense as bricks—an effect exacerbated in a few recipes by a curious kneading step. (Kneading helps develop the gluten in flour, providing structure to bread but rendering cakes and cookies tough.) In cakes so dry, the issue of wet, sunken centers never came up. Dejected, we bid our hosts a polite "good-morrow" and headed back to the test kitchen to regroup.

Cobbling together a basic working recipe from the best of the flawed versions we'd come across, we decided to put the structural problems on hold and focus on fixing flavor first.

Using a simple dump-and-stir method, we mixed the wet ingredients (molasses, water, melted butter, a couple of eggs) in one bowl and the dry ingredients (flour, baking soda, baking powder, brown sugar, salt) in another. For now, we opted for a purist's approach to the spice rack, expunging all options but a single tablespoon of ground ginger. After gently folding the wet ingredients into the dry, we poured the batter into an 8-inch square cake pan and baked it at 350 degrees for 40 minutes.

As expected, the cake's center collapsed. But with the extraneous spices out of the way, we were able to focus on the ginger. Bumping the ground ginger up to 2 tablespoons yielded an assertive bite, though it lacked complexity. We tried folding in grated fresh ginger with the dried. Sure enough, the pungent notes of the fresh root made the flavor sing.

As for other spices, options like cardamom, nutmeg, and cloves weren't terrible but shifted the gingerbread too far into spice-cake territory. In the end, only two made the cut: cinnamon and fresh-ground black pepper, which worked in tandem with all that potent ginger to produce a warm, complex, lingering heat.

Eyeing the liquid components, we suspected that using water was a missed opportunity. Buttermilk added tanginess but dulled the ginger. Ginger ale, ginger beer, and hard apple cider all seemed likely contenders, but baking rendered them undetectable. Dark stout, on the other hand, had a bittersweet flavor that brought out the caramel undertones of the molasses. To minimize its

NOTES FROM THE TEST KITCHEN

KEYS TO RICHER, ZINGIER FLAVOR

BITTERSWEET BEER
Dark stout contributes deep, caramelized notes.

FLAVOR-FREE FAT
Clean, neutral-tasting oil brings key flavors into clear relief.

A ROOTY BOOST
Fresh ginger kicks up the fiery, pungent notes of dried ginger.

BACKSEAT SPICES
Cinnamon and black pepper complement—without overwhelming—the ginger.

NOT SO GINGERLY WITH GINGERBREAD

Most cake batters require a gentle touch to avoid developing gluten in the flour and, thus, a tough crumb. But vigorous stirring actually gave our super-wet gingerbread batter the structure necessary to keep the center from collapsing.

GENTLY STIRRED BATTER = SUNKEN CAKE CENTER

booziness, we tried gently heating the stout to cook off some of the alcohol—a somewhat fussy step that side-by-side tests nonetheless proved worthwhile.

Finally, we found that swapping out the butter for cleaner-tasting vegetable oil and replacing a quarter of the brown sugar with granulated cleared the way to let all those spice flavors come through.

Now that the flavor was coming along nicely, we were more determined than ever to solve the sinking problem. Baking the cake in a Bundt pan might have alleviated the collapse, but not without the fussy steps of greasing and flouring the conical center and turning out the finished cake for serving. Not to mention the fact that not everybody has this type of pan. But we had another idea: Bucking the usual protocol for cakes, a few of the recipes we tested incorporated the baking soda with the wet ingredients instead of the other dry ones (including the baking powder). The reason? Too much acid in a batter lessens the baking powder's ability to leaven the cake. Baking powder contains just the right amounts of both acid and alkalai, which react to produce carbon dioxide for leavening. But if too much acid is present from other sources, it will neutralize some of the acid in the baking powder, reducing its effectiveness. Thus baking soda, an alkali, is used to neutralize acidic ingredients before they get incorporated into the batter. With gingerbread, the typical culprits are molasses and brown sugar, but our recipe also included stout—a triple threat of acidity that might well be thwarting the rise. We made the recipe again, this time stirring the half-teaspoon of baking soda right into the warm stout, followed by the molasses and brown sugar. It was a modest success. While the center still fell, it wasn't nearly as drastic—more of a buckle than a crater.

Our batter was quite loose, so we wondered if the flour-to-liquid ratio was off. Would a drier gingerbread be a sturdier gingerbread? We tried decreasing the stout and oil. No dice. An extra egg made the texture sturdier—but rubbery.

We were getting close to calling it quits—or at least calling for some blemish-masking sleight of hand involving powdered sugar—when we reached a breakthrough. It was a casual conversation with a colleague about that fruitless trip (weeks earlier) to Plimoth Plantation that

got us thinking about the gingerbread we'd made there. Structure, we mused, was about the only thing those tough little bricks had going for them. Which is when we remembered the unusual kneading step.

Kneading—as well as energetic beating—contributes strength and structure by developing the glutens in flour. But gluten development is the enemy of tenderness, which is why cake recipes generally incorporate the flour gently at the end of mixing, after the heavy-duty butter creaming is done. Tenderness we had in spades; structure, we could use. Could roughing up the batter a bit strengthen the crumb?

Departing from our current method of delicately folding the wet ingredients into the dry, we added only about a third of the liquid ingredients, then mixed vigorously to form a smooth paste. We incorporated the remaining wet ingredients in two more installments, mixing until smooth after each addition. We put the cake in the oven, crossed our fingers, and waited. Sure enough, this cake was a real looker—nary a crater in sight. Fragrant, moist, bold-flavored, and beautiful, this was the gingerbread cake we'd been dreaming of.

Silently, we made a mental note to respect our elders. Sometimes, it turns out, history bears repeating.

Classic Gingerbread Cake

SERVES 8

This cake packs potent yet well-balanced fragrant, spicy heat. If you are particularly sensitive to spice, you can decrease the amount of dried ginger to 1 tablespoon. Avoid opening the oven door until the minimum baking time has elapsed. Serve the gingerbread plain or with lightly sweetened whipped cream.

- **¾ cup stout, such as Guinness**
- **½ teaspoon baking soda**
- **⅔ cup molasses**
- **¾ cup packed (5¼ ounces) light brown sugar**
- **¼ cup (1¾ ounces) granulated sugar**
- **1½ cups (7½ ounces) all-purpose flour**
- **2 tablespoons ground ginger**
- **½ teaspoon baking powder**
- **½ teaspoon salt**
- **¼ teaspoon ground cinnamon**
- **¼ teaspoon pepper**
- **2 large eggs, room temperature**
- **⅓ cup vegetable oil**
- **1 tablespoon grated fresh ginger**

1. Adjust oven rack to middle position and heat oven to 350 degrees. Grease 8-inch square baking pan, line with parchment paper, grease parchment, then flour pan.

2. Bring stout to boil in medium saucepan over medium heat, stirring occasionally. Remove from heat and stir in baking soda (mixture will foam vigorously). When foaming subsides, stir in molasses, brown sugar, and granulated sugar until dissolved; set aside. Whisk flour, ground ginger, baking powder, salt, cinnamon, and pepper together in large bowl.

3. Transfer stout mixture to second large bowl. Whisk in eggs, oil, and grated ginger until combined. Whisk wet mixture into flour mixture in thirds, stirring vigorously until completely smooth after each addition.

4. Scrape batter into prepared pan, smooth top with rubber spatula, and gently tap pan on counter to release air bubbles. Bake until top of cake is just firm to touch and toothpick inserted into center comes out clean, 35 to 45 minutes. Let cake cool in pan on wire rack, about 1½ hours.

NEW YORK–STYLE *Pizza at Home*

CHAPTER 8

We use pizza peels in the test kitchen to remove hot pizza from the baking stone, but if you don't have one at home, simply use a wide spatula and an overturned baking sheet.

THERE'S NO DOUBT ABOUT IT: EVERYONE LOVES PIZZA. BUT WHAT makes a great pizza? Well, that question can provoke heated debate. Here in the test kitchen we love most any well-executed pizza, but we have a particular weakness for New York–style pizza, with its impossibly thin, crisp crust that still manages to be tender and chewy all at the same time. But home ovens don't reach any higher than 500 degrees, which makes this type of crust extremely difficult to achieve—the oven just doesn't get hot enough to produce a deeply browned crust before the interior dries out and toughens. Adding to your troubles is the dough, which can be nearly impossible to stretch thin, causing even the savviest home cook to struggle to produce a quality parlor pie. We were determined to change all that. So roll up your sleeves and follow us as we test our way—through trial and error, with a healthy dose of science mixed in—to the best foolproof thin-crust pizza. We promise you won't be disappointed.

THIN-CRUST PIZZA

WHY THIS RECIPE WORKS: With home ovens that reach only 500 degrees and dough that's impossible to stretch thin, even the savviest cooks can struggle to produce New York–style parlor-quality pizza. We were in pursuit of a simple-to-make pizza with a perfect crust—thin, crisp, and spottily charred on the exterior; tender yet chewy within. High-protein bread flour gave us a chewy, nicely tanned pizza crust and the right ratio of flour, water, and yeast gave us dough that would stretch and retain moisture as it baked. We kneaded the dough quickly in a food processor, then let it proof in the refrigerator for a few hours to develop its flavors. After we shaped and topped the pizza, it went onto a blazing hot baking stone to cook. Placing the stone near the top of the oven was a surprising improvement, allowing the top of the pizza to brown as well as the bottom. In minutes we had a pizza with everything in sync: a thoroughly crisp, browned crust with a slightly chewy texture, just like a good parlor slice.

PIZZA WAS THE FIRST FOOD MANY OF US LEARNED TO make as kids, and we've been determined to perfect it ever since. Over the years, our dogged pursuit of the ideal crust—thin, crisp, and spottily charred on the exterior; tender yet chewy within—has led us into exhaustive research and experiments, and even compelled us to extremes. We've been known to override the lock on our oven during its white-hot cleaning cycle. We've even built a wood-fired oven in the backyard.

But despite those efforts, we had yet to produce a recipe that was both reliable and reasonable for someone baking in a conventional oven. After the 10 to 12 minutes necessary to crisp the crust, the interior inevitably turns dry and tough. Plus, the raw dough itself is a devil to work with: Too wet and it becomes sticky; too dry and it's a stiff, dense wad. And forget stretching it into a neat circle; most of the time it either rips or springs back like a rubber band. If we were really going to bring home the kind of pizza we've come to crave when dining out, we'd have to take each element back to the drawing board.

Like other lean doughs, pizza dough has a short ingredient list (often just flour, water, salt, and yeast), so each element counts for a lot. Flour was the obvious first consideration, and we opted for high-protein (about 13 percent by weight) bread flour. It's a typical choice when a chewy, nicely tanned crust is the goal, since the proteins both encourage gluten development and brown easily.

The other major factor is the hydration level of the dough—in other words, the weight of the water in relation to the weight of the flour. From some work we've done on focaccia, we knew that low-hydration doughs (around 55 percent water) generally result in the type of tight, even crumb you might find in sandwich bread, whereas a higher hydration (70 percent and up) produces the looser, airier, more bubbly crumb typical of rustic artisan-style breads. Figuring our goal was somewhere in the middle, we started our testing by mixing together five moderately wet doughs (from 58 to 67 percent hydration), kneading all the ingredients with our preferred food-processor method. (A more conventional stand-mixer method might take 15 to 20 minutes before the dough turns into a shiny, elastic mass, but we've discovered that a food processor turns out comparably kneaded results in less than two minutes.) We let the dough proof at room temperature for a few hours, shaped and topped the pies with our quick no-cook pizza sauce (a placeholder at this stage) and a generous handful of shredded mozzarella, and shuttled them onto blazing hot (500-degree) baking stones to cook. We pulled them out roughly 10 minutes later, once the crusts had puffed up a bit and blistered in spots and the cheese was melted and spotty brown.

Just as we'd expected, the lower-hydration doughs were not only stiff and difficult to shape into even rounds when raw, but also tough to chew once baked. But really wet doughs weren't ideal either; though they emerged significantly more tender from the oven, all that water had made the raw dough so sticky and soft that it tended to tear when stretched. The best of the bunch fell at about 61 percent—enough to stretch easily without ripping or sticking to our fingers and retain moisture as it baked. With further experimentation, we found that we could raise the hydration level to 63 percent and still be able to handle this stickier dough by adding a little extra flour to the exterior as we shaped and stretched the pie.

THIN-CRUST PIZZA

Such a judicious use of "bench flour" allowed us to increase the hydration of the dough while still maintaining the ability to shape it easily.

With this dough we had a good jumping-off point, but pizza perfection was still a long way away. First off, instead of being thin and just a bit floppy, like a good parlor pie, our crust was bready and overinflated—more like focaccia than pizza—even when stretched as thin as possible. Even more troubling, the dough was lacking in flavor, save for a strong yeastiness.

Simply dialing back on the yeast seemed like an obvious test—and did help deflate the too-puffy crust just a bit. But it also wiped out what little flavor the dough started with. Since keeping the yeast to a minimum was a given, we clearly needed an altogether different approach to fermentation.

First, a little background on the relationship between fermentation and dough's texture and flavor. When dough is first mixed, tiny "seed" bubbles form that expand with carbon dioxide at two different junctures: once when the bread is proofed and again when a last burst of carbon dioxide is produced during the first few minutes of baking. The larger the bubbles in the dough prior to baking, the more open and puffy the final dough will be. One way to minimize the size of the bubbles is to chill the dough as it proofs. Aside from producing finer, tighter air bubbles, cold fermentation has the added benefit of creating more flavorful dough. Why? Because at lower temperatures, yeast produces less carbon dioxide and more of the initial side products of fermentation: flavorful sugars, alcohol, and acids.

With that in mind, we mixed up a new batch of dough and immediately placed it in the refrigerator to proof. The next day, we pulled it out, divided and shaped it into rounds, and let it warm to room temperature while we preheated our baking stone. We were skeptical at first; unlike the room temperature–proofed batch, this dough looked pretty unremarkable, showing none of the telltale signs of active fermentation such as an airy, bubbly structure. But one sniff of its heady, slightly boozy aroma clearly indicated that plenty had been happening beneath the surface. Furthermore, this tighter, smoother mass of dough proved much easier to work with, pulling effortlessly into a circle that gradually tapered in thickness from edge to center. We shouldn't have been surprised by this latter development. Besides slowing carbon dioxide production, chilling dough slows down gluten development so that dough literally stays looser, making it easier to stretch and hold its shape without snapping back. And the pizza it produced? Vastly better than previous attempts. Though not perfect, the dough was more complexly flavored and crisp than any other pie we'd made, with an interior that boasted decent tenderness and chew. Even the rim offered just the right degree of puffiness and functioned as an ample handle.

We had to wonder: If 24 hours of cold fermentation had such a dramatic effect on the dough, what would happen if we left it in the fridge even longer? Three days later, we had our answer. We'd mixed together and chilled a batch of dough each day over a 72-hour period, and the pizza bake-off proved that its flavor improved as time went by. (Push the fermentation beyond three days, however, and the yeast finally starts to produce a surplus of carbon dioxide, rendering the dough puffy.) True, cold-fermented dough wasn't exactly quick, but the recipe was a snap to make. Plus, the long rest wasn't altogether inconvenient; with a little planning, this dough had great make-ahead potential.

But the crust's crispness—or lack thereof—continued to nag us. Adding a tablespoon of oil to the dough helped a bit, but not enough. We had one other idea about how to encourage more crunch and color: sugar. We often sprinkle a spoonful over poultry skin to help it darken and crisp up in the oven, and we saw no reason the same trick couldn't be used here. We worked 2 teaspoons into the dough and, sure enough, the next pizza we pulled from the oven was tinged a slightly deeper shade of brown. But it still wasn't enough.

The real problem was the same one we'd been trying to address with all of our radical pizza-baking experiments over the years: the fact that home ovens simply don't get hot enough to produce a deeply browned crust before the interior crumb dries out and toughens. The best solution has always been the hottest setting on the oven dial and a pizza stone, which soaks up the radiating heat like a sponge. Following that logic, most recipes call for the stone to be placed as low in the oven as possible, where it gets maximum exposure to the main heating element. But when we thought about it, that technique didn't really make sense—and we even had an industry clue to prove it: commercial pizza ovens. These wide, shallow chambers quickly reflect heat from the floor back onto the top of the pie as it cooks, preventing the crust from drying out before the toppings have browned. Obviously we couldn't alter the shape of our oven—but we could move the stone up closer to the top to narrow the gap between the stone and the ceiling. After a series of tests with thermocouples and an infrared thermometer, we found the best position for the stone is really as close to the top of the oven as possible—about 4 inches or so from the ceiling, which left just enough headroom to comfortably house the pie. When we pulled this latest attempt from our newfangled setup, the results were a revelation: Everything had baked in sync, producing a pizza that was thoroughly crisp, well-browned on both top and bottom, and slightly chewy, just like a good parlor slice.

We had our perfect foundation; all we had left to do was tweak the toppings. The no-cook sauce we'd been using—canned whole tomatoes, garlic, olive oil, and spices pureed in the food processor—needed just a quick jolt of flavor, so we added a splash of red wine vinegar to enhance the tomatoes' bright acidity. As for the cheese, we supplemented the creamy, stretchy mozzarella with a fistful of sharp, salty, finely grated Parmesan. And that's where we stopped. Of course, additional toppings are fine (provided one doesn't use too heavy a hand); but for us, this simple-to-make, simply dressed pie bakes up perfect as is.

SCIENCE DESK

KEEPING INFLATION DOWN

The biggest factor contributing to a crust that turns out thick versus thin is the size of the air bubbles in the dough before it goes into the oven. The more the bubbles expand with carbon dioxide as the dough ferments (or "proofs"), the thicker the final crust. Could a longer rise in the refrigerator fix the problem?

THE EXPERIMENT

We made two batches of dough, leaving one to rise at room temperature for four hours and placing the other in the refrigerator for 24 hours, then baked them both according to our recipe.

THE RESULTS

The dough left to rise at room temperature produced a crust that puffed up like focaccia, while the dough that rose in the fridge baked up with smaller bubbles and boasted far more flavor.

THE EXPLANATION

Fermentation is a two-phase process: First, the carbohydrates in the dough are converted by the yeast to sugars, alcohol, and acids. Next, these convert to carbon dioxide, expanding the bubbles created in the dough when it was first mixed. At room temperature, the process moves rapidly to the production of carbon dioxide. But in the fridge, the process is slowed way down. With enough time, the complex-tasting sugars, alcohol, and acids form, but very little carbon dioxide gets converted, so the bubbles in the dough stay small and the crust bakes up both thin and more flavorful.

PUFFY AND BLAND

THIN AND FLAVORFUL

Thin-Crust Pizza

MAKES TWO 13-INCH PIZZAS, SERVING 4 TO 6

If you don't have a baking stone, bake the pizzas on an overturned and preheated rimmed baking sheet. You can shape the second dough round while the first pizza bakes, but don't add the toppings until just before baking. You will need a pizza peel for this recipe. It is important to use ice water in the dough to prevent it from overheating in the food processor. Semolina flour is ideal for dusting the peel; use it in place of bread flour if you have it. The sauce will yield more than needed in the recipe; extra sauce can be refrigerated for up to a week or frozen for up to a month.

DOUGH

- **3 cups (16½ ounces) bread flour**
- **2 teaspoons sugar**
- **½ teaspoon instant or rapid-rise yeast**
- **1⅓ cups ice water**
- **1 tablespoon vegetable oil**
- **1½ teaspoons salt**

SAUCE

- **1 (28-ounce) can whole tomatoes, drained**
- **1 tablespoon extra-virgin olive oil**
- **1 teaspoon red wine vinegar**
- **2 garlic cloves, minced**
- **1 teaspoon salt**
- **1 teaspoon dried oregano**
- **¼ teaspoon pepper**

CHEESE

- **1 ounce Parmesan cheese, grated (½ cup)**
- **8 ounces whole-milk mozzarella, shredded (2 cups)**

1. FOR THE DOUGH: Pulse flour, sugar, and yeast in food processor (fitted with dough blade if possible) until combined, about 5 pulses. With food processor running, slowly add water; process until dough is just combined and no dry flour remains, about 10 seconds. Let dough sit for 10 minutes.

2. Add oil and salt to dough and process until dough forms satiny, sticky ball that clears sides of bowl, 30 to 60 seconds. Transfer dough to lightly oiled counter and knead briefly by hand until smooth, about 1 minute. Shape dough into tight ball and place in large, lightly oiled bowl; cover bowl tightly with plastic wrap and refrigerate for at least 24 hours or up to 3 days.

3. FOR THE SAUCE: Process all ingredients in clean bowl of food processor until smooth, about 30 seconds. Transfer to bowl and refrigerate until ready to use.

4. TO BAKE THE PIZZA: One hour before baking, adjust oven rack to upper-middle position (rack should be about 4 to 5 inches from broiler), set baking stone on rack, and heat oven to 500 degrees. Transfer dough to clean counter and divide in half. With cupped palms, form each half into smooth, tight ball. Place balls of dough on lightly greased baking sheet, spacing them at least 3 inches apart; cover loosely with greased plastic and let sit for 1 hour.

5. Coat 1 ball of dough generously with flour and place on well-floured counter (keep other ball covered). Use fingertips to gently flatten dough into 8-inch disk, leaving 1 inch of outer edge slightly thicker than center. Using hands, gently stretch disk into 12-inch round, working along edges and giving disk quarter turns. Transfer dough to well-floured pizza peel and stretch into 13-inch round. Using back of spoon or ladle, spread ½ cup tomato sauce in thin layer over surface of dough, leaving ¼ inch border around edge. Sprinkle ¼ cup Parmesan evenly over sauce, followed by 1 cup mozzarella. Slide pizza carefully onto baking stone and bake until crust is well browned and cheese is bubbly and beginning to brown, 10 to 12 minutes, rotating pizza halfway through baking. Transfer pizza to wire rack and let cool for 5 minutes before slicing and serving. Repeat step 5 to shape, top, and bake second pizza.

VARIATION

Thin-Crust White Pizza

MAKES TWO 13-INCH PIZZAS, SERVING 4 TO 6

If you don't have a baking stone, bake the pizzas on an overturned and preheated rimmed baking sheet. You can shape the second dough round while the first pizza bakes, but don't add the toppings until just before baking. You will need a pizza peel for this recipe. It is important to use ice water in the dough to prevent it from overheating in the food processor. Semolina flour is ideal for dusting the peel; use it in place of bread flour if you have it.

DOUGH

- 3 cups (16½ ounces) bread flour
- 2 teaspoons sugar
- ½ teaspoon instant or rapid-rise yeast
- 1⅓ cups ice water
- 1 tablespoon vegetable oil
- 1½ teaspoons salt

WHITE SAUCE

- 8 ounces (1 cup) whole-milk ricotta cheese
- ¼ cup extra-virgin olive oil
- ¼ cup heavy cream
- 1 large egg yolk
- 4 garlic cloves, minced
- 2 teaspoons minced fresh oregano
- 1 teaspoon minced fresh thyme
- ½ teaspoon salt
- ¼ teaspoon pepper
- ⅛ teaspoon cayenne pepper
- 2 scallions, sliced thin, dark green tops reserved for garnish

CHEESE

- 1 ounce Pecorino cheese, grated (½ cup)
- 8 ounces whole-milk mozzarella cheese, shredded (2 cups)
- 4 ounces (½ cup) whole-milk ricotta cheese

1. FOR THE DOUGH: Pulse flour, sugar, and yeast in food processor (fitted with dough blade if possible) until combined, about 5 pulses. With food processor running, slowly add water; process until dough is just combined and no dry flour remains, about 10 seconds. Let dough sit for 10 minutes.

2. Add oil and salt to dough and process until dough forms satiny, sticky ball that clears sides of bowl, 30 to 60 seconds. Transfer dough to lightly oiled counter and knead briefly by hand until smooth, about 1 minute. Shape dough into tight ball and place in large, lightly oiled bowl; cover bowl tightly with plastic wrap and refrigerate for at least 24 hours and up to 3 days.

3. FOR THE SAUCE: Whisk all ingredients except scallion greens together in bowl; refrigerate until ready to use.

4. TO BAKE THE PIZZA: One hour before baking, adjust oven rack to upper-middle position (rack should

NOTES FROM THE TEST KITCHEN

ENSURING A THIN CRUST

1. ADD JUST ENOUGH WATER: Create relatively wet—but not too wet—dough, which stretches without tearing and stays tender once baked.

2. PROOF IN THE FRIDGE: Chill dough in refrigerator for at least 24 hours. (This leads to less rise, a more flexible dough that holds its shape, and a thinner and more flavorful final crust.)

3. DIVIDE: Halve dough and shape into balls. Place on lightly oiled baking sheet and cover with oiled plastic wrap. Let rest 1 hour to allow dough to return to room temperature.

4. FLATTEN: On well-floured surface and using fingertips, gently flatten dough into 8-inch disk, leaving outer edge slightly thicker than center to create a fatter "handle."

5. STRETCH: With hands, stretch dough into 12-inch round, working along edges and giving dough quarter turns. Transfer to well-floured peel and stretch to 13-inch round.

be about 4 to 5 inches from broiler), set baking stone on rack, and heat oven to 500 degrees. Transfer dough to clean counter and divide in half. With cupped palms, form each half into smooth, tight ball. Place balls of dough on lightly greased baking sheet, spacing them at least 3 inches apart; cover loosely with plastic wrap coated with vegetable oil spray and let sit for 1 hour.

5. Coat 1 ball of dough generously with flour and place on well-floured counter (keep other ball covered). Use fingertips to gently flatten dough into 8-inch disk, leaving 1 inch of outer edge slightly thicker than center. Using hands, gently stretch disk into 12-inch round, working along edges and giving disk quarter turns. Transfer dough to well-floured pizza peel and stretch into 13-inch round. Using back of spoon or ladle, spread ½ cup white sauce in thin layer over surface of dough, leaving ¼ inch border around edge. Sprinkle ¼ cup Pecorino evenly over sauce, followed by 1 cup mozzarella. Dollop ¼ cup ricotta in teaspoon amounts evenly over pizza. Slide pizza carefully onto baking stone and bake until crust is well browned and cheese is bubbly and beginning to brown, 10 to 12 minutes, rotating pizza halfway through baking. Transfer pizza to wire rack and let cool for 5 minutes before slicing and serving. Repeat step 5 to shape, top, and bake second pizza.

NOTES FROM THE TEST KITCHEN

A BETTER DUST FOR YOUR PEEL: SEMOLINA

One of the keys to success in making any pizza, including our Thin-Crust Pizza, is ensuring that your perfectly formed pie easily slides off the peel and onto the stone, without any rips or tears to the bottom of the crust. To prevent the dough from sticking, many recipes advise using cornmeal or bread crumbs. While both coatings work, they also leave a gritty or crunchy residue on the bottom of the pizza. We typically call for a generous dusting of flour, but even this isn't the perfect solution, as too much flour on the peel can lend a dusty, raw-flour taste to the crust, while too little will allow the dough to stick. The best approach is to spring for a bag of semolina flour. This coarsely ground wheat doesn't char as easily as all-purpose flour, so you can make two pies in succession without brushing off the stone. And almost any amount of semolina will allow pizza to release easily without leaving too gritty a residue.

SHRINK YOUR HEADROOM

Baking the pizza on the top rack—rather than the usual approach of placing it near the bottom of a home oven—means heat will hit the top of the pie, browning the toppings before the crust overcooks.

RATING RED WINE VINEGARS

As with balsamic vinegars, the number of red wine vinegars in the condiment aisle has exploded in the past decade. We asked tasters to sample several brands plain, in a simple vinaigrette, and in pickled onions. In the plain tasting, we assumed that tasters would be partial to the vinegars that were sweet and less harsh, but the favorite in this round fell right in the middle of the rankings for sweetness and harshness. In the vinaigrette tasting, some of the harsher vinegars were experienced as relatively sweet because of sugar in the vinaigrette. Less acidic vinegars, on the other hand, were pushed into the background, their flavor masked by the olive oil and mustard. In the end, our winner boasted a crisp red wine flavor balanced by stronger than average acidity and subtle sweetness. Tasters also exhibited a preference for vinegars that were a blend of multiple varieties of grapes, and therefore more complexly flavored. Brands are listed in order of preference. See www.americastestkitchen.com for updates to this testing.

RECOMMENDED

LAURENT DU CLOS Red Wine Vinegar

PRICE: $5.99 for 16.9 fl oz (35 cents per oz)
ACIDITY: 6.12% **SUGAR:** None detected
TYPE OF GRAPE: Vinifera, red and white
COMMENTS: "Good red wine flavor" won the day for this French import. Tasters liked the "nicely rich," "well-balanced," and "fruity" flavor that came through in the pickled onions, and they praised the "clean, light, pleasant taste" and "subtle zing" it added to the vinaigrette.

POMPEIAN Gourmet Red Wine Vinegar

PRICE: $3.99 for 16 fl oz (25 cents per oz)
ACIDITY: 5.14% **SUGAR:** 0.5%
TYPE OF GRAPE: Concord
COMMENTS: Tasters were enthusiastic about this "very mild, sweet, pleasant" red wine vinegar with "tang" that was in "harmonious balance." It was "not harsh at all," but had a "bright, potent taste" with "really pleasing red wine flavor."

RECOMMENDED WITH RESERVATIONS

SPECTRUM NATURALS Organic Red Wine Vinegar

PRICE: $5.99 for 16.9 fl oz (35 cents per oz)
ACIDITY: 6.06% **SUGAR:** None detected
TYPE OF GRAPE: Concord/Vinifera-type grapes
COMMENTS: Tasters praised our former favorite supermarket brand's "winy" and "fruity" taste with "buttery" and "briny" undertones, but it stumbled in the pickled onions, inspiring remarks about its "watery," "thin," and "wimpy" flavor.

HEINZ Gourmet Red Wine Vinegar

PRICE: $3.99 for 12 fl oz (33 cents per oz)
ACIDITY: 5.32% **SUGAR:** None detected
TYPE OF GRAPE: Concord
COMMENTS: Tasted on its own, this domestic red wine vinegar was deemed "bright and sweet with good red wine flavor." Once cooked, however, a few tasters noticed a "sour, almost fermented taste" that was "too harsh" to let the wine flavor through.

RECOMMENDED WITH RESERVATIONS *(cont.)*

HOLLAND HOUSE Red Wine Vinegar

PRICE: $2.89 for 12 fl oz (24 cents per oz)
ACIDITY: 5.2% **SUGAR:** 0.3%
TYPE OF GRAPE: Concord
COMMENTS: Some tasters liked its "tart," "fruity," and "cherry/nectarine" notes, but this vinegar also received the most complaints about its "acetone" or "nail polish remover" smell and taste.

REGINA Red Wine Vinegar

PRICE: $2.49 for 12 fl oz (21 cents per oz)
ACIDITY: 5.2% **SUGAR:** None detected
TYPE OF GRAPE: Vinifera
COMMENTS: Distinguishing itself with its perceived sweetness, this vinegar with "berry" and "floral" notes didn't offend, nor did it wow tasters, whose comments included "middle-of-the-road quality" and "no zip or zing."

COLAVITA Red Wine Vinegar

PRICE: $2.99 for 17 fl oz (18 cents per oz)
ACIDITY: 6.3% **SUGAR:** 0.9%
TYPE OF GRAPE: Vinifera
COMMENTS: Some tasters appreciated this vinegar's "winy and sweet" flavor and "nice balance" with "just the right tang." Others, however, found it "harsh," "sour," and "sharp" with a "saccharine aftertaste."

STAR Red Wine Vinegar

PRICE: $2.39 for 12 fl oz (20 cents per oz)
ACIDITY: 5.08% **SUGAR:** None detected
TYPE OF GRAPE: Vinifera
COMMENTS: This vinegar had a "bright and zippy" presence in vinaigrette and a "refreshing bite" in the pickled onions, but its lack of "real red wine taste" allowed the acidity to prevail, making it harsh for some.

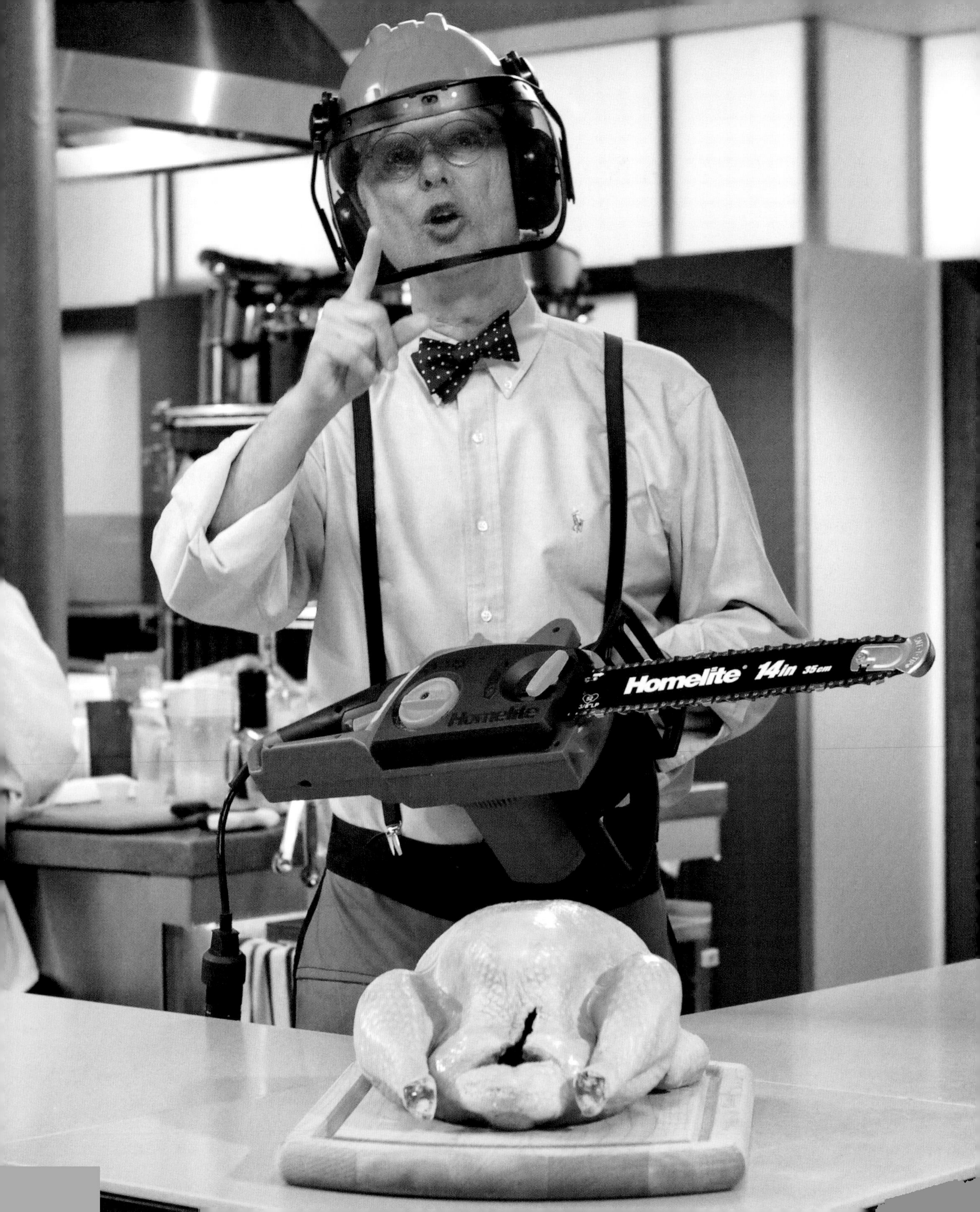
Homelite 14in 35cm
Homelite

A SLOW AND EASY *Thanksgiving*

CHAPTER 9

THE RECIPES

Braised Turkey

Baked Bread Stuffing with Fresh Herbs

- Baked Bread Stuffing with Leeks, Bacon, and Apple
- Baked Bread Stuffing with Sausage, Dried Cherries, and Pecans

EQUIPMENT CORNER

Oven Thermometers

Chris jokes that sometimes the Thanksgiving bird is so dried out, drastic measures need be taken come carving time—but not with the test kitchen's recipe.

TURKEY AND STUFFING ARE AS TRADITIONAL AS A MEAL GETS FOR Thanksgiving, and they're guaranteed crowd pleasers. But they're not without their problems. Everyone knows that getting the dark and white meat to cook at the same rate is a challenge, and although the stuffing cooked inside the bird is rich, moist, and flavorful, there is never enough to go around. This year we decided to tackle these problems head on. Instead of roasting a whole bird, we wanted to braise turkey parts. Simmering turkey parts in stock is a great way to achieve juicy, tender meat and ready-made gravy. The hitch? The oven temperature has to be just right. If we could find a temperature that would produce moist, juicy breast meat and well-cooked—but not tough—thighs, we'd have an easy method for preparing turkey we could turn to again and again.

The simple solution to the lack of stuffing would be to bake it in a dish. But stuffing baked in a dish usually lacks any turkey flavor. We wanted to find a way to bring that inside-the-bird taste to stuffing cooked outside it. First we'd tackle a basic recipe and then we could move on to the main event: infusing our baked stuffing with meaty turkey flavor.

BRAISED TURKEY

BRAISED TURKEY

WHY THIS RECIPE WORKS: Braising turkey parts can be a great way to keep them from drying out—simmering the meat in a covered pot is an inherently gentle cooking method, which helps ensure the delicate breast meat won't dry out. But braising doesn't necessarily guarantee moist meat; first, we'd have to find just the right temperature and cooking time. Braising the turkey parts in a roasting pan (rather than a Dutch oven) ensured they would all fit in a single layer. After trying higher and lower temperatures, we settled on cooking the parts at 325 degrees, which took a reasonable two hours. Brining the turkey seasoned the meat and helped it stay moist. Searing the pieces before adding the liquid added rich flavor to the stock. Adding some white wine, aromatics, and porcini mushrooms deepened the flavor of the stock further, which then allowed us to create a rich gravy.

THOUGH IT'S NOT AT ALL CLEAR THAT ROAST TURKEY, per se, was even on the menu when the Pilgrims gathered to prepare that first harvest feast in 1621, we'd like to think that at least a few savvy cooks raised the question of whether braising the bird wouldn't be the better way to go. This ancient adage would have been the perfect thing to call to their aid: "Turkey boiled is turkey spoiled/ And turkey roast is turkey lost/But for turkey braised, the Lord be praised."

Braising, after all, would have been uniquely suited to a tough wild fowl, as hours simmering in a covered pot would break down the dark meat's chewy connective tissue and turn it meltingly tender. But it's also a terrific way to cook today's mass-produced domestic turkey. Since the temperature in the pot can never rise above the boiling point of water (212 degrees), the method is inherently gentle, minimizing the risk of drying out the breast—the very definition of "turkey lost." On top of that, simmering the pieces in stock creates a flavor exchange between the meat and the liquid, giving the turkey a flavor boost and producing a rich, ready-made gravy. Braising parts instead of a whole bird makes the situation even more advantageous, providing extra insurance that the white and the dark meat cook at a more even rate.

But we knew a successful recipe would take more than just sticking some parts in stock, covering them up, and placing the whole thing in the oven. Contrary to what you might expect, simmering meat in liquid is no guarantee of juiciness. In fact, if cooked too long or at the wrong temperature, braised meat can dry out just as readily as roasted meat. The trick would be to find the optimal cooking time and oven temperature, and just the right ingredients to add deeper complexity to the meat.

Turkey parts are readily available at the supermarket, so we wouldn't have to bother with any butchering. We assembled enough bone-in, skin-on breasts, drumsticks, and thighs to total around 10 pounds per each batch—enough to feed a crowd of 10 to 12.

Before we figured out the nitty gritty of what would go in the braising liquid, we wanted to get the basics of the cooking method down. We arranged the parts skin side up in a roasting pan (the traditional vessel for braising—a covered casserole or Dutch oven—was out, as all the parts would never fit in one layer). We left the breast whole, as that was how it is most commonly available in our supermarket, plus splitting it into two pieces would allow more of its moisture to escape. We added enough chicken broth to come about ¾ of the way up the sides of the thighs, about 5 cups. That was as much liquid as we were willing to use to keep the flavor of the stock as concentrated as possible. We then covered the pan as tightly as we could with foil.

Now what about oven temperature? To help with the decision, we reviewed what we knew about braising. Despite the fact that it's sitting in liquid, braised meat never actually absorbs moisture. On the contrary, once its muscle fibers reach around 140 degrees, they begin to contract and wring out juices. But when the meat in the pot has a lot of collagen, this reaction is mitigated by a second reaction: Between 160 and 180 degrees, the collagen rapidly dissolves into gelatin, which then holds on to some of the juices squeezed from the muscle fibers.

If enough collagen dissolves, it lends something akin to tenderness to the meat. The challenge in braising turkey, however, is that the dark meat has collagen while the breast meat has almost none. We'd need to keep the thighs above the minimum for dissolving collagen long enough for most of it to turn into gelatin—but not so long that the breast dried out.

Playing it safe, we dialed the oven temperature to a very gentle 275 degrees and put the parts in. Without the insulating effect of the backbone and the breast, the thighs and drumsticks came up to their ideal temperature of 175 at the same time the breast reached its ideal 160 degrees, in about four hours. We pulled the turkey from the oven and called in tasters. Our colleagues raved that both types of meat were supremely tender and juicy. Even the very outermost layers of the breast were moist and succulent—an almost impossible feat when roasting. Still, as good as the turkey tasted, monopolizing the oven for four hours for a holiday meal was out of the question.

Wondering what would happen if we took the opposite tack and cranked the heat a lot higher, we prepped a new batch of turkey parts and braised them in a 400-degree oven. It took a little over an hour for the meat to come up to temperature, but the results were markedly inferior. The center of the breast was still juicy, but the outer layers were dried out and the thighs, though moist, were tough. Obviously, the higher heat caused the cooking liquid to rapidly come to a full boil, which in turn sped up the cooking. The upshot was that while the thighs didn't dry out, they didn't have enough time for the collagen to sufficiently break down. And despite the fact that the temperature inside the covered roasting pan was limited to 212 degrees, it was still hot enough to dry out the exterior of the breast. When we checked, we found the meat just below the surface of the breast had climbed a good 20 degrees higher than its center.

The compromise solution was 325 degrees. At this temperature, braising took a reasonable two hours, during which the thighs still had a chance to get tender while the breast meat remained relatively moist. But we couldn't get the super-juiciness of the batch cooked in the 275-degree oven out of our heads. Up to this point, we hadn't considered making brining part of the equation, but we knew it would guarantee that more juices stayed in the meat. The salt in a brine solution denatures the proteins, making them better able to hold on to moisture. It also thoroughly seasons meat—and bland turkey breast, especially, needs all the flavor it can get. A whole turkey takes at least six hours for a brine to be effective, but parts needed just three. Per our usual approach, we also added sugar to the salt solution, which boosts flavor.

Now that we had the meat where we wanted it, it was time to address the turkey's sallow skin. We had no expectations, of course, that truly crisp skin was in the cards, but browning was a must. Not only would it improve the look of the skin, it would add flavor that would make its way into the braising liquid. Searing the pieces in the oven would be the most efficient method. For our next batch, we cranked the heat to 500, brushed the parts with melted butter and roasted them for 20 minutes until lightly browned before adding liquid to the pan and returning the turkey to the oven. Though some of this color washed away during the long braise, it was worth it for the rich, roasted flavor it added to the stock.

Next up: refining the braising liquid. First we swapped out 1 cup of the chicken broth for white wine, which lent the stock a bright sweetness. (Since we've found even mild acid can eat holes in foil, we placed a layer of parchment between the foil and the turkey before wrapping the pan.) Next, we tossed chopped onions, celery, carrots, and garlic with melted butter and arranged them in the pan before placing the parts on top, and browned them in the oven along with the turkey. The addition of aromatic vegetables gave the finished stock a vegetal sweetness and further complexity. We deepened the flavor of the stock even more when we added pepper, bay leaves, thyme, parsley, and a handful of dried porcini mushrooms to the aromatics before browning them. Best of all, as the flavors of the stock improved, so did the flavor of the turkey itself.

All that remained was to turn this rich braising liquid into gravy. Once the turkey was cooked, we let the parts rest while we skimmed the stock and used some of the flavorful fat to produce a nice golden roux. We then whisked in a few cups of the stock and let the mixture simmer until it thickened into glossy gravy.

With its juicy, rich-tasting meat and sumptuous gravy, braised turkey is definitely worth celebrating. And who's to say an approach so good—and so tailor-made for turkey—didn't win out over roasting for that first Thanksgiving meal?

Braised Turkey

SERVES 10 TO 12

Instead of drumsticks and thighs, you may use 2 whole leg quarters, 1½ to 2 pounds each. The recipe will also work with turkey breast alone; in step 1, reduce the amount of salt and sugar to ½ cup each and the amount of water to 4 quarts. If you are braising kosher or self-basting turkey parts, skip the brining step, and instead season the turkey parts with 1½ teaspoons salt.

TURKEY

- **Salt and pepper**
- **1 cup sugar**
- **1 (5- to 7-pound) whole bone-in, skin-on turkey breast, trimmed**
- **4 pounds turkey drumsticks and thighs, trimmed**
- **3 onions, chopped**
- **3 celery ribs, chopped**
- **2 carrots, chopped**
- **6 garlic cloves, peeled and crushed**
- **2 bay leaves**
- **6 sprigs fresh thyme**
- **6 sprigs fresh parsley**
- **½ ounce dried porcini mushrooms, rinsed**
- **4 tablespoons unsalted butter, melted**
- **4 cups low-sodium chicken broth**
- **1 cup dry white wine**

GRAVY

- **3 tablespoons all-purpose flour**
- **Salt and pepper**

1. Dissolve 1 cup salt and sugar in 2 gallons cold water in large container. Submerge turkey pieces in brine, cover, and refrigerate for 4 to 6 hours.

2. Adjust oven rack to lower-middle position and heat oven to 500 degrees. Remove turkey from brine and pat dry with paper towels. Toss onions, celery, carrots, garlic, bay leaves, thyme, parsley, porcini, and 2 tablespoons butter in large roasting pan; arrange in even layer. Brush turkey pieces with remaining 2 tablespoons butter and season with pepper. Place turkey pieces, skin side up, over vegetables, leaving at least ¼ inch between pieces. Roast until skin is lightly browned, about 20 minutes.

3. While turkey is roasting, bring broth and wine to simmer in medium saucepan over medium heat. Cover and keep warm.

4. Remove turkey from oven and reduce temperature to 325 degrees. Pour broth mixture around turkey pieces (it should come about ¾ of the way up legs and thighs.) Place 16 by 12-inch piece of parchment paper over turkey pieces. Cover roasting pan tightly with aluminum foil. Return covered roasting pan to oven and cook until breast registers 160 degrees and thighs register

175 degrees, 1½ to 2 hours. Transfer turkey to carving board, tent loosely with foil, and let rest for 20 minutes.

5. FOR THE GRAVY: Strain vegetables and liquid from roasting pan through fine-mesh strainer set in large bowl. Press solids with back of spatula to extract as much liquid as possible. Discard vegetables. Transfer liquid to fat separator and allow to settle for 5 minutes. Reserve 3 tablespoons fat and measure off 3 cups broth (save any remaining broth for another use).

6. Heat 3 tablespoons reserved turkey fat in medium saucepan over medium-high heat; add flour and cook, stirring constantly, until flour is dark golden brown and fragrant, about 5 minutes. Whisk in 3 cups braising liquid and bring to boil. Reduce heat to medium-low and simmer, stirring occasionally, until gravy is thick and reduced to 2 cups, 15 to 20 minutes. Remove gravy from heat and season with salt and pepper to taste.

7. Carve turkey and serve, passing gravy separately.

RATING OVEN THERMOMETERS

Fact: Ovens are inaccurate. Since all ovens cycle on and off to maintain temperature, even the best models periodically deviate from the desired heat by at least a few degrees. And we've found they can be off by as much as 50 degrees unless they're recalibrated regularly. It doesn't make sense not to have an oven thermometer—they don't cost a lot, and a good one can literally save your dinner (plus everything else you cook or bake). We recently tested five brands of dial-face thermometers to find the best one. We used a super-precise instant-read thermocouple to check high and low readouts given by each thermometer. We also maneuvered pans and baking dishes in and out of the oven to gauge whether a thermometer stayed put and out of the way. Finally, we left a thermometer in every oven in the test kitchen and asked test cooks to provide feedback over six months of daily use. Brands are listed in order of preference. See www.americastestkitchen.com for updates to this testing.

RECOMMENDED

COOPER-ATKINS Oven Thermometer (model #24HP)
PRICE: $5.95 **TEMPERATURE ACCURACY:** ★★★ **DESIGN:** ★★★
COMMENTS: Basic, sturdy, accurate, and the least expensive model tested, this commercial-style thermometer (it provides food safety guidelines in small print on the face) rose to the top of our rankings. Designed to either sit on or hang from oven racks, it stayed safely out of our way as we baked and roasted. After six months of constant testing, the face was still easy to read and temperature readings remained spot-on.

CDN Pro Accurate Data Hold Oven Thermometer (model #PAT550)
PRICE: $11.99 **TEMPERATURE ACCURACY:** ★★★ **DESIGN:** ★★
COMMENTS: This model was especially accurate: It uses an oil-filled temperature chamber that delays readings as the oven cycles up and down. After months of testing, its dial was slightly yellowed but still very legible. Our one complaint: The mounting method—a flimsy and awkward clip—made it slightly difficult to attach to oven racks.

RECOMMENDED WITH RESERVATIONS

TAYLOR Connoisseur Series Oven Thermometer (model #503)
PRICE: $17.95 **TEMPERATURE ACCURACY:** ★★★ **DESIGN:** ★
COMMENTS: Although this thermometer was accurate, it was large and got in the way of our cooking. The company warns that prolonged use at over 440 degrees may lead to discoloration and cracking (which we did observe in the four copies of this model used in our testing)—an unacceptable caveat for an oven thermometer.

CDN Multi-Mount Oven Thermometer (model #MOT1)
PRICE: $7.95 **TEMPERATURE ACCURACY:** ★★ **DESIGN:** ★★
COMMENTS: This thermometer was once our favorite due to its accuracy and convenient magnet for easy attachment. But we noticed that over time the numbers started fading, making it almost impossible to read. What's more, new copies purchased for this testing were off by five degrees.

NOT RECOMMENDED

MAVERICK Oven Chek Large Dial Oven Thermometer (model #OT-02)
PRICE: $9.95 **TEMPERATURE ACCURACY:** ★ **DESIGN:** ★
COMMENTS: Big, clumsy, and top-heavy, this model fell to the bottom of the pack. After the first three months of testing, the dial became fogged and discolored, making it impossible to read. Accuracy was not its strong suit either; it was consistently 10 degrees below the oven's real temperature.

BAKED BREAD STUFFING

WHY THIS RECIPE WORKS: Stuffing baked in a dish definitely has appeal—you can make as much as you want and you don't have to time its doneness to coincide with the doneness of the meat—but it lacks the rich flavor from the bird's flavorful juices. As the base for our stuffing we chose ordinary sandwich bread, which we "staled" in a low oven; this allowed it to soak up plenty of liquid. To infuse the stuffing with meaty turkey flavor, we browned turkey wings on the stovetop, then used the same pan to sauté the aromatics. When we placed the stuffing in a baking dish, we arranged the seared wings on top—as they cooked, their rendered fat infused the stuffing with rich flavor. Covering the baking dish with foil prevented the top of the stuffing from drying out, while placing a baking sheet underneath the dish protected the bottom layer from the oven's heat.

BREAD STUFFING BAKED IN A LARGE DISH IS CERTAINLY plentiful, since you're not limited by the size of a turkey cavity, but does it usually taste as good as the stuffing baked inside a turkey, where it can absorb the bird's flavorful juices? Certainly not. We set out to revamp the stuffing cooked outside the turkey to give it the same ultra-savory rich flavor and soft texture of stuffing baked inside the bird.

We would start with the easy stuff: nailing down a basic recipe. The usual suspects in stuffing are store-bought chicken broth, celery and onion cooked in butter, eggs, fresh herbs—we chose time-honored thyme and sage—and, of course, dried cubes of bread. Many recipes call for drying the bread cubes by simply leaving them out for a few days. We already knew this was not an option. As bread stales at room temperature, its starch molecules undergo a process called retrogradation, causing it to become hard but not necessarily dry. Instead, we would "stale" the bread cubes in a 200-degree oven for an hour. This method actually removes moisture, ultimately leading to a drier structure that allows the bread to soak up more liquid for a better-tasting stuffing.

Normally, stuffing can be made with anything from cornbread to artisanal loaves, French baguettes, or Italian bread. But we wondered if one would prove better than another for achieving the moist texture we were shooting for. We didn't want to fool with making cornbread or hunting down a good ready-made batch, so we rounded up the other three candidates, along with sliced sandwich bread. We cut each bread into cubes and staled them in the oven. We were right to be concerned about the style of bread: Baguettes had too high a ratio of crust to interior, leading to a chewy stuffing. The super-fine crumb of Italian loaves became overly soggy and blown out, while artisanal breads like ciabatta were simply too tough. The best choice turned out to be ordinary, easy-to-find sandwich bread, which baked up soft but still retained some shape.

It was time to get on with our real goal: infusing the dressing with meaty turkey flavor. Ground sausage is a great way to impart an extra meaty dimension to stuffing, so what about simply adding ground turkey to the recipe? We browned 1 pound in a skillet, combined it with the other stuffing ingredients, threw everything in a baking dish, and put the whole thing in the oven. This got us nowhere. Unlike ground sausage, which, when added to stuffing, brings to the mix lots of flavorful fat and often herbs and spices, ground turkey is both relatively lean and bland. All it did was produce lumps of none-too-flavorful meat amid the bread cubes.

Next, we flirted with the idea of swapping the store-bought broth with a rich homemade turkey stock that we could reduce for extra intensity. That fantasy lasted about a minute as we tried to imagine ourselves tending to a pot of stock, all the while juggling the dozens of other things we needed to get done for the big feast. There had to be an easier way to re-create the rich fatty juices that trickle down inside the bird. Then it occurred to us: We could actually get that same trickle-down effect by covering the stuffing in the baking dish with turkey parts—in essence, creating a makeshift turkey cavity.

First we tried meaty turkey legs and thighs, which had the obvious advantage of exuding lots of flavorful juices (and fat). These proved a bit cumbersome, so we turned to turkey wings. To get every last bit of turkey juice and fat to render, we split the wings into sections and poked holes in the skin with a paring knife. We arranged the perforated wing pieces on the stuffing and baked it in a moderate oven—375 degrees—for an hour, until the wings reached a safe 175 degrees. We were on to something. The flavorful juices and fat from the roasted wings had penetrated deep into the stuffing. The only problem? The top layer had dried out in the oven.

The next time around, we covered the wings and stuffing with foil. This kept the stuffing moist, but the wings didn't get a chance to brown. Without all the new flavor compounds created by browning, the stuffing didn't have the richness we had noted in our previous attempt. If we wanted browning, the only other option was to sear the wings before placing them on the stuffing. We were happy to find that the 3 pounds of wings we'd been using fit into a skillet in one batch. After searing, we removed them, then sautéed the aromatics and added the chicken broth. Another benefit of this approach was that we could scrape up the flavorful fond that had built up on the bottom of the pan and incorporate it into the savory liquid. We combined the liquid with the aromatics and the bread, along with eggs and more chicken broth (to augment the juices from the wings), then placed the mixture in a baking dish, arranging the seared wings atop the stuffing. We covered the dish with foil and, to prevent the bottom of the stuffing from becoming crusty, we placed the baking dish on a baking sheet, which offered some protection against the oven's heat.

A little over an hour later, we had moist, tender stuffing that certainly looked the part—and our tasters declared it to be as rich and savory as any inside-the-bird stuffing they'd sampled.

With so much turkey flavor, the stuffing needed little else besides a handful of chopped parsley. But we also wanted to create a few variations that were a bit more dressed-up and complex, and offered some textural contrast. A version made with sausage, tart dried cherries, and toasted pecans won over our tasters, as did another, made with bacon, sautéed apples, and leeks.

Baked Bread Stuffing with Fresh Herbs

SERVES 10 TO 12

Two pounds of chicken wings can be substituted for the turkey wings. If using chicken wings, separate them into two sections (it's not necessary to separate the tips) and poke each segment four or five times. Also, increase the amount of broth to 3 cups, reduce the amount of butter to 2 tablespoons, and cook the stuffing for only 1 hour. Use the meat from the cooked wings to make salad or soup. If making the stuffing with Braised Turkey (page 93) bake stuffing first, then reheat while turkey is resting. To reheat, heat oven to 375 degrees, remove wings from top of stuffing, cover stuffing tightly with aluminum foil, and bake, still on rimmed baking sheet, for 20 to 25 minutes, until hot. Serve immediately.

- **2 pounds hearty white sandwich bread, cut into ½-inch cubes**
- **3 pounds turkey wings, divided at joints**
- **2 teaspoons vegetable oil**
- **6 tablespoons unsalted butter**
- **1 large onion, chopped fine**
- **3 celery ribs, minced**
- **Salt**
- **2 tablespoons minced fresh thyme**
- **2 tablespoons minced fresh sage**
- **1 teaspoon pepper**
- **2½ cups low-sodium chicken broth**
- **3 large eggs**
- **3 tablespoons minced fresh parsley**

1. Adjust oven racks to upper-middle and lower-middle positions and heat oven to 250 degrees. Spread bread cubes in even layer on 2 rimmed baking sheets. Bake until edges have dried but centers are slightly moist (cubes should yield to pressure), 45 minutes to 1 hour, stirring several times during baking. (Bread can be toasted up to 1 day in advance.) Transfer dried bread to large bowl and increase oven temperature to 375 degrees.

2. While bread dries, use paring knife to poke 10 to 15 holes in each wing segment. Heat oil in 12-inch skillet over medium-high heat until shimmering. Add wings in single layer and cook until golden brown on both sides, 8 to 12 minutes. Transfer wings to separate bowl and set aside.

3. Melt butter in now-empty skillet over medium heat. Add onion, celery, and ½ teaspoon salt and cook, stirring occasionally, until vegetables are softened, 7 to 9 minutes. Stir in thyme, sage, and pepper and cook until fragrant, about 30 seconds. Stir in 1 cup broth, scraping up any browned bits, and bring to simmer. Add vegetable mixture to bowl with dried bread and toss to combine.

4. Grease 13 by 9-inch baking dish. Whisk eggs, remaining 1½ cups broth, 1½ teaspoons salt, and any accumulated juices from wings together in bowl. Add egg mixture and parsley to bread mixture and toss to combine; transfer to prepared baking dish. Arrange wings on top of stuffing, cover tightly with aluminum foil, and place baking dish on rimmed baking sheet.

5. Bake on lower rack until wings register 175 degrees, 1 to 1¼ hours. Remove foil and transfer wings to dinner plate to reserve for another use. Using fork, gently fluff stuffing. Let rest for 5 minutes before serving.

VARIATIONS

Baked Bread Stuffing with Leeks, Bacon, and Apple

After browned turkey wings have been removed from skillet in step 2, cook 12 ounces bacon, cut into ½-inch pieces in skillet over medium-high heat until crisp, about 5 minutes. Remove bacon with slotted spoon and transfer to paper towel–lined plate; pour off all but 2 tablespoons fat from skillet. Proceed with recipe from step 3, reducing butter to 4 tablespoons, substituting 2 leeks, white and light green parts, sliced thin, for onion, and 3 Granny Smith apples, cut into ¼-inch pieces, for parsley.

Baked Bread Stuffing with Sausage, Dried Cherries, and Pecans

After browned turkey wings have been removed from skillet in step 2, cook 1 pound bulk pork sausage over medium-high heat, breaking sausage into ½-inch pieces with wooden spoon, until browned, 5 to 7 minutes. Transfer sausage to paper–towel lined plate, leaving rendered fat in skillet. Proceed with recipe from step 3, reducing butter to 4 tablespoons and substituting 1 cup dried cherries and 1 cup toasted, chopped pecans for the parsley.

NOTES FROM THE TEST KITCHEN

TURKEY WINGS TO THE RESCUE

Baking stuffing with browned turkey wings on top creates the same rich savoriness of stuffing cooked inside the bird.

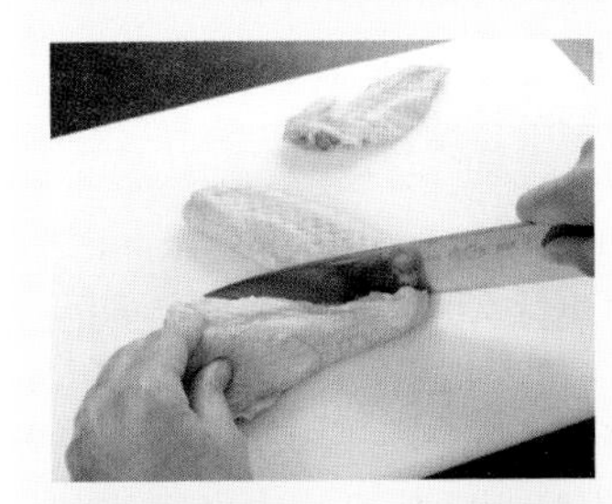

1. PREP WINGS: Cut through joint with sharp chef's knife. If turkey wing comes with tip, cut through this joint as well.

2. BROWN WINGS: Sear turkey wings to trigger flavor-producing Maillard reaction. Remove them from skillet.

3. SAUTÉ AROMATICS: Cook chopped onion and celery in rendered fat and butter to develop savory flavor base.

4. DEGLAZE WITH BROTH: Deglaze pan with broth to release fond and capture every last bit of flavor. Add mixture to dried bread cubes.

5. TOP, COVER, BAKE: Top stuffing with browned wings, cover with aluminum foil to trap moisture, and bake.

A LATIN *Celebration*

CHAPTER 10

THE RECIPES

Peruvian Roast Chicken with Garlic and Lime

Spicy Mayonnaise

Cuban-Style Black Beans and Rice

Vegetarian Cuban-Style Black Beans and Rice

TASTING LAB

Brown Rice

EQUIPMENT CORNER

Vertical Roasters

One step of adapting Peruvian Roast Chicken to the American home kitchen involves using a vertical roaster in place of a wood-fired rotisserie oven.

LATIN CUISINE IS AS WIDE AND VARIED AS THE CULTURES THAT encompass it, but one thing can be agreed upon: It is robust and flavorful, with an emphasis on spices and fresh herbs. Though perhaps not as well known as some other Latin American dishes, Peruvian garlic-lime chicken—boldly seasoned with garlic, spices, citrus, chiles, and a fresh mint paste—is a perfect example of this. Authentic versions of this bird are spit-roasted and boast an evenly bronzed exterior and moist meat. They also rely on ingredients that can be difficult to track down in this country. We wanted to re-create this lively dish at home—using a conventional oven and supermarket staples.

Black beans and rice is a dish you may be more familiar with. It is undoubtedly satisfying, but it often suffers from blandness—an unusual problem for this cuisine. Cuban versions remedy this with a heavy hand of aromatics, spices, and rich, flavorful fat, typically in the form of pork. But while cooking beans and rice in a single vessel sounds like a straightforward one-pot meal, getting the texture of both elements just right can be a challenge. We wanted to develop our own recipe that would give us flavorful, distinct grains of rice and creamy—not mushy—beans every time.

PERUVIAN ROAST CHICKEN

WHY THIS RECIPE WORKS: Authentic versions of Peruvian garlic-lime chicken require a wood-fired oven and hard-to-find ingredients. We wanted to replicate this robustly flavored dish using an oven and supermarket staples. A paste of salt, garlic, oil, lime zest, and cumin rubbed underneath and on top of the skin produced well-seasoned meat and a heady flavor. To this basic paste we added fresh mint (replacing the black mint paste called for in authentic recipes), oregano, pepper, and minced habanero chile for tangy spice, while a little smoked paprika subtly mimicked the smokiness we were missing from the rotisserie. Roasting the chicken vertically allowed it to cook evenly, while using two different oven temperatures helped us achieve both moist meat and well-browned skin.

PERUVIAN CHICKEN JOINTS HAVE RECENTLY DEVELOPED something of a cult following in the United States, and for good reason. The rotisserie bird that they serve, known as *pollo a la brasa* in the mother country, is deeply bronzed from its slow rotation in a wood-fired oven and impressively seasoned with garlic, spices, lime juice, chiles, and a paste made with *huacatay,* or black mint. Off the spit, the chicken is carved and served with a garlicky, faintly spicy, mayonnaise-like sauce.

We didn't want our lack of a rotisserie to stop us from re-creating this phenomenal dish at home. But when we started researching recipes, we realized that trying to achieve the smokiness and evenly browned skin of the authentic version wasn't going to be as simple as throwing a well-seasoned bird into the oven. We would also have to replicate the flavors of hard-to-find black mint paste, along with the Peruvian aji peppers that give both the chicken and the dipping sauce their signature subtle heat.

Hardly a piece of chicken passes through the test kitchen without being rubbed with salt or soaked in a brine. Since salting is our preferred technique when bronzed, well-rendered skin is the goal, we started there. (Both techniques render the bird flavorful and juicy, but while salting helps lock in the bird's existing juices, brining introduces extra moisture to the meat and yields comparatively flabby skin.) After letting the salt seep in for about an hour, we took cues from a few recipes we'd found and coated the exterior of the bird with a simple paste of garlic, extra-virgin olive oil, lime juice, and cumin that we had pureed in the blender. (We'd worry about the mint and smoke flavors later.) We then set the chicken on a V-rack in a roasting pan and cranked the oven to a blazing 450 degrees in hopes of replicating the rotisserie flame. About 45 minutes later the chicken was brown, all right—but only on one side. What's more, despite the salting treatment, the white meat was parched from all that high-heat exposure, and the punchy flavors from the paste were skin-deep at best.

Actually, the lack of flavor made sense. While developing our recipe for marinated beef kebabs, a test kitchen colleague learned that none of the flavors in a marinade (including garlic, spices, and acids) penetrate much beyond the exterior of the meat, no matter how long you leave it to soak—with one exception. Only salt and other compounds of sodium travel farther into the meat the longer it sits. The flavors of our wet paste would never be more than superficial, no matter how long we let the bird marinate, so two things—salt and plenty of time—would be key to heightening those heady flavors and seasoning the meat.

Since both the salt and the paste were being rubbed onto the chicken, we combined the two flavor components into one step, this time mixing a generous 2 tablespoons of kosher salt into the paste. Instead of merely rubbing it over the skin, we also spread the paste under the skin directly against the meat for maximum penetration; we then let the bird rest for six hours before roasting. The result? Much improved taste. Though our marinade was still missing a few of the trademark elements, the salt in the paste had worked its magic and ramped up the chicken's flavor from skin to bone. (Further testing revealed that it was fine to marinate the bird for up to 24 hours.)

PERUVIAN ROAST CHICKEN WITH GARLIC AND LIME

Our next test took us back to the supermarket, where we shopped for a replacement for the herbaceous, slightly earthy black mint paste. Fresh ordinary mint was the best option, so we worked a handful of the leaves into our next batch of paste, along with some dried oregano, grated lime zest (to satisfy those who'd requested more citrus flavor but didn't want too much acidity), black pepper, sugar, and just a teaspoon of finely minced habanero chile (a little of this fiery pepper goes a long way). Now the tangy spice flavors of our chicken were popping.

Back to our other major hurdle: replacing the rotisserie. While our goal wasn't necessarily crisp skin—the skin on the chicken we'd eaten in restaurants was well rendered but not crackly—we did want it evenly browned, and the V-rack just wasn't working. One option was to flip the chicken several times during cooking, but with a hefty amount of wet paste slathered on the bird, this turned out to be a messy proposition—not to mention an outright pain. Our other idea was a vertical roaster, which cooks the chicken standing upright and allows the heat to circulate freely around the bird for evenly cooked results. We proceeded with our recipe, placing the marinated bird over the roaster's tall cone and setting the whole package on a baking sheet to cook. We knew we were on to something this time: There was no awkward flipping, and the fat dripped freely out of the bird, allowing the skin to render and brown. But it wasn't a perfect solution: The rotisserie's subtle smokiness was predictably absent, and without the roasting-pan walls to shield it from the blasting heat, the white meat was still dry.

There was only one way to keep the chicken from dehydrating: lowering the oven temperature. Indeed, when we roasted the next bird at a relatively gentle 325 degrees, the meat was tender and juicy—but the skin was only lightly tanned. Stuck between these two opposing ideals, we opted for a two-pronged approach that we've used before in the test kitchen. Once the low-roasted chicken was almost cooked through, we let it rest briefly at room temperature, cranked the oven to 500 degrees, added a little water to the roasting pan (to prevent the rendered fat from smoking), and returned the chicken to the much-hotter oven to brown thoroughly. At last: perfectly cooked meat and skin. That left just the missing smoke flavor to resolve.

NOTES FROM THE TEST KITCHEN

APPROXIMATING THE FLAVORS OF PERU

MINT AND OREGANO
The combination of fresh mint and dried oregano replicates the clean, faintly woodsy flavor of Peruvian black mint (huacatay) paste.

TWO TYPES OF CHILE
Spicy aji peppers are integral to the marinade and dipping sauce. We replaced the aji with a fiery habanero in the marinade and pickled jalapeño in the sauce.

SMOKED PAPRIKA
The smoked version of this brick-red powder imitates the wood-fired flavors of a rotisserie.

Nothing about our roasting technique was going to infuse smokiness—but we did have something in our spice cabinet that might help. Smoked paprika, which has recently become widely available, isn't a traditional part of the Peruvian marinade, but 2 teaspoons mixed into the paste turned out to be a pretty close approximation of the real thing.

Finally, there was the sauce. The ideal texture is thinner than traditional mayonnaise but still viscous enough to coat the chicken when dunked. With that in mind, we whipped a whole egg (instead of just a yolk, as in traditional mayonnaise) and vegetable oil in the food processor with a little water, onion, lime juice, cilantro, yellow mustard, and garlic. The consistency was right—but it lacked the punch of those elusive aji peppers. The next best thing? A pickled jalapeño, which kicked up the acidity a notch, too.

Looking over our recipe, we were surprised at how easily we'd been able to replicate the authentic flavors with a few supermarket staples and a vertical roaster. But we weren't surprised that among our fellow test cooks, this Peruvian mainstay had developed a cult following of its own.

Peruvian Roast Chicken with Garlic and Lime

SERVES 3 TO 4

If habanero chiles are unavailable, 1 tablespoon of minced serrano chile can be substituted. Wear gloves when working with hot chiles. This recipe calls for a vertical poultry roaster. If you don't have one, substitute a 12-ounce can of beer. Open the beer and pour out (or drink) about half of the liquid. Spray the can lightly with vegetable oil spray and proceed with the recipe.

- **¼ cup fresh mint leaves**
- **3 tablespoons extra-virgin olive oil**
- **6 garlic cloves, chopped coarse**
- **1 tablespoon salt**
- **1 tablespoon pepper**
- **1 tablespoon ground cumin**
- **1 tablespoon sugar**
- **2 teaspoons smoked paprika**
- **2 teaspoons dried oregano**
- **2 teaspoons grated lime zest plus ¼ cup juice (2 limes)**
- **1 teaspoon minced habanero chile**
- **1 (3½- to 4-pound) whole chicken, giblets discarded**
- **1 recipe Spicy Mayonnaise (recipe follows)**

1. Process all ingredients except chicken and mayonnaise in blender until smooth paste forms, 10 to 20 seconds. Use your fingers to gently loosen skin covering breast and thighs; place half of paste under skin, directly on meat of breast and thighs. Gently press on skin to distribute paste over meat. Spread entire exterior surface of chicken with remaining paste. Tuck wings behind back. Place chicken in gallon zipper-lock bag and refrigerate at least 6 hours or up to 24 hours.

2. Adjust oven rack to lowest position and heat oven to 325 degrees. Place vertical roaster on rimmed baking sheet. Slide chicken onto vertical roaster so drumsticks reach down to bottom of roaster, chicken stands upright, and breast is perpendicular to bottom of pan. Roast chicken until skin just begins to turn golden and breast registers 140 degrees, 45 to 55 minutes. Carefully remove chicken and pan from oven and increase oven temperature to 500 degrees.

3. Once oven has come to temperature, place 1 cup water in bottom of baking sheet and continue to roast until entire chicken skin is browned and crisp, breast registers 160 degrees, and thighs register 175 degrees, about 20 minutes, rotating pan halfway through roasting. Check chicken halfway through roasting; if top is becoming too dark, place 7-inch square piece of aluminum foil over neck and wingtips of chicken and continue to roast (if pan begins to smoke and sizzle, add additional water to pan).

4. Carefully remove chicken from oven and let rest, still on vertical roaster, for 20 minutes. Using 2 large wads of paper towels, carefully lift chicken off vertical roaster and onto carving board. Carve chicken and serve, passing Spicy Mayonnaise separately.

NOTES FROM THE TEST KITCHEN

PASTE IT ON

Distributing the flavorful paste both over and under the skin ensures the best taste, and storing the chicken in a zipper-lock bag helps contain the mess. Be sure to wear gloves when working with chiles.

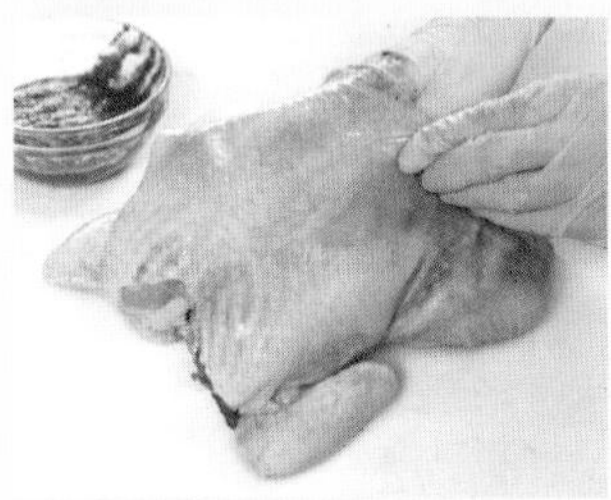

1. SLIP IT UNDER: Loosen skin from over thighs and breast and rub half of paste directly on meat.

2. RUB IT OVER: Spread remaining paste over skin of entire chicken.

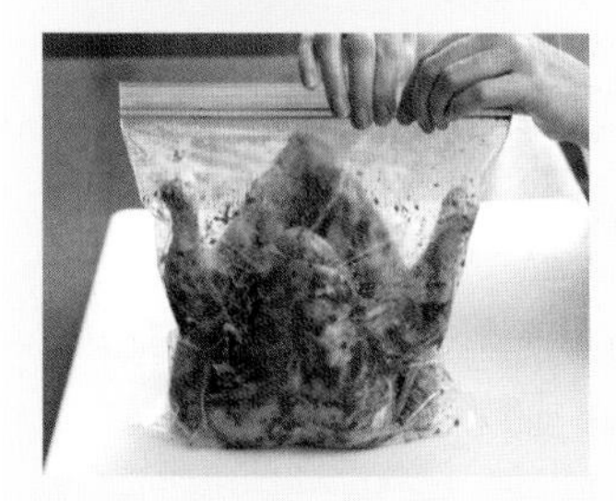

3. CHILL THE BIRD: Place chicken in 1-gallon zipper-lock bag and refrigerate for 6 to 24 hours.

Spicy Mayonnaise

MAKES ABOUT 1 CUP

If you have concerns about consuming raw eggs, ¼ cup of an egg substitute can be used in place of the egg.

- **1 large egg**
- **2 tablespoons water**
- **1 tablespoon minced onion**
- **1 tablespoon lime juice**
- **1 tablespoon minced fresh cilantro**
- **1 tablespoon minced jarred jalapeños**
- **1 garlic clove, minced**
- **1 teaspoon yellow mustard**
- **¼ teaspoon salt**
- **1 cup vegetable oil**

Process all ingredients except oil in food processor until combined, about 5 seconds. With processor running, slowly drizzle in oil in steady stream until mayonnaise-like consistency is reached, scraping down bowl as necessary.

RATING VERTICAL ROASTERS

Vertical roasters promise to cook poultry evenly and crisp the skin all over—and you don't have to turn the bird the way you would on a traditional V-rack. We tested six models priced from $11.99 to $180, in materials from metal to porcelain to clay. A few came attached to their own oval roasting pans, one was a simple tube, and others had shallow metal trays and infusers for adding liquids before roasting. We downgraded models that seemed flimsy, as this created concerns about the chicken tipping over, and we didn't like designs where the chicken sat in its own fat. Our two top performers excelled in even roasting and sturdiness. For a cheaper option, you can always substitute a 12-ounce beer can, emptied of about half its liquid. Brands are listed in order of preference. See www.americastestkitchen.com for updates to this testing.

RECOMMENDED

NORPRO Vertical Roaster with Infuser (model #303876)
PRICE: $30.95
ROASTING: ★★★ **STURDINESS:** ★★★ **CLEANUP:** ★★
COMMENTS: With the longest shaft of the lineup (8 inches), this roaster makes the chicken sit tall without any chance of getting soggy from slumping into the fat. Its open design helps the bird brown evenly and makes it easy to remove when all done. While the metal basin is slightly shallow compared to some of the other models, it catches enough drippings to make a good pan sauce. Cleanup was a little messy, but chicken grease scrubbed off relatively easily. Two curved metal bars that form the shaft detach from the tray for cleaning, and lie flat for storage.

ELIZABETH KARMEL'S GRILL FRIENDS Porcelain Chicken Sitter (model #60514)
PRICE: $11.99 BEST BUY
ROASTING: ★★★ **STURDINESS:** ★★ **CLEANUP:** ★★
COMMENTS: This lampshade-shaped roaster was designed by the creator of a website called Girls at the Grill. We set it in a roasting pan before putting it in the oven. Sturdy and solid, it kept a large 6-pound chicken from wobbling even though the shaft was only 5 inches tall. Cleanup was messy.

RECOMMENDED WITH RESERVATIONS

RECO INTERNATIONAL Romertopf 12-inch Chicken Roaster, Terra Cotta (model #01202)
PRICE: $35
ROASTING: ★★ **STURDINESS:** ★★★ **CLEANUP:** ★
COMMENTS: This terra-cotta roaster shaped like a bowl with a raised central 7-inch shaft was sturdy enough to hold a 6-pound chicken upright. It has a pouring spout, a good feature for handling grease that pools in the basin. Cleanup was difficult and awkward due to its large size.

RECOMMENDED WITH RESERVATIONS *(cont.)*

ALL-CLAD Stainless Steel Ultimate Chicken Roaster (model #1481530)
PRICE: $179.95
ROASTING: ★★ **STURDINESS:** ★★ **CLEANUP:** ★★
COMMENTS: This pricey "horizontal" roaster has a detachable arm that promises to hold the chicken up for even cooking, while you roast vegetables in the pan below. While it sounded good in theory, the low-placed arm meant that any chicken bigger than 4 pounds draped over the vegetables, interfering with air circulation and causing the vegetables to drown in drippings and the chicken to steam, not brown. Smaller chickens worked better, although they didn't weigh enough to keep the arm anchored firmly in place.

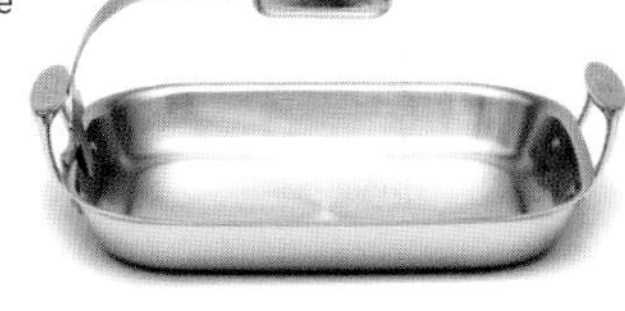

NOT RECOMMENDED

STEVEN RAICHLEN Best of Barbecue Stainless Beer Can Chicken Rack with Drip Pan (model #SR8016)
PRICE: $24.99
ROASTING: ★★ **STURDINESS:** ★ **CLEANUP:** ★★
COMMENTS: Created for the grill, but fine for use in the oven, this roaster developed by the author of the bible on beer-can cooking had design flaws. The frame and tray felt flimsy, tippy, and thin, and it had the shortest shaft of the lineup (4¾ inches) for holding up the chicken. The shallow grease tray filled quickly, leaving the chicken sitting in its own fat, and making cleanup a greasy process.

STAUB Vertical Roaster, Black (model #1200018)
PRICE: $110
ROASTING: ★ **STURDINESS:** ★★ **CLEANUP:** ★
COMMENTS: The roasting dish of this enameled cast-iron roaster was not deep enough, and filled up quickly with chicken grease, and the 5-inch shaft couldn't lift the chicken high enough, leaving the bird sitting in its own fat. Its hefty weight, more than 5 pounds, made it difficult to lift in and out of the oven, causing us to splash hot grease.

BLACK BEANS AND RICE

WHY THIS RECIPE WORKS: Beans and rice is a familiar combination the world over, but Cuban black beans and rice is unique in that the rice is cooked in the inky concentrated liquid left over from cooking the beans, which renders the grains just as flavorful. For our own superlative version, we reserved a portion of the sofrito (the traditional combination of garlic, bell pepper, and onion) and simmered it with our beans to infuse them with flavor. Instead of just draining off and throwing away the flavorful bean cooking liquid, we used it again to cook our rice and beans together. Lightly browning the remaining sofrito vegetables and spices with rendered salt pork added complex, meaty flavor, and baking the dish in the oven eliminated the crusty bottom that can form when the dish is cooked on the stove.

RICE AND BEANS HAS ALWAYS BEEN A SUSTENANCE DISH to us—satisfying, surely, but a bit mundane. So we were intrigued when a friend returned from a trip to Miami and raved about a Cuban version in which black beans and rice are cooked together with aromatic vegetables, spices, and pork to create either a hearty main course or a flavorful side dish. Traditionally called *Moros y Cristianos,* this dish is unique in that the rice is cooked in the inky concentrated liquid left over from cooking the beans, which renders the grains just as flavorful. This was definitely a dish we wanted to cook at home.

Most of the recipes that we found followed the same method: Sauté pork (usually salt pork or bacon) in a Dutch oven until crisp; lightly brown aromatic vegetables and spices in the rendered fat; then stir in uncooked rice, followed by the already cooked black beans and their cooking liquid. Cover and gently simmer until the liquid has been absorbed and the rice is tender.

Sounded easy enough. But after cooking up a few pots, our problems became clear: Sometimes we had bland rice studded with insipid beans—hardly worth the effort. Other times we ended up with poorly cooked rice: either a moist, gluey mash or grains scorched on the bottom but still undercooked on the top (the liquid having boiled away). Our goal was to make a dish that was not just richly flavorful, but foolproof.

To get the flavor right, we knew we needed to perfect the sofrito. This mixture of aromatic vegetables, spices, and herbs is a cornerstone of Latin cooking and the starting point for this dish. The specific elements in the mix differ from one Latin cuisine to another, but a Cuban sofrito usually consists of a "holy trinity" of onion, green pepper, and garlic, typically flavored with cumin and oregano.

We quickly found that pureeing the vegetables for the sofrito before combining them with the beans and rice was not the way to go here; the resulting paste muddied the texture of the dish and eliminated the possibility of browning the sofrito in a skillet first. Chopping the vegetables (or pulsing them in a food processor) into quarter-inch dice was a better option. After crisping 6 ounces of diced salt pork (bacon made an acceptable substitute), we added the onion, pepper, cumin, and oregano, and sautéed the sofrito for 15 minutes in the rendered fat and a splash of extra-virgin olive oil until the mixture was golden brown and flavorful. Then we added some garlic to the mix.

The only problem? There just wasn't enough of that rich flavor. We needed this sofrito to be the backbone to a big pot of beans and rice, not just give it a mild overtone. Increasing the spices helped, but only to a point; overdoing it made the dish dusty and harsh. We thought that doubling the amount of sofrito would do the trick—and flavorwise, it did—but the sheer volume of moist vegetables weighed down the rice and beans in a kind of sofrito sludge. Did all of the veggies have to go directly into the sofrito? Since we had been precooking the soaked beans in plain water, we wondered if we could use the extra veggies to infuse the beans and thereby increase the overall flavor of the dish. With that in mind, we put half an onion, half a green pepper, half a garlic head, and bay leaves in with the beans to simmer. When the beans were just cooked, we sampled them. It turned out to be a good idea—both the beans and their cooking liquid were full-flavored and would lend that quality to the rice as well. The results were even better when we swapped half of the water for chicken broth.

With the flavor of the dish where we wanted it, we turned to the rice. We had hoped to forgo the traditional extra step of rinsing the rice before cooking, but a side-by-side comparison clearly showed that washing off the excess starch from the grains helps prevent them from turning sticky and clumping together. Plus, we were already using the starchy black bean cooking liquid to cook the rice, so removing the extra surface starch from the rice grains was particularly important.

Fixing the scorched-yet-undercooked rice was a little trickier. The line between gummy rice and undercooked rice is a fine one because the beans, sofrito, and pork all add moisture to the pot. We tinkered around a bit with extra liquid; after a few sodden pots of beans and rice, we found that 2½ cups was the correct amount of bean liquid to get 1½ cups of rice cooked through in about 30 minutes. But even at the lowest heat setting, we found that the mixture at the bottom of the pot was still scorching while the rice grains at the top remained almost crunchy. The problem made sense: With the stove's flame hitting only the underside of the pot, the bottom layer of rice burned while the grains at the top barely cooked at all. That's when we recalled our oven-baked rice technique, in which the all-around, indirect heat cooks the pot's contents gently and evenly. We brought the rice, beans, and liquid (including a splash of red wine vinegar for brightness) to a simmer, gave the mixture a stir, covered the vessel, and slid it into a 350-degree oven. After about the same time as it took to cook on the stove, we removed the pot, fluffed the contents with a fork, and let it sit for five minutes. Finally, perfectly cooked rice from top to bottom.

As a final touch, a sprinkling of thinly sliced scallions and a squeeze of lime brought the dish to life. And for a meatless version, a tablespoon of tomato paste cooked with the sofrito laced the dish with a savory presence. Forget about packing your bags—this was a taste of Cuba that you could make in any kitchen.

NOTES FROM THE TEST KITCHEN

WHAT'S A SOFRITO?

A sofrito serves as the fundamental flavor base for many Cuban dishes, including this one. The combination of onion, green pepper, and garlic (and often cumin and oregano) is a close relative of the French mirepoix, which features onion, carrot, and celery.

CUBAN FLAVOR BASE

Cuban-Style Black Beans and Rice

SERVES 6 TO 8

It is important to use lean—not fatty—salt pork. If you can't find it, substitute 6 slices of bacon. If using bacon, decrease the cooking time in step 4 to 8 minutes. You will need a Dutch oven with a tight-fitting lid for this recipe.

- Salt
- 1 cup dried black beans, picked over and rinsed
- 2 cups low-sodium chicken broth
- 2 cups water
- 2 large green bell peppers, stemmed, seeded, and halved
- 1 large onion, halved at equator and peeled, root end left intact
- 1 head garlic, 5 cloves minced, remaining head halved at equator with skin left intact
- 2 bay leaves
- 1½ cups long-grain white rice
- 2 tablespoons extra-virgin olive oil
- 6 ounces lean salt pork, cut into ¼-inch dice
- 4 teaspoons ground cumin
- 1 tablespoon minced fresh oregano
- 2 tablespoons red wine vinegar
- 2 scallions, sliced thin
- Lime wedges

1. Dissolve 1½ tablespoons salt in 2 quarts cold water in large bowl or container. Add beans and soak at room temperature for at least 8 hours or up to 24 hours. Drain and rinse well.

2. In Dutch oven, stir together drained beans, broth, water, 1 pepper half, 1 onion half (with root end), halved garlic head, bay leaves, and 1 teaspoon salt. Bring to simmer over medium-high heat, cover, and reduce heat to low. Cook until beans are just soft, 30 to 35 minutes. Using tongs, remove and discard pepper, onion, garlic, and bay leaves. Drain beans in colander set over large bowl, reserving 2½ cups bean cooking liquid. (If you don't have enough bean cooking liquid, add water to equal 2½ cups.) Do not wash out Dutch oven.

3. Adjust oven rack to middle position and heat oven to 350 degrees. Place rice in large fine-mesh strainer and rinse under cold running water until water runs clear, about 1½ minutes. Shake strainer vigorously to remove all excess water; set rice aside. Cut remaining peppers and onion into 2-inch pieces and process in food processor until broken into rough ¼-inch pieces, about 8 pulses, scraping down bowl as necessary; set vegetables aside.

4. In now-empty Dutch oven, heat 1 tablespoon oil and salt pork over medium-low heat and cook, stirring frequently, until lightly browned and fat is rendered, 15 to 20 minutes. Add remaining 1 tablespoon oil, chopped peppers and onion, cumin, and oregano. Increase heat to medium and continue to cook, stirring frequently, until vegetables are softened and beginning to brown, 10 to 15 minutes longer. Add minced garlic and cook, stirring constantly, until fragrant, about 1 minute. Add rice and stir to coat, about 30 seconds.

5. Stir in beans, reserved bean cooking liquid, vinegar, and ½ teaspoon salt. Increase heat to medium-high and bring to simmer. Cover and transfer to oven. Cook until liquid is absorbed and rice is tender, about 30 minutes. Fluff with fork and let rest, uncovered, for 5 minutes. Serve, passing scallions and lime wedges separately.

VARIATION

Vegetarian Cuban-Style Black Beans and Rice

Substitute water for chicken broth and omit salt pork. Add 1 tablespoon tomato paste with vegetables in step 4 and increase amount of salt in step 5 to 1½ teaspoons.

NOTES FROM THE TEST KITCHEN

KEYS TO DEEPLY FLAVORED BLACK BEANS AND RICE

1. ENRICH BEANS: Simmering the beans in water and chicken broth bolstered with salt, garlic, bell pepper, onion, and garlic adds extra flavor.

2. RINSE RICE: Washing excess starch off the rice with plenty of cool running water helps the grains cook up fluffy, not sticky.

3. DEEPEN SOFRITO FLAVOR: Lightly browning the sofrito vegetables and spices with the rendered salt pork adds complex, meaty flavor.

4. ADD BEAN COOKING LIQUID: Cooking the rice and beans in the reserved bean cooking liquid plus red wine vinegar imbues the dish with flavor.

5. BAKE IN OVEN: Baking the beans and rice eliminates the crusty bottom that can form when the dish is cooked on the stove.

RATING BROWN RICE

Brown rice is essentially a less-processed version of white rice. Every grain of rice is made up of an endosperm, germ, bran, and a hull or husk; white rice is stripped of all but the endosperm, while brown rice also retains the germ and bran. Because it is less processed than white rice, brown rice has almost three times the amount of fiber and more vitamins. We wondered if brand really mattered when it came to a product that had undergone so little processing. To find out, we tasted five brands of long-grain brown rice prepared two ways: simply steamed in a rice cooker and baked in the oven. In both tastings, one brand came out on top; this rice was praised for its firm yet tender grains and bold, nutty flavor. Tasters found all but one brown rice acceptable; that brand was the only rice in the lineup that's parboiled for quicker cooking. Unfortunately, this treatment was detrimental to the rice's texture and flavor. Brands are listed in order of preference. See www.americastestkitchen.com for updates to this testing.

RECOMMENDED

GOYA Brown Rice Natural Long Grain Rice
PRICE: $1.49 for 16 oz (9 cents per oz)
COMMENTS: "Earthy," "grassy," "toasty," "nutty," "buttery," and "sweet" were all used to describe our favorite brown rice. One taster even identified a "popcorn" aftertaste we associate with aromatic varieties of rice. It had firm yet tender grains that one taster described as having a "nice pop." With both a pleasing flavor and texture, this brown rice won both our tastings.

LUNDBERG Organic Long Grain Brown Rice
PRICE: $4.04 for 32 oz (13 cents per oz)
COMMENTS: Slightly less flavorful than our winner, this rice, though moderately nutty and buttery with "mineral" notes, was often described as "neutral" and "mild" by our tasters. But even tasters who were lukewarm on its flavor praised its firm, "al dente" texture.

RECOMMENDED WITH RESERVATIONS

CAROLINA Brown Rice (Whole Grain)
PRICE: $2.99 for 28 oz (11 cents per oz)
COMMENTS: Tasters described this rice as a good "blank slate" for other flavors, describing it as "neutral rather than bland," with a texture that was "al dente" with "good starchiness." In other words, this rice was average in every way, neither offensive nor special.

SHILOH FARMS Organic Brown Rice Long Grain
PRICE: $5.60 for 32 oz (18 cents per oz)
COMMENTS: Like Carolina brown rice, this rice was average through and through, with a "buttery, decent taste, but maybe not the best," and "decent overall texture and flavor, but bland." Tasters commented on the "chewiness" of the grains, one saying they had "good chew" while another taster complained they were "too chewy."

NOT RECOMMENDED

UNCLE BEN'S Natural Whole Grain Brown Rice
PRICE: $2.39 for 16 oz (15 cents per oz)
COMMENTS: "Unremarkable in every way," was the highest praise our tasters could muster for this rice that was also described as "bland and a tad spongy." The only rice to be parboiled for quicker cooking, its treatment was detrimental to the texture and flavor. Its fatal flaw was the aftertaste, with tasters complaining of "dirty oil," "cardboard-y," "soapy," "plastic," "yeasty," "sour," "chemical," and "slightly metallic" notes.

Gnocchi AND PANZANELLA

CHAPTER 11

THE RECIPES

Potato Gnocchi with Browned Butter and Sage Sauce

- Gorgonzola-Cream Sauce
- Parmesan Sauce with Pancetta and Walnuts
- Porcini Mushroom Broth

Italian Bread Salad (Panzanella)

- Italian Bread Salad with Peppers and Arugula
- Italian Bread Salad with Olives and Feta
- Italian Bread Salad with Garlic and Capers

EQUIPMENT CORNER

Rotary Graters

Gadget guru Lisa McManus tests out rotary graters and discovers that all models are not created equal.

ITALIAN COOKING, AT LEAST IN THIS COUNTRY, TYPICALLY CONJURES up images of pasta and red sauce, or perhaps heavily breaded cutlets smothered in mozzarella. But two of our favorite Italian dishes—gnocchi and panzanella—are an exercise in simplicity. Both are made from very few ingredients, which means that even the slightest variation in technique or assembly can mean the difference between mediocre and memorable. Potato gnocchi are nothing more than mashed potatoes and a little bit of flour kneaded into a dough. When done right, they cook up into light, pillowy dumplings that need little adornment other than a simple sauce. But finding just the right ratio of flour to potato is typically a guessing game, and overworked dough leads to dense, heavy dumplings. We wanted a foolproof recipe and technique that would guarantee light, fluffy gnocchi.

Panzanella is a rustic tomato-bread salad that has thrifty roots as a way to use up leftover, stale bread. That means the other ingredients—tomatoes, herbs, and extra-virgin olive oil—should be of the highest quality. The bread soaks up the dressing and juices from the tomatoes, which allows the flavors of the dish to meld. But the bread can quickly become over-saturated if each component is not handled just right. We wanted a bright dressing, just the right combination of supporting ingredients, and chunks of bread that were pleasantly soft and chewy—not soggy.

GNOCCHI AT HOME

WHY THIS RECIPE WORKS: The method for making gnocchi is simple: Knead the mashed potatoes into a dough with a minimum of flour; shape; and boil for a minute. And yet the potential pitfalls are numerous (lumpy mashed potatoes, too much or too little flour, a heavy hand when kneading, and bland flavor). We wanted a foolproof recipe for impossibly light gnocchi with unmistakable potato flavor. Baking russets after parcooking them in the microwave produced intensely flavored potatoes—an excellent start to our gnocchi base. To avoid lumps, which can cause gnocchi to break apart during cooking, we turned to a ricer for a smooth, supple mash. While many recipes offer a range of flour, which ups the chances of overworking the dough (and producing leaden gnocchi), we used an exact amount based on the ratio of potato to flour so that our gnocchi dough was mixed as little as possible. And we found that an egg, while not traditional, tenderized our gnocchi further, delivering delicate pillowlike dumplings.

IN ITALY, GNOCCHI CAN MEAN ANY NUMBER OF DIFferent styles of dumpling, from ricotta to semolina, and most good cooks have at least two or three types in their repertoire. In this country, gnocchi more often than not means the potato-based type. At their best, these thimble-size dumplings boast a pillowy texture and an earthy flavor that needs nothing more than a gloss of browned butter sauce to be fit for the table. Creating them always looks straightforward enough: Just mash the cooked potatoes; bind them with flour and knead into dough; shape into dumplings; and boil. And yet, the abundance of mediocre versions of gnocchi is astonishing. Most of the time, these dumplings turn out dense, gluey, or rubbery—and sometimes all of the above.

The fact is that even in a seemingly simple recipe such as this, there's plenty of room for error. First, the moisture in the potato will impact how much flour the dough absorbs—and, in turn, will affect the density of the gnocchi. Second, mashing the potatoes presents a Catch-22. While obviously necessary, the action of mashing bursts starch cells in the potatoes, and the more that they burst, the more gluey the gnocchi will be. Third, developing a modest amount of gluten is what lends these dumplings their pleasantly faint chew—but add too much flour or water, or overknead the dough, and you'll end up with leaden sinkers. Add to this the fact that sometimes even the most perfectly textured gnocchi can lack distinct potato flavor, and the challenge looms even larger.

Surely there was some way to make this simple recipe foolproof so that light, delicate, and potato-y gnocchi were not just a happy accident, but a guarantee.

We weren't surprised to find that the majority of gnocchi recipes we surveyed called for russet potatoes, since their low-moisture flesh absorbs less flour than Yukon gold or waxy creamer spuds. The trouble is, russets are also comparatively bland. We tried out the other two kinds but the resulting dumplings we fished out of the water were as dense as rubber balls. Clearly russets were the way to go.

No need to give up on potato flavor just yet, however. The pre-cooking step was our opportunity to enhance the spuds' earthiness, and we quickly set up a side-by-side test between baked and boiled samples. Not surprisingly, the oven deepened the potatoes' flavor, while the hot water bath washed them out. Even better, the oven's dry heat evaporated some of the spuds' moisture, yielding fluffier results. The only drawback was the lengthy baking time. We pulled out an old test kitchen trick to hasten the process. We zapped the potatoes in the microwave for 10 minutes before moving them into a hot 450-degree oven, where they needed just 20 minutes to finish cooking. We then pulled the spuds from the oven and hurriedly grabbed an oven mitt and paring knife to remove the skins. Again, since the drier the potatoes, the better, working quickly was essential if we were going to ensure that they gave off as much steam as possible.

For mashing, we needed the gentlest method possible. In the past, we've found that the repeated motion of hand mashing ruptures far more cells than a ricer does, as the utensil compresses the potatoes only once. After pushing our warm peeled russets through this tool, we followed the lead of many recipes and spread the fine threads onto a baking sheet, where they continued to release steam.

Once the potatoes had cooled slightly, the flour could be incorporated—but exactly how much was not clear.

The existing recipes we'd tried didn't specify an amount of flour, but offered a range that varied by as much as 1 cup in some cases. The idea is to form the dough with the lesser amount of flour and boil a few test dumplings to see if it's enough. If the gnocchi fall apart, gradually work more flour into the dough. But therein lies the problem: Because you're starting on the low end of the scale, the dough invariably requires more flour, which means extra kneading—and more gluten development—as you work it in. To limit the dough manipulation, the trick would be to weigh out an exact amount of cooked potato, and then determine the precise amount of flour that corresponds to it. Not only would we avoid guesswork during mixing, but the dough would turn out the same way every time.

To determine the minimum amount of flour required to bind the potato together, we made several batches of dough, using a fork to gently stir different amounts into each and kneading them for just a minute. The magic number turned out to be 5 ounces; any less and the gnocchi feathered apart in the water. But although these gnocchi cooked up relatively light and airy, they still weren't the delicate-yet-substantial puffs we had envisioned.

Reasoning that we could do no more than we already had with the potatoes and flour, we pulled out what we thought might be a ringer from our pantry: baking powder. This batch definitely puffed up, but, unfortunately, also absorbed some cooking water and turned mushy. And the same was true for baking soda. With so little gluten, the dough couldn't hold the gases created by leavening, and it blew apart, allowing water to seep in.

We were running low on ideas when a colleague asked why we hadn't tried incorporating an egg, a relatively common addition. We have to admit that this omission wasn't entirely accidental; we'd deliberately avoided recipes containing calling for egg because we thought its proteins would coagulate during cooking and bind the dough together too firmly. But at this point, we had nothing to lose.

We whipped up another batch of dough, this time stirring in a beaten egg before adding the 5 ounces of flour. Predictably, the dough was a little wetter than usual. Because we resisted compensating with flour, we were skeptical about the gnocchi holding together when they hit the boiling water. We needn't have feared. These gnocchi not only held their shape, but also emerged from the water puffed and tender. The egg turned out to be exactly what the dough needed after all: a more tender replacement for some of the gluten-rich flour, with the proteins creating just the right amount of structure.

We wondered if we could press this advantage even further, and we made another batch, dropping the flour to a mere 4 ounces. After 90 seconds of simmering, the gnocchi had just the impossibly light texture and rich potato flavor we'd been aiming for.

As for shaping, we kept our method traditional: Cut the dough into eight pieces, roll each into a ½-inch-thick rope, and cut ¾-inch lengths. From there, we simply pressed each dumpling against the back of a fork to create an indentation, then rolled it down the tines to create ridges. This classic technique serves two purposes: The ridges trap sauce, while the indentation helps each gnocchi cook more evenly.

These potato-y puffs were good enough to eat straight from the pot, drizzled with a little extra-virgin olive oil, but we also wanted to whip up a few simple sauces. The classic traditional nutty browned butter with shallot and fresh sage was a must. We also threw together an equally indulgent Gorgonzola-cream sauce brightened with white wine and chopped chives.

In the end, it turns out that you don't need to be Italian or an accomplished cook to make perfect gnocchi. All it takes is a little precision—and an egg.

NOTES FROM THE TEST KITCHEN

SECRETS TO AIRY, EARTHY-TASTING POTATO GNOCCHI

1. BAKE, DON'T BOIL FOR BETTER FLAVOR: For a quicker "bake," nuke the russets in the microwave, then finish in the oven.

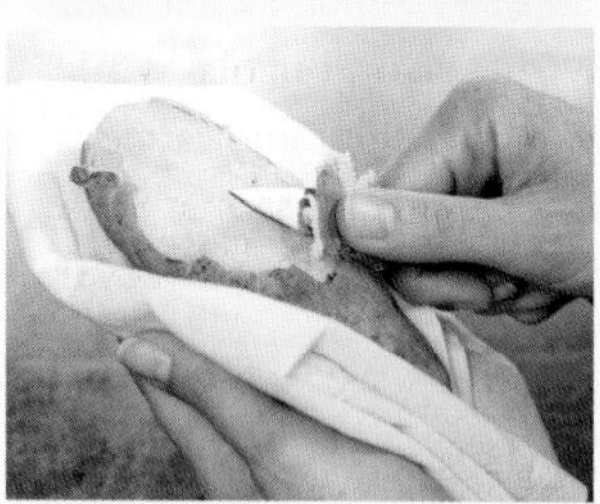

2. PEEL 'EM WHILE THEY'RE HOT: Peel hot potatoes to release steam. The drier the potatoes, the less flour needed to hold them together, and the lighter the texture.

3. SPREAD OUT: Press cooked potatoes through a ricer, which bursts fewer gluey starch cells than hand mashing does. Evaporate more steam by spreading the potatoes over a sheet pan.

4. BE PRECISE: Instead of adding flour a little at a time until the dough holds together, start with the exact amount of cooked potato and exact amount of flour, so you knead only once.

5. ADD AN EGG: Egg helps the dough hold its shape with less flour, for lighter results.

Potato Gnocchi with Browned Butter and Sage Sauce

SERVES 4

Gnocchi require accurate measurement in order to achieve the proper texture; it's best to weigh the potatoes and flour. After processing, you may have slightly more than the 3 cups (1 pound) of potatoes required for this recipe; do not be tempted to use more than 3 cups. Eat or discard any extra. If you prefer, replace the browned butter sauce with Gorgonzola-Cream Sauce, Parmesan Sauce with Pancetta and Walnuts, or Porcini Mushroom Broth (recipes follow).

POTATO GNOCCHI

- **2 pounds russet potatoes**
- **1 large egg, lightly beaten**
- **¾ cup plus 1 tablespoon (4 ounces) all-purpose flour**
- **Salt**

BROWNED BUTTER AND SAGE SAUCE

- **4 tablespoons unsalted butter, cut into 4 pieces**
- **1 small shallot, minced**
- **1 teaspoon minced fresh sage**
- **1½ teaspoons lemon juice**
- **¼ teaspoon salt**

1. FOR THE GNOCCHI: Adjust oven rack to middle position and heat oven to 450 degrees. Poke each potato 8 times with paring knife over entire surface. Place potatoes on plate and microwave until slightly softened at ends, about 10 minutes, flipping potatoes halfway through cooking. Transfer potatoes directly to oven rack and bake until skewer glides easily through flesh and potatoes yield to gentle pressure, 18 to 20 minutes.

2. Hold potato with potholder or kitchen towel and peel with paring knife. Process potato through ricer or food mill onto rimmed baking sheet. Repeat with remaining potatoes. Gently spread potatoes into even layer and let cool for 5 minutes.

3. Transfer 3 cups (1 pound) warm potatoes to large bowl. Using fork, gently stir in egg until just combined. Sprinkle flour and 1 teaspoon salt over potato mixture. Using fork, gently combine until no pockets of dry flour remain. Press mixture into rough dough, transfer to lightly floured counter, and gently knead until smooth but slightly sticky, about 1 minute, lightly dusting counter with flour as needed to prevent sticking.

4. Line 2 rimmed baking sheets with parchment paper and dust liberally with flour. Cut dough into 8 pieces. Lightly dust counter with flour. Gently roll 1 piece of dough into ½ inch-thick rope, dusting with flour to prevent sticking. Cut rope into ¾-inch lengths. Hold fork, with tines facing down, in 1 hand and press side of each piece of dough against ridged surface with thumb to make indentation in center; roll dough down and off tines to form ridges. Transfer formed gnocchi to prepared sheets and repeat with remaining dough.

5. FOR THE SAUCE: Melt butter in 12-inch skillet over medium-high heat, swirling occasionally, until butter is browned and releases nutty aroma, about 1½ minutes. Off heat, add shallot and sage, stirring until shallot is fragrant, about 1 minute. Stir in lemon juice and salt and cover to keep warm.

6. Bring 4 quarts water to boil in large pot. Add 1 tablespoon salt. Using parchment paper as sling, add half of gnocchi and cook until firm and just cooked through, about 1½ minutes (gnocchi should float to surface after about 1 minute). Remove gnocchi with slotted spoon, transfer to skillet with sauce, and cover to keep warm. Repeat with remaining gnocchi and transfer to skillet. Gently toss gnocchi with sauce to combine and serve.

NOTES FROM THE TEST KITCHEN

MAKING RIDGES ON GNOCCHI

Hold fork with tines facing down. Press each dough piece against tines (cut side down) with thumb to create indentation in middle and ridges on back. Use thumb to roll dumpling down tines to create ridges on sides.

Gorgonzola-Cream Sauce

MAKES ABOUT 1 CUP; ENOUGH FOR 1 RECIPE POTATO GNOCCHI

Adjust the consistency of the sauce with up to 2 tablespoons cooking water before adding it to the gnocchi.

- **¾ cup heavy cream**
- **¼ cup dry white wine**
- **4 ounces Gorgonzola cheese, crumbled (1 cup)**
- **2 tablespoons minced fresh chives**
- **Salt and pepper**

Bring cream and wine to simmer in 12-inch skillet over medium-high heat. Gradually add Gorgonzola while whisking constantly and cook until melted and sauce is thickened, 2 to 3 minutes. Stir in chives and season with salt and pepper to taste. Remove from heat and cover to keep warm.

Parmesan Sauce with Pancetta and Walnuts

MAKES ABOUT 1 CUP; ENOUGH FOR 1 RECIPE POTATO GNOCCHI

Serve with extra grated Parmesan cheese on the side.

- **½ cup low-sodium chicken broth**
- **1 ounce Parmesan cheese, grated (½ cup)**
- **¼ cup heavy cream**
- **2 large egg yolks**
- **⅛ teaspoon pepper**
- **2 teaspoons olive oil**
- **3 ounces pancetta, chopped fine**
- **½ cup walnuts, chopped coarse**
- **Salt**

Whisk broth, Parmesan, cream, egg yolks, and pepper together in bowl until smooth. Heat oil in 12-inch skillet over medium heat until shimmering. Add pancetta and cook until crisp, 5 to 7 minutes. Stir in walnuts and cook until golden and fragrant, about 1 minute. Off heat, gradually add broth mixture, whisking constantly. Return skillet to medium heat and cook, stirring often, until sauce is thickened slightly, 2 to 4 minutes. Season with salt to taste. Remove from heat and cover to keep warm.

Porcini Mushroom Broth

MAKES ABOUT 1¼ CUPS; ENOUGH FOR 1 RECIPE POTATO GNOCCHI

Serve with grated Parmesan cheese.

- **1¾ cups low-sodium chicken broth**
- **½ ounce dried porcini mushrooms, rinsed**
- **3 tablespoons extra-virgin olive oil**
- **1 small shallot, minced**
- **2 garlic cloves, sliced thin**
- **⅓ cup dry white wine**
- **2 tablespoons minced fresh parsley**
- **Salt and pepper**

1. Microwave broth and porcini in covered bowl until steaming, about 1 minute. Let sit until softened, about 5 minutes. Drain mushrooms through fine-mesh strainer lined with coffee filter, reserve liquid, and finely chop mushrooms.

2. Heat 1 tablespoon oil in 12-inch skillet over medium heat until shimmering. Add chopped mushrooms, shallot, and garlic and cook until lightly browned, 2 to 4 minutes. Stir in reserved porcini soaking liquid, wine, and remaining 2 tablespoons oil, scraping up any browned bits. Bring mixture to boil and cook, whisking occasionally, until reduced to 1¼ cups, 6 to 9 minutes. Stir in parsley and season with salt and pepper to taste. Remove from heat and cover to keep warm.

RATING ROTARY GRATERS

Rather than risk scraping our knuckles on a box or rasp-style grater, we prefer to shred Parmesan cheese tableside with a rotary grater. To find a tool that works quickly with the least amount of pressure possible, we asked testers with various hand sizes to try four models, priced from $9.99 to $34.99, handing them everything from hard Parmesan to semisoft cheddar, soft mozzarella, and even chocolate. Not surprisingly, the biggest factor turned out to be the size of the barrel: Models with larger barrels zipped through the cheese in seconds. We preferred classic designs—where one hand presses a clamp against the cheese to hold it in place while the other rotates the handle—to gimmicky devices that twist like a peppermill or require brute strength. Brands are listed in order of preference. See www.americastestkitchen.com for updates to this testing.

RECOMMENDED

ZYLISS All Cheese Grater (model #11355)
PRICE: $19.95 **PARMESAN:** ★★★ **CHEDDAR:** ★★★
MOZZARELLA: ★★ **CHOCOLATE:** ★★ **DESIGN:** ★★★
COMMENTS: This simply designed, dishwasher-safe grater, with an extra-wide barrel and comfortable handle, blasted through chunks of cheddar and Parmesan and produced perfect chocolate shavings and mozzarella shreds even after stiffening up a bit. Our only complaint: The plastic body created static that made chocolate shavings jump from the barrel onto our hands and clothes.

RECOMMENDED WITH RESERVATIONS

CUISIPRO Rotary Cheese Grater (model #746607)
PRICE: $24.50 **PARMESAN:** ★★ **CHEDDAR:** ★★
MOZZARELLA: ★★ **CHOCOLATE:** ★★★ **DESIGN:** ★★
COMMENTS: This simple stainless steel model easily shaved chocolate and did a fine job with the cheeses. But it suffered from two design problems. For starters, it came with only one relatively fine-bladed grinder drum (inserts for other sizes are sold separately). What's more, its ropy metal handle became slightly uncomfortable after prolonged use.

NOT RECOMMENDED

SWISSMAR Rotary Cheese Grater Set (model #S3170)
PRICE: $9.99 **PARMESAN:** ★★ **CHEDDAR:** ★
MOZZARELLA: ★ **CHOCOLATE:** ★ **DESIGN:** ★
COMMENTS: Though this model came equipped with the largest grinding barrel, its peppermill-like design demanded considerable effort in exchange for very little output. Parmesan was no big deal and neither was cheddar (though it required more effort), but both softer mozzarella and dense chocolate clogged the mechanism and required us to twist with extra force—and even then results were scrappy.

RÖSLE Cheese Mill (model #16684)
PRICE: $34.99 **PARMESAN:** ★ **CHEDDAR:** ★
MOZZARELLA: ★ **CHOCOLATE:** ★ **DESIGN:** ★
COMMENTS: In a prime example of price not equaling performance, this most-expensive, gimmicky model was an all-around disappointment. Its small grinder drum struggled with chocolate and all three cheeses. Even worse, its T-shaped design made handling awkward. We had to hold the mill in one hand while turning the crank with the other, and our two hands inevitably smacked into each other.

PANZANELLA

WHY THIS RECIPE WORKS: When the rustic Italian bread salad panzanella is done well, the sweet juice of the tomatoes mixes with a bright-tasting vinaigrette, moistening chunks of thick-crusted bread until they're soft and just a little chewy—but the line between lightly moistened and unpleasantly soggy is very thin. Toasting fresh bread in the oven, rather than using the traditional day-old bread, was a good start. The bread lost enough moisture in the oven to absorb the dressing without getting waterlogged. A 10-minute soak in the flavorful dressing yielded perfectly moistened, nutty-tasting bread ready to be tossed with the tomatoes, which we salted to intensify their flavor. A thinly sliced cucumber and shallot for crunch and bite plus a handful of chopped fresh basil perfected our salad.

RIPE SUMMER TOMATOES REQUIRE NOTHING MORE than to be sliced, drizzled with fruity extra-virgin olive oil, and sprinkled with sea salt and fresh pepper. But when we need a side dish that's a little more substantial, we're often tempted by panzanella, the rustic Italian tomato-bread salad in which the fruit is cut into chunks, tossed with bread pieces, and dressed with olive oil and vinegar. When done well, the tomatoes give up some of their sweet juices, which mix with the tangy dressing and moisten the dry bread until it's soft and just a little chewy.

In our experience, the line between lightly moistened and unpleasantly soggy is very thin, even when we start with a good-quality bakery loaf. We were determined to aim higher. Besides using ripe, juicy tomatoes (nothing but farmers' market–quality specimens would do), we'd get the bread just right: a thick-crusted loaf cut into chunks and moderately soaked—not drenched—with a bright vinaigrette.

Like many other peasant dishes, panzanella started out as a way to make use of day-old bread. But in the test kitchen, we've stopped cooking with naturally stale bread. Instead, we prefer to cut up a fresh loaf and "quick-stale" the pieces by drying them in a low oven. Here's why: As bread stales naturally, its starch molecules recrystallize in a process called retrogradation, causing the bread to become hard and crumbly but not necessarily dry. Oven-dried bread, on the other hand, loses a fair bit of moisture, thereby enhancing its ability to soak up any added liquid.

We cobbled together a working recipe by cutting a rustic loaf into bite-size (1-inch) pieces, tossing them with a little olive oil and salt, spreading them in an even layer on a baking sheet, and sliding the tray into a 225-degree oven. After about 15 minutes, we took the bread out of the oven, let it cool, and then combined it with the tomato chunks and a 2:1 ratio of olive oil to red wine vinegar. The results? Not bad, but not stellar. The bread was a little dry and unevenly moistened, and the whole thing tasted a smidge flat. Plus, the salad didn't come together as a whole: The bread and tomatoes seemed like two separate components occupying the same bowl.

Leaving the bread alone for the moment, we switched gears to focus on the tomatoes. Since not enough of the juices from the ripe, sweet fruit were making it into the bread, maybe it would work better if we removed some of the juices first and added them directly to the salad. We tossed the cut-up tomatoes with ½ teaspoon of salt and set them over a colander to drain. Fifteen minutes later, they'd shed a good bit of juice, into which we whisked the oil and vinegar. We added the bread and tomatoes and summoned our colleagues for a tasting. Everyone agreed that the bread still hadn't absorbed much of the dressing's flavor.

Reviewing our research, we remembered that the traditional approach to panzanella calls for giving the bread a lengthy soak in water before tossing it with the other ingredients—a frugal step that meant cooks didn't have to rely as much on tomatoes and olive oil to moisten the stale loaf. We weren't about to dilute the flavor of the bread with water, but what if we gave it a few extra minutes in the dressing before adding the other components? We mixed up the dressing, added the bread, and let it soak for about 10 minutes before stirring in the tomatoes. Our tasters said that the bread was now perfectly moistened, but they clamored for just a bit more flavor from the bread itself.

When making bruschetta, we always toast the bread first, since browning brings out fuller flavor. Figuring

ITALIAN BREAD SALAD (PANZANELLA)

that the technique would translate here, we cranked up the oven to 400 degrees and baked the bread until it turned light golden brown before proceeding with our recipe. This was the winning batch: The browned bread pieces were nutty-tasting and lightly saturated with the flavorful dressing.

Now for the finishing touches. Thinly sliced cucumber and shallot made the cut for their crunch and fresh bite, as did chopped basil. And because we knew that this salad would become a staple, we whipped up a few variations: one with sweet red bell pepper and spicy arugula, another with briny olives and tangy feta, and one flavored with garlic and capers.

Italian Bread Salad (Panzanella)

SERVES 4

The success of this recipe depends on high-quality ingredients, including ripe, in-season tomatoes and fruity olive oil. Fresh basil is also a must. Your bread may vary in density, so you may not need the entire loaf for this recipe.

- **1 (1-pound) loaf rustic Italian or French bread, cut or torn into 1-inch pieces**
- **½ cup extra-virgin olive oil**
- **Salt and pepper**
- **1½ pounds tomatoes, cored, seeded, and cut into 1-inch pieces**
- **3 tablespoons red wine vinegar**
- **1 cucumber, peeled, halved lengthwise, seeded, and sliced thin**
- **1 shallot, sliced thin**
- **¼ cup chopped fresh basil**

1. Adjust oven rack to middle position and heat oven to 400 degrees. Toss bread pieces with 2 tablespoons oil and ¼ teaspoon salt; arrange bread in single layer on rimmed baking sheet. Toast bread pieces until just starting to turn light golden, 15 to 20 minutes, stirring halfway through baking. Set aside and let cool to room temperature.

2. Gently toss tomatoes and ½ teaspoon salt in large bowl. Transfer to colander set over bowl; set aside to drain for 15 minutes, tossing occasionally.

3. Whisk remaining 6 tablespoons oil, vinegar, and ¼ teaspoon pepper into tomato juices. Add bread pieces, toss to coat, and let stand for 10 minutes, tossing occasionally.

4. Add tomatoes, cucumber, shallot, and basil to bowl with bread pieces and toss to coat. Season with salt and pepper to taste and serve immediately.

VARIATIONS

Italian Bread Salad with Peppers and Arugula

Substitute 1 thinly sliced red bell pepper for cucumber and 1 cup coarsely chopped baby arugula for basil.

Italian Bread Salad with Olives and Feta

Add ⅓ cup coarsely chopped kalamata olives and ½ cup crumbled feta cheese to salad in step 4.

Italian Bread Salad with Garlic and Capers

Add 1 minced garlic clove, 2 minced anchovy fillets, and 2 tablespoons rinsed capers to dressing in step 3.

America's

BISTRO-STYLE
Steak and Potatoes

CHAPTER 12

THE RECIPES

EQUIPMENT CORNER

Viewers often write in to report back on the recipes they make from the test kitchen.

STEAK AND POTATOES MAY BE A SIMPLE MEAL AT HEART, BUT THE French sure do know how to dress them up. The ultra-rich flavor and glossy consistency of the classic reduction known as a demi-glace make it one of the hallmarks of fine French cuisine—and when spooned over a simple pan-seared steak, a demi-glace elevates the dish to four-star status. But making this savory, full-bodied sauce is a full-blown production, one that requires roasting veal bones, deglazing pans, and hours of simmering. We wanted all the flavor and silkiness of this classic French sauce without all the fuss.

Potato galette is another classic French dish that takes something so utterly simple—potatoes—and turns them into special occasion fare. This crisp, earthy-tasting potato cake would be the perfect side dish if it weren't for all the fussy layering. The potatoes must be sliced exceptionally thin and carefully layered into the dish—a time-consuming process, to say the least. Just as frustrating, the cake has a tendency to fall apart as soon as you slice into it. We wanted to find a way to get the same creamy center and crisp, beautifully browned exterior in a fraction of the time. And while we were at it, we'd find a way to remove a slice in one cohesive piece.

PAN-SEARED STEAK WITH HERB SAUCE

RESTAURANT-STYLE SAUCES FOR PAN-SEARED STEAKS

WHY THIS RECIPE WORKS: We love the ultra-rich flavor and glossy consistency that a classic French demi-glace (a savory, full-bodied reduction traditionally made from veal bones and stock) adds to a sauce, but making it is a time-consuming process usually left to the expertise of professional cooks. We wanted to find a shortcut for making demi-glace at home, so that we could use it as the base of a sauce for crusty, pan-seared steaks. Chopping up vegetables (to increase their surface area, thus providing more opportunity for flavorful browning) as well as adding mushrooms, tomato paste, and seasonings to red wine and beef broth was a good start, but it wasn't enough. To replicate the meaty flavor and unctuous gelatin given up by roasted bones, we sautéed ground beef with the tomato paste and stirred powdered gelatin into the final reduction.

IT'S EASY ENOUGH TO FINISH A SEARED STEAK WITH A quick pan sauce or a knob of flavored butter, but anyone who's dined in a fine French restaurant knows that nothing compares to a sauce made with the ultra-savory, full-bodied reduction known as demi-glace. The preparation has been a hallmark of haute cuisine since the days of the 19th-century French chef Auguste Escoffier, and chefs trained in classic French technique tend to keep a supply on hand not only to dress up steak, but as a meaty flavor foundation for soups, sauces, and sautés.

But making demi-glace is another matter. The time-consuming process is really only feasible in a restaurant kitchen. The process in a nutshell: Veal bones are roasted for a couple of hours with aromatics; the roasting pan is deglazed, releasing all the flavorful browned bits that will help enrich the stock; the whole works are transferred to a stock pot with wine and several quarts of water where it all gurgles gently for at least six hours. The stock is then strained and reduced to an ultra-concentrated, glossy, silky essence.

We weren't about to delve into such fussy work in our own kitchen. But this rich, velvety sauce is too good to be left only to restaurant chefs. Surely with some experimenting we could find a shortcut.

The test kitchen already has a good technique for pan-searing steaks (our preferred cuts are strip and rib eyes), so we immediately got to work on the demi-glace. We started by browning carrot, onion, and garlic chunks in a Dutch oven before deglazing the pot with a little red wine and beef broth. Once the mixture had boiled down and thickened a bit, we took a taste. The result wasn't terrible, but its flavor was thin and it had no real body to speak of—hardly something that could stand as the backbone to a sauce.

We had one quick idea for amping up the flavor: In a traditional demi-glace, the vegetables are usually cut into large chunks, which break down and release flavor over the course of roasting and simmering. But since we needed big flavor fast, we pulsed the aromatics in the food processor until they were roughly chopped, figuring their increased surface area would offer more opportunity for flavorful browning. We also added mushrooms and tomato paste (another component common in traditional demi-glace), knowing that both ingredients' meat-mimicking glutamates would increase the savory flavor. Sure enough, this batch—which we further enhanced with thyme, bay leaves, and peppercorns, then deglazed with red wine and a quart of beef broth and reduced for about 25 minutes—showed definite flavor improvement. But it still didn't win over our tasters. Even after we'd worked this latest version into a classic herb pan sauce, they unenthusiastically pushed pieces of steak around in the still-thin reduction. Our faux base still wasn't fooling anybody.

There was no doubt what was missing: Without the meatiness and unctuous gelatin given up by roasted veal bones, our attempt would never be as savory or silky-textured as the real deal. We were at a loss for our next move, when a colleague reminded us of a similar conundrum when we tried to make full-bodied chicken soup without the time-consuming step of slow-simmering a chicken carcass. Our secret there? Ground chicken. The choice actually makes a lot of sense, as the goal with any stock is to extract as much flavor from

the meat as possible—and the finer the bits, the quicker the flavor is extracted. Figuring the same principle would apply here, we grabbed a half pound of ground beef and browned it along with tomato paste for about 10 minutes before adding the vegetables. This was the breakthrough we'd been looking for: Though still not as full-bodied as we'd like, this base more than hinted at the flavor of roasted bones.

The consistency issue was a little trickier. Calves' bones are particularly rich in collagen, which prolonged roasting and simmering breaks down into rich gelatin. Even when we reduced our base to a near-syrupy consistency, the effect wasn't at all the same. But we did have something in our kitchen cupboard that might help: powdered gelatin. We stirred two packages into the final reduction (after straining the solids) and boiled it down to half a cup. As we'd hoped, this was all it took to turn our quick demi-glace silky and viscous.

This time, when we worked the base into our final steak sauces—fresh herbs, brandy with green peppercorns, and port wine were our favorites—tasters mopped up every last drop. Admittedly, classically trained French chefs might be able to tell the difference between our "semi demi" and the true approach—but we'd bet they'd still want the recipe.

Pan-Seared Steaks with Herb Sauce

SERVES 4

We like this sauce with strip or rib-eye steaks, but it will work with any type of pan-seared steak.

- **1 tablespoon vegetable oil**
- **4 (8-ounce) boneless strip or rib-eye steaks, 1 to 1¼ inches thick**
- **Salt and pepper**

- 1 small shallot, minced
- ½ cup white wine
- ¼ cup Sauce Base (½ recipe; recipe follows)
- ¼ teaspoon white wine vinegar
- 1½ teaspoons minced fresh chives
- 1½ teaspoons minced fresh parsley
- 1 teaspoon minced fresh tarragon
- 1 tablespoon unsalted butter

1. Heat oil in 12-inch skillet over medium-high heat until just smoking. Meanwhile, pat steaks dry with paper towels and season with salt and pepper. Lay steaks in pan, leaving ¼ inch between them. Cook, not moving steaks, until well browned, about 4 minutes. Using tongs, flip steaks and continue to cook until meat registers 120 to 125 degrees (for rare to medium-rare), 3 to 7 minutes. Transfer steaks to platter and tent loosely with aluminum foil while preparing herb sauce.

2. Return now-empty skillet to medium-low heat; add shallot and cook, stirring constantly, until lightly browned, about 2 minutes. Add wine and bring to simmer, scraping up any browned bits. Add Sauce Base, vinegar, and any accumulated juices from steak; return to simmer and cook until slightly reduced, about 1 minute. Off heat, whisk in chives, parsley, tarragon, and butter; season with salt and pepper to taste. Spoon sauce over steaks and serve.

VARIATIONS

Pan-Seared Steaks with Brandy and Green-Peppercorn Sauce

Substitute brandy for white wine and red wine vinegar for white wine vinegar. Omit chives, parsley, tarragon, and butter. Add ¼ cup heavy cream, 2 tablespoons rinsed green peppercorns, and ¼ teaspoon chopped fresh thyme to skillet along with Sauce Base and vinegar.

Pan-Seared Steaks with Port Wine Sauce

Substitute ruby port for white wine and balsamic vinegar for white wine vinegar. Substitute ¼ teaspoon chopped fresh thyme for chives, parsley, and tarragon.

Sauce Base

MAKES ½ CUP

The sauce base recipe yields more than called for in the steak recipe; leftovers can be refrigerated for up to 3 days or frozen for up to 1 month.

- 1 small onion, peeled and cut into rough ½-inch pieces
- 1 small carrot, peeled and cut into rough ½-inch pieces
- 8 ounces cremini mushrooms, trimmed and halved
- 2 garlic cloves, peeled
- 1 tablespoon vegetable oil
- 8 ounces 85 percent lean ground beef
- 1 tablespoon tomato paste
- 2 cups dry red wine
- 4 cups beef broth
- 4 sprigs fresh thyme
- 2 bay leaves
- 2 teaspoons whole black peppercorns
- 5 teaspoons unflavored gelatin

1. Pulse onion, carrot, mushrooms, and garlic in food processor into ⅛-inch pieces, 10 to 12 pulses, scraping down bowl as necessary.

2. Heat oil in Dutch oven over medium-high heat until shimmering; add beef and tomato paste and cook, stirring frequently, until beef is well browned, 8 to 10 minutes. Add vegetable mixture and cook, stirring occasionally, until any exuded moisture has evaporated, about 8 minutes. Add wine and bring to simmer, scraping up any browned bits. Add broth, thyme, bay leaves, and peppercorns; bring to boil. Reduce heat and gently boil, occasionally scraping bottom and sides of pot and skimming fat from surface, until reduced to 2 cups, 20 to 25 minutes.

3. Strain mixture through fine-mesh strainer set over small saucepan, pressing on solids with rubber spatula to extract as much liquid as possible (you should have about 1 cup stock). Sprinkle gelatin over stock and stir to dissolve. Place saucepan over medium-high heat and bring stock to boil. Gently boil, stirring occasionally, until reduced to ½ cup, 5 to 7 minutes. Remove from heat and cover to keep warm.

POTATO GALETTE

WHY THIS RECIPE WORKS: Pommes Anna, the classic French potato cake (or galette) in which thinly sliced potatoes are tossed with clarified butter, tightly shingled in a skillet, and cooked slowly on the stovetop, delivers showstopping results, but it requires so much labor and time that we're willing to make it only once a year. We wanted a potato galette with a crisp, deeply bronzed crust encasing a creamy center that tasted of earthy potatoes and sweet butter—and we wanted one we could make on a weeknight. We started by neatly arranging just the first layer of potatoes in the skillet, and casually packed the rest of the potatoes into the pan; once the galette was inverted onto the plate, only the tidy layer was visible. We swapped the traditional cast-iron skillet for a nonstick pan and achieved superior browning by starting the galette on the stovetop, then transferring it to the bottom rack of the oven. Regular melted butter was just as good as clarified and less work, and for a galette that held together but wasn't gluey, we rinsed the potatoes to rid them of excess starch, then incorporated a little cornstarch for just the right amount of adhesion. And in lieu of occasionally tamping down on the galette during cooking as in traditional recipes, we simply filled a cake pan with pie weights and set it on the galette for a portion of the baking time.

ABOUT ONCE A YEAR, WE FEEL COMPELLED TO MAKE pommes Anna, the classic French potato cake in which thin-sliced potatoes are tossed with clarified butter, tightly shingled in a skillet, and cooked slowly on the stovetop. The results can be glorious: a crisp, deeply bronzed crust encasing a creamy center that tastes of earthy, well-seasoned potatoes and sweet butter. It's about as good as non-deep-fried potatoes can get.

But despite our fondness for it, the galette is strictly special-occasion fare as far as we're concerned. It's not the ingredient list—that part's brief. But thinly slicing and then diligently layering all those potato disks takes more time and attention to detail than we usually want to spend.

That said, plenty of existing recipes promise to make the dish "easy," "simple," and "foolproof," but we have yet to find one that really delivers on all counts. Only one that we've tried produced anything resembling the classic potato galette, and it differed from the others in two ways: First, it was roasted in a very hot (450-degree) oven, where the steady, ambient heat cooked the three-odd pounds of potatoes evenly (no chalky bits of raw tuber) and colored them nicely brown. Second, only the first layer of ⅛-inch-thick potato slices was neatly arranged; the rest were casually packed into the pan, eliminating most of the usual tedious layering work. Then, following tradition, the cooked galette was inverted out of the skillet, its crisp, golden exterior hiding the haphazard arrangement within.

But the recipe got us only halfway to our goal. The whole operation was still fussier than we wanted, and while the exterior of this improvised galette more or less looked the part, the tightly fused, striated layers that are the hallmark of classic pommes Anna were gone. And as soon as the knife hit the crust, the underlying slices slid apart.

So, there was obvious potential in roasting, and we had a simple (if not totally foolproof) assembly method for the cake—but everything else in the recipe was up for consideration. For starters, there was the pan. Pommes Anna is traditionally cooked in a cast-iron skillet, which absorbs heat beautifully and turns out a galette with a substantial, deeply browned crust. But considering that this new iteration was cooked in the oven—and that inverting the already heavy vessel when it's full and searing hot can be intimidating—wasn't a baking pan worth a try? But as we tested our way through square, round, ovoid, rectangular, and springform pans, every one either warped in the hot oven or failed to generate much of a crust. A skillet really was the best tool for the job, though for convenience's sake—and to avoid a risk of the cake sticking to the pan bottom—we opted to forgo cast iron in favor of an ovensafe nonstick model.

Of course we'd need to compensate for the lighter, thinner pan's browning inadequacies, so we started fiddling with the placement of the oven rack on which the potatoes were cooking. Not surprisingly, the farther we lowered the rack toward the main heating element, the deeper the spuds browned. On the advice of several

SIMPLIFIED POTATO GALETTE

colleagues, we tried to eke out even more color and flavor by placing a pizza stone under the skillet. Sure enough, the thick slab (which absorbs heat in much the same way as a cast-iron skillet) guaranteed even browning—but it also required preheating for an hour and more heavy lifting than we wanted. Ultimately, we devised a much simpler two-pronged approach that worked equally well: First we got the galette cooking on the stovetop (where the direct flame jump-started the browning process), then we slid the pan onto the bottom rack of the hot oven. That gave us great browning with no stone.

Then there was the laborious clarifying step required by most recipes. This traditional technique involves barely simmering the butter until its water has just cooked off, then removing its milk solids. The idea is that milk solids in whole butter can cause the potatoes to stick to the bottom of the pan. But when we whipped up batches of our working recipe with clarified and whole butter, we couldn't tell the difference between the two. One more complication out of the way.

We were pleased with our progress—the galette was deeply bronzed—but one lingering problem remained: How to keep the potatoes from sliding away from each other into a messy heap when we sliced it? One contributing factor, we realized, was our informal assembly method. Simply dumping most of the potatoes into the skillet may have been easy, but the bond between the piled-on slices was fairly haphazard. Still, the lack of

NOTES FROM THE TEST KITCHEN

HOW TO MAKE GALETTE EASIER

1. Place 1 potato slice in center of skillet, then overlap potato slices in circle around center slice.

2. Continue to layer potato slices in overlapping fashion to form layer that covers bottom of pan. Then gently place remaining potatoes on top to form second layer, making sure to form cake of even thickness.

3. Finally, press down on galette with cake pan full of pie weights. Transfer skillet to oven, keeping cake pan on top for first 20 minutes of baking.

INVERTING POTATO GALETTE

1. Slide loosened galette out of skillet onto large plate.

2. Gently place cutting board over galette. Do not use overly heavy board, which may crush it.

3. Carefully flip plate over so board is on bottom. Remove plate and slice and serve galette.

adhesiveness often seemed exacerbated by the potatoes themselves. Sometimes they seemed to have more starchy glue, other times they cooked up overly dry. Up to this point we'd been using russet potatoes, which virtually every pommes Anna recipe, classic or otherwise, calls for. Switching to Yukon Golds didn't help. Though tasters preferred their buttery, sweet flavor, their texture was just as unreliable as the russets, and they weren't any better at keeping the layers together.

After giving it some thought, we realized that the variable "stick-ability" of the potatoes—whether Yukons or russets—had a simple explanation: The starch in any potato is always going to be a wild card, since it changes considerably depending how long the potato has been out of the ground. To eliminate this as a variable, one of our colleagues had a suggestion: Wash away the potato starch and find another means of gluing the slices together. Though counterintuitive, the idea was not entirely unfamiliar. A few years back we developed a recipe for potato roesti (pommes Anna's Swiss cousin, made with shredded spuds) in which we first rinsed the potatoes of their surface starch, then tossed them with a smidge of cornstarch to ensure cohesion.

Hopeful that the technique might transfer to our sliced potatoes (we decided to stick with the more flavorful Yukons) we proceeded with our working recipe, swirling the slices in a bowl of cold water to wash away their starch, then thoroughly patting them dry. (Excess moisture also impedes bonding.) Then we added a tablespoon of cornstarch to the melted butter, tossed the two components together, and proceeded with assembly. The result? Big improvement. Though the galette still wasn't quite as dense and compact as a meticulously layered pommes Anna is, at least the slices adhered to one another more reliably.

So what could we do about that loose layering of potatoes? Some recipes suggest occasionally tamping down on the galette as it cooks to compress the slices, but we wondered if more constant contact might be better. We placed a foil-wrapped brick on top of the cake for the first part of the cooking, and the layers did indeed stick together somewhat better, but unevenly—the outer rim was still loose. Rummaging around for something broader and rounder, we spied the cake pan we'd discarded earlier in our testing and thought of a novel deployment. We filled the center with pie weights, placed it on the cake, pressed down firmly, and left it on during the first 20 minutes of baking (with a sheet of aluminum foil sprayed with vegetable oil in between to prevent the pan bottom from sticking). After removing the cake pan halfway through cooking to allow the top layer of potatoes to take on a little color, we were delighted to find the cake not only uniformly browned, but nicely compacted as well.

The exhaustive testing paid off. Once flipped out of the pan, our crispy potato cake revealed itself to be perfectly browned and, better yet, perfectly whole. A few cuts with a serrated knife and it was ready to serve—completely looking the part of a classic pommes Anna. We, however, knew the truth: It took an easy few minutes to assemble, cooked largely unattended, and, best yet, was foolproof.

Simplified Potato Galette

SERVES 6 TO 8

In order for the potato cake to hold together, it is important to slice the potatoes no more than ⅛ inch thick and to make sure the slices are thoroughly dried before assembling the cake. Use a mandoline slicer or the slicing attachment of a food processor to slice the potatoes uniformly thin. A pound of dried beans, rice, or coins can be substituted for the pie weights. You will need a 10-inch ovensafe nonstick skillet for this recipe.

- **2½ pounds Yukon Gold potatoes, sliced ⅛ inch thick**
- **5 tablespoons unsalted butter, melted**
- **1 tablespoon cornstarch**
- **1½ teaspoons chopped fresh rosemary (optional)**
- **1 teaspoon salt**
- **½ teaspoon pepper**

1. Adjust oven rack to lowest position and heat oven to 450 degrees. Place potatoes in bowl and fill with cold water. Using hands, swirl to remove excess starch, drain, then spread potatoes onto kitchen towels and dry thoroughly.

2. Whisk 4 tablespoons butter, cornstarch, rosemary, if using, salt, and pepper together in large bowl. Add dried potatoes and toss to thoroughly coat. Place remaining 1 tablespoon butter in 10-inch ovensafe nonstick skillet and swirl to coat. Place 1 potato slice in center of skillet, then overlap slices in circle around center slice, followed by outer circle of overlapping slices. Gently place remaining sliced potatoes on top of first layer, arranging so they form even thickness.

3. Place skillet over medium-high heat and cook until sizzling and potatoes around edge of skillet start to turn translucent, about 5 minutes. Spray 12-inch square of aluminum foil with vegetable oil spray. Place foil, sprayed side down, on top of potatoes. Place 9-inch cake pan on top of foil and fill with 2 cups pie weights. Firmly press down on cake pan to compress potatoes. Transfer skillet to oven and bake 20 minutes.

4. Remove cake pan and foil from skillet. Continue to bake until potatoes are tender when paring knife is inserted in center, 20 to 25 minutes. Return skillet to stovetop and cook over medium heat, gently shaking pan, until galette releases from sides of pan, 2 to 3 minutes.

5. Off heat, place cutting board over skillet. Using oven mitts or potholders, hold cutting board in place with one hand and with other hand on skillet handle, carefully invert skillet and cutting board together. Lift skillet off galette. Using serrated knife, gently cut into wedges and serve immediately.

RATING WINE OPENERS

Lever-style corkscrews are designed to use leverage rather than muscle power to pull the cork, but many such models are unwieldy and bulky. We wanted a wine opener that could cleanly and effortlessly remove any type of cork, took minimal cajoling (the fewer steps, the better), and fit neatly in a drawer. So we gathered 17 models ranging from $8 to $100 and opened cases of wine until we narrowed our choices to seven. Besides lever-style openers, we opened our testing to waiter's corkscrews (in which the lever rests on one side of the lip of the bottle), twisting pull models, and winged designs. After wine-opening novices and experts alike test-drove our finalists on both natural and synthetic corks, we had our winner. Not only is it compact and easy to use, but it's also not expensive—so we have more money to spend on a good bottle. Brands are listed in order of preference. See www.americastestkitchen.com for updates to this testing.

RECOMMENDED

OGGI Nautilus Corkscrew (model #7305)
PRICE: $24.99
COMMENTS: Compact and easy to use, this lever-style model fits securely over the bottle and sports a long handle for plenty of leverage. It even features a foil cutter and an extra corkscrew worm. The cork emerged from the bottle cleanly and easily, and came neatly off the worm with a second pump of the handle.

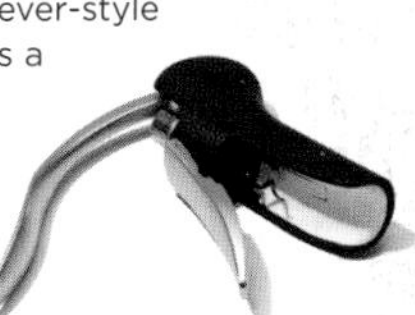

METROKANE Vertical Rabbit (model #6907)
PRICE: $59.99
COMMENTS: Very similar to our winner in design and performance, this pricier lever-style model was "sleek enough for James Bond to use" and effortlessly removed the cork with a simple push-pull motion. The only downfall? It's on the bulky side for storage.

RECOMMENDED WITH RESERVATIONS

TRUDEAU Double Lever Corkscrew (model #099508)
PRICE: $10.99
COMMENTS: Many of our more experienced testers favored this compact, waiter-style model, which opened bottles quickly and cleanly. The trick was nailing the motion—a series of pulls, flips, and snaps to engage the lever and worm. Once opened, the two-part lever streamlined the pulling effort, and the serrated cutter effortlessly sliced through the bottle's foil seal.

STARFRIT Gourmet Stainless Corkscrew (model #93023)
PRICE: $7.99
COMMENTS: Though not as intuitive, sleek, or quick as our winners, this opener removed corks through continuous turning, forcing the cork up the worm and out of the bottle. With a little patience, it proved to be functional, cleanly uncorking each bottle.

RECOMMENDED WITH RESERVATIONS *(cont.)*

SCREWPULL Original Table Corkscrew (model #TM-100)
PRICE: $25
COMMENTS: Intuitively designed, this opener slips over the top of the bottle and features a long, handled worm that extracted the cork with a few simple twists. Simple, that is, if you've got some hand strength; slighter testers were outmuscled. Plus, it proved awkward for left-handed testers.

NOT RECOMMENDED

SCREWPULL Compact Corkscrew (model #CM-100)
PRICE: $24.95
COMMENTS: Though this opener calls itself the "compact" model, it's no smaller than most of the others we tested. It uses the same mode of extraction as the Screwpull Original Table Corkscrew, except that its handle is hinged and awkward to use. It also required a bit of pressure to insert the worm without damaging the cork.

ANOLON Advanced Corkscrew (model #55709)
PRICE: $21.99
COMMENTS: The only wing-style opener to reach the final round of testing, this model mangled a number of corks—even a plastic one. The hinges on the wings pinched some testers, and though it did successfully uncork the bottle every time, there were far more user-friendly models to choose from.

A MOROCCAN *Feast*

CHAPTER 13

THE RECIPES

EQUIPMENT CORNER

Test Kitchen Director Erin McMurrer checks in on the progress of two test cooks as they ready food for a scene.

THE FLAVORS AND SPICES OF MOROCCAN CUISINE ARE WARM, LIVELY, and inviting. The process of preparing authentic Moroccan dishes, however, is often a laborious task calling on hard-to-find ingredients, unusual equipment, and time-consuming methods. One of our favorite dishes is chicken tagine, which features briny olives, bright citrus, fragrant herbs, and bold spices. Considering that tagine at heart is really just a stew, we wanted to find a way to make it more accessible to the American home cook by streamlining the process and relying only on supermarket ingredients.

Couscous is a staple of North African cuisine and typically serves as a base for stews and braises such as tagine. Actually tiny grains of pasta made from semolina granules, couscous is a lighter, fluffier alternative to rice or potatoes, and it readily absorbs the rich flavors of the main course. But while back-of-the package instructions may be simple, they too often yield a tasteless, soggy mess. To cook couscous properly, we'd have to think outside the box. Join us as we uncover the secrets to these two Moroccan favorites.

MOROCCAN CHICKEN

WHY THIS RECIPE WORKS: Time-consuming techniques and esoteric ingredients make cooking authentic Moroccan chicken a daunting proposition. We wanted a recipe that was ready in an hour and relied on supermarket staples. For depth and flavor, we used a mix of white and dark chicken and browned the meat first. After removing the chicken from the pot, we sautéed onion, strips of lemon zest, garlic, and a spice blend in the leftover brown bits and some oil; this ensured that no flavor went to waste. A number of everyday spices were necessary to recreate the authentic notes in Moroccan chicken, including paprika, cumin, cayenne, ginger, coriander, and cinnamon; honey contributed a missing sweetness. Greek green olives provided the meatiness and piquant flavor of hard-to-find Moroccan olives. Chopped cilantro, stirred in right before serving, was the perfect finishing touch to our exotic dinner.

WHEN MOST PEOPLE THINK OF MOROCCO, THEY envision dusty souks, spindly minarets, and men in flowing djellabas. Not us—we think with our stomachs and see tagine. Tagines are exotically spiced, assertively flavored stews slow-cooked in earthenware vessels of the same name. They can include all manner of meats, vegetables, and fruit, though our hands-down favorite combines chicken with briny olives and tart lemon.

While we love tagine, it's not a dish we ever conceived of as American home cooking. Why? The few traditional recipes we had seen required time-consuming, labor-intensive cooking methods, a special pot (the tagine), and hard-to-find ingredients. We're usually game for a day in the kitchen or a hunt for exotica, but isn't tagine, at its most elemental level, just stew?

A little research proved that we weren't the first to take a stab at making tagine more accessible. While most of the recipes we tried lacked the depth of an authentic tagine, they did hold promise, proving that a Western cooking method (braising in a Dutch oven) was a serviceable substitution for stewing for hours in a tagine. We also discovered that the flavors we associated with Moroccan cooking weren't necessarily "exotic"—they were a strategic blending of ingredients we already had in our cupboard.

Almost all of the recipes we collected specified a whole chicken—broken down into pieces—and we soon found out why. Batches made entirely with white meat lacked the depth and character of those made with a blend of dark and white.

But when we cooked the white and dark meat in the same way—simmered partially submerged in broth—the white meat turned dry and stringy. Pulling out the white meat when it had just cooked through solved matters, but the close attention required was bothersome. There had to be an easier way.

That's when we thought of carrots. They were added to many of the recipes we had found and, if cut large enough, could raise the white meat pieces above the simmering broth. So we piled several large carrot pieces into the bottom of the pot with the dark meat and set the white meat on top. With this method—and a five-minute head start for the dark meat—all the chicken was perfectly cooked and ready at the same time.

Some recipes called for rubbing the chicken with lemon and salt and letting the meat marinate before cooking; others employed salt alone or blended with spices. We found that adding spices at this point resulted in a muddy-flavored broth. Finally, while leaving the skin on the meat to brown it gave the braising liquid a deep flavor, pulling it off before simmering kept the dish free of rubbery skin.

A large sliced onion and a few minced garlic cloves rounded out the basic flavors of the stew, and we finally felt ready to tackle the defining ingredients: spices, olives, and lemon. Many recipes called for a spice blend called ras el hanout, which translates loosely as "top of the shop" and may contain upward of 30 spices. We experimented with a broad range of spices until we landed on a blend that was short on ingredients but long on flavor. Cumin and ginger lent depth, cinnamon brought warmth that tempered a little cayenne heat, and citrusy coriander boosted the stew's lemon flavor. Paprika added sweetness and, perhaps more important, colored the broth a deep, attractive red. Thoroughly toasting the spices in hot oil brought out the full depth of flavors.

MOROCCAN CHICKEN WITH OLIVES AND LEMON

Finding the right olives proved harder than we anticipated. Big, meaty, green Moroccan olives were the obvious choice for the stew, but they were a rarity at any of our local markets. Other meaty green olives, like Manzanilla, Cerignola, and Lucques, were either too mild or too assertive to match the other flavors in the stew. Greek "cracked" olives, however, tasted great and were easy to find. When we added the olives to the stew too soon, their flavor leached out into the braising liquid, rendering them bland and bitter. Stirring in the olives just a few minutes before serving proved a better approach, as they retained their piquant flavor and firm texture.

The lemon flavor in authentic tagines comes from preserved lemon, a long-cured Moroccan condiment that's hard to find outside of specialty stores. "Quick" preserved lemons can be produced at home in a few days, but we wanted to keep our recipe as simple as possible. Part tart citrus, part pickled brine, traditional preserved lemon has a unique flavor that's tough to imitate. So we chose not to try; instead, we aimed for a rich citrus backnote in the dish. We added a few broad ribbons of lemon zest along with the onions, and the high heat coaxed out the zest's oils and mellowed them. Adding a lemon's worth of juice just before serving reinforced the bright flavor.

A spoonful of honey further balanced things, and chopped cilantro leaves freshened the flavors, but we felt the stew still lacked a certain spark. A last-minute addition of raw garlic and finely chopped lemon zest seemed to clinch it, as the sharpness brought out the best in each of the stew's components.

Moroccan Chicken with Olives and Lemon

SERVES 4

Bone-in chicken parts can be substituted for the whole chicken. For best results, use four chicken thighs and two chicken breasts, each breast split in half; the dark meat contributes valuable flavor to the broth and should not be omitted. Use a vegetable peeler to remove wide strips of zest from the lemon before juicing it. Make sure to trim any white pith from the zest, as it can impart bitter flavor. If the olives are particularly salty, give them a rinse. Serve with Classic Couscous (page 140).

1¼ teaspoons paprika
½ teaspoon ground cumin
½ teaspoon ground ginger
¼ teaspoon cayenne pepper
¼ teaspoon ground coriander
¼ teaspoon ground cinnamon
3 (2-inch) strips lemon zest
5 garlic cloves, minced
1 (3½- to 4-pound) whole chicken, cut into 8 pieces (4 breast pieces, 2 thighs, 2 drumsticks), trimmed, wings discarded
Salt and pepper
1 tablespoon olive oil
1 large onion, halved and sliced ¼ inch thick
1¾ cups low-sodium chicken broth
1 tablespoon honey

2 carrots, peeled and cut crosswise into ½ inch-thick rounds, very large pieces cut into half-moons
1 cup cracked green olives, pitted and halved
3 tablespoons lemon juice
2 tablespoons chopped fresh cilantro

1. Combine paprika, cumin, ginger, cayenne, coriander, and cinnamon in bowl and set aside. Mince 1 strip lemon zest, add 1 teaspoon minced garlic, and mince together until reduced to fine paste; set aside.

2. Season both sides of chicken pieces with salt and pepper. Heat oil in Dutch oven over medium-high heat until just beginning to smoke. Brown chicken pieces, skin side down, until deep golden, about 5 minutes; using tongs, flip chicken pieces and brown on second side, about 4 minutes longer. Transfer chicken to plate; when cool enough to handle, remove and discard skin. Pour off and discard all but 1 tablespoon fat from pot.

3. Add onion and 2 remaining lemon zest strips to pot and cook, stirring occasionally, until onion slices have browned at edges but still retain their shape, 5 to 7 minutes (add 1 tablespoon water if pan gets too dark). Add remaining garlic and cook, stirring, until fragrant, about 30 seconds. Add spices and cook, stirring constantly, until darkened and very fragrant, 45 seconds to 1 minute. Stir in broth and honey, scraping up any browned bits. Add thighs and drumsticks, reduce heat to medium, and simmer for 5 minutes.

4. Add carrots and breast pieces with any accumulated juices to pot, arranging breast pieces in single layer on top of carrots. Cover, reduce heat to medium-low, and simmer until breast pieces register 160 degrees, 10 to 15 minutes.

5. Transfer chicken to plate and tent with aluminum foil. Add olives to pot; increase heat to medium-high and simmer until liquid has thickened slightly and carrots are tender, 4 to 6 minutes. Return chicken to pot and stir in garlic mixture, lemon juice, and cilantro; season with salt and pepper to taste. Serve.

VARIATION

Moroccan Chicken with Chickpeas and Apricots

Substitute 1 cup dried apricots, halved, for 1 of the carrots, and substitute one 15-ounce can chickpeas, rinsed, for the olives.

RATING COMPOST BUCKETS

Compost buckets offer a "green" way to deal with the odor of food scraps mingling in the kitchen trash: A carbon filter on the lid keeps the smells in but still allows oxygen to enter so decomposition can occur, cutting down on trips to the compost heap. These buckets fit beneath the sink; some are attractive enough for the counter. We had test cooks use three different compost buckets (lined with BioBag biodegradable bags, $5.99 for 25 bags; buckets can be used with or without liners) over several weeks, recording how easy they were to fill and empty, if they let out odors, and how often they needed to be emptied (or the liner replaced). Brands are listed in order of preference. See www.americastestkitchen.com for updates to this testing.

HIGHLY RECOMMENDED

EXACO TRADING KITCHEN Compost Waste Collector (model #ECO-2000)
PRICE: $19.98 **CAPACITY:** 2.4 gallons
COMMENTS: This inexpensive green plastic pail is 8½ inches wide at the base and fits on the counter or in a cabinet under the sink. Food scraps broke down as expected, and odors were completely contained. We fit an average of 12 recipes' worth of waste before having to empty the bucket. The hinged lid was easy to flick open and closed with a single hand, and the latch kept the lid secure. (A pack of three replacement filters is $7.95; the filter is supposed to be changed every three months.)

RECOMMENDED

NORPRO Stainless Steel Composter Keeper (model #94)
PRICE: $38.99 **CAPACITY:** 1 gallon
COMMENTS: This stainless steel pail is durable and cleans quickly and easily with a little soapy water. The charcoal filter on this unit can pop off if toppled over. The brushed steel finish does not show fingerprints. With less than half the capacity of our winner, this pail needed to be emptied after preparing three to six recipes.

RSVP INTERNATIONAL Endurance Stainless Steel Compost Pail (model #PAIL)
PRICE: $41.95 **CAPACITY:** 1 gallon
COMMENTS: This one is almost identical to the Norpro compost bucket in every way. It's easy to clean, durable, traps odors, and holds three to six recipes' worth of kitchen waste. Fingerprints and dribbles from wet scraps show up easily on its polished steel finish.

COUSCOUS

WHY THIS RECIPE WORKS: Couscous, granules of semolina, traditionally serves as a sauce absorber under stews and braises, but it can also be a quick and flavorful side dish for a variety of foods. We wanted to develop a classic version for saucy dishes as well as a handful of flavor-packed versions, as convenient as the boxed kind, but much fresher tasting. Toasting the couscous grains in butter deepened their flavor and helped them cook up fluffy and separate. And to bump up the flavor even further, we replaced half of the cooking liquid with chicken broth. For our enriched variations, dried fruit, nuts, and citrus juice added textural interest and sweet, bright notes.

ALTHOUGH COUSCOUS TRADITIONALLY FUNCTIONS as a sauce absorber beneath North African stews and braises, it works equally well as a lighter, quicker alternative to everyday side dishes like rice pilaf and mashed potatoes. The tiny grains of pasta, made by rubbing together moistened semolina granules, readily adapt to any number of flavorful add-ins, from grassy fresh herbs like cilantro and parsley to heady spices like cumin and coriander and sweeter elements like raisins and dates. Best of all, the whole operation, from box to bowl, takes about five minutes.

At least that's what the back-of-the-box instructions say. We quickly realized that such convenience comes at a cost. No matter how precisely we followed the directions—measure and boil water, stir in couscous, cover and let stand off heat for five minutes, fluff with fork—the results were discouragingly similar to wet sand: bland, blown-out pebbles that stuck together in clumps. And it wasn't just one brand's poor instruction: Every box we bought spelled out the same steps.

We're no experts on North African cuisine, but we'd read enough about couscous to know that it has far more potential than our efforts were suggesting. Then, as we were researching how the grains are made, we realized our problem: the box—both its contents and its cooking instructions. According to traditional couscous-making practices, the uncooked grains are steamed twice in a double boiler–shaped vessel called a couscoussière, from which the grains emerge fluffy and separate. The commercial staple we find on grocery store shelves, however, is far more processed: The grains are flash-steamed and dried before packaging. When exposed to the rigors of further cooking, this parcooked couscous—more or less a convenience product—turns to mush. That's why the box instructions are so simple: A quick reconstitution in boiling water is all the grains can stand.

To bring some much-needed flavor to the dish, we tried a popular trick used on another grain that, without some finesse, can also cook up woefully bland: rice. The "pilaf method," according to widely accepted rice and grain cookery, calls for briefly sautéing the grains in hot fat before liquid is introduced. So for our next batch of couscous, we melted a small amount of butter, which, as we'd hoped, coated the grains nicely, allowing them to brown gently and uniformly and helping them cook up fluffy and separate. (Plus, with butter in the pan, we could briefly sauté all sorts of add-ins, like spices, garlic, shallots, and even grated carrot.) To bump up the flavor even further, we replaced half of the water called for in the box instructions with chicken broth. Now we were getting somewhere: After absorbing the hot stock-based liquid, the couscous grains were flavorful enough to stand on the plate without a sauce. With our technique established, we developed simple flavor variations by adding dried fruit, nuts, and zest to the couscous.

Satisfied with our recipe, we figured our work was just about done—until we spied the two dirty pans in the sink. Given that the dish took all of five minutes to cook, we were determined to do better when it came to cleanup. Then it dawned on us: Since our saucepan was already hot from toasting the grains, why not simply add room-temperature liquid to it instead of going to the trouble to heat the liquid in a separate pan? Sure enough, that did it. The residual heat from the pan boiled the liquid almost instantly—it was like deglazing a skillet after searing. On went the lid, and after a brief rest and a quick fluff with a fork, our couscous was done—with much better flavor (and just minutes' more effort) than we got from the box method.

CLASSIC COUSCOUS

Classic Couscous

SERVES 4 TO 6

- **2 tablespoons unsalted butter**
- **2 cups couscous**
- **1 cup water**
- **1 cup low-sodium chicken broth**
- **1 teaspoon salt**
- **Pepper**

Melt butter in medium saucepan over medium-high heat. Add couscous and cook, stirring frequently, until grains are just beginning to brown, about 5 minutes. Add water, broth, and salt and stir briefly to combine. Cover and remove pan from heat. Let stand until grains are tender, about 7 minutes. Uncover and fluff grains with fork. Season with pepper to taste and serve.

VARIATIONS

Couscous with Dates and Pistachios

Increase butter to 3 tablespoons and add ½ cup chopped dates, 1 tablespoon grated fresh ginger, and ½ teaspoon ground cardamom to saucepan with couscous. Increase amount of water to 1¼ cups. Stir ¾ cup coarsely chopped toasted pistachios, 3 tablespoons minced fresh cilantro, and 2 teaspoons lemon juice into couscous before serving.

Couscous with Dried Cherries and Pecans

Increase butter to 3 tablespoons and add ½ cup coarsely chopped dried cherries, 2 minced garlic cloves, ¾ teaspoon garam masala, and ⅛ teaspoon cayenne pepper to saucepan with couscous. Increase amount of water to 1¼ cups. Stir ¾ cup coarsely chopped toasted pecans, 2 thinly sliced scallions, and 2 teaspoons lemon juice into couscous before serving.

Couscous with Carrots, Raisins, and Pine Nuts

Increase butter to 3 tablespoons and add 2 grated carrots and ½ teaspoon ground cinnamon; cook, stirring frequently, until carrot softens, about 2 minutes. Add ½ cup raisins to saucepan with couscous and increase water to 1¼ cups. Stir ¾ cup toasted pine nuts, 3 tablespoons minced fresh cilantro, ½ teaspoon grated orange zest, and 1 tablespoon orange juice into couscous before serving.

Couscous with Shallots, Garlic, and Almonds

Increase butter to 3 tablespoons and add 3 thinly sliced shallots; cook, stirring frequently, until softened and lightly browned, about 5 minutes. Before adding couscous, add 1 minced garlic clove and cook until fragrant, about 30 seconds. Stir ¾ cup toasted sliced almonds, ¾ cup minced fresh parsley, ½ teaspoon grated lemon zest, and 2 teaspoons lemon juice into couscous before serving.

RATING STEAMER BASKETS

What could be simpler than a steamer basket, whose sole purpose is to sit in a pot over simmering water? We wanted to find out if there were any differences in performance when it came to various brands and models and rounded up eight baskets of varying shapes and materials (stainless steel, bamboo, and silicone). To test them, we steamed broccoli, fish fillets, and dumplings. We ended up with a list of criteria for the best basket: tall enough to clear the simmering water, but not too bulky; strong enough to support food, yet flexible enough to collapse for easy storage. In the end, we preferred a classic collapsible stainless steel model with a new twist: an adjustable center rod that allows for easier removal from the pot. Brands are listed in order of preference. See www.americastestkitchen.com for updates to this testing.

RECOMMENDED

PROGRESSIVE Easy Reach Steamer Basket (model #2090L)
PRICE: $8.95 **MATERIAL:** Stainless steel
DISHWASHER SAFE: Yes **COOKING:** ★★★
DESIGN: ★★★ **CAPACITY:** ★★ **STORAGE:** ★★★
COMMENTS: This collapsible stainless steel basket steams evenly and features an adjustable center rod that unscrews for storage. Though not as practical for large quantities of food, it's great for smaller amounts.

JOYCE CHEN 3-Piece Steamer Set (model #J26-0013)
PRICE: $18.95 **MATERIAL:** Bamboo
DISHWASHER SAFE: No **COOKING:** ★★★
DESIGN: ★★★ **CAPACITY:** ★★★ **STORAGE:** ★★
COMMENTS: This sturdy two-level steamer offers twice as much room as most other models: 25 dumplings fit comfortably on its two slatted shelves. The only drawback is that you need plenty of room to store it. But the double-decker design is a great choice if you do lots of steaming.

OXO Good Grips Pop-Up Steamer (model #067247)
PRICE: $16.99 **MATERIAL:** Stainless steel
DISHWASHER SAFE: Yes **COOKING:** ★★★
DESIGN: ★★ **CAPACITY:** ★★ ½ **STORAGE:** ★★★
COMMENTS: This basket comfortably held fish, broccoli, and 16 dumplings. Our only quibble? To cover the pot we had to depress the pop-up handle; removing the basket meant reaching into the hot steam to pop it back up.

RECOMMENDED WITH RESERVATIONS

CUISINART Chef's Classic Stainless Universal Steamer (model #7116-20)
PRICE: $39.95 **MATERIAL:** Stainless steel
DISHWASHER SAFE: Yes **COOKING:** ★★★
DESIGN: ★★★ **CAPACITY:** ★★ **STORAGE:** ★
COMMENTS: This universal steamer, shaped like a saucepan, fits into 2-, 3-, and 4-quart pots, but not Dutch ovens. Sturdily built, it comes with a solid-fitting top. This sturdy universal steamer's 7½-inch handle ensures easy loading and burn-free maneuvering. Tall sides mean the steamer can double as a colander, but created minor difficulties when removing flat foods that require delicate handling such as fish fillets.

RECOMMENDED WITH RESERVATIONS *(cont.)*

PROGRESSIVE Bamboo 3-Piece Steamer Basket (model #CWBS-04)
PRICE: $10.99 **MATERIAL:** Bamboo
DISHWASHER SAFE: No **COOKING:** ★★
DESIGN: ★ **CAPACITY:** ★★★ **STORAGE:** ★★
COMMENTS: This bamboo steamer was similar in capacity to the Joyce Chen model, but not as sturdily made; it warped after a few uses. While it fit 25 dumplings, the uneven surface of the steamer shelves tipped several over.

NOT RECOMMENDED

NORPRO Deluxe Double Steamer (model #172)
PRICE: $15.50 **MATERIAL:** Stainless steel
DISHWASHER SAFE: Yes **COOKING:** ★
DESIGN: ★ **CAPACITY:** ★★ **STORAGE:** ★★★
COMMENTS: A two-tiered failure. When we placed dumplings on the bottom basket and attached the top one, its metal feet dug into the dumplings below, tearing their wrappers. Worse, removing the hot top basket after cooking burned our fingers.

TRUDEAU Silicone Vegetable Steamer (model #998004)
PRICE: $9.99 **MATERIAL:** Silicone
DISHWASHER SAFE: Yes **COOKING:** ★
DESIGN: ½ star **CAPACITY:** ★★ **STORAGE:** ★★★
COMMENTS: Lightweight and small, this floppy lily pad look-alike presented issues from start to finish. Its short legs and flimsy frame meant that food ended up in the water. And lifting up the basket by its handle—made of two opposing loops that fold over the top of the basket and lock together—caused the entire contraption to buckle, tipping dumplings over and spilling out broccoli florets.

CHEF'N Sleekstor Veggisteam (model #VGST-750CH)
PRICE: $12 **MATERIAL:** Silicone
DISHWASHER SAFE: Yes **COOKING:** ★
DESIGN: ½ star **CAPACITY:** ★★ **STORAGE:** ★★★
COMMENTS: Similar to the Trudeau but without the long, floppy handles, this silicone answer to the traditional metal steamer had an intriguingly quirky design. Unfortunately, the stubby handles made it difficult and dangerous to remove the basket from a hot pot of water. Short legs and a floppy body also let water leak into its basket. One plus: the flat surface design allowed for clean removal of delicate fish fillets.

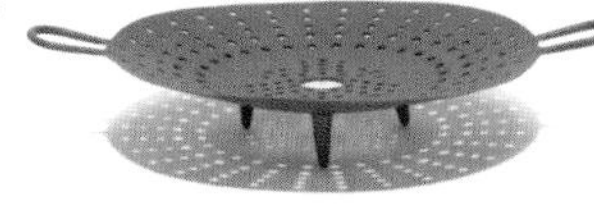

America's

Pasta, PLEASE

CHAPTER 14

THE RECIPES

Classic Spaghetti and Meatballs for a Crowd

Spring Vegetable Pasta

EQUIPMENT CORNER

Sous-Vide

Chris shows that you don't necessarily need a pasta fork to serve spaghetti; all-purpose tongs work just fine.

PASTA IS UNDOUBTEDLY QUICK AND SATISFYING. BUT THE TRUTH IS A truly great pasta dish requires a little more effort than just tossing pasta together with sauce. One dish that's truly a labor of love is spaghetti and meatballs. Meatballs and tomato gravy are the ultimate comfort food, except when you're the cook—the traditional approach of preparing and then frying the meatballs a few at a time is a process that can take the better part of a day, particularly if you're making enough to feed a crowd. We wanted to find a way to cut the fuss without losing any of the slow-cooked flavor.

For warmer weather, pasta primavera is another popular, time-consuming classic. We found that the original primavera method takes hours, only to produce washed-out vegetables and a stodgy sauce that tastes nothing like spring—not to mention it leaves behind a mountain of dirty dishes. We set out to revamp this restaurant standby to create a pasta dish with clean vegetable flavor and a full-bodied yet bright sauce. Join us as we streamline a cold-weather comfort and a springtime favorite.

SPAGHETTI AND MEATBALLS

WHY THIS RECIPE WORKS: Making spaghetti and meatballs to serve a crowd can try the patience of even the toughest Italian grandmother. We sought an easier way. We found that roasting the meatballs on a wire rack, rather than frying them in batches, made our recipe faster and cleaner. Adding some powdered gelatin to a mix of ground chuck and ground pork served to plump the meatballs and lent them a soft richness. Prosciutto gave the meatballs extra meatiness and a panade, which we made with panko, kept the meat moist and prevented it from getting tough. To create a rich, flavorful sauce, we braised the meatballs in marinara sauce for about an hour. And to make sure the sauce didn't overreduce, we swapped half of the crushed tomatoes in our marinara recipe for an equal portion of tomato juice.

MAYBE IF ANY OF US HAD AN ITALIAN GRANDMOTHER, we would have a better opinion of spaghetti and meatballs. But frankly, we've always been a little surprised that this dish is so popular. Eating it is one thing; making it is quite another. Too many of the recipes we've followed yield meatballs that are crumbly and bland and a sauce that's one-dimensional and barely coats the pasta. Furthermore, the typical approach of frying a few at a time is slow going and leaves a grease-spattered mess on your stovetop. It also severely limits the number of meatballs you can make within a reasonable amount of time—and as long as you're making meatballs, you might as well make them for a crowd.

We may not be able to trace our roots back to Sicily, but we've been cooking long enough to know that moist, tender meatballs in a flavorful, full-bodied tomato gravy is an achievable goal that shouldn't require a huge amount of fuss. We wanted a recipe that would feed an extended family of 12, that we could get on the table in no more than an hour and a half, and that didn't leave our kitchen looking like a disaster.

One amendment we would definitely make: roasting the meatballs instead of frying them, which would be easier and faster and would hopefully create good, even browning. But first we needed to figure out the best way to make the meatballs.

Meatballs are basically mini meatloaves: ground meat bound together and lightened with a variety of ingredients such as eggs, milk, and bread. Many recipes call for "meatloaf mix," a prepackaged combination of ground beef, pork, and veal. Though its convenience is appealing, we knew from experience that the fat content and the size of the meat grind vary from package to package, leading to inconsistent results. Instead, we tried another simple approach: all-beef meatballs made with 85 percent lean ground chuck (anything less fatty would almost certainly produce a dry, bland meatball). We seasoned the meat with salt, pepper, and a little grated Parmesan and, following our plan, roasted the meatballs on sheet pans in a 450-degree oven. While these were decently moist and flavorful, swapping out some of the beef with ground pork (we liked a 3:1 ratio) made for a markedly richer, meatier taste.

As long as we were adding pork, we figured we might as well consider veal, which has lots of gelatin and could add extra suppleness to the meatballs. While the veal did add suppleness, another problem arose: Ultra-lean veal is usually ground very fine, and these meatballs lacked the pleasantly coarse texture of the beef-and-pork batch. But veal wasn't the only way to address the texture. Following a trick we've used for meatloaf, we added 1½ teaspoons of powdered gelatin moistened in a little water to the meatballs. As they cooked, they plumped up nicely with help from the gelatin, which also lent them the soft richness they'd been lacking. And for yet another dimension of meatiness, we chopped up several ounces of prosciutto, which is packed with glutamates that enhance savory flavor, and incorporated it into the meat mixture.

As for the binder, we tried a series of egg tests—both whole eggs and just yolks mixed into the meat—and landed on a simple formula: one whole egg per pound of meat. The fat and emulsifiers from the yolk enriched the meat, while the protein boost from the egg white kept the meatballs nicely glued together, but not rubbery.

CLASSIC SPAGHETTI AND MEATBALLS FOR A CROWD

Milk-soaked bread, called a panade, was also a must. When added to ground meat, starches from the bread absorb the milk to form a gel that, like fat, coats and lubricates the protein molecules in the meat, keeping them moist and preventing them from linking together into a tough matrix. The bread also absorbs juices from the meat and keeps it from draining away. But not just any form of bread will do. Cubes of sandwich bread contributed too much of their own moisture and turned the texture pasty. Ditto for commercial bread crumbs, which were too fine to soak up much of the milk. Drying bread cubes in the oven and then pulsing them in a food processor to create large crumbs worked far better, but was fussy. Then a colleague suggested we try panko—supercrunchy Japanese bread crumbs with a coarser texture than regular crumbs. Sure enough, after a 10-minute soak, these crumbs absorbed all the milk and left no trace of their presence when mixed into the meatballs. One last tweak: We swapped regular milk for buttermilk, which added pleasant tang.

Now to nail down the roasting technique. In an ideal world, we would simply place the meatballs on a sheet pan, stick 'em in a 450-degree oven, and come back when they were done. When we tried this, the meatballs were cooked through after 20 minutes—but their bottoms were tough and overly browned while their tops had no color at all. Turning them with tongs every few minutes got us the deep, even color we wanted but felt just as tedious as frying them in a skillet. The problem, of course, was that the part of the meatball touching the hot pan was always going to brown faster. But what if no part of the meatballs was in direct contact with the pan? To find out, we propped up the meatballs on a wire rack set inside the pan. This worked beautifully to produce meatballs that browned evenly with no turning required. We found we could roast two trays at a time, a total of 40 meatballs, in just 30 minutes.

Our next challenge: Create a rich, flavorful sauce without the benefit of pan drippings. The meatballs had browned nicely, so we figured those meaty flavors could beef up our simple marinara, provided the two components spent enough time together. Most of the recipes we found called for quick-simmering the meatballs in the sauce, but a few backed up our idea for a longer braise. Once the sauce had bubbled away for about 15 minutes, we dropped in the roasted meatballs, slid the whole pot into a low oven (our preferred hands-off braising technique), and let it simmer for about an hour. As we'd hoped, the sauce now boasted meaty richness; even better, the meatballs had absorbed some sauce, giving them a plump, firm tenderness.

But the technique wasn't perfect. As the meatballs absorbed liquid, the sauce overreduced and became too thick to amply coat the pasta. We considered thinning

NOTES FROM THE TEST KITCHEN

KEY INGREDIENTS FOR TENDER, FLAVORFUL MEATBALLS

PANKO
Absorbent Japanese bread crumbs hold on to meat juices.

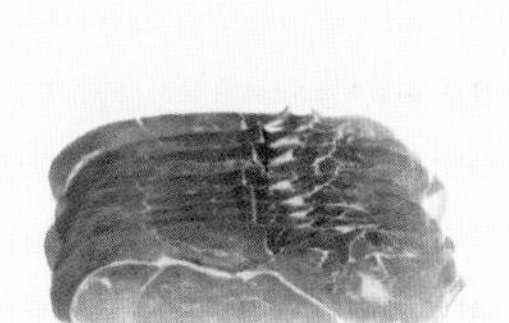

PROSCIUTTO
Bits of glutamate-rich prosciutto boost meatiness.

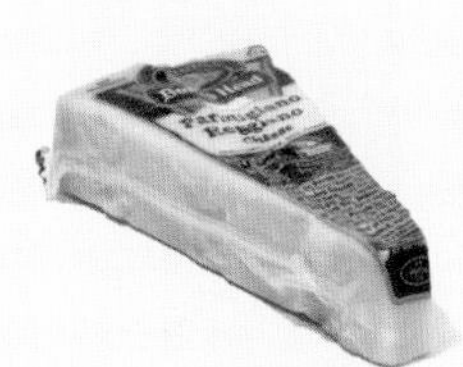

PARMESAN
Also packed with glutamates, Parmesan builds savor.

BUTTERMILK
Tangy buttermilk lends more flavor than regular milk.

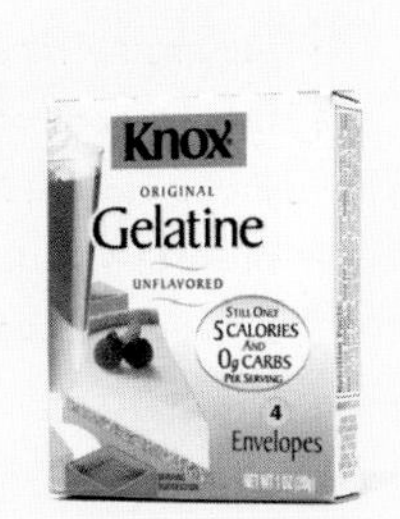

GELATIN
Gelatin helps the meatballs plump up and adds suppleness.

it with water or adding extra tomatoes until we recalled an unusual recipe that actually called for braising the meatballs in tomato juice. We swapped half of the crushed tomatoes for an equal portion of juice, and the results were great: By the time the meatballs had plumped up, the sauce was full-bodied but not sludgy. Once we brightened the flavors with a little white wine, parsley, and basil, we put on a big pot of water for pasta and recruited a group of tasters to come and enjoy. They loved this traditional spaghetti dinner made according to our untraditional technique—and we'd done it all without so much as breaking a sweat.

Classic Spaghetti and Meatballs for a Crowd

SERVES 12

If you don't have buttermilk, you can substitute 1 cup plain whole-milk yogurt thinned with ½ cup whole milk. Grate the onion on the large holes of a box grater. You can cook the pasta in two separate pots if you do not have a large enough pot to cook all of the pasta together. The ingredients in this recipe can be reduced by two-thirds to serve 4.

MEATBALLS

- **2¼ cups panko bread crumbs**
- **1½ cups buttermilk**
- **1½ teaspoons unflavored gelatin**
- **3 tablespoons water**
- **2 pounds 85 percent lean ground beef**
- **1 pound ground pork**
- **6 ounces thinly sliced prosciutto, chopped fine**
- **3 large eggs**
- **3 ounces Parmesan cheese, grated (1½ cups)**
- **6 tablespoons minced fresh parsley**
- **3 garlic cloves, minced**
- **1½ teaspoons salt**
- **½ teaspoon pepper**

SAUCE

- **3 tablespoons extra-virgin olive oil**
- **1 large onion, grated**
- **6 garlic cloves, minced**
- **1 teaspoon dried oregano**
- **½ teaspoon red pepper flakes**
- **3 (28-ounce) cans crushed tomatoes**
- **6 cups tomato juice**
- **6 tablespoons dry white wine**
- **Salt and pepper**
- **½ cup chopped fresh basil**
- **3 tablespoons minced fresh parsley**
- **Sugar**

- **3 pounds spaghetti**
- **2 tablespoons salt**
- **Grated Parmesan cheese**

1. FOR THE MEATBALLS: Adjust oven racks to lower-middle and upper-middle positions and heat oven to 450 degrees. Set wire racks in 2 aluminum foil–lined rimmed baking sheets and spray racks with vegetable oil spray.

2. Combine bread crumbs and buttermilk in large bowl and let sit, mashing occasionally with fork, until smooth paste forms, about 10 minutes. Meanwhile, sprinkle gelatin over water in small bowl and allow to soften for 5 minutes.

3. Mix ground beef, ground pork, prosciutto, eggs, Parmesan, parsley, garlic, salt, pepper, and gelatin mixture into bread-crumb mixture using hands. Pinch off and roll mixture into 2-inch meatballs (about 40 meatballs total) and arrange on prepared wire racks. Roast until well browned, about 30 minutes, switching and rotating baking sheets halfway through roasting.

4. FOR THE SAUCE: While meatballs cook, heat oil in Dutch oven over medium heat until shimmering. Add onion and cook until softened and lightly browned, 5 to 7 minutes. Stir in garlic, oregano, and pepper flakes and cook until fragrant, about 30 seconds. Stir in crushed tomatoes, tomato juice, wine, 1½ teaspoons salt, and ¼ teaspoon pepper, bring to simmer, and cook until thickened slightly, about 15 minutes.

5. Remove meatballs from oven and reduce oven temperature to 300 degrees. Gently nestle meatballs into sauce. Cover, transfer to oven, and cook until meatballs are firm and sauce has thickened, about 1 hour. (Sauce and meatballs can be cooled and refrigerated for up to 2 days. To reheat, drizzle ½ cup water over sauce, without stirring, and reheat on lower-middle rack of 325-degree oven for 1 hour.)

6. Meanwhile, bring 10 quarts water to boil in 12-quart pot. Add pasta and salt and cook, stirring often, until al dente. Reserve ½ cup cooking water, then drain pasta and return it to pot.

7. Gently stir basil and parsley into sauce and season with sugar, salt, and pepper to taste. Add 2 cups sauce (without meatballs) to pasta and toss to combine. Add reserved cooking water as needed to adjust consistency. Serve, topping individual portions with more tomato sauce and several meatballs and passing Parmesan separately.

NOTES FROM THE TEST KITCHEN

TWO STEPS TO EASIER, BETTER MEATBALLS

1. BROWN IN OVEN: Roasting meatballs is far easier than messy, time-consuming batch-frying. Elevating the meatballs on a wire rack allows heat to circulate underneath for even browning.

2. COOK IN SAUCE: Most meatballs are simply warmed in the sauce. Allowing them to finish cooking in it adds richness to the sauce and juiciness to the meat.

SPRING VEGETABLE PASTA

WHY THIS RECIPE WORKS: In pasta primavera, the vegetables and pasta are tossed together in a cream sauce made with broth and heavy cream. We love this classic, but sometimes we want a lighter, brighter version—one with a creamy sauce, but without the cream. As for the vegetables, we wanted true spring vegetables. To start, we chose asparagus and green peas, adding chives for bite and garlic and leeks for depth and sweetness. For a deeply flavored sauce that would unify the pasta and vegetables, we borrowed a technique from risotto, lightly toasting the pasta in olive oil before cooking it in broth and white wine. The sauce flavored the pasta as it cooked while the pasta added starch to the sauce, thickening it without the need for heavy cream. This nontraditional approach gave us a light but creamy sauce with sweet, grassy flavors that paired perfectly with the vegetables for a dish that truly tasted like spring.

YOU'D NEVER KNOW THAT PASTA PRIMAVERA, A pseudo-Italian dish that appears on virtually every chain restaurant menu, actually has roots in French haute cuisine. The usual reproduction—a random jumble of produce tossed with noodles in a heavy, flavor-deadening cream sauce—tastes nothing like spring. Surprisingly, when we dug up the original recipe from New York's famed Le Cirque restaurant, our colleagues found it wasn't all that inspiring either, despite taking about two hours to prepare and dirtying five pans. First, the vegetables (which had been painstakingly blanched one by one) were bland. Second, the cream-, butter-, and cheese-enriched sauce dulled flavor and didn't really unify the dish. If we wanted a true spring vegetable pasta—with a few thoughtfully chosen vegetables and a light, but full-bodied sauce that clung well to the noodles and brought the dish together—we'd have to start from the beginning.

Before we began cooking, we had some produce shopping to do. Freely testing our way through various spring staples, we landed on a pair of classics, asparagus and green peas, and then added garlic and leeks for their aromatic depth and sweetness, chives for their fresh bite and onion-y overtones, and mint, a natural match for peas.

We also decided at the outset to do away with the tedious blanching step. We found that by sautéing the vegetables in stages in a large Dutch oven, we were able to ensure that each one maintained its crisp-tender texture while taking on a touch of flavorful browning. First went the leeks, followed by the chopped asparagus, the minced garlic, and finally the frozen baby peas, which needed only a minute over the heat to lend sweetness to the mix.

But as we'd learned from the original recipe, simply tossing sautéed vegetables with the pasta didn't add up to a dish any greater than the sum of its parts. What we needed was a way to tie the dish together and give it depth of flavor—a job that's usually reserved for the sauce. The chicken broth used in the original recipe didn't seem like the best way to enhance the vegetable flavor, so we swapped it for vegetable broth. To give it depth, we simmered the broth with the pile of scraps we'd peeled and trimmed away from the vegetables (the green parts of the leeks and the woody ends of the asparagus), along with some extra garlic and peas. But once we'd strained the broth and added the cream and butter—necessary to give the sauce body—any flavor advantage we had gained was lost. We tried cutting back on the dairy, but the result was so thin that it just slid off the pasta. The bottom line: The vegetables alone weren't enough to give the dish flavor.

We were thinking of calling it quits when a colleague reminded us that Italian cookery has a tradition of parboiling pasta in water and then letting it finish cooking for a minute or two in whatever sauce is being served. The technique has a twofold benefit: As the pasta cooks, it absorbs some of the sauce and takes on its flavors. In exchange, the noodles release some of their starches into the sauce, which helps build body. It wouldn't hurt to try this approach. We prepared another batch, this time boiling the pasta (spaghetti, for now) for a couple of minutes in the water, draining it, and then allowing it to finish cooking in our enhanced vegetable broth. Everyone agreed that while this was a step in the right direction, the results were still too subtle.

Then a thought occurred to us: If we were going to add the pasta to the broth eventually, why not get the full benefit of the broth's flavor and use it to cook the pasta

SPRING VEGETABLE PASTA

from the start? The concept was nothing new, of course: It's a classic risotto technique, in which the rice and broth work together to produce a glossy, full-bodied "sauce" that thoroughly flavors and coats each grain. When we tried the approach with pasta, the results weren't quite perfect, but they were promising: The noodles, which we had boiled in a modest 5 cups of liquid (4 cups of broth, 1 cup of water) until they were al dente and the Dutch oven was almost dry, emerged more flavorful and lightly coated with the silky, starchy pot liquor. In fact, the sauce was thick enough that we didn't even need to add any cream or butter to give it body.

Now that we were on a roll, we wondered if we couldn't stretch the risotto technique even farther. Traditionally, the raw rice grains "toast" for a few minutes in some hot fat before the liquid is added, taking on a nutty richness. Adapting this technique for our pasta recipe seemed like a natural move, except for the problem of the long spaghetti strands, which we'd need to break up first. It seemed easier to just change the shape of the noodle. After testing half a dozen shorter shapes, we opted for bell-shaped campanelle: They held on to the sauce nicely, without clinging to one another or compressing into a mass. (Bow tie–shaped farfalle and penne quills made fine substitutes.)

Now that we had the right pasta shape, we went back to the cooking technique. After sautéing the vegetables, we wiped out the pot, added a splash of extra-virgin olive oil, and toasted the pasta until it started to color. Continuing with the classic risotto method, we poured in some dry white wine (its crisp acidity would brighten the sauce), stirring the mixture until most of the liquid had cooked off, and added the hot broth and cranked up the heat to a boil. When we stuck in our fork about 10 minutes later, the results were remarkably improved: tender pasta pieces coated with a light but lustrous and creamy sauce that more than hinted at the sweet, grassy flavors of the vegetables.

Once the sautéed vegetables were incorporated, all the dish needed was a little flavor tweaking here and there. Along with the minced garlic, we added a dash of hot pepper flakes and, just before serving, a handful of grated Parmesan. Finally, we brightened the whole lot with a

EQUIPMENT CORNER

SOUS-VIDE

Recently, sous-vide has become a hugely popular restaurant technique. Literally "under vacuum," sous-vide is the process of vacuum-sealing food in plastic, immersing it in water, and cooking it slowly at the temperature at which it's meant to be served (e.g., 130 degrees for medium steaks). Unlike standard high-heat methods, with this technique, there's no risk of overcooking the food. Even better, you can hold it at the desired temperature for hours; keeping meat at 130 degrees or higher for a prolonged period of time kills most bacteria. Plus slow cooking can turn tough cuts of meat incredibly tender (though they still need a quick sear in a hot pan for a nicely browned crust). When we came across the **SousVide Supreme**, a $399 machine that brings water-bath cooking into the home kitchen, we had to give it a try. We followed the simple setup instructions and cooked fish, chicken, and steaks—all with perfect results. We had only one gripe: A vacuum sealer—another pricey investment—is necessary but not included. That said, the machine makes a great splurge if you want to try sous-vide at home.

splash of lemon juice plus a handful of combined fresh chopped mint, chives, and lemon zest.

Nothing against the folks at Le Cirque, mind you, but unlike their original primavera, our recipe—a match-up of grassy, bright-tasting vegetables and nutty pasta in a complex, richly flavored sauce—truly tasted like spring, and came together in a fraction of the time.

NOTES FROM THE TEST KITCHEN

FOR BETTER FLAVOR, COOK PASTA LIKE RISOTTO
To deepen the overall flavor of our Spring Vegetable Pasta and add body to the sauce, we cooked the pasta like rice.

1. TOAST PASTA: Sautéing the raw pasta in oil, as you would raw rice for risotto, gives it a golden brown color and nutty, rich flavor.

2. ADD WINE: A cup of white wine introduced to the pot gets absorbed by the pasta, further contributing to the dish's flavor.

3. ADD BROTH: Instead of using water, we boil the pasta in vegetable broth (simmered first with vegetable peelings to concentrate its flavor).

4. COOK UNTIL CREAMY: As the pasta cooks, it gets coated in the creamy, starch-thickened broth. No need to add any actual cream.

Spring Vegetable Pasta

SERVES 4 TO 6

Campanelle is our pasta of choice in this dish, but farfalle and penne are acceptable substitutes.

- **1½ pounds leeks, white and light green parts halved lengthwise, sliced ½ inch thick, and washed thoroughly; 3 cups dark green parts chopped coarse and washed thoroughly**
- **1 pound asparagus, tough ends trimmed, chopped coarse, and reserved; spears cut on bias into ½-inch lengths**
- **2 cups frozen peas, thawed**
- **4 garlic cloves, minced**
- **4 cups vegetable broth**
- **1 cup water**
- **2 tablespoons minced fresh mint**
- **2 tablespoons minced fresh chives**
- **½ teaspoon grated lemon zest plus 2 tablespoons juice**
- **6 tablespoons extra-virgin olive oil**
- **Salt and pepper**
- **¼ teaspoon red pepper flakes**
- **1 pound campanelle**
- **1 cup dry white wine**
- **1 ounce Parmesan cheese, grated (½ cup), plus extra for serving**

1. Bring dark leek greens, asparagus trimmings, 1 cup peas, half of garlic, broth, and water to simmer in large saucepan. Reduce heat to medium-low and simmer gently for 10 minutes. While broth simmers, combine mint, chives, and lemon zest in bowl; set aside.

2. Strain broth through fine-mesh strainer into large liquid measuring cup, pressing on solids to extract as much liquid as possible (you should have 5 cups broth; add water as needed to measure 5 cups). Discard solids and return broth to saucepan. Cover and keep warm.

3. Heat 2 tablespoons oil in Dutch oven over medium heat until shimmering. Add leeks and pinch salt and cook, covered, stirring occasionally, until leeks begin to brown, about 5 minutes. Add asparagus and cook until asparagus is crisp-tender, 4 to 6 minutes. Add remaining garlic and pepper flakes and cook until fragrant, about 30 seconds. Add remaining 1 cup peas and continue to

cook 1 minute longer. Transfer vegetables to plate and set aside. Wipe out pot.

4. Heat remaining ¼ cup oil in now-empty pot over medium heat until shimmering. Add pasta and cook, stirring often, until just beginning to brown, about 5 minutes. Add wine and cook, stirring constantly, until absorbed, about 2 minutes.

5. When wine is fully absorbed, add warm broth and bring to boil. Cook, stirring frequently, until most of liquid is absorbed and pasta is al dente, 8 to 10 minutes. Off heat, stir in half of herb mixture, vegetables, lemon juice, and Parmesan. Season with salt and pepper to taste and serve immediately, passing additional Parmesan and remaining herb mixture separately.

NOTES FROM THE TEST KITCHEN

TRIMMING ASPARAGUS: IT'S A SNAP

Even the most thin, delicate asparagus spears still have tough, woody ends that must be removed. To break off the ends at precisely the right point, all you need is your hands.

Grip the stalk about halfway down; with the other hand, hold the stalk between the thumb and index finger about an inch or so from the bottom and bend the stalk until it snaps.

SOUTHEAST ASIAN *Favorites*

CHAPTER 15

THE RECIPES

Grilled Thai Beef Salad

Indonesian-Style Fried Rice (Nasi Goreng)

Faux Leftover Rice

SCIENCE DESK

A Thai Trick for Grilling Steak

EQUIPMENT CORNER

Smoker Boxes

Test cook Dan Zuccarello puts the finishing touches on Indonesian-Style Fried Rice just before the camera rolls.

WHEN A CRAVING FOR SOUTHEAST ASIAN FOOD STRIKES, MOST OF US simply head out to a nearby restaurant for a fix of this highly seasoned, boldly flavored cuisine because tracking down hard-to-find ingredients simply seems like more work than it's worth, and unfamiliar cooking techniques can be daunting. But sometimes curiosity gets the better of us, and we decided it was time to find out for ourselves how to prepare a couple of our favorite dishes: Thai grilled beef salad and Indonesian-style fried rice. Thai grilled beef salad is a mix of thinly sliced, charred steak, shallots, fresh mint and cilantro, and a lively dressing—an irresistible combination of the cuisine's flavor elements: hot, sour, salty, sweet, and bitter. Our goal was to look no further than the supermarket to replicate this salad's complex range of flavors and textures. And we hoped to learn a thing or two about grilling along the way.

Indonesian fried rice is a far cry from the typical Chinese takeout versions. Rather than being loaded with meat and vegetables and tossed with a nondescript brown sauce, the Indonesian version is garnished more simply with shallots, egg, and crisp vegetables, then seasoned with a pungent chili paste balanced with a sweet soy sauce. As with the Thai beef salad, we hoped to stick to supermarket staples for this dish, but the real challenge would be producing firm grains of rice without the overnight chill (fried rice dishes are typically based on leftover rice, something we rarely have on hand).

GRILLED THAI BEEF SALAD

GRILLED THAI BEEF SALAD

WHY THIS RECIPE WORKS: This traditional Thai salad features slices of deeply charred steak tossed with thinly sliced shallots and handfuls of torn mint and cilantro in a bright, bracing dressing. We started on developing our own version at the grill, choosing flank steak for its generous marbling, beefy flavor, and moderate price. Grilling the steak over a modified two-level fire and flipping it just when moisture beaded on the surface yielded perfectly charred, juicy meat. Adding a fresh Thai chile and a mix of toasted cayenne and paprika gave the dressing a fruity, fiery heat. Toasted rice powder, a traditional tableside condiment that gives the dressing fuller body and a subtle crunch, is not widely available, but we found it easy enough to make our own.

IN WINTER WHEN WE CRAVE THAI FOOD, IT'S OFTEN A rich, coconut milk–based curry or a wok-charred noodle dish. But in the summer months, we're more tempted by the country's famous salads, particularly the grilled-beef rendition known as *nahm tok*. Served warm or at room temperature, this preparation features an irresistible contrast of flavors and textures: blackened steak, crisp sliced shallots, and a generous amount of fresh mint and cilantro, all tossed with a lively dressing. In the best versions, the cuisine's five signature flavor elements—hot, sour, salty, sweet, and bitter—come into balance, making for a light but satisfying dish that's traditionally served with steamed jasmine rice.

We paged through the test kitchen's stack of Thai cookbooks for some nahm tok recipes to try and were pleased to find that both the shopping list and the cooking time—about half an hour from start to finish—were very manageable. The most unusual ingredient was toasted rice powder, which we knew would be easy enough to make at home. Still, the salads that we produced in the test kitchen, while not bad, fell short of the versions that we've eaten in good Thai restaurants. Either the dressing's flavors were unbalanced—too sweet, too salty, too sour—or the beef itself didn't boast enough char to give the salad its hallmark smoky, faintly bitter edge. Clearly, we had some tinkering to do.

The obvious place to start our testing was with the beef. Surprisingly, the recipes that we consulted were all over the map. Some specified lean cuts like tenderloin, others more marbled choices like skirt steak or New York strip steak. A few recipes called for marinating the meat before grilling; others suggested simply seasoning it with salt and white pepper (a staple ingredient in Thai cuisine). Most of them didn't even specify a grilling method. As a starting point, we built a standard single-level fire—a full chimney's worth of coals spread in an even layer over the kettle—and seared a variety of beef cuts: New York strip steak, boneless short ribs, tenderloin, and flank steak, each one sprinkled with salt and white pepper. Once each piece had developed a thick, dark crust, we pulled it off the fire, let it rest briefly (to allow the interior juices to be reabsorbed), cut thin slices, and tossed them in a standard dressing of equal parts fresh lime juice and fish sauce, a little sugar, and a thinly sliced Thai chile.

Just as we had expected, the more marbled pieces of beef fared better than the lean tenderloin, which started out woefully bland and ended up overcooked by the time it developed even the barest crust. Flavorwise, any of these fattier cuts would have been a fine choice, but two came with a caveat. Boneless short ribs vary in quality: Some are evenly marbled and ideally shaped, almost like small strip steaks, while others are misshapen and full of interior fat and connective tissue that requires trimming. Meanwhile, New York strip steaks boast good flavor and pleasantly tender chew but don't come cheap. We settled on flank steak. The uniformly shaped, moderately priced slab was also beefy, juicy, and sliced neatly.

Next decision: whether or not to marinate the meat in a mixture of the dressing ingredients. A quick side-by-side test made our decision easy. Since moisture thwarts browning, the crust on the marinated flank steak was markedly thin and pale compared with that on the non-marinated sample. Besides, once the slices of grilled steak were tossed with the dressing, they were plenty flavorful.

With the cut of meat decided, we could now focus our attention on the grilling method. The single-level fire had produced decently charred results, but for this salad, the contrast of a crisp, smoky, faintly bitter crust and a juicy center was a must, and we knew we could do better. To get a true blaze going, we turned to the test kitchen's favorite high-heat grill method: a modified two-level fire, in which all the coals are concentrated in an even layer over half of the grill. This way, the meat's exterior would caramelize almost on contact and would cook more rapidly, ensuring that the interior would stay medium-rare.

The recipes that we consulted may have been vague about the fire setup, but they did offer one grilling pointer: As the steak cooks, beads of moisture will appear on its surface—an indication that the meat is ready to be flipped. In fact, the dish is named for this visual cue: "nahm tok" translates as "water falling." Grateful for the cue, we flipped the meat as soon as beads of moisture showed up, let it sear another five minutes on the second side, and pulled it off the grill. To our delight, this steak was not only perfectly charred on the exterior, but also spot-on medium-rare within.

With perfectly grilled and subtly, satisfyingly bitter meat in hand, we moved back indoors to address the other four flavor elements: hot, sour, salty, and sweet. Everyone agreed that our initial dressing needed some tweaking—a bit more sweetness, a more balanced (and less heady) salty-sour punch, and more complex heat. The first two requests were easy to fix: We quickly landed on a 2:3 ratio of fish sauce to lime juice, plus ½ teaspoon of sugar and 2 tablespoons of water to tone it all down a touch. But the chile situation required a bit more attention. A fresh chile was a given, and we'd been using a Thai bird chile; when sliced thin and tossed with the other vegetable components, it adds a fruity, fiery blaze to each bite. So why did something still seem to be missing? We found the answer in a recipe from Thai cuisine guru David Thompson: His grilled-beef salad calls for not only fresh Thai bird chile, but also a toasted powder made from the dried pods.

Hoping that regular old cayenne powder toasted in a skillet would suffice, we compared its effects on the salad with that of a powder made with ground, toasted chiles following Thompson's instructions. The consensus was unanimous: The powder made from the dried Thai bird chiles added a deeper, earthier complexity than the hotter, more one-dimensional cayenne. Just ½ teaspoon of cayenne, in fact, overpowered the meat's smoky char. We were about to resign ourselves to the extra step of grinding our own powder when we spied a jar of sweet paprika in the spice cabinet. Could this give us the earthy, fruity red pepper flavor that was missing from the cayenne? As it turned out, a 50–50 mix of cayenne and paprika did the trick. We added just a dash of the toasted spice mixture to the dressing and put the rest aside as a seasoning for those who wanted to kick up the heat another notch.

The other condiment that we had to address was the *kao kua,* or toasted rice powder. These days, most Thai recipes call for the commercially made product, but it can be hard to find. It was simple enough to make our own by toasting rice in a dry skillet and pulverizing it in a spice grinder. Tossing half of the powder with the salad components gave the dressing fuller body, while sprinkling on the rest at the table added faint but satisfying crunch.

SCIENCE DESK

A THAI TRICK FOR GRILLING STEAK

This salad's Thai name, nahm tok (literally "water falling"), refers to the beads of moisture that form on the surface of the steak as it cooks—an age-old Thai cookery cue that the meat is ready to be flipped. While this method sounded imprecise, during testing we found it to be a surprisingly accurate gauge of when the flank steak is halfway done. Here's why: As this steak's interior gets hotter, its tightly packed fibers contract and release some of their interior moisture, which the fire's heat then pushes to the meat's surface. When turned at this point and cooked for an equal amount of time on the second side, the steak emerged deeply charred on the outside and medium-rare within. (Note: We do not recommend this technique across the board for steaks; since the thickness and density of the meat fibers vary from cut to cut.)

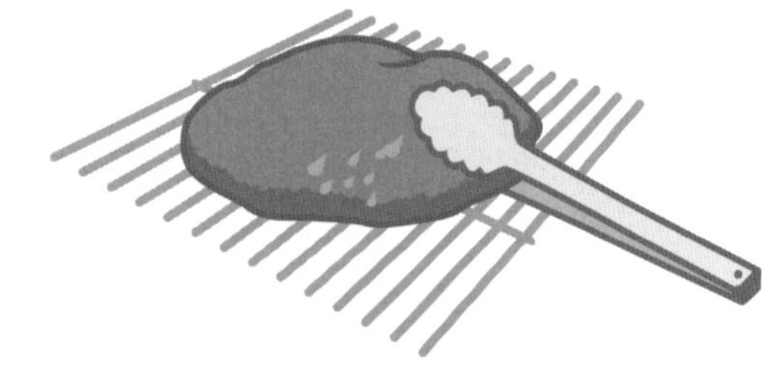

TIME TO FLIP
For perfectly cooked meat, flip the steak when beads of moisture appear on its surface.

As for the vegetable components, it was really a matter of personal taste. Some salads called for incorporating only the requisite sliced shallots and torn mint leaves and cilantro, while others required adding green beans, cabbage, cucumbers, and lettuce. Our tasters agreed that any accoutrements should complement—not compete with—the grilled beef. We settled on just one extra: a thinly sliced cucumber, which contributed a cool crispness to this nicely balanced, complexly flavored Thai classic.

Grilled Thai Beef Salad

SERVES 4 TO 6

Serve with rice, if desired. If fresh Thai chiles are unavailable, substitute ½ serrano chile. Don't skip the toasted rice; it's integral to the texture and flavor of the dish. Any variety of white rice can be used. Toasted rice powder (kao kua) can also be found in many Asian markets; substitute 1 tablespoon rice powder for the white rice.

- **1 teaspoon paprika**
- **1 teaspoon cayenne pepper**
- **1 tablespoon white rice**
- **3 tablespoons lime juice (2 limes)**
- **2 tablespoons fish sauce**
- **2 tablespoons water**
- **½ teaspoon sugar**
- **1 (1½-pound) flank steak, trimmed**
- **Salt and coarsely ground white pepper**
- **1 seedless English cucumber, sliced ¼ inch thick on bias**
- **4 shallots, sliced thin**
- **1½ cups fresh mint leaves, torn**
- **1½ cups fresh cilantro leaves**
- **1 Thai chile, stemmed, seeded, and sliced thin into rounds**

1. Heat paprika and cayenne in 8-inch skillet over medium heat; cook, shaking pan, until fragrant, about 1 minute. Transfer to bowl. Return skillet to medium-high heat, add rice and toast, stirring constantly, until deep golden brown, about 5 minutes. Transfer to separate bowl and let cool 5 minutes. Grind rice with spice grinder, mini food processor, or mortar and pestle until it resembles fine meal, 10 to 30 seconds (you should have about 1 tablespoon rice powder).

NOTES FROM THE TEST KITCHEN

FIVE TASTES OF GRILLED THAI BEEF SALAD—AND ONE MORE

One of the keys to this salad is balancing the signature flavor elements of Thai cuisine. In addition to achieving this, we added one more complementary flavor: the earthiness of toasted cayenne and sweet paprika.

HOT

A fresh Thai bird chile creates bright, fruity heat in the dressing.

SOUR

A generous 3 tablespoons of fresh lime juice adds bracing acidity.

SALTY

Derived from salted, fermented fish, pungent fish sauce acts as a rich flavor enhancer.

SWEET

A half-teaspoon of sugar tames the dressing's salty-sour flavors without becoming cloying.

BITTER

Thoroughly charred steak adds both a pleasing textural contrast and a subtle bitter edge.

EARTHY

Though nontraditional, ground cayenne and sweet paprika add earthy flavor without too much heat.

2. Whisk lime juice, fish sauce, water, sugar, and ¼ teaspoon toasted paprika mixture in large bowl and set aside.

3A. FOR A CHARCOAL GRILL: Open bottom vent completely. Light large chimney starter filled with charcoal briquettes (6 quarts). When top coals are partially covered with ash, pour in even layer over half of grill. Set cooking grate in place, cover, and open lid vent completely. Heat grill until hot, about 5 minutes.

3B. FOR A GAS GRILL: Turn all burners to high, cover, and heat grill until hot, about 15 minutes. Leave primary burner on high and turn off other burner(s).

4. Clean and oil cooking grate. Season steak with salt and pepper. Place steak on grate over hot part of grill and cook until beginning to char and beads of moisture appear on outer edges of meat, 5 to 6 minutes. Flip steak; continue to cook on second side until meat registers 120 to 125 degrees (for medium-rare), about 5 minutes longer. Transfer to carving board, tent loosely with aluminum foil, and rest for 10 minutes (or allow to cool to room temperature, about 1 hour).

5. Line large platter with cucumber slices. Slice meat, against grain, on bias, into ¼-inch-thick slices. Transfer sliced steak to bowl with fish sauce mixture, add shallots, mint, cilantro, chile, and half of rice powder and toss to combine. Arrange steak over cucumber-lined platter. Serve, passing remaining rice powder and toasted paprika mixture separately.

RATING SMOKER BOXES

To infuse gas-grilled food with a smoky flavor, we usually wrap soaked wood chips in an aluminum foil packet and place it over the burners. We wondered if vented metal smoker boxes, which can be filled with soaked wood chips, would do a better job. We smoked chickens using four models as well as our tried-and-true foil packet method. All the boxes were easy to fill and use, and all but one fit neatly under the grill grates. The real test came when we tasted the chickens. All but one smoker box produced chicken at least as good as the chicken smoked with a foil packet. The winner cost less than $10—a worthy, reusable investment. Brands are listed in order of preference. See www.americastestkitchen.com for updates to this testing.

HIGHLY RECOMMENDED

GRILLPRO Cast Iron Smoker Box made by Onward Manufacturing Company (model #00150)

PRICE: $8.50

COMMENTS: Tasters preferred the smoke flavor produced by this box, describing it as "good, sweet, and balanced." Its cast iron heated slowly and let the chips smolder steadily a long while, producing chicken with a clean smoky taste. Slightly over an inch tall, it will fit in almost any grill. It was easy to fill, empty, and clean.

RECOMMENDED

CHARCOAL COMPANION Platinum Gas Grill V-Shape Smoker Box, short (model #CC4065)

PRICE: $11.88

COMMENTS: This box helped to infuse the chicken with a "welcome amount" of "sweet, pleasing" smokiness. Its stainless steel finish discolored during a single smoking session, but this had no impact on the box's effectiveness.

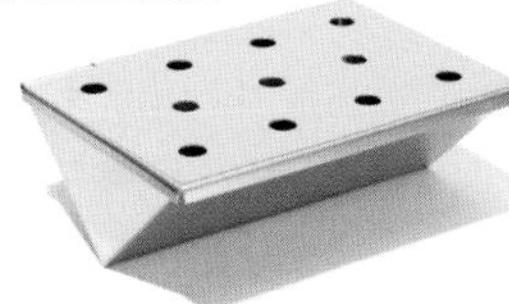

RECOMMENDED *(cont.)*

KINGSFORD Wood Chip Smoking Box made by Outset (model #KSA77)

PRICE: $12

COMMENTS: Bearing the "Kingsford" logo, this stainless steel box is attractive and functional. Slightly larger than our winner, it heated the chips a bit faster and hotter, which produced lots of smoke quickly. This resulted in more pronounced smokiness, which most tasters liked, though a minority found the effect bitter.

NOT RECOMMENDED

FIRE MAGIC Smoker Box (model #3561)

PRICE: $82.45

COMMENTS: This pricey stainless steel box with an adjustable vent didn't fit under the grill grates and had to be set on top. (More than twice the size of the other boxes, it could be useful for very long-smoked recipes if filled completely, but it's unnecessarily large for most applications.) Though we only opened the vent an inch, this box bellowed smoke faster than the others and the smoke flavor produced was "harsh," "acrid," and "ashy."

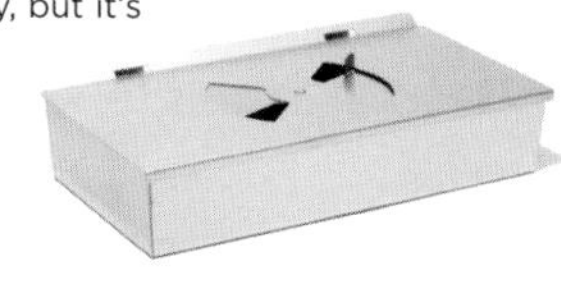

INDONESIAN-STYLE FRIED RICE

WHY THIS RECIPE WORKS: Chinese takeout versions of fried rice are satisfying, to be sure, but frequently leave little to the imagination. We wanted to create a less heavy version of fried rice featuring the pungent, complex flavors of Indonesia—without heading to specialty markets for all of our ingredients. The primary source of this dish's flavor is chili paste, and we were happy to discover that the ingredients for this paste are readily available at the average supermarket. To replicate the flavor of shrimp paste—another key but hard-to-find ingredient—we used a combination of fish sauce and chopped shrimp, which we added to the skillet with the chili paste. This dish requires chilled, firm rice, but most of us don't have leftover rice sitting in our fridge. For rice with the proper consistency, we cooked it in less water and then spread it out on a baking sheet to allow it to chill quickly in the fridge.

FRIED RICE HAS ALWAYS BEEN THE FRUGAL CHEF'S template for using up leftovers: Take cold cooked rice, stir-fry it with whatever meat, vegetables, and aromatics are on hand, and toss it in a sauce that lightly coats the mixture and rehydrates the grains. When done well, the result is a satisfying one-dish meal.

And yet after years of eating the typical Chinese takeout versions—in which the rice is chock-full of meat and vegetables cut to the same size, cooked together, and tossed in a garden-variety "brown sauce"—we often crave something a bit more inspired. Indonesia's spin on the approach, *nasi goreng,* provides an answer. In this Southeast Asian rendition, the grains themselves are more thoroughly seasoned with a pungent chile paste called sambal oelek, along with fermented shrimp paste and a syrupy-sweet soy sauce known as kecap manis. Then, instead of being loaded up with a hodgepodge of meats and vegetables, the rice is garnished with crunchy fried shallots, egg, and crisp fresh vegetables. The final product boasts so much complexity in flavor and texture that it hardly seems like the typical afterthought. But how best to replicate the dish in our own kitchen?

A quick survey of Indonesian fried rice recipes revealed the source of this dish's heady flavor: chile paste. This coarse mixture is nothing more than a puree of shallots, garlic, and fresh Thai chiles. In most recipes, sautéing the chile paste in oil is the first step in the process. This way, the paste develops complexity and heat before the other ingredients hit the pan. (Note: The test kitchen prefers a skillet for stir-frying, since its flat bottom is better suited to a Western-style burner than a wok.)

The chile paste, we discovered, isn't hard to reproduce. We easily found the ingredients at the supermarket, and the paste was a snap to make, requiring just a few quick pulses in the food processor. As for duplicating the flavors of the shrimp paste, glutamate-rich anchovies packed a rich, salty punch but were a little too fishy. Pungent fish sauce made a better substitute, but didn't single-handedly capture the paste's brininess. For that, we ended up going directly to the source, sautéing 12 ounces of chopped extra-large shrimp with the chili paste.

Bottled versions of kecap manis consist of palm sugar, which has a rich, almost caramelized flavor, and soy sauce. But simply adding brown sugar, which also has caramel notes, to soy sauce didn't quite replicate this condiment's complex flavor and viscosity. We had the best luck sweetening the soy with equal amounts of dark brown sugar and molasses.

In a series of quick motions, we added the shrimp to the pan in which we had been sautéing the paste, followed by the sweet soy mixture (including the fish sauce) and, finally, the rice. Each bite of this fried rice revealed that famously addictive balance of sweetness, heat, and pungency. A scattering of sliced scallions and a squirt of lime juice gave the dish a fresh finish.

With the flavors of this dish locked down, we moved on to tackle a more fundamental fried rice problem: hastening the crucial rice-chilling step. Unlike freshly cooked rice, which forms soft, mushy clumps when stir-fried too soon, chilled rice undergoes a process called retrogradation, in which the starch molecules form crystalline structures that make the grains firm enough to withstand a second round of cooking. That's why this dish is tailor-made for last night's leftover rice: After hours in the fridge, the grains are cold and firm. But since cold

INDONESIAN-STYLE FRIED RICE

cooked rice is something that we rarely have on hand, we had to take the extra step of cooking the rice the day before—a process that required more forethought than we wanted to give the dish.

We wondered: Was the 12 to 24 hours in the fridge really necessary? Hoping that we could get away with less chill time, we tried our recipe with rice that had been refrigerated for two, three, and four hours. While the results weren't bad, they hardly compared with the batches made with stiffer, drier grains that had chilled overnight. The freezer was no help: Although the rice felt cold and dry, it cooked up surprisingly mushy. Our science editor offered an explanation: Once the rice freezes, retrogradation comes to a halt, since freezing prevents the starch from crystallizing.

If we couldn't figure out a way to speed up retrogradation, maybe we could produce similarly firm, dry results by cooking the rice in less water. Getting the amount of liquid just right took some fiddling; the standard 3:2 ratio of water to rice was saturating the grains too much, so we drained varying amounts of water from the pot before achieving the ideal texture with just a third of a cup less liquid in the mix. Then we briefly rested the pot on the counter with a kitchen towel under the lid (to absorb excess moisture), spread the rice on a baking sheet, and popped the tray in the fridge. Twenty minutes later, the rice felt almost as firm as the overnight-chilled batches. The only holdup: The grains were a bit sticky. Our two-pronged solution? Rinsing the raw rice and then briefly sautéing it in a splash of oil to form a greasy barrier before adding the water.

All that remained was adding the traditional trimmings: a fried egg or omelet, frizzled shallots, and fresh-cut cucumbers and tomatoes. The latter three were no problem, but we had to decide how to prepare the egg, and everyone agreed that avoiding the last-minute work of egg frying would be a plus. With that in mind, we whipped up a quick omelet, which we rolled into a tight log, sliced into spirals, and set aside until we were ready to garnish.

With its sweet-salty flavors, spicy kick, and contrasting textures, this take on fried rice had officially eclipsed the more familiar humdrum versions. And since we didn't even have to wait a day to make it, it was a recipe that we'd turn to again and again.

NOTES FROM THE TEST KITCHEN

RE-CREATING THE FLAVORS OF INDONESIA
No need to hunt down esoteric ingredients. The various components that give this dish complex flavors and textures can be found at your local supermarket.

DARK BROWN SUGAR, SOY SAUCE, MOLASSES
Soy sauce sweetened with dark brown sugar and molasses approximates the flavors of the Indonesian condiment kecap manis.

GARLIC, SHALLOT, THAI CHILES
We create an Indonesian chili paste by coarsely pureeing these aromatics and sautéing them in oil to develop their flavors.

FISH SAUCE AND FRESH SHRIMP
The combination of fish sauce and fresh shrimp captures the rich, briny essence of hard-to-find Asian shrimp paste.

SIMPLE OMELET
A thin Asian-style omelet that gets rolled into a log and sliced into spirals brings tender texture to the dish.

CRISP SHALLOTS
Sliced thin and fried until golden, a traditional topping of shallot rings adds sweetness and addictive crunch.

Indonesian-Style Fried Rice (Nasi Goreng)

SERVES 4 TO 6

If Thai chiles are unavailable, substitute two serranos or two medium jalapeños. Reduce the spiciness of this dish by removing the ribs and seeds from the chiles. This dish progresses very quickly at step 4; it's imperative that your ingredients are in place by then and ready to go. If desired, serve the rice with sliced cucumbers and tomato wedges.

- **5 green or red Thai chiles, stemmed**
- **7 large shallots, peeled**
- **4 large garlic cloves, peeled**
- **2 tablespoons packed dark brown sugar**
- **2 tablespoons molasses**
- **2 tablespoons soy sauce**
- **2 tablespoons fish sauce**
- **Salt**
- **4 large eggs**
- **½ cup vegetable oil**
- **1 recipe Faux Leftover Rice (recipe follows)**
- **12 ounces extra-large shrimp (21 to 25 per pound), peeled, deveined, tails removed, and cut crosswise into thirds**
- **4 large scallions, sliced thin**
- **2 limes, cut into wedges**

1. Pulse chiles, 4 shallots, and garlic in food processor until coarse paste forms, about 15 pulses, scraping down bowl as necessary. Transfer mixture to bowl and set aside. In second bowl, stir together brown sugar, molasses, soy sauce, fish sauce, and 1¼ teaspoons salt. Whisk eggs and ¼ teaspoon salt together in third bowl.

2. Slice remaining 3 shallots thin and place in 12-inch nonstick skillet with oil. Fry over medium heat, stirring constantly, until shallots are golden and crisp, 6 to 10 minutes. Using slotted spoon, transfer shallots to paper towel–lined plate and season with salt to taste. Pour off oil and reserve. Wipe out skillet with paper towels.

3. Heat 1 teaspoon reserved oil in now-empty skillet over medium heat until shimmering. Add half of eggs to skillet, gently tilting pan to evenly coat bottom. Cover and cook until bottom of omelet is spotty golden brown and top is just set, about 1½ minutes. Slide omelet onto cutting board and gently roll up into tight log. Using sharp knife, cut log crosswise into 1-inch segments (leaving segments rolled). Repeat with another 1 teaspoon reserved oil and remaining eggs.

4. Remove rice from refrigerator and break up any large clumps with fingers. Heat 3 tablespoons reserved oil in now-empty skillet over medium heat until just shimmering. Add chile mixture and cook until mixture turns golden, 3 to 5 minutes. Add shrimp, increase heat to medium-high, and cook, stirring constantly, until exterior of shrimp is just opaque, about 2 minutes. Push shrimp to sides of skillet to clear center; stir molasses mixture to recombine and pour into center of skillet. When molasses mixture bubbles, add rice and cook, stirring and folding constantly, until shrimp is cooked, rice is heated through, and mixture is evenly coated, about 3 minutes. Stir in scallions, remove from heat, and transfer to serving platter. Garnish with egg segments, fried shallots, and lime wedges; serve immediately.

NOTES FROM THE TEST KITCHEN

HOW TO MAKE FRIED RICE WITHOUT LEFTOVERS

Leftover white rice that's been thoroughly chilled—essential to making fried rice—is a staple in Asian households but not something that most of us keep on hand. To condense the overnight chilling process, we came up with a three-pronged approach that produces comparably dry, firm rice in less than an hour.

1. COAT WITH OIL: Sautéing the rinsed rice in oil before steaming helps keep the grains from clumping.

2. USE LESS WATER: Cooking the rice in slightly less water yields more rigid grains that don't require an overnight chill.

3. REST AND CHILL: Resting and then briefly refrigerating the rice ensures that it is dry and firm enough for a second round of cooking.

Faux Leftover Rice

MAKES 6 CUPS; ENOUGH FOR 1 RECIPE INDONESIAN-STYLE FRIED RICE

To rinse the rice, place it in a fine-mesh strainer and rinse under cool water until the water runs clear.

- **2 tablespoons vegetable oil**
- **2 cups jasmine or long-grain white rice, rinsed**
- **2⅔ cups water**

Heat oil in large saucepan over medium heat until shimmering. Add rice and stir to coat grains with oil, about 30 seconds. Add water, increase heat to high, and bring to boil. Reduce heat to low, cover, and simmer until all liquid is absorbed, about 18 minutes. Off heat, remove lid and place clean kitchen towel folded in half over saucepan; replace lid. Let stand until rice is just tender, about 8 minutes. Spread cooked rice onto rimmed baking sheet, set on wire rack, and let cool for 10 minutes. Transfer to refrigerator and chill for 20 minutes.

America's
America's

Vegetarian PASTA NIGHT

CHAPTER 16

THE RECIPES

Vegetable Lasagna

Spaghetti al Limone

TASTING LAB

Whole Wheat Lasagna Noodles

In preparation for combating the problems of overly wet vegetable lasagnas, Becky and Chris have fun demonstrating how much water eggplant contains—by putting the vegetable through a duck press.

WHEN WE WANT A MEAT-FREE MEAL, PASTA IS TYPICALLY OUR GO-TO main course. But vegetarian pastas frequently disappoint with soggy, overcooked vegetables and washed out flavor, making for a bland and underwhelming dish. Vegetable lasagna is a prime example of this, something that is usually prepared as an afterthought to its meaty counterpart. The vegetables exude water and the end result is a loose casserole in which the cheese and sauce—not the vegetables—take center stage. We aimed to create a cohesive vegetable lasagna that put the emphasis back on the vegetables; one that would be every bit as satisfying as a meat lasagna, with the flavors and textures of the vegetables front and center.

Spaghetti al limone is an Italian vegetarian pasta with which you may be less familiar, but it's a dish we think is worth getting to know—its simple ingredient list belies its bold, bright flavor. However, this dish is all about balance; unaccustomed to the spotlight, lemon can quickly turn temperamental—unless you provide it with the perfect costars. Our goal was to temper the tart lemon juice without masking its flavor by adding just the right supporting layers, for a clingy sauce that would perfectly coat the long strands of pasta.

VEGETABLE LASAGNA

WHY THIS RECIPE WORKS: For a complex vegetable lasagna with bold flavor, we started with a summery mix of zucchini, yellow squash, and eggplant, salting and microwaving the eggplant and sautéing the vegetables to cut down on excess moisture and deepen their flavor. Garlic, spinach, and olives added textural contrast and flavor without much work. We dialed up the usual cheese filling by replacing mild-mannered ricotta with tangy cottage cheese mixed with heavy cream for richness and Parmesan and garlic for added flavor. Our quick no-cook tomato sauce brought enough moisture to our lasagna that we found that we could skip the usual step of soaking the no-boil noodles before assembling the dish.

WE'VE RARELY COOKED A VEGETABLE LASAGNA THAT we've been moved to make again. Some versions look tempting enough, with a topcoat of bubbly cheese and thick tomato gravy, but cutting out a square invariably reveals trouble at the core. Often placed between the pasta sheets raw, the zucchini and squash turn out steamy and limp, flooding the dish with their juices—or, in some instances, remain undercooked and crunchy. Then there's the eggplant, which is typically both soggy and greasy from prefrying. Add to that the usual patches of dry, grainy ricotta, and it's a wonder this dish ever became an Italian-American standard.

So what would it take to make a full-flavored lasagna with vegetables that could stand up to—not wash out—the cheese and sauce? Ridding the produce of some of its moisture and boosting its flavor before adding it to the dish would be steps in the right direction.

We first focused our efforts on the eggplant. Besides being full of water, eggplant is extremely porous and readily soaks up any available liquid (or oil). It therefore requires some sort of pretreatment that not only rids the flesh of water, but also breaks down its absorbent air pockets. Fortunately, the test kitchen had already devised an effective approach to both problems for another eggplant dish. Following these instructions, we cut the eggplant into ½-inch cubes, sprinkled them with salt, placed the pieces on a double layer of coffee filters, and then microwaved them for 10 minutes. This process expedites the elimination of moisture triggered by salt, plus it collapses the air pockets, leaving the eggplant shrunken, wrinkled, and less prone to absorbing liquid. When we sautéed the pretreated eggplant to give it more flavor and color, it hardly picked up any oil at all.

We considered salting the zucchini and yellow squash to remove their excess water, but we were fairly certain that a turn in the skillet would burn off enough fluid and deepen their flavor. We cubed the squashes and, to save ourselves an extra step, combined them with the microwaved eggplant before sautéing the whole mixture in two batches with minced garlic. About seven minutes later, the pieces had good color and garlicky flavor, but we knew we could do better. We minced more garlic, this time letting the bits soak in a tablespoon of olive oil along with some minced fresh thyme. Added to the skillet as each batch of vegetables finished cooking, this garlicky, herbal-infused mixture gave the eggplant and squash so much flavor, they were good enough to eat straight from the pan.

Now it was time to see how the vegetables would fare in the lasagna. Keeping things simple, we layered a dozen no-boil noodles with a placeholder tomato sauce (crushed tomatoes, garlic, olive oil, basil, and a dash of pepper flakes, simmered briefly), the sautéed vegetables, and generous helpings of ricotta, mozzarella, and Parmesan cheese. We then baked the casserole until golden and bubbly. The good news was that starting with precooked vegetables allowed us to cut the baking time from the usual hour-plus down to about 35 minutes. But improvements were still needed here and there. Instead of a creamy binder, the ricotta had cooked up into grainy pockets, and some tasters wanted the dairy element to be even richer. Plus, the tomato sauce tasted a bit flat.

We had one quick idea about the ricotta from prior recipe development for baked ziti: substituting cottage cheese. When we made the switch with our next batch, everyone agreed that it was a step in the right direction,

VEGETABLE LASAGNA

To fix the curdling problem, we whisked 1 teaspoon of cornstarch in with the other dairy ingredients (the cornstarch gels and prevents the dairy proteins from curdling when heated).

As for the tomato sauce, we couldn't help but wonder if a similar no-cook approach might not liven up its dull flavor—and save a few extra minutes at the stove. We prepared another batch, this time simply stirring together the ingredients and adding the sauce to the casserole without simmering it first. The results were better than ever. Even after baking and cooling, the sauce still tasted bright, punching up the filling with just enough acidity.

And yet balancing the complexity of the dairy-rich "béchamel" with the fruity tomato sauce didn't quite perk up tasters' interest in the filling. We needed something bolder and fresher to complement the eggplant and squash. Rummaging through the refrigerator for ideas, we decided to add a bag of baby spinach (sautéed briefly until wilted) for freshness and a handful of briny chopped kalamata olives—two small additions that made a big difference. At last we had produced a dish flavorful and substantial enough to please even a meat lover.

but that the cheese was still a bit dry and lean-tasting. In fact, this round of testing convinced us that what we all really wanted was the richness of a béchamel sauce, the classic roux-thickened milk mixture found in countless meat and vegetable lasagna recipes. Our only hesitation was that it involved extra work. We didn't want to add more fuss to the dish by cooking a third element, so we tried a lazy man's approach and whipped up a no-cook cheese sauce with 1 cup each of milk and cottage cheese, a generous 2 cups of Parmesan, and a couple of minced garlic cloves.

We weren't expecting much from this experiment, but the result was surprisingly good. All that cheese produced a "sauce" that was considerably richer, if still a bit thin and curdled. The first problem we easily fixed by swapping the milk for an equal amount of heavy cream.

Vegetable Lasagna

SERVES 8 TO 10

Part-skim mozzarella can also be used in this recipe, but avoid preshredded cheese, as it does not melt well. We prefer kosher salt because it clings best to the eggplant. If using table salt, reduce salt amounts by half. To make assembly easier, the roasted vegetable filling can be made and stored in the refrigerator for up to a day.

TOMATO SAUCE

- **1 (28-ounce) can crushed tomatoes**
- **¼ cup chopped fresh basil**
- **2 tablespoons extra-virgin olive oil**
- **2 garlic cloves, minced**
- **1 teaspoon kosher salt**
- **¼ teaspoon red pepper flakes**

CREAM SAUCE

- **8 ounces (1 cup) whole-milk cottage cheese**
- **1 cup heavy cream**
- **4 ounces Parmesan, grated (2 cups)**
- **2 garlic cloves, minced**
- **1 teaspoon cornstarch**
- **½ teaspoon kosher salt**
- **½ teaspoon pepper**

VEGETABLE FILLING

- **1½ pounds eggplant, peeled and cut into ½-inch pieces**
- **Kosher salt and pepper**
- **Vegetable oil spray**
- **1 pound zucchini, cut into ½-inch pieces**
- **1 pound yellow squash, cut into ½-inch pieces**
- **5 tablespoons plus 1 teaspoon extra-virgin olive oil**
- **4 garlic cloves, minced**
- **1 tablespoon minced fresh thyme**
- **12 ounces (12 cups) baby spinach**
- **½ cup pitted kalamata olives, minced**
- **12 ounces whole-milk mozzarella cheese, shredded (3 cups)**

- **12 no-boil lasagna noodles**
- **2 tablespoons chopped fresh basil**

1. FOR THE TOMATO SAUCE: Whisk all ingredients together in bowl; set aside.

2. FOR THE CREAM SAUCE: Whisk all ingredients together in separate bowl; set aside.

3. FOR THE FILLING: Adjust oven rack to middle position and heat oven to 375 degrees. Toss eggplant with 1 teaspoon salt in large bowl. Line surface of large plate with double layer of coffee filters and lightly spray with vegetable oil spray. Spread eggplant in even layer over coffee filters; wipe out and reserve bowl. Microwave eggplant, uncovered, until dry to touch and slightly shriveled, about 10 minutes, tossing halfway through cooking. Cool slightly. Return eggplant to bowl and toss with zucchini and summer squash.

NOTES FROM THE TEST KITCHEN

FIXING WHAT AILS VEGETABLE LASAGNA

1. PROBLEM: Bland zucchini and squash
SOLUTION: We sautéed the microwaved eggplant with the zucchini and squash to burn off some of their moisture and develop flavorful browning. A shot of garlic-thyme oil stirred in near the end of cooking added depth.

2. PROBLEM: Grainy ricotta cheese
SOLUTION: Ricotta cheese bakes up into dry, chalky patches. We swapped it for creamier cottage cheese and blended it with cream and Parmesan cheese (and a touch of cornstarch) for extra richness.

3. PROBLEM: Dull-tasting red sauce
SOLUTION: Don't cook it. Our no-cook sauce made with crushed tomatoes, fresh basil, and garlic preserves its bright flavors—and saves time at the stove, too.

4. PROBLEM: Watery eggplant
SOLUTION: To rid the spongy eggplant of its excess moisture, we salted and then microwaved the cubed pieces on a coffee filter-lined plate for 10 minutes.

4. Combine 1 tablespoon oil, garlic, and thyme in bowl. Heat 2 tablespoons oil in 12-inch nonstick skillet over medium-high heat until shimmering. Add half of eggplant mixture, ¼ teaspoon salt, and ¼ teaspoon pepper and cook, stirring occasionally, until vegetables are lightly browned, about 7 minutes. Clear center of skillet, add half of garlic mixture, and cook, mashing with spatula, until fragrant, about 30 seconds. Stir garlic mixture into vegetables and transfer to medium bowl. Repeat with 2 tablespoons oil, remaining eggplant mixture, and remaining garlic mixture; transfer to bowl.

5. Heat remaining 1 teaspoon oil in now-empty skillet over medium-high heat until shimmering. Add spinach and cook, stirring frequently, until wilted, about 3 minutes. Transfer spinach to paper towel–lined plate and drain for 2 minutes. Stir into eggplant mixture.

6. Grease 13 by 9-inch baking dish. Spread 1 cup tomato sauce evenly over bottom of dish. Arrange 4 noodles on top of sauce (noodles will overlap). Spread half of vegetable mixture over noodles, followed by half of olives. Spoon half of cream sauce over top and sprinkle with 1 cup mozzarella. Repeat layering with 4 noodles, 1 cup tomato sauce, remaining vegetables, remaining olives, remaining cream sauce, and 1 cup mozzarella. For final layer, arrange remaining 4 noodles on top and cover completely with remaining tomato sauce. Sprinkle with remaining 1 cup mozzarella.

7. Cover dish tightly with aluminum foil that has been sprayed with vegetable oil spray and bake until edges are just bubbling, about 35 minutes, rotating dish halfway through baking. Let lasagna cool for 25 minutes, then sprinkle with basil and serve.

RATING WHOLE WHEAT LASAGNA NOODLES

Good whole wheat pasta should have a pleasantly nutty flavor and tender-firm chew. To find a whole wheat lasagna noodle with both, we sampled four brands—three made from 100 percent whole wheat flour and one whole wheat/white flour blend—plain and in our Vegetable Lasagna. Three samples were traditional noodles that must be cooked before layering into the casserole; the fourth was a no-boil product. Though we usually prefer no-boil noodles (which are precooked and dehydrated before packaging) for their thinner, more delicate texture, tasters' likes and dislikes centered on wheat flavor. They panned noodles that were too gritty and cardboard-y, but pasta that bore too much of a resemblance to white pasta—including the no-boil noodle—wasn't their top pick either. Brands are listed in order of preference. See www.americastestkitchen.com for updates to this testing.

RECOMMENDED

BIONATURAE Organic 100% Whole Wheat Lasagna
PRICE: $3.99 for 12 oz
COMMENTS: These 100 percent whole wheat lasagna sheets won us over with their "nutty," "rich" wheat flavor and a texture that was pleasantly "chewy" without being gritty.

DELALLO 100% Organic Whole Wheat Lasagna
PRICE: $4.48 for 9 oz
COMMENTS: Thin and waferlike, these 100 percent whole wheat no-boil noodles won fans for their delicate texture, which "rivals that of traditional pasta." Flavorwise, tasters were torn. Some liked that these sheets could "pass for white flour noodles"; others wished they tasted more wheaty.

RONZONI Healthy Harvest Whole Grain Lasagna
PRICE: $2.29 for 13.25 oz
COMMENTS: The only blended pasta of the bunch (only 54 percent whole wheat), these noodles had "good structure that holds up well to sauce and cheese." But as they had with the DeLallo lasagna, tasters criticized the noodles for a flavor that wasn't white—but wasn't whole wheat either.

RECOMMENDED WITH RESERVATIONS

HODGSON MILL Whole Wheat Whole Grain Lasagna
PRICE: $2 for 8 oz
COMMENTS: The dark tan color of these 100 percent whole wheat noodles was the first indication that they were seriously wheaty. A few tasters praised their "nutty" flavor, but most found the whole grain flavor overwhelming. As one taster summed it up: "This is like eating burlap."

SPAGHETTI AL LIMONE

WHY THIS RECIPE WORKS: Unaccustomed to the spotlight, lemon can turn temperamental in this quick-hit Italian classic—unless you provide it with the perfect costars. We wanted a dish bursting with bright, bracing lemon flavor, moistened with just enough fruity olive oil to coat each delicate strand. Starting with the lemon flavor, we found the window for the right amount of juice per pound of pasta was extremely small, and if we leaned more to either side, the lemon flavor became either too tart or barely noticeable. To boost the lemon's power without extra acidity, we added some grated zest to the sauce. As for the base of the sauce, we relied on an olive oil–cream sauce—the cream neutralized some of the acids in the juice while augmenting the oils responsible for the fruity, floral notes.

SPAGHETTI AL LIMONE IS A GREAT EXAMPLE OF SIMPLE Italian cooking at its best—a few basic ingredients are combined to create a boldly flavored, satisfying meal. In this dish, the al dente noodles barely seem sauced at all. Yet every forkful bursts with bright, bracing lemon flavor, moistened with just enough fruity olive oil to coat each delicate strand.

But our attempts to create this simple pasta dish in the test kitchen were exercises in frustration. The sauce came out greasy—or worse, slid right off the pasta. And the lemon was unreliable: bright and tangy one batch, harshly acidic the next.

We wanted a clingy sauce with loads of lemon flavor, not mouth-puckering sourness. A survey of the literature revealed that spaghetti al limone recipes run the gamut from dairy-laden Alfredo variants to complicated reductions of citrus and wine. But the style we were after was more like a warm pasta salad: a basic vinaigrette of lemon juice and olive oil tossed with hot pasta.

Lemon was the star of this show, so we started there. We found that anything less than ¼ cup of juice per pound of pasta and the flavor faded into the background. But the threshold was ruthlessly small: Even a bit beyond that had tasters puckering. To boost the lemon's power without extra acidity, we stirred in a generous dose of grated zest, which added fragrant floral notes.

Unfortunately, to balance out the acidity of even this modest amount of lemon juice, we needed a whopping 1½ cups of olive oil—excessive for a dish meant for the weeknight-dinner rotation. Rolling back the oil, we tried tempering the sourness instead with garlic, shallot, even sugar. While the sweet, pungent complexity of the shallot was a keeper, the sauce remained too tart.

So far we'd been steadfast in our purist approach, keeping the lemon and olive oil at center stage. But we were hitting a wall. We were looking for spaghetti al limone, not spaghetti al olio, we reasoned. Would tasters prefer all that heady lemon flavor in one of the dairy-based sauces we'd dismissed?

We made two versions of our working recipe—one with olive oil, the other substituting cream—and had tasters sample them side by side. The cream really did a number on the lemon flavor, mitigating the sourness. On the other hand, tasters missed the fruity olive oil flavor. Even the leftovers (an unofficial gauge of taster enthusiasm) offered no clues: Exactly half a batch of each remained.

Defeated, we dumped all the leftovers into one container, and ate it the next day. To our surprise, this two-batch hybrid tasted great: The sourness was gone, the flavor of the olive oil came through, and the spaghetti wasn't greasy. And remarkably, the lemon flavor also seemed more pronounced than in any version thus far. On further research, we learned that dairy fat does double duty with lemon flavor. First, it dampens the sourness by neutralizing some of the acids in the juice. But it also augments the part of a lemon's flavor profile (the oils) responsible for the fruity, floral notes by working in tandem with the olive oil to emulsify those flavors into a form that really coats the tastebuds. By combining the dairy fat with the olive oil fat, at least in theory, we could solve all our problems.

To find out, we whipped up a batch using both oil and cream. As tasters sang our praises, we knew we were on the right track. Fiddling with the proportions of oil to cream, we found that 1:1 was the ideal ratio. To keep the

SPAGHETTI AL LIMONE

fat reasonably low while still yielding enough sauce to coat the spaghetti, we incorporated some of the starchy pasta water, an age-old Italian trick.

One last problem: The sauce wasn't clinging to the pasta well. Tinkering with the cooking method, we let the sauced pasta sit, covered, for two minutes to absorb the flavors and let the sauce thicken. We finished the dish with nutty Parmesan cheese (a common addition), chopped fresh basil, and a drizzle of olive oil. Bright, floral, and balanced, with a fruity olive oil bite, our final dish tasted as pure and simple as it's meant to be.

Spaghetti al Limone

SERVES 4

Let the dish rest briefly before serving so the flavors develop and the sauce thickens.

- **1 pound spaghetti**
- **Salt and pepper**
- **¼ cup extra-virgin olive oil, plus extra for drizzling**
- **1 shallot, minced**
- **¼ cup heavy cream**
- **1 ounce Parmesan cheese, grated (½ cup), plus extra for serving**
- **2 teaspoons grated lemon zest plus ¼ cup juice (2 lemons)**
- **2 tablespoons chopped fresh basil**

1. Bring 4 quarts water to boil in large pot. Add pasta and 1 tablespoon salt and cook, stirring often, until al dente. Reserve 1¾ cups cooking water, then drain pasta.

2. Heat 1 tablespoon oil in now-empty pot over medium heat until shimmering. Add shallot and ½ teaspoon salt and cook until softened, about 2 minutes. Stir in 1½ cups reserved cooking water and cream, bring to simmer, and cook for 2 minutes. Off heat, add drained pasta, remaining 3 tablespoons oil, Parmesan, lemon zest, lemon juice, and ½ teaspoon pepper and toss to combine.

3. Cover and let pasta rest for 2 minutes, tossing frequently and adding remaining cooking water as needed to adjust consistency. Stir in basil and season with salt and pepper to taste. Drizzle individual portions with oil and serve, passing Parmesan separately.

America's
TEST KITCHEN
CROCK·POT

SLOW-COOKER *Revolution*

CHAPTER 17

THE RECIPES

Old-Fashioned Chicken Noodle Soup

Pork Loin with Cranberries and Orange

Nutella Bread Pudding

EQUIPMENT CORNER

Slow Cookers

To prevent our Nutella Bread Pudding from scorching in the slow cooker, we line the insert with aluminum foil. The foil, sprayed with vegetable oil spray, also makes the pudding a cinch to remove.

A SLOW COOKER IS NO DOUBT A CONVENIENCE ITEM, BUT IF YOU expect to simply dump a bunch of ingredients into it and walk away for the day to return home to a satisfying, home-cooked meal, you are bound to be disappointed. Prepping your ingredients, choosing the right temperature setting, and building flavor from the get-go are easy steps that can turn a somewhat ordinary dish into something extraordinary. Take chicken noodle soup for example; recipes for slow-cooker versions are plentiful, but a good one is hard to come by, with most producing a bland, watery, unremarkable soup. Our goal was to create a slow-cooker chicken noodle soup with rich chicken flavor, tender—not disintegrated—vegetables, and hearty noodles with just the right amount of chew.

Many slow-cooker recipes are custom-made for a busy weeknight, but sometimes we want to apply the convenience of the slow-cooker to a dish that's better suited for company. Tender pork loin with a sweet-tart cranberry glaze is just what we had in mind. Since pork loin is naturally mild and easily overcooked, our main goals would be to build flavor before the pork even went into the slow cooker, and to determine the best time and temperature setting for cooking it.

And while desserts aren't typically thought of as slow-cooker fare, we saw no reason to rule them out. We narrowed down our challenge to bread pudding, one of our favorite all-time desserts. If we could figure out a way to make it work, using the slow cooker to make bread pudding would give us the ultimate entertaining trick—a way to have a warm dessert ready without any last-minute fuss.

OLD-FASHIONED CHICKEN NOODLE SOUP

WHY THIS RECIPE WORKS: Making chicken noodle soup with a deep, satisfying flavor requires a few tricks when using a slow cooker. First, we used a combination of bone-in chicken thighs and breasts. The cooked and shredded breast meat tasted nice in the final soup, but the bone-in thighs really gave the broth its flavor during the long cooking time. And for maximum flavor, we found it necessary to brown the chicken thighs (and remove the skin) before adding them to the slow cooker. To prevent the breast meat from overcooking (which happens when there is a lot of liquid in the slow cooker), we wrapped the chicken breast inside a foil packet. Boiling the noodles separately was a quick and easy way to make sure they had just the right texture.

RECIPES FOR SLOW-COOKER CHICKEN NOODLE SOUP abound. Simply combine chicken, vegetables, noodles, and water in a slow cooker to render a rich broth and tender meat, right? Unfortunately, it's not that easy. We made a handful of recipes following this method, and they were, at best, watery and bland. Clearly, we were going to have to build a better recipe from the ground up if we wanted soup with rich chicken flavor, tender vegetables and noodles, and big bites of succulent meat.

Since we were looking for intense chicken flavor, we chose to use bone-in cuts of chicken. Not sure which cut to use, however, we ran a head-to-head test between chicken thighs and chicken breasts. While we found that the bone-in thighs were certainly tender and flavorful, we were surprised to find that the bone-in breasts offered comparable flavor and texture. The bones had not only helped the body of the broth, but they also kept the breast meat relatively moist and flavorful. Since many people enjoy both dark meat and white meat, we decided to include both, settling on 1½ pounds of chicken thighs and one 12-ounce chicken breast.

Now that we had chosen our chicken, we began to consider how to prepare it for the slow cooker. Many slow-cooker recipes call for browning the chicken ahead of time. While this helps develop a deeper flavor, we wondered if we could avoid the extra work. So we set up a side-by-side test. For one batch of soup we seared the chicken in a skillet, removed the skin, then nestled the pieces in the slow cooker along with chicken broth and sautéed aromatics. The other batch went into the slow cooker cold. Not too surprisingly, tasters favored the flavor of the soup made with seared chicken. Since bold chicken flavor was the focal point of this soup, the additional flavor achieved by browning helped to enrich the broth. The only trick we found necessary for using browned chicken was to remove the skin prior to cooking to ensure that the final stew didn't become greasy.

Our final tests with the chicken focused on timing. Chicken is notorious for drying out with extended cooking times, even in the moist environment of a slow cooker. After several tests, we found that cooking the soup on high was a terrible idea: After only two to three hours, the chicken had turned into a dry rubbery mess. Fortunately, the thighs cooked through perfectly in four to six hours on the low setting. The chicken breast, on the other hand, was cooking unevenly.

To iron out the cooking issue, we decided to skip the browning process for the breast meat since it accelerates cooking. To insulate and protect the tender meat, one taster suggested wrapping it in a foil packet as well. This time, the breast cooked at just the same rate as the thighs, giving us consistently juicy and tender meat throughout the soup.

We were now ready to turn our attention to finishing the soup base. Tasters liked the classic combination of sautéed carrots, celery, and onion the best. To this mixture we also decided to add a tablespoon of tomato paste—to encourage browning and add depth of flavor—as well as some garlic, thyme, and red pepper flakes for further savory notes. We deglazed the skillet with a little chicken broth, scraping up the browned bits (the fond) left over from browning. Transferring the mixture to the slow cooker, we then stirred in the remaining chicken broth and some

OLD-FASHIONED CHICKEN NOODLE SOUP

bay leaves before adding the chicken thighs and breast. After four hours, we shredded the chicken and returned it to the slow cooker along with some peas for good measure.

The noodles were the last remaining element. Egg noodles are the obvious choice for a traditional chicken noodle soup, and we assumed that all we'd have to do was stir in the uncooked noodles several minutes before serving time. When we put this theory to the test, however, the egg noodles softened slightly but never really cooked through; they merely tasted raw and mushy. We realized that the soup wasn't hot enough to actually cook the egg noodles. To fix this problem, we simply boiled the egg noodles in a separate pot, and then stirred them into the soup right before serving. Finished with a pinch of fresh parsley for a bright, fresh touch, our soup was now rich, satisfying, and packed with chicken flavor.

NOTES FROM THE TEST KITCHEN

SHREDDING CHICKEN

To shred chicken into bite-size pieces that fit easily onto a soupspoon, simply hold a fork in each hand (tines facing down), insert the forks into the cooked meat, and gently pull the meat apart.

MAKING A FOIL PACKET

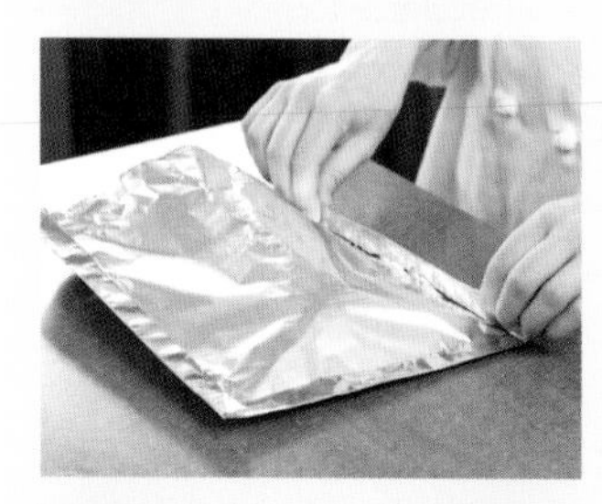

1. Place chicken on 1 side of large piece of aluminum foil. Fold foil over and crimp to seal edges.

2. Place packet on top of soup, pressing gently as needed.

Old-Fashioned Chicken Noodle Soup

SERVES 6 TO 8

- **1½ pounds bone-in chicken thighs, trimmed**
- **Salt and pepper**
- **1 tablespoon vegetable oil**
- **3 carrots, peeled and chopped**
- **2 celery ribs, chopped**
- **1 onion, chopped fine**
- **3 garlic cloves, minced**
- **1 tablespoon tomato paste**
- **2 teaspoons minced fresh thyme or ½ teaspoon dried**
- **⅛ teaspoon red pepper flakes**
- **8 cups low-sodium chicken broth**
- **2 bay leaves**
- **1 (12-ounce) bone-in split chicken breast, trimmed**
- **1½ ounces (1 cup) wide egg noodles**
- **½ cup frozen peas**
- **2 tablespoons minced fresh parsley**

1. Dry chicken thighs with paper towels and season with salt and pepper. Heat oil in 12-inch skillet over medium-high heat until just smoking. Brown chicken thighs well on both sides, 6 to 8 minutes. Transfer to plate, let cool slightly, and discard skin.

2. Pour off all but 1 tablespoon fat left in pan. Add carrots, celery, and onion and cook over medium heat until vegetables are softened, 7 to 10 minutes. Stir in garlic, tomato paste, thyme, and pepper flakes and cook until fragrant, about 30 seconds. Stir in 1 cup chicken broth, scraping up any browned bits; transfer to slow cooker.

3. Stir remaining 7 cups broth and bay leaves into slow cooker. Nestle browned chicken with any accumulated juices into slow cooker. Season chicken breast with salt and pepper. Place breast on 1 side of large piece of aluminum foil, fold foil over, and crimp to seal edges. Lay foil packet on top of soup. Cover and cook until chicken is tender, 4 to 6 hours on low.

4. Remove foil packet, open it carefully (watch for steam), and transfer chicken breast to cutting board. Transfer chicken thighs to cutting board. Let all chicken cool slightly, then shred into bite-size pieces, discarding skin and bones. Let soup settle for 5 minutes, then remove fat from surface using large spoon. Discard bay leaves.

5. Bring 4 quarts water to boil in large pot. Add noodles and 1 tablespoon salt and cook, stirring often, until al dente, then drain. Stir cooked noodles, shredded chicken, and peas into soup and let sit until heated through, about 5 minutes. Stir in parsley, season with salt and pepper to taste, and serve.

PORK LOIN WITH CRANBERRIES AND ORANGE

WHY THIS RECIPE WORKS: Pork loins are typically roasted, but we wanted to find a way to prepare this cut in a slow cooker. To ensure that it would even fit in our slow cooker, we found it important to shop carefully—only a boneless pork loin that was wide and short (rather than long and narrow) would do. Browning the roast prior to placing it in the slow cooker was essential for flavor, as this step allowed the fat cap to melt and flavor the roast throughout. It was also important to cook our pork loin on the low setting; a high setting resulted in dry, leathery meat. The tart flavor of cranberries was the ideal complement to our mild pork loin, which we added to our dish in the form of a whole cranberry sauce accented with a little orange and cinnamon. Simmering the sauce on the stovetop created a clingy glaze that perfectly coated our pork.

OPEN UP YOUR TYPICAL SLOW-COOKER COOKBOOK, and you'll find dozens of recipes for comforting soups, stews, and chilis. While these homey dishes are worth making during the workweek, we wanted to see if we could create a meal worthy of company. We turned to the dinner-party friendly pork loin roast for inspiration.

When developing other slow-cooker recipes, we've learned that we need to focus on building a lot of flavor from the get-go since the long cooking times and moist cooking environment of the slow cooker tend to mute flavor. To ensure a flavorful pork loin, we decided to pair this naturally mild meat with the bold flavor of cranberries. The first step in building our roast was to see if we could even fit a pork loin into our slow cooker! We quickly learned that bone-in cuts wouldn't fit, so we focused on boneless pork loin. We found that narrow pork loins don't fit as easily into the slow cooker and are prone to overcooking because they cook through

PORK LOIN WITH CRANBERRIES AND ORANGE

more quickly, so we settled on a 4½- to 5-pound roast that is wide and short.

Our cut selected, we now turned to the question of whether or not to brown our roast. Since we wanted this recipe to be as easy as possible, we decided to first try cooking a pork loin added to the slow cooker totally raw. Unfortunately, our unbrowned slow-cooked roast did not fare so well. Cooked in the relatively low heat of the slow cooker, the fat cap on top of the roast couldn't render. Our roast emerged not only pale in color, but also topped with an unpleasantly chewy layer of fat. After this failed test, we decided to brown the roast in a skillet before adding it to the slow cooker. Luckily it only took 10 minutes of cooking to effectively brown the roast, and this step made a world of difference. The pork was now golden brown, and the fat cap had melted into the meat, flavoring the roast throughout.

Next we moved on to the matter of cooking time. Since pork loin is a naturally lean cut, we knew that we would need to keep our cooking time relatively short. But could we get away with cooking it on both the high and low settings? Cooking the loin on high was disastrous—this meat was leathery, dry, and borderline inedible. The low setting worked much better, as long as we watched it carefully, and pulled it out right when it reached 140 degrees (this turned out to be about four hours).

Now that we had found the best way to cook the pork, we moved on to our cranberry sauce. To find the ultimate cranberry flavor, we tested various combinations of jellied cranberry sauce, whole berry cranberry sauce, cranberry juice, and dried cranberries. A few tests revealed that both the jellied cranberry sauce and cloying cranberry juice added minimal flavor with loads of sugar, so we axed them both. On the other hand, tasters gave the thumbs-up to whole berry cranberry sauce, which lent texture and a truer cranberry flavor, as well as to ½ cup of dried cranberries, which added bright pockets of tart chew.

While we were pleased with the cranberry flavor, tasters wanted a more complex sauce. Savory additions like Dijon mustard, onions, and vinegar muddied the flavor. Instead, we liked the inclusion of mildly acidic orange juice. We added ½ cup juice to our sauce, and further bolstered the flavor with a few strips of orange peel.

A small amount of cinnamon lent a little spice and depth.

At this point, our pork was perfectly cooked and our sauce tasted great, but we thought we could improve the dish by turning our sauce into a clingy glaze. Since we knew we'd need to let the pork rest before serving, we decided to take advantage of this waiting time and reduce the sauce on the stovetop. Twelve minutes of simmering turned our runny cranberry sauce to a glossy glaze. Drizzled over the pork, the glaze added the finishing touch to a company-worthy dinner that was so bright in flavor, no one would guess it came from a slow cooker.

Pork Loin with Cranberries and Orange

SERVES 6

- **1 (4½- to 5-pound) boneless pork loin roast, trimmed and tied at 1-inch intervals**
- **Salt and pepper**
- **1 tablespoon vegetable oil**
- **1 (14-ounce) can whole berry cranberry sauce**
- **½ cup dried cranberries**
- **½ cup orange juice**
- **3 (3-inch-long) strips orange zest, trimmed of white pith**
- **⅛ teaspoon ground cinnamon**

1. Dry pork with paper towels and season with salt and pepper. Heat oil in 12-inch skillet over medium-high heat until just smoking. Brown pork well on all sides, 7 to 10 minutes.

2. Stir cranberry sauce, cranberries, orange juice, orange zest, and cinnamon into slow cooker. Nestle browned pork into slow cooker. Cover and cook until pork is tender and registers 140 degrees, about 4 hours on low.

3. Transfer pork to carving board, tent loosely with aluminum foil, and let rest for 10 minutes. Let braising liquid settle for 5 minutes, then remove fat from surface using large spoon. Discard orange zest. Transfer braising liquid to medium saucepan and simmer until reduced to 2 cups, about 12 minutes. Season with salt and pepper to taste.

4. Remove twine from pork, slice into ½-inch-thick slices, and arrange on serving platter. Spoon 1 cup sauce over meat and serve with remaining sauce.

NOTES FROM THE TEST KITCHEN

BUYING PORK LOIN ROASTS

Buying the right pork loin will make all the difference in this slow-cooker recipe. Look for a 4½- to 5-pound pork loin roast that is wide and short and steer clear from those that are long and narrow. Narrow pork loins don't fit as easily into the slow cooker and are prone to overcooking because they cook through more quickly.

LONG AND NARROW

WIDE AND SHORT

MAKING ZEST STRIPS

Use a vegetable peeler to remove long, wide strips of citrus zest from the fruit. Try not to remove any of the white pith beneath the zest, as it is bitter.

NUTELLA BREAD PUDDING

WHY THIS RECIPE WORKS: Getting the texture of this company-worthy dessert—Nutella bread pudding—just right was the real challenge; early tests yielded mushy or dry bread puddings, not the creamy and moist texture we were after. After extensive testing of different types of bread, we settled on challah for its rich flavor. We cut it into cubes, which we toasted until dry before combining them with our custard (a combination of egg yolks, milk, heavy cream, sugar, and vanilla). Pressing the bread into the custard ensured every cube soaked up its share. We loved the addition of chocolate chips, which added a chocolaty boost that the Nutella couldn't without adding too much sweetness. Once cooked, the chocolate chips melted and added a decadent gooeyness that had tasters diving in for seconds. After four hours in the slow cooker, we had an easy-to-prepare bread pudding that rivaled our oven versions.

SINCE WE ARE HUGE FANS OF BREAD PUDDING, WE wanted to see if we could develop one that would work in a slow cooker. And while this task seemed daunting (we envisioned all manner of issues with the texture), success would mean a hands-off dessert that could be served up warm and creamy when entertaining with no last-minute timing required.

To tackle this challenge, we first decided to outline and try the basic recipe technique for bread pudding. A recent test kitchen recipe for bread pudding calls for cubes of bread, dried out in the oven, and soaked for 30 minutes in a mixture of 2 cups milk, 2 cups cream, 9 egg yolks, 1 cup sugar, ½ cup raisins, and warm spices. The mixture is then baked slowly in a low oven. To replicate this technique in the slow cooker, we hypothesized that we could skip the soaking step (since the slow cooker takes about 30 minutes to heat up anyway), and cook the pudding for several hours on low heat.

We dried out a loaf of white bread, whipped up a custard base, and layered it all into our slow cooker, gently pressing the bread into the custard to encourage absorption. After about four hours on low, the eggs were set, and our custard was ready to eat. And while the bread had certainly soaked up all of the custard, we were faced with a major problem: half of our pudding had burned. Making matters worse, even the unburned portions of pudding had stuck to the insert.

Not wanting to give up on our pudding just yet, we took a closer look at our slow cooker to see if we could find the source of the burning. In the slow cooker we use in the test kitchen, the heating element is located in the rear of the cooker opposite the controls. (Other slow cooker models have elements in the front or bottom of the cooker.) When preparing a dish with a fair amount of liquid, such as a soup or stew (or even a braise), the heat is distributed evenly throughout the insert and burning or sticking is a nonissue. But since our bread pudding was so dense (not to mention full of easily burned sugar), the heating element overheated the mixture, leading to our burnt pudding—especially on the side of the insert adjacent to the heating element.

To solve this problem, we figured that our pudding just needed a little bit of insulation. We folded up a couple sheets of foil and lined the interior side of the slow cooker insert facing the heating element with a foil collar. Luckily, the foil proved to be an effective barrier. To make our pudding easier to remove, we also lined our bolstered slow cooker with a foil sling and sprayed it with vegetable oil spray for good measure. This time, we were able to scoop our bread pudding out of the slow cooker with ease, and, best of all, it was burn-free.

With our method finally settled, we examined the bread. We had been using plain old white sandwich bread, but we wanted to see if there was a better option. We compared puddings made with French bread, Italian bread, challah, and the requisite sandwich bread. The French bread pudding was, surprisingly, too coarse and rustic to yield the refined texture we had in mind. The airy Italian loaf suffered the opposite ill of disintegrating into the custard, leaving zero distinction between bread and pudding. As it turned out, challah was the winner: This soft, braided loaf swelled nicely, absorbing liquid without disintegrating, and its deep gold crust retained a satisfying chew.

While the original custard base translated well to the slow cooker, tasters were finding the final outcome a bit boring. We decided to take our bread pudding in a new (and chocolate) direction. Out went the raisins and warm spices. In went a whole cup of Nutella (a common European breakfast spread of hazelnuts, skim milk, and cocoa) and a handful of chocolate chips. The Nutella offered instant chocolaty, nutty complexity, and the chips gave the pudding a rich, gooey decadence. These changes made, we found we just needed to drop the amount of milk in our original custard to keep the bread moist and creamy.

NOTES FROM THE TEST KITCHEN

PREPARE YOUR SLOW COOKER

Most slow cookers have a hotter side (typically the back side, opposite the side with the controls) that can cause dense dishes like bread pudding to burn. To solve this problem we lined the slow-cooker insert with an aluminum foil collar. Since we wanted to lift the bread pudding out of the insert intact, we first lined the slow cooker with a foil collar, then lined it with a foil sling.

TO MAKE A FOIL COLLAR: Layer and fold sheets of heavy-duty foil until you have a 6-layered foil rectangle that measures roughly 16 inches long by 4 inches wide. (Depending on the width of the foil, you will need either 2 or 3 sheets of foil.) Press the collar into the back side of the slow-cooker insert; the food will help hold the collar in place during cooking.

TO MAKE A FOIL SLING: Line the slow-cooker insert with a foil collar. Then fit 2 large sheets of heavy-duty foil into the slow cooker, perpendicular to one another, with the extra hanging over the edges of the cooker insert. Before serving, these overhanging edges can be used as handles to pull the dish out of the slow cooker fully intact.

Transformed from a burned sticky mess into a luscious chocolate confection, our Nutella Bread Pudding had tasters clamoring for more. Topped with softly whipped cream, it was now not only a great slow-cooker recipe, but also a wonderful (and easy) dessert.

Nutella Bread Pudding

SERVES 8 TO 10

- **1 (14-ounce) loaf challah bread, cut into 1-inch cubes (12 cups)**
- **½ cup chocolate chips**
- **2 cups heavy cream**
- **2 cups whole milk**
- **9 large egg yolks**
- **1 cup Nutella**
- **¾ cup (5¼ ounces) plus 1 tablespoon granulated sugar**
- **4 teaspoons vanilla extract**
- **¾ teaspoon salt**
- **2 tablespoons packed light brown sugar**

1. Layer and fold sheets of heavy-duty aluminum foil until you have 6-layered foil rectangle that measures roughly 16 inches long by 4 inches wide. (Depending on width of foil, you will need either 2 or 3 sheets of foil.) Press collar into back side of slow-cooker insert. Fit 2 large sheets of heavy-duty foil into slow cooker, perpendicular to one another, with extra hanging over edges of cooker insert. Coat collar and sling with vegetable oil spray. Adjust oven rack to middle position and heat oven to 225 degrees. Spread bread over rimmed baking sheet and bake, shaking pan occasionally, until dry and crisp, about 40 minutes. Let bread cool slightly, then transfer to very large bowl.

2. Mix chocolate chips into dried bread; transfer to prepared slow cooker. Whisk cream, milk, egg yolks, Nutella, ¾ cup granulated sugar, vanilla, and salt together in bowl, then pour mixture evenly over bread. Press gently on bread to submerge.

3. Mix remaining 1 tablespoon granulated sugar with brown sugar then sprinkle over top of casserole. Cover and cook until center is set, about 4 hours on low. Let cool for 30 minutes before serving.

RATING SLOW COOKERS

The winner of our previous slow-cooker testing, made by All-Clad, costs nearly $200. We recently pitted it against six new, less expensive models to see if we could save money without sacrificing performance. We limited our lineup mainly to oval slow cookers, which can fit a large roast, with capacities of 6 quarts or more, and judged the cookers on design and performance. Six models had programmable timers and warming modes, features we like. Ideally, a slow cooker should produce perfect results on all settings. But when we made pot roast, meaty tomato sauce, and French onion soup, some of the models variously gave us pot roast with dry, tough meat or juicy, sliceable meat, tomato sauces that were extra-thick or thin and watery, and soup with burnt onions or nicely browned onions. We devised a test to measure the maximum temperatures of the models on high and low settings and found that some just didn't get hot enough, whereas others reached the boiling point; the best models fell somewhere in between. Brands are listed in order of preference. See www.americastestkitchen.com for updates to this testing.

HIGHLY RECOMMENDED

CROCK-POT Touchscreen Slow Cooker (model #SCVT650-PS)
PRICE: $129.99 **COOKING:** ★★★ **DESIGN:** ★★★
MAXIMUM TEMPERATURE: 199°F on low, 204.5°F on high
COMMENTS: The control panel is extremely easy to use, and the timer counted up to 20 hours, even on high. Sunday gravy thickened to the correct consistency, pot roast was tender and sliceable, and onions caramelized perfectly.

RECOMMENDED

ALL-CLAD Slow Cooker with Ceramic Insert (model #99009)
PRICE: $199.95 **COOKING:** ★★★ **DESIGN:** ★★
MAXIMUM TEMPERATURE: 195°F on low, 207°F on high
COMMENTS: Pot roast and gravy cooked to the correct consistency, and temperatures fell into the right ranges. But we got equally good results from our top-ranked model at a much lower price. The button controls are easy to use, but the timer could not be set for more than six hours on high.

RECOMMENDED WITH RESERVATIONS

BREVILLE Slow Cooker with EasySear (model #BSC560XL)
PRICE: $179.95 **COOKING:** ★★ **DESIGN:** ★★
MAXIMUM TEMPERATURE: 209°F on low, 212°F on high
COMMENTS: Although this large cooker ran hot, the tight seal of its metal lid yielded fall-apart meat in Sunday gravy. Pot roast overcooked, though, and onions for the soup burned. We couldn't see the food through the steel lid. For this price, we expected a timer and warm cycle.

RECOMMENDED WITH RESERVATIONS *(cont.)*

KITCHENAID Slow Cooker (model #KSC700SS)
PRICE: $129.99 **COOKING:** ★★ **DESIGN:** ★★
MAXIMUM TEMPERATURE: 187°F on low, 187°F on high
COMMENTS: The meat in Sunday gravy was tender, but the pot roast was dry. The onions didn't cook evenly. The heavy insert's square shape made pouring easy. The control panel has five cooking settings, but the timer stops after eight hours on high.

NOT RECOMMENDED

CUISINART Programmable Slow Cooker (model #PSC-650)
PRICE: $99.95 **COOKING:** ★★ **DESIGN:** ★
MAXIMUM TEMPERATURE: 177°F on low, 205°F on high
COMMENTS: The first model wouldn't turn on; the second struggled to cook the onions evenly. The construction was flimsy, the buttons hard to push. The low setting produced tough meat. Sunday gravy fared better on high.

ELITE CUISINE by Maxi-Matic Programmable LED Slow Cooker (model #MST-6000)
PRICE: $39.99 **COOKING:** ★ **DESIGN:** ★
MAXIMUM TEMPERATURE: 188°F on low, 204°F on high
COMMENTS: This cooker produced tender meat but broke after two uses. The settings were confusing; we thought we'd turned the machine on, but an hour later we found that the timer hadn't begun to count down (the only way to know if it's working).

KALORIK Slow Cooker (model #SC11048)
PRICE: $29.98 **COOKING:** ★ **DESIGN:** ★
MAXIMUM TEMPERATURE: 182°F on low, 213°F on high
COMMENTS: This timer-less machine ran the hottest on high, meaning onions burned, and Sunday gravy was dry. On low, it took almost eight hours to reach its high temperature and failed to reach the food-safe temperature of 140 degrees within two hours.

TIME TO *Grill*

CHAPTER 18

THE RECIPES

Grill-Roasted Bone-In Pork Rib Roast

Orange Salsa with Cuban Flavors

Grilled Sea Scallops

Bacon and Brown Butter Vinaigrette

Basil Vinaigrette

Chile-Lime Vinaigrette

Barbecue Sauce Vinaigrette

SCIENCE DESK

Boning Up on Flavor

EQUIPMENT CORNER

Grilling Baskets for Whole Fish

Innovative Kitchen Gadgets

GRILLING SEASON MEANS BURGERS AND DOGS. WE'VE GOT NOTHING against these standbys, but sometimes we want to put ourselves to the test and prove that we've got a more varied grilling repertoire than just flipping a patty of ground meat. Our thoughts first turned to a large roast—boneless pork roast, to be specific. Yet while there's no denying the convenience of a boneless pork roast, we couldn't help but wonder if something important is lost (say, flavor?) when those bones are cut away. With that in mind, we stepped our challenge up a notch and set out to uncover the secrets to grilling a bone-in roast, one that would be juicy, rich, and packed with flavor.

Moving to the other end of the spectrum, we next decided to tackle infuriatingly delicate, quick-cooking scallops. A blazing-hot fire can render scallops beautifully crisp on the outside and juicy within—or cement them to the grate like carbonized hockey pucks. Hoping to avoid the latter, we were determined to master the elusive technique for grilling scallops—the one that would render them lightly charred on the outside and tender and juicy within—without a single scallop sticking to the grill. Join us as we take on these grilling challenges.

Chris shows that by using two spatulas, a big piece of meat like our pork rib roast is easy to lift off the grill.

GRILLED BONE-IN PORK ROAST

WHY THIS RECIPE WORKS: Grilling a bulky cut of meat like a pork rib roast may sound difficult, but it's not. We found that a tender, quick-cooking center-cut rib roast and a simple salt rub were all that we needed for a juicy grilled roast with a thick mahogany crust. We grilled it over indirect heat (on the cooler side of the grill) so it could cook through slowly, adding a single soaked wood chunk for a subtle tinge of smoke flavor. After little more than an hour on the grill, our roast was tender and juicy, with plenty of rich, deep flavor. A fresh orange salsa was the perfect counterpoint to the roast's richness.

MOST OF US CONSIDER BONELESS PORK ROASTS TO BE a welcome modern convenience, like automatic transmissions. Why deal with a clutch and a stick shift—or with bones—if you don't have to? We can't complain about the convenience of a boneless pork roast—little to no butchering on the front end, and fuss-free slicing at the table—but we also know that meat cooked on the bone just tastes better. Plus, for many people, gnawing on the bone is a satisfying way to finish off a meal.

With those reflections in mind, we decided to reacquaint ourselves with the pleasures of grilling a bone-in roast. We wanted a succulent, flavor-packed roast with a thick, well-browned crust and subtle smokiness. And while we figured out the best way to achieve those results, we also hoped to learn exactly why it is that bones make meat taste juicier and richer.

The obvious starting place was our supermarket butcher case, where we focused on tender, quick-cooking roasts from the loin section of the animal. From this region, we had our choice of three roasts: the blade-end (sometimes called the rib-end) roast, the center-cut rib roast, and the confusingly named center-cut loin roast. From all the taste tests done in our test kitchen over the years, we already knew that the center-cut loin roast offers the least impressive flavor of the three. So we narrowed our choices to the blade-end and center-cut rib roasts, settling on the center-cut roast for its great ease of preparation: Because the meat is a single muscle attached along one side to the bones, there is no need to tie the roast for a tidy presentation.

We began by rubbing the meat with a generous handful of kosher salt and letting it rest in the refrigerator for six hours before starting the fire—a technique we prefer to soaking the meat in a brine when our goal is a deeply browned, crisp crust. Next we built a modified two-level fire, banking all the coals on one side of the kettle. This left a cooler area where the meat could cook through slowly by indirect heat without risk of burning the exterior. Then we threw the roast on the grate, covered the grill, and walked away.

A little more than an hour later, the roast's internal temperature measured 140 degrees (we knew it would rise to the requisite 150 degrees as it rested). We expected to pull the roast over to the grill's hot side for a quick sear before we took it off the grill, but to our delight the meat's exterior had already formed a thick mahogany crust.

Now that we'd picked the best cut and cooking method for the job, we moved on to consider possible tweaks to the flavorings—though, to be honest, we weren't sure that the roast needed much improvement. The meat was tender and remarkably juicy and had plenty of rich, deep flavor. Even our dead-simple salt rub enhanced the pork's taste without distraction.

But, being skeptics and perfectionists, we wanted to rule out all other options. So we set up a side-by-side test for our colleagues, pitting our plain salt-rubbed roast against identical specimens crusted with black pepper and a range of other spices and herbs. We also tested varying strengths of wood smoke. When the votes were tallied, our original intuition was confirmed: Simpler was better. Our tasters opted for nothing more than a little sprinkling of black pepper just before cooking and a subtle tinge of smoke flavor. The latter was easy enough: We soaked one wood chunk, placed it on top of the hot coals, positioned the lid vent over the meat, and opened it halfway to draw smoke over the roast.

Our testing was nearly done, but we still wanted to know exactly what makes a bone-in roast so flavorful and juicy. We consulted our science editor as well as a number of unaffiliated meat scientists and experts, and several

of them advanced similar theories about the enhanced juiciness and flavor of bone-in meat.

First, there is extra fat and connective tissue around the bones. As the roast cooks, that fat melts and bastes the meat while the connective tissues break down into gelatin, lending the meat perceived juiciness. (We score the fat on the surface of the roast for this reason.) Second, the bones act as insulation. Because they conduct heat poorly, they inhibit evaporation and moisture loss from the meat attached to them, keeping the meat around them juicier. Our science editor also pointed out that many of the flavor compounds in smoke vapor are fat-soluble, and since there is extra fat in the roast—courtesy of the bones—the meat is likely to absorb and retain more flavor from the smoke.

But another, more intriguing theory, and one we had never heard before, credited the bone marrow. Two experts thought some of the flavorful compounds of the marrow might migrate through the porous bone and into the surrounding meat, though they knew of no experiments that proved it. This hypothesis seemed promising, so we asked our science editor to help the test kitchen devise an experiment to test it (see "Boning up on Flavor"). As it turned out, the theory held up.

With all the flavor and tenderness those bones provided, all that this roast needed was a simple orange salsa to provide a counterpoint to its richness. As the man once said, "If it ain't broke, don't fix it."

SCIENCE DESK

BONING UP ON FLAVOR

We've long known that the fat and connective tissue that surround bones lend moisture and richness to bone-in meats, while the mere presence of bones slows cooking and limits evaporation of juices. But it seemed to us that there must be other reasons why bone-in meat tastes better than the boneless kind. So when two meat experts suggested that some flavor might migrate from the rich marrow at the center of bones through the porous bone itself and right into the meat, our curiosity was piqued. We devised a test to see if this theory made any sense.

EXPERIMENT

To fabricate a neutral-flavored pork substitute, we made a big batch of mashed potatoes and seasoned it with 8 percent butter and 1 percent salt by weight, amounts that mimic the fat and salt found in our pork roast. Then we formed the potatoes into two equal-size, oblong shapes on a baking sheet. Next we scraped three pork rib bones clean of all fat and connective tissue, so that the only flavor would be from the marrow, and placed these bones over the top of one of the roasts and left the other alone. Then we cooked both in a 425-degree oven for 1½ hours. After a 20-minute rest, we compared the samples.

RESULTS

A majority of tasters found that the sample cooked with bones tasted noticeably meaty.

EXPLANATION

As bones are heated, they expel moisture, salt, amino acids, and nucleotides (the last two being responsible for the "meatiness" that tasters detected) from the richly flavored marrow. However, since those water-soluble flavor molecules must penetrate through a thick layer of bone to reach the meat, the diffusion process is slow and the amount of flavor contributed is not enormous. Nevertheless, when coupled with the considerable moisture- and flavor-enhancing benefits of the fat and connective tissue around the bones, the process certainly provides another good reason to opt for bone-in.

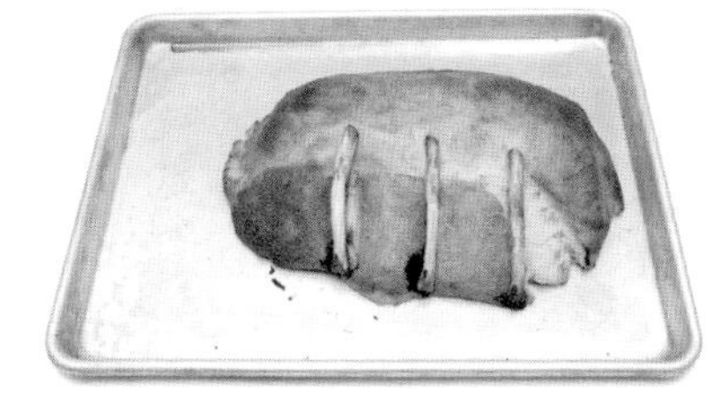

BONE-IN MASHED POTATO "ROAST"
Crazy as it sounds, our imitation roast proved that some flavor from the bone can migrate into the meat.

GRILL-ROASTED BONE-IN PORK RIB ROAST

Grill-Roasted Bone-In Pork Rib Roast

SERVES 6 TO 8

If you buy a blade-end roast, tie it into a uniform shape with kitchen twine at 1-inch intervals; this step is unnecessary with a center-cut roast. For easier carving, ask the butcher to remove the tip of the chine bone and to cut the remainder of the chine bone between the ribs. One medium wood chunk, soaked in water for 1 hour, can be substituted for the wood chip packet on a charcoal grill.

- **1 (4- to 5-pound) bone-in pork center-cut rib- or blade-end roast, tip of chine bone and membrane removed, fat trimmed to ¼-inch thickness**
- **4 teaspoons kosher salt**
- **1 cup wood chips, soaked in water for 15 minutes and drained**
- **1½ teaspoons pepper**
- **1 recipe Orange Salsa with Cuban Flavors (optional; recipe follows)**

1. Pat roast dry with paper towels. Using sharp knife, cut slits in surface fat layer, spaced 1 inch apart, in crosshatch pattern, being careful not to cut into meat. Season roast with salt. Wrap with plastic wrap and refrigerate for at least 6 hours or up to 24 hours.

2. Using large piece of heavy-duty aluminum foil, wrap soaked chips in foil packet and cut several vent holes in top.

3A. FOR A CHARCOAL GRILL: Open bottom vent halfway. Light large chimney starter filled with charcoal briquettes (6 quarts). When top coals are partially covered with ash, pour into steeply banked pile against side of grill. Place wood chip packet on 1 pile of coals. Set cooking grate in place, cover, and open lid vent halfway. Heat grill until hot and wood chips are smoking, about 5 minutes.

3B. FOR A GAS GRILL: Place wood chip packet over primary burner. Turn all burners to high, cover, and heat grill until hot and wood chips are smoking, about 15 minutes. Turn primary burner to medium-high and turn off other burner(s). (Adjust primary burner as needed during cooking to maintain grill temperature around 350 degrees.)

4. Clean and oil cooking grate. Unwrap roast and season with pepper. Place roast on grate with meat near, but not over, coals and flames and bones facing away from coals and flames. Cover (position lid vent over meat if using charcoal) and cook until meat registers 140 degrees, 1¼ to 1½ hours.

5. Transfer roast to carving board, tent loosely with foil, and let rest for 30 minutes. Carve into thick slices by cutting between ribs. Serve, passing salsa, if using, separately.

NOTES FROM THE TEST KITCHEN

THE BEST BONE-IN PORK ROAST

The three most common pork loin roasts offer markedly different results in terms of flavor and texture.

TOP CHOICE: CENTER-CUT RIB ROAST

A cut from the center of the loin that contains mostly loin muscle attached to a neat row of curved rib bones.

PROS: Good flavor; easy availability; no tying necessary

CONS: Tendency to dry out when boneless

CLOSE SECOND: BLADE-END ROAST

Also known as the "rib-end roast," this cut from the shoulder end of the loin is a hodgepodge of small muscles.

PROS: Exceptionally rich flavor

CONS: Spotty availability; must be tied; tricky to slice cleanly

DISTANT THIRD: CENTER-CUT LOIN ROAST

A narrow section of loin muscle fused with a larger section of tenderloin, cut from the rear of the loin. The bones are mostly T-shaped vertebrae, not ribs.

PROS: Tender; decent flavor

CONS: Carving is difficult; less flavorful than other options.

REMOVING THE MEMBRANE OF PORK RIB ROAST

Nick membrane at edge of roast with tip of knife to loosen it, then grab loose bit using paper towel and slowly pull off membrane.

GRILLED SEA SCALLOPS

WHY THIS RECIPE WORKS: In theory, the blazing-hot fire of a grill is perfect for cooking scallops with an extra-crisp crust and moist interior, but in practice they're usually rubbery and overcooked by the time they develop a good sear, and they inevitably stick to the grate. For great grilled scallops, we needed to figure out how to build the biggest fire possible. The solution was a disposable aluminum pan—it allowed us to corral the coals in just the center of the grill for a tall, even, super-hot fire that gave us scallops with impressive char and juicy centers. Drying the scallops with kitchen towels before cooking helped ensure browning, and threading them on double metal skewers made them easy to flip all at once. To combat the problem of sticking, we lightly coated the scallops with a mixture of flour, cornstarch, oil, and sugar. With this simple coating, our scallops were crisp-crusted, moist and tender within, and released without hesitation.

Orange Salsa with Cuban Flavors

MAKES ABOUT 2½ CUPS; ENOUGH FOR 1 RECIPE GRILL-ROASTED BONE-IN PORK RIB ROAST

To make this salsa spicier, add the reserved chile seeds.

- ½ **teaspoon grated orange zest plus 5 oranges peeled and segmented; each segment quartered crosswise**
- ½ **cup minced red onion**
- 1 **jalapeño chile, stemmed, seeds reserved, and minced**
- 2 **tablespoons lime juice**
- 2 **tablespoons minced fresh parsley**
- 1 **tablespoon extra-virgin olive oil**
- 2 **teaspoons packed brown sugar**
- 1½ **teaspoons distilled white vinegar**
- 1½ **teaspoons minced fresh oregano**
- 1 **garlic clove, minced**
- ½ **teaspoon ground cumin**
- ½ **teaspoon salt**
- ½ **teaspoon pepper**

Combine all ingredients in bowl.

PAN-SEARING SCALLOPS IS OUR FAVORITE WAY TO cook them indoors: The quick blast of heat deeply browns their exteriors while leaving their centers plump and moist. We've always figured the bivalves would be tailor-made for the grill, too. In theory, the blazing-hot fire would produce even better results than a stove, rendering the scallop crusts extra-crisp, with a hint of smoke. Unfortunately, our outdoor efforts have suggested otherwise. By the time the scallops develop a good sear, they're usually overcooked and rubbery. And then there's the more general problem of trying to flip them: No matter how diligently we coat the scallops with oil before cooking, they inevitably end up sticking to the grate.

Maybe we should be more discouraged by those results, but we just can't shake the idea of savoring scallops at their best: lightly charred on the outside, tender and juicy inside, and tinged with smoke flavor. We set ourselves up with a charcoal kettle and dozens of scallops, determined to find a way around these pitfalls.

The test kitchen has already tackled the issue of shopping for scallops. Not only did we want the largest sea specimens we could find—sold as U10s or U20s, which indicates that there are about 10 to 20 per pound—but we would also make sure that we were purchasing "dry," not "wet," scallops. Although pricier and harder to find, dry scallops are worth seeking out because they have not been treated with a preservative solution of water and sodium tripolyphosphate, which gives them a soapy, metallic flavor and causes them to leach water during cooking, which in turn thwarts browning.

We also already had a trick to help ensure good browning: blotting the scallops dry between layers of kitchen towels before cooking. From there, we threaded the scallops onto doubled metal skewers, which ensured that all of the scallops could be flipped at the same time and wouldn't spin in the process. Then we brushed them with oil, seasoned them with salt and pepper, and considered our grill setup. To avoid overcooking the scallops but still develop a brown crust, we needed a quick blast of blazing heat. Since most grill grates aren't adjustable, we brainstormed ways to build the biggest fire possible. Our first thought was to load the grill with two chimneys full of briquettes, which brought the coals 2 inches from the grate. In four minutes, our scallops were beautifully seared, with succulent interiors. The only problem? Four hours later, the fire was still burning—a ridiculous waste of 200 briquettes.

Our next idea was a trick we borrowed from celebrity chef Alton Brown: He grills tuna steaks on a wire rack set directly atop a chimney full of hot coals. Searing food over such a small surface works fine for a piece of fish (if you don't mind the slightly precarious setup), but after grilling our sixth batch of scallops, we realized the idea was absurd for skewers.

Had we dismissed the oversize-fire idea too quickly? Two chimneys were too much, but what if we piled as many coals as possible into a single chimney (7 quarts instead of the usual 6) and made a fire in the center of the grill? We gave it a whirl, and the results were encouraging, though still not ideal. Without anything to contain them, the coals didn't form an even layer, meaning that the skewers set over the center of the fire cooked faster than those sitting over the perimeter. We needed a way to corral the coals and make the fire as level as possible. We rummaged through the test kitchen's grilling equipment and found the simple solution: a disposable aluminum pan. When grilling a roast, we often set one of these deep basins alongside the coals, where it can catch rendered fat, but this time we placed one in the center of the grill, piled in the lit coals from the chimney, and proceeded with our recipe. The result? Scallops with impressive char and juicy centers.

The only problem: We still couldn't get the scallops off the grill in one piece. Then we remembered that we already had a solution at hand. To keep fish fillets from sticking when grilled, the test kitchen uses a two-step approach: We superheat the grates by briefly covering them with a piece of aluminum foil and then paint them with multiple coats of oil. The latter step creates a super-slick cooking surface that won't instantly burn off, much like the coating on a well-seasoned cast-iron skillet. We applied both techniques here and, sure enough, the scallops released more easily. But if we were going to pay $18 per pound for these scallops, we had to do better.

That's when we decided to try coating the scallops with something more protective than just oil. One suggestion—a spice rub—didn't pan out, since the scallops' delicate flavor was lost and the spices themselves tended to burn. But a trick that another colleague developed to protect lean chicken breasts from drying out during pan-searing sounded at least a little promising: lightly coating the meat with a slurry of melted butter, flour, and cornstarch. This seemed worth trying, although we wondered if such a coating would actually hold up in the much-hotter fire of a grill. To our delight, it worked beautifully—with two quick tweaks. To save ourselves the trouble of melting the butter, we swapped it for vegetable oil, and we added a little sugar to the mixture to expedite browning. When we went to pull this last batch of scallops off the grill, they were crisp-crusted but moist and tender within—and they released without hesitation.

Everyone agreed that these scallops tasted just about perfect with nothing more than a squeeze of lemon. But since scallops aren't everyday fare for most of us, we whipped up a few boldly flavored vinaigrettes—one featuring bacon and brown butter, one with basil, a chile and lime version, and finally a barbecue-inspired variation—for more dressed-up occasions.

Grilled Sea Scallops

SERVES 4

We recommend buying "dry" scallops, those without chemical additives. Dry scallops will look ivory or pinkish and feel tacky; wet scallops look bright white and feel slippery. If using wet scallops, soak them in a solution of 1 quart water, ¼ cup lemon juice, and 2 tablespoons salt for 30 minutes before step 1, and do not season with salt in step 3. Double-skewering the scallops makes flipping easier. To skewer, thread 4 to 6 scallops onto one skewer and then place a second skewer through the scallops parallel to and about ¼ inch from the first. You will need eight to twelve 12-inch metal skewers for this recipe. You will also need a deep (at least 2¾ inches) disposable 13 by 9-inch aluminum roasting pan. Gas grills typically have enamel- or ceramic-coated cooking grates, so we do not recommend heating gas grills with aluminum foil pressed against the grates—the extreme heat levels can damage the grates.

- **1½ pounds large sea scallops, tendons removed**
- **1 (13 by 9-inch) disposable aluminum roasting pan**
- **2 tablespoons vegetable oil**
- **1 tablespoon all-purpose flour**
- **1 teaspoon cornstarch**
- **1 teaspoon sugar**
- **Salt and pepper**
- **Lemon wedges**
- **1 recipe vinaigrette (optional; recipes follow)**

1. Place scallops on rimmed baking sheet lined with clean kitchen towel. Place second clean kitchen towel on top of scallops and press gently on towel to blot liquid. Let scallops sit at room temperature, covered with towel, for 10 minutes. With scallops on work surface, thread onto doubled skewers so that flat sides will directly touch cooking grate, 4 to 6 scallops per doubled skewer. Return skewered scallops to towel-lined baking sheet; refrigerate, covered with second towel, while preparing grill.

2A. FOR A CHARCOAL GRILL: Loosely cover cooking grate with large piece of heavy-duty aluminum foil. Light large chimney starter mounded with charcoal briquettes (7 quarts) and allow to burn until coals are fully ignited and partially covered with thin layer of ash, about 25 minutes. Remove and discard foil. Meanwhile, poke twelve ½-inch holes in bottom of disposable aluminum roasting pan and place in center of grill. Empty coals into pan.

2B. FOR A GAS GRILL: Turn all burners to high, cover, and heat grill until hot, about 15 minutes.

3. While grill is heating, whisk oil, flour, cornstarch, and sugar together in bowl. Remove towels from scallops. Brush both sides of skewered scallops with oil mixture and season with salt and pepper.

4. Clean cooking grate, then repeatedly rub grate with well-oiled paper towels until grate is black and glossy, 5 to 10 times. Place skewered scallops directly over hot coals (covered if using gas). Cook without moving scallops until lightly browned, 2½ to 4 minutes. Carefully flip skewers and continue to cook until second side is browned, sides of scallops are firm, and centers are opaque, 2 to 4 minutes longer. Serve immediately with lemon wedges and vinaigrette, if using.

Bacon and Brown Butter Vinaigrette

MAKES ABOUT 1 CUP; ENOUGH FOR 1 RECIPE GRILLED SEA SCALLOPS

- **8 tablespoons unsalted butter**
- **1 slice bacon, diced**
- **3 tablespoons sherry vinegar**
- **3 tablespoons vegetable oil**
- **1 shallot, minced**
- **1 tablespoon maple syrup**
- **2 teaspoons Dijon mustard**

1. Heat 6 tablespoons butter in 10-inch skillet over medium-high heat until melted. Continue to cook, swirling pan constantly until butter is dark golden brown and has nutty aroma, 1 to 3 minutes. Remove skillet from heat and transfer browned butter to large heatproof bowl. Stir remaining 2 tablespoons butter into hot butter to melt. Wipe skillet clean with paper towels.

2. Cook bacon in now-empty skillet over medium heat, stirring occasionally, until crisp, 5 to 7 minutes. Using slotted spoon, transfer bacon to paper towel–lined plate. Pour off any bacon fat into browned butter. Add vinegar, oil, shallot, maple syrup, and mustard to browned butter mixture; whisk until emulsified. Stir in reserved bacon.

Basil Vinaigrette

MAKES ABOUT 1 CUP; ENOUGH FOR 1 RECIPE GRILLED SEA SCALLOPS

- **1 cup packed fresh basil leaves**
- **3 tablespoons minced fresh chives**
- **2 tablespoons champagne vinegar**
- **2 garlic cloves, minced**
- **2 teaspoons sugar**
- **1 teaspoon salt**
- **½ teaspoon pepper**
- **⅔ cup vegetable oil**

Pulse basil, chives, vinegar, garlic, sugar, salt, and pepper in blender until roughly chopped, 5 to 7 pulses. With blender running, slowly drizzle in oil until emulsified, about 1 minute, scraping down blender jar as necessary.

Chile-Lime Vinaigrette

MAKES ABOUT 1 CUP; ENOUGH FOR 1 RECIPE GRILLED SEA SCALLOPS

- **1 teaspoon grated lime zest plus 3 tablespoons juice (2 limes)**
- **1 tablespoon sriracha sauce**
- **2 tablespoons honey**
- **2 teaspoons fish sauce**
- **½ cup vegetable oil**

Whisk lime zest and juice, sriracha sauce, honey, and fish sauce together in bowl until combined. Whisking constantly, slowly drizzle in oil until emulsified.

Barbecue Sauce Vinaigrette

MAKES ABOUT 1 CUP; ENOUGH FOR 1 RECIPE GRILLED SEA SCALLOPS

- **3 tablespoons barbecue sauce**
- **2 tablespoons cider vinegar**
- **1 tablespoon ketchup**
- **2 teaspoons sugar**
- **½ teaspoon salt**
- **½ cup vegetable oil**

Whisk barbecue sauce, vinegar, ketchup, sugar, and salt together in bowl until combined. Whisking constantly, slowly drizzle in oil until emulsified.

NOTES FROM THE TEST KITCHEN

DID YOU BUY "WET" SCALLOPS?

We strongly recommend purchasing dry scallops (those without chemical additives). To determine if your scallops are dry or wet, place one scallop on a paper towel-lined, microwave-safe plate and microwave on high power for 15 seconds. If the scallop is dry, it will exude very little water. If it is wet, there will be a sizable ring of moisture on the paper towel. In this case, soak the scallops in a solution of 1 quart cold water, ¼ cup lemon juice, and 2 tablespoons salt for 30 minutes to help disguise any chemical taste before proceeding with step 1, and season only with pepper in step 3.

RATING GRILLING BASKETS FOR WHOLE FISH

Fish baskets can make the task of wrestling whole fish off the grill a lot less dicey. These oblong, two-piece metal cages keep skin from sticking to the grill and corral your catch for easier flipping. We grilled large whole striped bass and smaller whole red snapper in six heavy-gauge wire baskets costing $11 to $25, most featuring nonstick coatings and two with removable handles. Only the two largest baskets easily cradled a 2½-pound striped bass; of these, only one also allowed successful turning of fish as small as ¾ pound (the other had wide-set wires that let little fish get away). And because this model's handle is removable, we could lay the basket flat and, if necessary, close the grill lid. A removable handle was a must for another reason: It allowed the basket to fit easily in the dishwasher. Brands are listed in order of preference. See www.americastestkitchen.com for updates to this testing.

RECOMMENDED

CHARCOAL COMPANION Ultimate Nonstick Fish-Grilling Basket (model #CC3036)
PRICE: $24.99 **CAPACITY:** ★★★ **MANEUVERABILITY:** ★★½
STICKING: ★★★ **CLEANUP:** ★★★
COMMENTS: A heavy-gauge metal cage treated with a black nonstick coating, this large fish-shaped basket easily accommodated a 2½-pound whole striped bass as well as smaller fish, thanks to wires set less than 2 inches apart. The two pieces latched firmly together and kept the fish securely in place during turning, and the nonstick coating released the fish with the skin intact. The perpendicular removable handle, which is made of rosewood, stayed cool, felt sturdy, and allowed the cage to fit in the dishwasher.

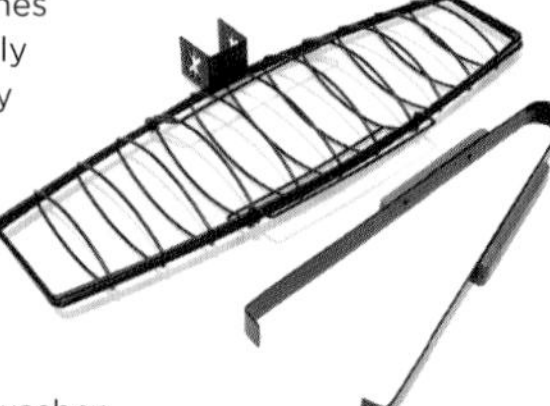

NOT RECOMMENDED

CUISINART Simply Grilling Nonstick Fish Fillet Basket (model #CNFB-432)
PRICE: $12.99 **CAPACITY:** ★ **MANEUVERABILITY:** ★★★
STICKING: ★★★ **CLEANUP:** ★★
COMMENTS: There was a lot to like about this basket: It closed securely and held the fish tightly in place, and its rubber-coated handle made the tool easy to flip. But it was too small for fish larger than 1 pound, which severely limits its usefulness. (If you can't make enough fish to adequately feed two people, what's the point?) Furthermore, the handle, which can't be removed, protruded past the edge of the grill, raising the end of the basket (and the fish) above the grates and preventing the lid from closing.

ONWARD Grill Pro Nonstick Fish Basket (model #24794)
PRICE: $11.16 **CAPACITY:** ★ **MANEUVERABILITY:** ★★
STICKING: ★★★ **CLEANUP:** ★★
COMMENTS: As with the other small grill baskets, this model's handle extended past the edge of the grill, raising part of the fish 2 inches from the grate, and it could only accommodate small fish (no more than 1 pound). Its closing mechanism was also faulty, making us fear that the cage might open as we flipped.

NOT RECOMMENDED *(cont.)*

STEVEN RAICHLEN Best of Barbecue Nonstick Large Fish Grilling Basket (model #SR8073)
PRICE: $24.99 **CAPACITY:** ★ **MANEUVERABILITY:** ★
STICKING: ★★★ **CLEANUP:** ★★★
COMMENTS: Although large enough to hold a 2½-pound whole fish, the cage on this model was hard to securely close because the latches did not line up (a backup sample shared the problem). The removable handle has a fussy clip that must be held open to reattach it, putting our fingers too close to the fire. The wires on this basket are very far apart (at 2½ inches, more than half an inch farther apart than those of our winner), which let any fish weighing less than ¾ pound slip right through when we turned the basket.

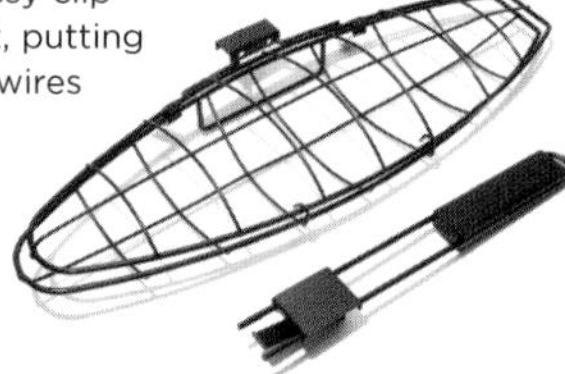

OUTSET 22-Inch Fish Basket (model #QN74)
PRICE: $25 **CAPACITY:** ★ **MANEUVERABILITY:** ★★
STICKING: ★★★ **CLEANUP:** ★★
COMMENTS: This small basket uses a copper-colored nonstick coating, which may account for its higher price but made no perceptible difference in how the fish came out. The design resembles all the other smaller fish baskets, with a nonremovable handle at one end that rests on the grill edge, raising part of the fish away from the grates. For a device that can hold only smaller fish, it's not worth the price.

GRILLFINITY Large Fish Basket (model #760105)
PRICE: $16.50 **CAPACITY:** ★ **MANEUVERABILITY:** ★★
STICKING: ★ **CLEANUP:** ★
COMMENTS: This basket uses the same design as the rest of the smaller models in our lineup, except its stainless-steel wires lack a nonstick coating. Even fish coated with oil before grilling got stuck on the wires of the cage, which, when opened after grilling, ripped pieces of skin away and compromised the appeal of the finished dish. The wires required scrubbing, even after going through the dishwasher.

INNOVATIVE KITCHEN GADGETS

There's cookware that's absolutely essential in every kitchen—think nonstick skillet, rubber spatula, and chef's knife—and then there are those that may not be must-haves, but are worth a second look. These innovative gadgets sold us on both their usability and fun design. See www.americastestkitchen.com for updates to this testing.

SILICONE SALT PIG

The Prepara Pop Savor ($19.99) improves upon the design of a traditional "salt pig"—a small, hooded ceramic vessel that cooks use to grab salt for seasoning—and fashions the cover from soft silicone to make a closeable lid that keeps out dirt and moisture. To test its usefulness, we filled the cavity with salt, sugar, and ice cream sprinkles and left the container next to the stove while frying a pound of bacon. As promised, the durable "pop" top easily flipped open and kept its contents shielded from splattered grease when closed. The ceramic base has a 1-cup capacity and the included ½-teaspoon measure is accurate and fits nicely in the silicone loop at the rear of the container. Our only gripe? The 3½-inch opening was a little cramped for a few testers with large hands.

WINNER: PREPARA POP SAVOR

COMPACT SELTZER MAKER

Home seltzer makers that transform still water into sparkling promise clear advantages: no more heavy bottles to lug home from the store or clutter up the landfill. But many models cost upward of $100 and take up precious counter space. Now there's a more affordable and easier-to-store alternative. The iSi Twist 'n Sparkle ($49.95) has a contained carbonation system, so it doesn't require a whole station atop the counter. Instead, it uses a twist-top design to release carbon dioxide bubbles into a carafe holding 4 cups of water, juice, or any other nondairy beverage. Just take note of which CO_2 chargers you buy; this seltzer maker runs on single-use chargers ($19.95 for twenty-four 4-cup units, or about 20 cents per cup), but there are equally effective generic chargers available that work just as well for a fraction of the cost.

WINNER: ISI TWIST 'N SPARKLE

QUICK POPSICLE MAKER

No matter your age or the temperature outside, popsicles make a refreshing treat. We recently came across the Zoku Quick Pop Maker ($49.95), which makes popsicles in under 10 minutes. When we poured a homemade fruit blend into the three 2-ounce slots, it took just seven minutes for the mixture to turn rock solid—the cue to insert the special key in each pop handle to release the treat. The process can be repeated for two more rounds of pops (nine pops in total) before the unit needs to be refrozen; note that although the first round of pops is quite speedy, pops in the second and third rounds took six to 10 extra minutes to freeze. While we love the quick gratification this nifty gadget provides, it doesn't entirely eliminate the need for planning ahead: The console, which contains a proprietary liquid that gets colder than ice, must be placed in the freezer 24 hours before use.

WINNER: ZOKU QUICK POP MAKER

SILICONE MICROWAVE LID

Heating up splatter-prone food, like soups or saucy dishes, in the microwave can be annoying—if you don't cover every inch of the container, you're guaranteed to spend some time cleaning up. We found a whimsical and functional way to avoid this hassle: The Japanese-made Piggy Steamer ($18), a 7-inch circle of thin silicone with a thicker, raised center shaped like the face of a pig. For microwave reheating, we rested it directly on rice on a plate and across the tops of bowls of soup and pasta sauce. The rice became steamy without drying out; the soup and pasta sauce emerged piping hot, and the lid kept the microwave splatter-free. The Piggy Steamer is unbreakable and stays cool, with protruding ears that serve as convenient handles. (The nostrils vent steam—and can be used for lifting the lid with chopsticks.) This funny, floppy lid easily washes clean and is also effective for opening jar lids.

WINNER: PIGGY STEAMER

America
TEST

Mediterranean SPECIALS

CHAPTER 19

THE RECIPES

Grilled Beef Kebabs with Lemon and Rosemary Marinade

Grilled Beef Kebabs with North African Marinade

Greek Spinach and Feta Pie (Spanakopita)

SCIENCE DESK

A New Way to Grill High and Low

TASTING LAB

Greek Yogurt

Bryan shows how squeezing the excess water from the spinach in our Spanakopita helps the layers of phyllo bake up light and crisp.

WE HAVE A WEAKNESS FOR MEDITERRANEAN FOOD—PARTICULARLY crisp, juicy kebabs and rich, flaky spanakopita—but unfortunately, mediocre versions of these dishes abound stateside. That's not to say we don't still gobble them up, but we're frequently disappointed. Really great renditions do exist, but a kebab joint or authentic Greek pastry shop isn't always right around the corner. So we couldn't help but wonder: Could we have any success creating these favorites ourselves? Beef kebabs seem simple enough, but we already knew from experience that grilling relatively small chunks of meat usually results in a charred exterior and tough, chewy interior. For thoroughly seasoned meat with a thick, caramelized crust and tender-crisp vegetables, we were pretty sure that the typical marinade—and the typical grill setup—would have to go.

Ideally, spanakopita is a hot and flavorful one-dish meal encased in a crispy, buttery crust. A filling of tender spinach and tangy feta is accented with plenty of lemon, garlic, and a healthy dose of fresh herbs, then layered between a flaky phyllo crust. Yet most versions (at least in this country) fall flat—a Greek tragedy in need of a happy ending. We set out to create an authentic-tasting version of spanakopita without making it a multi-day project.

GRILLED BEEF KEBABS WITH LEMON AND ROSEMARY MARINADE

BEEF KEBABS

WHY THIS RECIPE WORKS: Most beef kebabs are disappointing, with overcooked meat and vegetables that are either raw or mushy. We wanted to develop a foolproof approach to creating meaty kebabs that looked and tasted like the real thing: chunks of beef with a thick, caramelized char on the outside and a juicy, pink interior, all thoroughly seasoned by a marinade and paired with nicely browned, tender-firm vegetables. For the meat, we chose well-marbled steak tips, with their beefy flavor and tender texture. For the marinade, we included salt for moisture, oil for flavor, and sugar for browning. For even more depth, we used tomato paste, a host of seasonings and herbs, and beef broth. We chose three grill favorites for the vegetables: peppers, onions, and zucchini. Grilling the beef kebabs and vegetables on separate skewers over a two-level fire, which has hotter and cooler areas, allowed us to cook the vegetables over a lower temperature while the beef seared over the hotter area.

IF YOU'VE EVER HAD A KEBAB FROM AN AUTHENTIC kebab joint, you'll understand why the tradition of skewering meat and searing it over a blazing live fire has persisted through the centuries. The presentation is spectacular—the kebabs arrive on a skewer the size of a sword. Even more impressive is the beef: meaty 2-inch chunks with a thick, caramelized char on the outside and a juicy pink interior, all of it thoroughly seasoned by a marinade.

Over the years, we've had mixed success trying to re-create that perfect combination of flavor and fire. Too often, our attempts resemble the meat-and-vegetable sticks we grew up eating at family barbecues, with beef that's either chalky with black spots or practically incinerated with a red, raw interior. And the vegetables? These usually turn out torched on the outside and still crunchy on the inside. We were determined to nail a foolproof approach to putting that smoke, char, and flavor into the beef and achieving nicely browned, tender-firm vegetables at the same time.

Our testing started at the butcher case, where we rounded up five possible cuts of meat for skewering, ranging from bottom round to tenderloin. Virtually every recipe we consulted advised cutting the meat into 1-inch chunks. Instead, we took a cue from the kebab restaurants we've frequented, cubing the meat into generous 2-inch pieces. We then skewered the cubes and seasoned them with salt and pepper (we'd worry about the veggies and a marinade later) before throwing them onto the fire—for the moment, 6 quarts of briquettes spread into a single layer. Lean, pricey tenderloin was a waste of money, since tasters found it predictably bland, while bottom round was too chewy. The more marbled cuts—skirt steak, blade steak, and steak tips—all boasted respectable flavor, but the looser-grained steak tips outdid the others in both beefiness and tender texture.

As for a marinade, the test kitchen has developed a number of tricks to maximize its impact, so we had a head start. First, we've found that salt is one of the few ingredients that penetrate to season the center of the meat, so we use a lot of it. As it does in a simple brine, salt also swells and dissolves some of the proteins, allowing them to hold on to their moisture for juicier results. Second, we always include oil. Though it won't seep beyond the meat's surface, oil is a key player when herbs and spices are part of the mix, since their flavor compounds are mostly fat-soluble. Third, we add a little sugar to lend a hint of sweetness and help the meat develop flavorful browning.

Soy sauce is a common choice for the liquid base of the marinade (if we used it, it would replace the salt), and for good reason: It's packed with flavor enhancers called glutamates that can also travel deep into meat chunks to make them taste more savory. But we find that meat soaked in soy sauce always ends up tasting like teriyaki; we wanted a more neutral base. As we mentally ticked off other common pantry staples, we thought of tomato paste, also full of glutamates. Though an unorthodox addition to marinade, its fruity taste could be just the ticket for a soaking liquid thinned with water. We used the blender to mix up a simple marinade of thinned tomato paste, onion, oil, salt, pepper, sugar, rosemary, lemon zest, and roughly half a head of garlic.

Next question: How long should the beef marinate? After some trial and error, we found just an hour gave the chunks all the seasoning they needed. As for our tomato paste–based marinade, tasters found it amplified the beef's meaty flavor nicely without overpowering the other seasonings. We wondered, though, if instead of thinning the tomato paste with water we should try a more flavorful liquid like beef broth.

When we made this simple swap, tasters raved about the new depth of flavor. Intrigued, we consulted our science editor. It turns out that many commercial broths (including our new favorite, Rachael Ray Stock-in-a-Box) contain yeast extract, a powerhouse of not one but two kinds of flavor enhancers: glutamates and nucleotides. The latter work in synergy with the naturally occurring glutamates in meat to ramp up savory taste by as much as 20 times. Even the tiny amount of yeast extract in ⅓ cup of beef broth was enough to impress tasters.

For the vegetables, we singled out three grill favorites—peppers, onions, and zucchini—and marinated them for 30 minutes. Our 2-inch beef chunks were staying on a hot fire for 12 to 16 minutes, which gave the vegetables ample time to turn tender, but it also ensured a blackened exterior that tasted like charcoal. Clearly, the veggies would do better cooked over more gentle heat. The obvious solution was to place the two components on separate skewers and build a two-level fire, where they could cook simultaneously but over their own optimal degree of heat.

Our usual approach to a modified two-level fire (half the coals banked to one side of the kettle) wouldn't work, because the beef skewers occupied more than half the grill space. Instead, we tweaked the two-level setup by spreading all the coals in the center of the grill (with veggies no longer a consideration, we piled on a seventh quart of coals to further enhance the char on the beef), leaving a 2-inch gap between the grill wall and the charcoal. The heat flamed up the center, bonfire-style, and charred the beef pieces perfectly. Meanwhile, the veggies rested on the perimeter of the coals, where they slowly bronzed and charred at the tips over the less intense heat (for a gas grill, we simply turned down the heat after the beef skewers came off the grill). At last, in our own backyard we could enjoy kebabs as good as any we've had at an authentic kebab joint.

NOTES FROM THE TEST KITCHEN

MARINADE POWER BROKERS

Contrary to popular opinion, almost none of the flavors in a marinade penetrate to the center of the meat, no matter how long you soak it. But studies published in the *Journal of Food Science* indicate that salts—ordinary table salt as well as sodium glutamates, the naturally occurring flavor enhancers found in many foods—are the exception, traveling far into meat chunks and beefing up taste as they go. With this in mind, we created a turbo-charged marinade with three key ingredients:

SALT: Not only does it penetrate meat to thoroughly season it, salt also swells and dissolves some of the proteins, allowing them to retain juices.

TOMATO PASTE: This condiment is a potent source of naturally occurring glutamates. Just 3 tablespoons ramp up savory flavor.

BEEF BROTH: Many commercial beef broths contain yeast extract, a rich source of two flavor-enhancing molecules: glutamates and nucleotides. The latter amplify flavor 20-fold, so that even ⅓ cup of broth in the marinade has a big impact.

Grilled Beef Kebabs with Lemon and Rosemary Marinade

SERVES 4 TO 6

If you can't find sirloin steak tips, sometimes labeled "flap meat," substitute 2½ pounds blade steak; if using blade steak, cut each steak in half to remove the gristle. You will need four 12-inch metal skewers for this recipe. If you have long, thin pieces of meat, roll or fold them into approximate 2-inch cubes before skewering.

MARINADE

- **1 onion, chopped**
- **⅓ cup beef broth**
- **⅓ cup vegetable oil**
- **3 tablespoons tomato paste**
- **6 garlic cloves, chopped**
- **2 tablespoons chopped fresh rosemary**
- **2 teaspoons grated lemon zest**
- **2 teaspoons salt**
- **1½ teaspoons sugar**
- **¾ teaspoon pepper**

BEEF AND VEGETABLES

- 2 **pounds sirloin steak tips, trimmed and cut into 2-inch chunks**
- 1 **large zucchini or summer squash, halved lengthwise and sliced 1 inch thick**
- 1 **large red or green bell pepper, stemmed, seeded, and cut into 1½-inch pieces**
- 1 **large red or sweet onion, peeled, halved lengthwise, each half cut into 4 wedges and each wedge cut crosswise into thirds**

1. FOR THE MARINADE: Process all ingredients in blender until smooth, about 45 seconds. Transfer ¾ cup marinade to large bowl and set aside.

2. FOR THE BEEF AND VEGETABLES: Place remaining marinade and beef in 1-gallon zipper-lock bag and toss to coat; press out as much air as possible and seal bag. Refrigerate for 1 to 2 hours, flipping bag every 30 minutes.

3. Add zucchini, bell pepper, and onion to bowl with reserved marinade and toss to coat. Cover and let sit at room temperature for at least 30 minutes.

4. Remove beef from bag and pat dry with paper towels. Thread beef tightly onto two 12-inch metal skewers. Thread vegetables onto two 12-inch metal skewers, in alternating pattern of zucchini, bell pepper, and onion.

5A. FOR A CHARCOAL GRILL: Open bottom vent completely. Light large chimney starter mounded with charcoal briquettes (7 quarts). When top coals are partially covered with ash, pour evenly over center of grill, leaving 2-inch gap between grill wall and charcoal. Set cooking grate in place, cover, and open lid vent completely. Heat grill until hot, about 5 minutes.

5B. FOR A GAS GRILL: Turn all burners to high, cover, and heat grill until hot, about 15 minutes.

6. Clean and oil cooking grate. Place vegetable skewers on grill (near edge of coals if using charcoal and turn burners to low if using gas) and cook (covered if using gas), turning kebabs every 4 to 5 minutes, until tender and lightly charred, 17 to 21 minutes. Transfer skewers to serving platter and tent loosely with aluminum foil.

7. Meanwhile, place meat skewers on grill (in center if using charcoal) and cook (covered if using gas), turning kebabs every 3 to 4 minutes, until well browned and beef registers 120 to 125 degrees (for medium-rare) or 130 to 135 degrees (for medium), 12 to 16 minutes. Transfer meat skewers to platter with vegetable skewers, tent loosely with foil, and let rest for 5 to 10 minutes before serving.

VARIATION

Grilled Beef Kebabs with North African Marinade

Substitute 20 cilantro sprigs, 2 teaspoons paprika, 1½ teaspoons ground cumin, and ½ teaspoon cayenne pepper for lemon zest and rosemary.

SCIENCE DESK

A NEW WAY TO GRILL HIGH AND LOW

Meat and vegetables need different levels of heat to grill properly, so it's no wonder they cook unevenly on the same skewer. We created a new approach to direct and indirect heat—placing veggie skewers at the perimeter of the grill and meat skewers over the center of the coals—that allows each component to cook at its own pace.

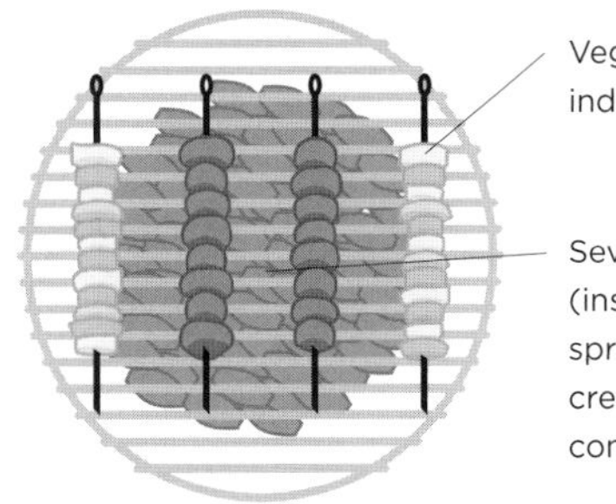

Vegetables cook over indirect heat on outer edge.

Seven quarts of charcoal (instead of the usual 6) spread in center of grill create a large area of direct concentrated heat for meat.

GREEK SPINACH AND FETA PIE

WHY THIS RECIPE WORKS: The roots of this savory spinach and feta pie, with its trademark layers of flaky, crisp phyllo, run deep in Greek culture, yet most stateside versions are nothing more than soggy layers of phyllo with a sparse, bland filling. We wanted a casserole-style pie with a perfect balance of zesty spinach filling and shatteringly crisp phyllo crust—and we didn't want to spend all day in the kitchen. Using store-bought phyllo was an easy timesaver. Among the various spinach options (baby, frozen, mature curly-leaf), tasters favored the bold flavor of fresh curly-leaf spinach that had been microwaved, coarsely chopped, then squeezed of excess moisture. Crumbling the feta into fine pieces ensured a salty tang in every bite, while the addition of Greek yogurt buffered the assertiveness of the feta. We found that Pecorino Romano (a good stand-in for a traditional Greek hard sheep's-milk cheese) added complexity to the filling and, when sprinkled between the sheets of phyllo, helped the flaky layers hold together. Using a baking sheet rather than a baking dish allowed excess moisture to easily evaporate, ensuring a crisp crust.

SPANAKOPITA'S ROOTS RUN DEEP IN GREEK CULTURE, and it's not hard to understand the enduring appeal. This savory spinach "pie" trades on a flaky phyllo crust—wafer-thin sheets of oven-crisped dough—that gives way to a delectably moist filling of tender greens and salty feta, kicked up with lemon, garlic, herbs, and spices. What's not to love?

Plenty, at least stateside. The lackluster versions served at unambitious Greek-American diners bear more resemblance to lukewarm lawn clippings encased in a wet paper bag than the crispy-pillowy pride of Hellenic home cooking. A step up from there, the tidy spinach-and-phyllo turnovers found in supermarket freezers at least get the crispiness right. Yet the paltry ratio of filling to buttery crust places these tasty bites squarely in hors d'oeuvre territory.

Our goal was to bring back the features that made spanakopita such a mealtime favorite in the first place—a casserole-style pie with a perfect balance of zesty spinach filling to shatteringly crisp phyllo crust—and we didn't want it to require an all-day stint in the kitchen. To that end, we decided to go with frozen phyllo sheets rather than homemade pastry: we wanted a weeknight meal, not a weeklong project.

Most recipes for spanakopita follow the same basic series of steps: Transparently thin sheets of phyllo—unleavened dough made from flour, water, and lemon juice or vinegar—are layered to form a bottom crust, usually in a 13 by 9-inch baking pan. Each layer receives a brush of melted butter to contribute rich flavor and boost browning. On top of that goes the cheesy spinach filling, followed by another layering of delicate phyllo sheets, which forms the top crust. Baked at a high temperature (to ensure a golden-brown top), the piping-hot pie is cooled and sliced into serving portions.

To get our bearings, we baked several versions that we came across in various Greek cookbooks (as well as a few family recipes kindly offered up from colleagues), confirming that store-bought frozen phyllo dough was plenty reliable, save for some niggling texture issues involving the bottom crust. (We would deal with those later.) But the filling, by contrast, needed some serious work.

We decided to start with the main ingredient—the spinach—and come up with the perfect filling from there. To our surprise, many of the recipes we came across in our research called for canned spinach—but knowing the sad, lifeless state of most canned fruits and vegetables, we refused to go there. Instead, we narrowed our options to frozen spinach, fresh baby leaves, and fresh adult greens. After loading up our cart, we headed back to the test kitchen for a daylong spinach-tasting extravaganza.

Using a bare-bones filling of spinach, feta, and egg (for binding), we needed but one test to rule out frozen. The weak flavor and woody, stringy texture were nonstarters. In the end, tasters favored the bolder flavor of the mature fresh spinach. Happily, all the methods we tried for precooking it (sautéing, boiling, microwaving, steaming)

GREEK SPINACH AND FETA PIE

worked well for these hearty leaves, so we went with the push-button convenience of the microwave. Follow-up tests revealed that coarsely chopping the spinach and thoroughly squeezing out its excess moisture yielded superior texture and maximum flavor.

With the green stuff in good shape, we moved on to the other major component: the dairy. Feta rides shotgun to spinach in spanakopita, and the right amount can make or break the dish. We found that simply crumbling the rich, pungent cheese (in the end, 12 ounces) into fine pieces helped it spread evenly through the sea of green, ensuring a salty tang in every bite. To buffer the assertiveness of the feta and add textural contrast, many recipes incorporate soft dairy into the mix as well. We tried everything. Cream cheese gave the spanakopita the consistency of spinach dip; ricotta and cottage cheese cooked up into rubbery curds. Sour cream and yogurt fared better, but thicker Greek yogurt—go figure!—turned out the best batch to date.

Some of the recipes we tested even included a third dairy component in the filling: a hard sheep's-milk cheese called *kefalograviera,* which builds complexity. We wanted depth of flavor, but not the hassle of scouring specialty markets for such an obscure item. In the end, another, far more readily available hard sheep's-milk cheese, Pecorino Romano, made a stand-up substitute.

A few final flavor tweaks: Grassy scallions trumped onions, leeks, and shallots; the more-robust flavor of raw minced garlic beat out sautéed; a generous scattering of dill and mint provided a burst of freshness. A little nutmeg, cayenne, and a dose of lemon (juice plus grated zest) added fragrant warmth and brightness, respectively.

With a filling worthy of Mount Olympus, we were ready to move on to that one maddening texture issue: the crust. The top crust was flaky and golden brown. But no matter how we sliced it, the bottom crust ended up soggy. We tried adjusting the oven temperature, to no avail. Had we missed a clue during our initial survey of spanakopita recipes, too distracted by the lousy fillings to pick up on some clever trick? No—reviewing our notes, we realized every recipe we had tested was plagued by the same problem.

In fact, the store-bought frozen turnovers were the only versions to achieve crisp bottom crusts. Though we were reluctant to take on the labor-intensive task of turning spanakopita into bite-size triangles for the purposes of weeknight dinner (the triangles didn't really add up to a meal anyway), we decided to bake a batch just to see what made them work so well. Aside from their cunning shape, the big difference here was the ratio of phyllo to filling in each bite. While not nearly enough filling for our purposes, it was hard to argue with the crispiness of the triangles.

But could adjusting the ratio of phyllo to filling be the key to success in a casserole version as well? Studying our

NOTES FROM THE TEST KITCHEN

SPANAKOPITA GONE WRONG

The average square of spinach pie served up in a Greek diner is so flawed, we're surprised anyone ever orders it.

1. PROBLEM: Top sheets of phyllo fall off when pie is sliced, leaving filling virtually exposed
SOLUTION: A sprinkling of grated Pecorino Romano between some of the top layers of phyllo glues them together more firmly than the usual butter alone, so the top crust stays put.

2. PROBLEM: Dull-tasting, woody filling made with frozen spinach
SOLUTION: We use chopped fresh mature spinach precooked in the microwave, squeezed of excess moisture, and brightened with fresh herbs, lemon juice, and zest.

3. PROBLEM: Soggy bottom crust
SOLUTION: A thinner layer of filling cuts down on moisture, and baking the pie on a baking sheet helps the crust can crisp up.

current recipe, we measured the height of the spinach layer: just shy of 2 inches. We supposed dialing it back was worth a shot. But when we tried this, we didn't start seeing increased crispiness on the bottom of the crust until the filling was reduced to almost half its original volume—and at that point, we were cutting into the number of servings. Plus the bottom, while improved, was still nowhere close to where we wanted it to be.

Then it occurred to us that no matter how much we reduced the filling, the thick, high walls of the baking dish would still trap any moisture coming off it, in effect helping to "steam" the crust instead of crisping it. So, what if we moved the pie to the flat surface of a baking sheet, which would allow excess liquid to evaporate far more readily? Sure enough, this proved to be an excellent move.

For starters, the assembly was easier. In the baking dish, the phyllo sheets, which were bigger than the vessel, would bunch up on the sides and corners. (And trimming them to fit was far too fussy.) A typical 18 by 13-inch baking sheet, on the other hand, was plenty big enough to accommodate the full size of the 14 by 9-inch dough sheets. We layered 10 pieces of phyllo for the bottom crust, carefully painting each sheet with butter, then spread our spinach filling over top, which was now about ¾ inch thick—more than the paltry smear in those spanakopita triangles but less than half as much as the filling in the casserole dish. We covered the spinach with eight more buttered layers of phyllo. As a last-minute brainstorm, we also took the grated Pecorino Romano we were using in the filling and sprinkled it between the first six layers instead, which helped glue them together and fixed the annoying, recurrent problem of having this tissue-thin pastry slide off when sliced. We scored the top few layers of phyllo with the tip of our knife to make it easier to cut once cooked, and transferred the baking sheet to a 425-degree oven.

Twenty-five minutes later, what emerged from the oven was a beautiful spanakopita with crispness on the top and—sure enough—on the bottom. In the end, all this classic needed was a modern twist to make it great. What started as a Greek tragedy was now a real showstopper.

Greek Spinach and Feta Pie (Spanakopita)

SERVES 6 TO 8 AS A MAIN COURSE OR 10 TO 12 AS AN APPETIZER

It is important to rinse the feta; this step removes some of its salty brine, which would overwhelm the spinach. Full-fat sour cream can be substituted for whole-milk Greek yogurt. Phyllo dough is also available in larger 18 by 14-inch sheets; if using, cut them in half to make 14 by 9-inch sheets. Don't thaw the phyllo in the microwave; let it sit in the refrigerator overnight or on the countertop for 4 to 5 hours.

FILLING

- **1¼ pounds curly-leaf spinach, stemmed**
- **¼ cup water**
- **12 ounces feta cheese, rinsed, patted dry, and crumbled into fine pieces (3 cups)**
- **¾ cup whole-milk Greek yogurt**
- **4 scallions, sliced thin**
- **2 large eggs, beaten**
- **¼ cup minced fresh mint**
- **2 tablespoons minced fresh dill**
- **3 garlic cloves, minced**
- **1 teaspoon grated lemon zest plus 1 tablespoon juice**
- **1 teaspoon ground nutmeg**
- **½ teaspoon pepper**
- **¼ teaspoon salt**
- **⅛ teaspoon cayenne pepper**

PHYLLO LAYERS

- **7 tablespoons unsalted butter, melted**
- **8 ounces (14 by 9-inch) phyllo, thawed**
- **1½ ounces Pecorino Romano cheese, grated (¾ cup)**
- **2 teaspoons sesame seeds (optional)**

1. FOR THE FILLING: Place spinach and water in large bowl. Cover and microwave until spinach is wilted and decreased in volume by half, about 5 minutes. Using potholders, remove bowl from microwave and keep covered for 1 minute. Transfer spinach to colander. Using back of rubber spatula, gently press spinach against colander to release excess liquid. Transfer spinach to cutting board and chop coarse. Transfer spinach to clean kitchen

towel and squeeze to remove excess water. Place drained spinach in large bowl. Add feta, yogurt, scallions, eggs, mint, dill, garlic, lemon zest and juice, nutmeg, pepper, salt, and cayenne and mix until thoroughly combined.

2. FOR THE PHYLLO LAYERS: Adjust oven rack to lower-middle position and heat oven to 425 degrees. Line rimmed baking sheet with parchment paper. Using pastry brush, lightly brush 14 by 9-inch rectangle in center of parchment with melted butter to cover area same size as phyllo. Lay 1 phyllo sheet on buttered parchment and brush thoroughly with melted butter. Repeat with 9 more phyllo sheets, brushing each with butter (you should have total of 10 layers of phyllo).

3. Spread spinach mixture evenly over phyllo, leaving ¼-inch border on all sides. Cover spinach with 6 more phyllo sheets, brushing each with butter and sprinkling each with about 2 tablespoons Pecorino cheese. Lay 2 more phyllo sheets on top, brushing each with butter (do not sprinkle these layers with Pecorino).

4. Working from center outward, use palms of your hands to compress layers and press out any air pockets. Using sharp knife, score spanakopita through top 3 layers of phyllo into 24 equal pieces. Sprinkle with sesame seeds, if using. Bake until phyllo is golden and crisp, 20 to 25 minutes. Cool on baking sheet 10 minutes, or up to 2 hours. Slide spanakopita, still on parchment, onto cutting board. Cut into squares and serve.

TO MAKE AHEAD: Filling can be made up to 24 hours in advance and refrigerated. Freeze assembled, unbaked spanakopita on baking sheet, wrapped well in plastic wrap, or cut spanakopita in half crosswise and freeze smaller sections on plate. Bake spanakopita frozen, increasing baking time by 5 to 10 minutes.

NOTES FROM THE TEST KITCHEN

TIPS FOR TAMING PHYLLO

Frozen packaged phyllo dough functions as light, flaky pastry in traditional Greek dishes such as baklava and spanakopita and as a ready-made tart crust or wrapper for both sweet and savory fillings. But the tendency of these paper-thin sheets to tear, dry out quickly, or stick together can be maddening. Here are some tips for mastering this delicate dough.

1. TRIM STUCK EDGES: When phyllo sheets emerge from the box fused at their edges, don't try to separate the sheets. Instead, trim the fused portion and discard.

2. COVER WITH PLASTIC AND A DAMP TOWEL: The usual approach to prevent phyllo from cracking is to cover the stack with a damp towel. But it's easy to turn the dough sticky. We cover the stack with plastic wrap and then a damp towel.

3. STAGGER THE CRACKS: Some sheets of phyllo may crack and even tear while still in the box. Don't worry about rips, just make sure to adjust the orientation of the sheets as you stack them so that cracks in different sheets don't line up.

RATING GREEK NONFAT YOGURT

A few years ago, you might have found just one or two brands of Greek yogurt; nowadays, supermarkets carry nearly a dozen brands with a variety of fat levels. To find out if any of these brands lived up to the hype, we sampled 18 different plain nonfat Greek yogurts. Some yogurts were stiff, others watery. Flavors ranged from bland to lightly tangy to strongly sour. A little research into the yogurt-making process helped us understand these variations. The major difference between ordinary yogurt and Greek-style yogurt is that true Greek yogurt is strained to remove most of its liquid whey; the result is a thicker yogurt that is higher in protein. But some manufacturers are using shortcuts, such as skipping the straining and adding gelatin or pectin to accomplish a thicker, creamier product. Our tasters caught on and downgraded these yogurts for their gelatinous texture. Brands are listed in order of preference; protein is per 6-ounce serving. See www.americastestkitchen.com for updates to this testing.

HIGHLY RECOMMENDED

OLYMPUS Traditional Greek Nonfat Yogurt Strained, Plain
PRICE: $1.99 for 6 oz **PROTEIN:** 15g
INGREDIENTS: Grade A pasteurized nonfat milk. Contains yogurt cultures.
COMMENTS: This yogurt—the lone Greek import—won raves for its "smooth, fatty," "seriously creamy" consistency and "pleasantly tangy," well-balanced flavor. In sum: "Hard to believe it's nonfat."

RECOMMENDED

VOSKOS Greek Yogurt Plain Nonfat
PRICE: $2.69 for 8 oz **PROTEIN:** 18g
INGREDIENTS: Grade A pasteurized skim milk. Contains live active cultures
COMMENTS: Though a bit on the runny side for some tasters, this "creamy" yogurt was "bright, clean, and rich," with the kind of "nice tang" and "complex flavor" that you'd "expect from Greek yogurt."

BROWN COW Greek Yogurt 0% Fat, Plain
PRICE: $0.99 for 5.3 oz **PROTEIN:** 17g
INGREDIENTS: Cultured pasteurized nonfat milk. Contains live active cultures.
COMMENTS: Most tasters found this Greek-style relative of our favorite regular plain yogurt "very thick," "super silky," and "smooth." Many noted that its "good, rich tang" reminded them of sour cream and cream cheese. Others found this sample "a bit too acidic."

DANNON Greek Plain 0% Fat
PRICE: $1.39 for 5.3 oz **PROTEIN:** 17g
INGREDIENTS: Cultured Grade A nonfat milk. Contains active yogurt cultures.
COMMENTS: Most tasters agreed that this yogurt's consistency was "ideal": "thick, smooth, and lush." One happy taster even called it "a guilty pleasure" and compared it to ice cream. Still, others felt its richness wasn't enough to temper its "super-duper sour" flavor and "slightly chalky aftertaste."

RECOMMENDED *(cont.)*

OIKOS Organic Greek Yogurt 0% Fat, Plain
PRICE: $1.99 for 5.3 oz **PROTEIN:** 17g
INGREDIENTS: Cultured pasteurized organic nonfat milk. Contains live active cultures.
COMMENTS: This Greek-style offering from the folks at Stonyfield Farm boasted "lots of tang," a quality that some found "distracting." Texture-wise, this product was on the "watery" side, with a "puddle-y" consistency.

FAGE Total 0% Greek Strained Yogurt
PRICE: $1.99 for 6 oz **PROTEIN:** 15g
INGREDIENTS: Grade A pasteurized skimmed milk. Contains live active yogurt cultures.
COMMENTS: Unlike other samples, this well-known Greek brand (by the way, it's pronounced "fa-yeh"), which now produces yogurt in the U.S., met no criticism for excessive tanginess. In fact, most tasters found it a tad "muted." Others described it as "nice and creamy, with just enough tang to remind you, 'Yes, this is yogurt.'"

RECOMMENDED WITH RESERVATIONS

CHOBANI Greek Yogurt Plain Nonfat
PRICE: $1.25 for 6 oz **PROTEIN:** 18g
INGREDIENTS: Cultured pasteurized nonfat milk. Contains live active cultures.
COMMENTS: While some tasters found this yogurt's texture "buttery" and like "clotted cream," others deemed it "ricotta-like." Several tasters also inquired about the missing "tang," noting that it "would work to cool down a spicy dish" but wasn't worth eating on its own.

NOT RECOMMENDED

ATHENOS Greek Strained Nonfat Plain Yogurt
PRICE: $3.29 for 16 oz **PROTEIN:** 16g
INGREDIENTS: Cultured pasteurized nonfat milk
COMMENTS: As we like to say in Boston, this sample from Kraft was "wicked sour." The texture was "wrong," too. Tasters described it as "smooth" but "runny," "thin," and "on a par with regular yogurt."

BACKYARD *Chicken Dinner*

CHAPTER 20

THE RECIPES

Smoked Chicken

Salt-Baked Potatoes with Roast Garlic and Rosemary Butter

Salt-Baked Potatoes with Roast Shallot and Thyme Butter

SCIENCE DESK

Don't Oversmoke Your Chicken

EQUIPMENT CORNER

Coolers

During filming, the test kitchen fires up at least 6 grills at one time to prep for the grilling episodes.

ROAST CHICKEN AND POTATOES IS A CLASSIC COOL WEATHER PAIRING, but sometimes we want the comfort of this combo mid-summer. We wanted something different than such grilling season stand-bys as barbecued chicken parts or a grill-roasted whole chicken, so we decided to try our hand at smoked chicken. We knew that the key to success would require a careful balancing act between heat level, timing, and most importantly, just the right amount of smoke flavor. We wondered if the trick to perfecting smoke flavor would be to let the wood smolder for as long as possible or perhaps just the opposite: knowing when to let it burn out.

Potatoes are a well-loved accompaniment to most any dish, and smoked chicken is no exception. We've heard a lot about salt-baked potatoes, a process which is said to produce extremely moist, well-seasoned potatoes. A new twist on the classic baked potato sounded intriguing, but really, we had to wonder: What could 2 pounds of salt do to a potato that an oven alone can't? We decided to cast our doubts aside to find out if burying potatoes in salt could really make that much of a difference. Join us as we attempt to put a new spin on a familiar pairing.

SMOKED CHICKEN

SMOKED CHICKEN

WHY THIS RECIPE WORKS: When done right, smoking produces chicken with moist, tender, pleasantly smoky meat and an attractively browned exterior. But smoking a chicken is no easy feat—if the heat level isn't just right, the delicate breast meat inevitably dries out and with too much exposure to the smoke, the flavor of the chicken becomes harsh and bitter. Brining the bird ensured the meat would remain moist, and building a slow-burning moderate fire (by piling lit coals on top of unlit coals) allowed us to extend the life of the fire without having to tend to it. A pan of water underneath the chicken helped control the level of heat. Using chicken parts (rather than a whole bird) allowed each piece to be infused with smoke flavor. Finally, we discovered that using wood chunks and smoking the chicken for only half of the cooking time produced chicken with a pleasant—not overpowering—smoke flavor.

THOUGH THEY ARE COOKED UNDER SEEMINGLY similar conditions, grill-roasted chickens and smoked chickens are birds of very different feathers. Grill-roasting is a relatively fast, hot cooking method that produces chicken with crisp skin and subtle smoke flavor. Smoking is a gentler process in which a low fire burns slowly to keep pieces of wood smoldering while cooking the chicken more gradually. When done right, the meat is juicy, tender, and imbued throughout with insistent yet balanced smokiness. The skin is just as well rendered as you'd find on a good grilled bird, but instead of being crackly-crisp, it's moist, supple, and stained a deep brown.

Early tests, however, taught us that smoking a chicken is definitely the more challenging proposition. When grill-roasting, it's tricky enough to balance the relationship between the heat level and the cooking time. Add smoke to the equation, and the situation becomes even more complicated. When we built a fire that was too hot, the delicate breast meat overcooked before the smoke had a chance to penetrate beyond the skin. When the fire wasn't hot enough, the heat dwindled too quickly and forced us to refuel the charcoal multiple times. And the smoke flavor was fickle—sometimes barely there, other times harsh and bitter. Our task was clear: Nail down a fire setup and a specific window of smoking time that would produce tender, juicy meat with clean, full-bodied smoke flavor.

As with all chicken recipes, we had a preliminary decision to make: brine or salt the bird? Both treatments season the meat and help it retain its own juices; the difference is that brining plumps up the bird with additional moisture, which we knew would be a boon in a recipe in which the meat is prone to drying out.

While the chicken soaked, we stepped outside to figure out the grill setup. It seemed to us that our best bet would be to adopt the method that we devised for a brisket recipe. Rather than bank a full chimney's worth of hot coals to one side of the kettle while leaving the other side empty—a traditional indirect setup known as a modified two-level fire—we mounded a smaller pile of unlit briquettes against one side of the grill and added a batch of lit coals on top. Over time, the heat from the lit briquettes trickles down and lights the cold coals, thereby extending the life of the fire without the need for opening the grill to refuel and allowing precious heat to escape.

The other trick we borrowed from that brisket recipe: stowing a pan of water under the chicken on the cool side of the grill. The humidity provided by the water stabilizes the temperature of the grill and (along with brining) helps prevent the delicate breast meat from drying out. Set up this way (for now, we'd stick with 3 quarts each of lit and unlit coals), the grill jumped to 375 degrees early on and then quickly dropped to the 300 to 325 range, where it held steady.

Now came the harder part: incorporating well-balanced smoke flavor into a whole chicken. We already knew that we'd use wood chunks, since they smolder more steadily and evenly than smaller chips do, and that we'd soak them in water for at least 30 minutes before cooking, since the absorbed moisture keeps the wood from burning too quickly.

Several of the recipes that we found called for keeping up the smolder for the duration of cooking, so we followed their lead, adding two soaked wood chunks to the coals and throwing two more onto the coals when the smoke died out after about 45 minutes. After two hours of indirect cooking, the chicken was up to temperature (160 degrees for the breast and 175 degrees for the leg quarters); we pulled it off the grill, let it rest briefly to ensure that the juices redistributed, and called over our colleagues for a tasting. The results? Unimpressive. The delicate breast meat was parched, and the smoke flavor was uneven. We soon realized that the problem was actually fundamental to all whole chickens grill-roasted in a kettle-style vessel: With an indirect fire, a good bit of the heat travels up and under the lid and then bounces back down onto the meat, so that the top of the chicken cooks faster than the side closest to the grate. Trying to compensate for this effect, we started another bird breast side down and flipped it halfway through cooking, but that got us nowhere. The smoke flavor was still uneven, and now the bird was unattractively branded from the grill grate. Plus, heat escaped when we opened the grill, adding 15 minutes to the cooking time.

There was an easy answer to these problems: Forget the whole bird and start with parts. That way, the white meat could sit as far from the heat as possible, and the smoke could evenly surround the smaller individual pieces. We gave it a whirl and saw immediate progress. Not only were the dark and white components evenly tender and juicy, but we were able to cut down the cooking time from two hours to an hour and a half, and the unlit briquettes from 3 quarts to 2 quarts.

Unfortunately, the one problem we still had to contend with—the smoke flavor—had just gone from bad to worse. Whereas smoke only spottily infused the whole chicken, it now so heavily saturated the smaller pieces that tasters likened their flavor to a wet ashtray. We tried adding only one extra wood chunk midway through cooking, but the improvement was negligible. We even tested a slightly hotter fire so that the chicken would get a brief blast of smoke, but this batch was barely tinged with smoke. The problem was that the chicken could absorb only so much smoke flavor at one time, so although the wood was smoldering heavily around the meat, the meat was taking in only a small bit of that smoke and the rest was blowing right out the vent.

At this point we wondered if continuously smoking the meat wasn't the best idea after all, so we tried an altogether different approach: We prepared another batch of chicken, and when the initial pair of chunks burned out, we let the meat finish cooking without refueling the wood. We had our doubts—smoking the meat for only half of the cooking time sounded inadequate—but to our delight, this batch was markedly better. The meat was deeply smoky but not overpoweringly so. In fact, the results were so improved that we mentioned the test to

SCIENCE DESK

DON'T OVERSMOKE YOUR CHICKEN

To infuse our chicken pieces with full-bodied smoke flavor, we figured it was necessary to keep the wood chunks smoldering for the entire time that the meat was on the grill. But when the finished product tasted not just smoky, but also harsh and ashy, we wondered: Was there a limit to the amount of smoke that the chicken could take?

EXPERIMENT

We smoked two batches of chicken. For the first, we added two soaked wood chunks to the fire at the beginning of cooking; when those had burned out about 45 minutes later, we added two more soaked chunks to keep the smoldering going for the duration of cooking. For the second batch, we didn't replenish the wood after the initial chunks had burned out.

RESULTS

The chicken exposed to smoke the entire time tasted bitter and sooty, while the pieces that were exposed to smoke for only 45 minutes or so (about half of the overall cooking time) had just enough smoky depth.

EXPLANATION

Smoke contains both water- and fat-soluble compounds. As the chicken cooks, water evaporates and fat drips away, eventually halting meat's capacity to continue absorbing smoke flavor. Once that happens, any additional smoke flavor that's not absorbed by the meat gets deposited on the exterior of the chicken, where the heat of the grill breaks it down into harsher-flavored compounds.

ONE ROUND OF WOOD CHUNKS = BALANCED SMOKINESS

our science editor. He explained that while the smoke flavor that meat develops early on during cooking is fresh and clean-tasting, those pleasant flavors will turn harsh if the meat is exposed to smoke for too long.

Lesson learned, we had just one holdover issue to resolve: the skin, which had been rendering nicely but was a tad leathery and not quite as glossy as we'd hoped. The obvious fix? A little extra fat. When we brushed the pieces with a coat of vegetable oil just before cooking, the skin emerged supple and tender, with a polished mahogany sheen.

This, finally, was the smoked chicken we'd been working toward: moist and juicy, richly (but not harshly) infused with smoke, and beautifully tanned. And since most of the cooking time was unattended and there was no fussy carving to worry about, the recipe was dead simple.

Smoked Chicken

SERVES 6 TO 8

If using kosher chicken, do not brine in step 1, and season with salt along with the pepper. Avoid mesquite wood chunks for this recipe; we find that the meat can turn bitter if they smolder too long.

- **1 cup salt**
- **1 cup sugar**
- **6 pounds bone-in chicken parts (breasts, thighs, and drumsticks), trimmed**
- **3 tablespoons vegetable oil**
- **Pepper**
- **Large disposable aluminum roasting pan (if using charcoal) or disposable aluminum pie plate (if using gas)**
- **2 wood chunks soaked in water for 30 minutes and drained (if using charcoal) or 3 cups wood chips, half of chips soaked in water for 30 minutes and drained (if using gas)**

1. Dissolve salt and sugar in 4 quarts cold water in large container. Submerge chicken in brine, cover, and refrigerate for 30 minutes to 1 hour. Remove chicken from brine and pat dry with paper towels. Brush both sides of chicken with oil and season with pepper.

2A. FOR A CHARCOAL GRILL: Open bottom vent halfway. Arrange disposable pan filled with 2 cups water on 1 side of grill and 2 quarts unlit charcoal briquettes against empty side of grill. Light large chimney starter filled halfway with charcoal briquettes (3 quarts). When top coals are partially covered with ash, pour on top of unlit briquettes, keeping coals steeply banked against side of grill. Place wood chunks on top of coals. Set cooking grate in place, cover, and open lid vent halfway. Heat grill until hot and wood chunks begin to smoke, about 5 minutes.

2B. FOR A GAS GRILL: Using large piece of heavy-duty aluminum foil, wrap soaked chips in foil packet and cut several vent holes in top. Wrap unsoaked chips in second foil packet and cut several vent holes in top. Place wood chip packets directly on primary burner. Place disposable pie plate with 2 cups water on other burner(s). Turn all burners to high, cover, and heat grill until hot and wood chips begin to smoke, about 15 minutes. Turn primary burner to medium-high and turn off other burner(s).

3. Clean and oil cooking grate. Place chicken, skin side up, as far away from fire as possible with thighs closest to fire and breasts furthest away. Cover (positioning lid vent over chicken if using charcoal) and cook until breasts register 160 degrees and thighs/drumsticks register 175 degrees, 1¼ to 1½ hours.

4. Transfer chicken to cutting board, tent loosely with foil, and let rest for 5 to 10 minutes before serving.

SALT-BAKED POTATOES WITH ROAST GARLIC AND ROSEMARY BUTTER

SALT-BAKED POTATOES

WHY THIS RECIPE WORKS: Baked potatoes are simple and satisfying, but let's be honest: sometimes they could use a flavor boost. And then there's the texture issue—instead of light and fluffy, they turn out dense and crumbly. The process of salt-baking potatoes promises solutions to these problems, producing a well-seasoned, moist, and fluffy potato. After a promising initial test, we set out to test the most important variables—temperature, pan size, and amount of salt. Using a hot 500-degree oven and uncovering the potatoes toward the end of cooking ensured dry skin. A 13 by 9-inch baking dish provided plenty of space so we didn't crowd the potatoes, and 2½ cups of salt allowed us to thoroughly cover the bottom of the pan.

WE HAD ALWAYS ASSUMED THAT SALT-BAKED POTATOES were a novelty act akin to dishwasher-steamed salmon or manifold-roasted meatloaf. How could burying a potato beneath pounds of salt possibly improve on basic baking? Well, if you believe the press, all that salt intensifies the potato's flavor and makes its texture particularly moist and fluffy. Despite our doubts, we managed to compartmentalize our skepticism, bought a sack of russets, and set to work separating fact from fiction.

Besides potatoes being buried in salt and baked, we found two other credible recipe styles (there were some really odd ducks out there): potatoes brushed in an egg wash and encrusted in salt before being baked and potatoes roasted on a bed of salt and sealed in a foil-wrapped baking dish. The "buried" potatoes had an appealingly fluffy texture, but the skin was as tough and desiccated as an old baseball mitt. The crusted potatoes were far better, though the egg wash was messy and chiseling off the crust at the table was inelegant at best. The potatoes cooked in the sealed dish, however, were good—really good. The skins were paper-thin and tender (a far cry from a conventional baked potato skin, but utterly enjoyable), the inside was fluffy and very moist, and the flavor was deep and well seasoned, though by no means salty. They were some of the best baked potatoes we had ever tasted. Our doubts were erased.

Interestingly, the salt directly beneath each potato had caked firm, as if it had been soaked with water. Where was all the moisture coming from? And why was the skin so wet?

According to our science editor, this cooking method creates a unique environment ideally suited to bringing out the best in potatoes. A conventionally baked potato can be too dry due to moisture loss, and a baked potato wrapped directly in foil can be too wet from retaining moisture. A potato that's baked atop salt in a foil-covered pan, however, is neither too dry nor too wet. The moisture that escapes from the potato is contained in the pan and is then absorbed by the salt crystals (hence the salt clumping beneath the potatoes). The salt, in turn, releases some of the moisture due to the heat, whereby the potato reabsorbs it.

For comparison's sake, we baked a potato in a covered pan without salt, and the result was wet and dense-textured. And a potato cooked directly on the rack weighed about 1½ ounces (the equivalent of about 3 tablespoons of water) less than one baked on salt in a covered pan.

Feeling better informed, we tested all the possible variables—temperature, pan size, amount of salt, etc.—and, to be honest, every test delivered pretty good potatoes. We had the best results in a 450-degree oven, using a 13 by 9-inch baking dish (so the potatoes didn't touch) and 2½ cups of either kosher or table salt (the minimum amount necessary to cover the pan bottom with a thick layer of salt).

The potato's wet skin, however, remained troubling. Sensing a bit of dry heat could burn off some of that moisture, we removed the foil once the potatoes were almost cooked and let them finish uncovered. Our hunch paid off and the skin improved. Boosting the oven temperature to 500 degrees quickly wicked off the skin's excess moisture without ill effect to the interior. Brushing the potatoes with olive oil (after removing the foil) intensified the skin's flavor and gave the potatoes a glossy appeal.

Wondering if adding herbs would work with our revamped method, we retested a handful of flavorings. We had little success until we tried fresh rosemary sprigs, which infused the potatoes with their highly aromatic flavor. While we were at it, we roasted a head of garlic in the pan alongside the potatoes and whipped up a quick roasted garlic butter for a topping.

Salt-Baked Potatoes with Roast Garlic and Rosemary Butter

MAKES 4 POTATOES

Kosher or table salt can be used in this recipe. The salt may be sifted through a strainer to remove any solid bits and reused to make this recipe another time. These potatoes can be prepared without the roast garlic butter and topped with your favorite potato toppings, such as sour cream, chives, crumbled bacon, or shredded cheese.

2½ cups plus ⅛ teaspoon salt
4 russet potatoes (8 ounces each), well scrubbed and dried
2 sprigs fresh rosemary plus ¼ teaspoon minced leaves
1 whole head garlic, outer papery skin removed and top quarter of head cut off and discarded
4 teaspoons olive oil
4 tablespoons unsalted butter, softened

1. Adjust oven rack to middle position and heat oven to 450 degrees. Spread 2½ cups salt into even layer in 13 by 9-inch baking dish. Gently nestle potatoes in salt, broad side down, leaving space between each potato. Add rosemary sprigs and garlic, cut side up, to baking dish. Cover baking dish with aluminum foil and crimp edges to tightly seal. Bake for 1 hour and 15 minutes; remove pan from oven.

2. Carefully remove foil. Remove garlic head from baking dish and set aside to cool. Brush exposed portion of each potato with 1 teaspoon oil. Increase oven temperature to 500 degrees and return uncovered baking dish to oven. Continue to bake until potatoes are tender and skins are glossy, 15 to 20 minutes.

3. Meanwhile, once garlic is cool enough to handle, squeeze root end until cloves slip out of their skins. Using fork, mash garlic, butter, ⅛ teaspoon salt, and minced rosemary to smooth paste. Remove any clumped salt from potatoes (holding potatoes with kitchen mitt or towel if necessary), split lengthwise, top with portion of butter and serve.

VARIATION

Salt-Baked Potatoes with Roast Shallot and Thyme Butter

Substitute 5 crumbled bay leaves for rosemary sprigs and 1 teaspoon minced fresh thyme leaves for minced rosemary. Substitute 2 large shallots for garlic head. Proceed with recipe, removing shallots from pan after removing foil. When cool enough to handle, squeeze shallots out of their skins onto cutting board and chop finely. Using fork, mash shallots, butter, ⅛ teaspoon salt, and thyme to smooth paste. Top potatoes with portion of butter and serve.

RATING COOLERS

The first modern cooler, dating back to the 1950s, was a simple insulated box. Nowadays, coolers come in a variety of shapes, sizes, and materials. Bells and whistles range from wheels and telescoping handles to removable dividers and cup holders. Modern innovations aside, we wanted to know how effectively coolers were at keeping things cold and securely contained. We tested five models, ranging in price from $4 to $75. Every model kept prechilled sodas at the same temperature (45 degrees) for four hours; two models even dropped the sodas to a colder temperature. Beyond chilling capacity, coolers had to be durable, which we tested by dropping them from a car tailgate. Models had to be sturdy but not heavy or awkward to move when full. We also liked brands that were easy to clean and didn't pick up food odors; to gauge odor retention, we left fish in the coolers over a weekend and scrubbed the vessels with various cleaning solutions. Brands are listed in order of preference. See www.americastestkitchen.com for updates to this testing.

RECOMMENDED

CALIFORNIA Cooler Bags T-Rex Large Collapsible Rolling Cooler (model #20109KYC)
PRICE: $75
INTERIOR DIMENSIONS: 15 in high, 16 in wide, 14.5 in deep
KEEPING IT COLD: ★★★ **PORTABILITY:** ★★★
COOLING ABILITY: ★★★ **DURABILITY:** ★★★ **CLEANUP:** ★★
COMMENTS: Thanks to an ultra-insulating layer of plastic lining, this was the only nonelectric model to not only keep the sodas cool, but also chill them to 40 degrees. Wheels, a telescoping handle, a hatch in the lid to limit airflow, and a collapsible frame earned it plenty of convenience points, too. The only downside was cleaning its zip-in lining: Crumbs got caught in the teeth and a very slight fishy odor clung to the fabric.

CALIFORNIA Cooler Bags Large 48-52 Classic Collapsible Cooler (model #5-22010KYC)
PRICE: $36.40
INTERIOR DIMENSIONS: 12 in high, 16 in wide, 12 in deep
KEEPING IT COLD: ★★★ **PORTABILITY:** ★★★
COOLING ABILITY: ★★ **DURABILITY:** ★★★ **CLEANUP:** ★
COMMENTS: This collapsible cooler isn't equipped with its larger sibling's insulating lining, but it still cooled sodas to 42 degrees. It also scored big for portability (a padded shoulder strap), space efficiency (stretchy fabric), and ruggedness. Odors clung to this cooler's interior.

RECOMMENDED WITH RESERVATIONS

RUBBERMAID 5-Day Wheeled Cooler (model #802697)
PRICE: $48
INTERIOR DIMENSIONS: 14.5 in high, 20 in wide, 10.5 in deep
KEEPING IT COLD: ★★★ **PORTABILITY:** ★★★
COOLING ABILITY: ★ **DURABILITY:** ★ **CLEANUP:** ★★★
COMMENTS: While this hard plastic tub sports bells and whistles like a split lid and cup holders, and cleanup-friendly features like a spout for emptying liquid, it isn't as durable as it looks. When we dropped it, one of the wheels came loose.

COLEMAN Collapsible Chest Cooler (model #2000004139)
PRICE: $39.99
INTERIOR DIMENSIONS: 12 in high, 22 in wide, 13 in deep
KEEPING IT COLD: ★★★ **PORTABILITY:** ★
COOLING ABILITY: ★ **DURABILITY:** ★★★ **CLEANUP:** ★★★
COMMENTS: This cooler's spacious interior may seem like a perk, but once it's loaded up with food and drink, its wheel-free body is almost impossible to move by the short loop handle. That said, it can take a good bit of wear and tear and cleans up nicely, thanks to its smooth sides and antimicrobial fabric.

LIFOAM Styrofoam Cooler (model #3542)
PRICE: $4
INTERIOR DIMENSIONS: 12 in high, 17 in wide, 10 in deep
KEEPING IT COLD: ★★★ **PORTABILITY:** ★★★
COOLING ABILITY: ★ **DURABILITY:** ★ **CLEANUP:** ★½
COMMENTS: You can't beat the price—but you don't get much for it. Though this Styrofoam cube kept drinks cool, it was too small to hold more than a few items. And given the crack that developed on the side during cleaning, it clearly wasn't meant for multiple uses.

Summertime SUPPER

CHAPTER 21

THE RECIPES

Grilled Stuffed Pork Tenderloin

- Piquillo Pepper and Manchego Stuffing
- Olive and Sun-Dried Tomato Stuffing
- Porcini and Artichoke Stuffing

Lighter Corn Chowder

EQUIPMENT CORNER

Liquid Measuring Cups

Don't use a cutting board when slicing corn off the cob, unless you want a mess all over your counter—a deep bowl will neatly corral all the kernels.

WHEN GRILLING SEASON STRIKES, WE BEGIN TO FEEL ADVENTUROUS, so we're always on the lookout for new spins on some of our favorite summertime recipes and ingredients. Take pork tenderloin: it cooks fast, requires minimal prep, and is elegant enough for entertaining. But it's also lean, making it prone to drying out, and mild (some might say downright bland). A savory filling is a great way to boost flavor and help this lean cut stay moist on the grill—if you can keep the stuffing from leaking out. We set out to find a way to get the stuffing to stay put, and hoped to come up with a few flavor variations for a versatile weeknight main course.

Corn is an ingredient that practically screams summer. But sometimes we want something different than the crowd-pleasing yet somewhat unremarkable corn on the cob. Corn chowder fits the bill, but its heaviness is a problem. Usually awash in a glut of dairy, sweet corn doesn't stand a chance in this classic summer soup. We decided to put the squeeze on the traditional approach, and see if we couldn't find a way to lighten up this dish—we wouldn't be satisfied unless the sweet flavor of summer corn was front and center.

GRILLED STUFFED PORK TENDERLOIN

WHY THIS RECIPE WORKS: Pork tenderloin has many advantages that make it an ideal candidate for the grill: It's quick-cooking, extremely tender, and has a uniform shape which allows for even cooking. But this cut is also mild and lean, making it prone to drying out. Stuffing this roast solves these problems by adding flavor and moisture. Pounding and rolling the tenderloins created more surface area for the filling and helped prevent leaks. Pulsing bold ingredients—such as olives, sun-dried tomatoes, and porcini mushrooms—in a food processor produced an intense paste that stayed put and didn't ooze out. A two-level fire, with the coals spread over half the grill, allowed the pork to cook evenly without drying out, while a sprinkling of sugar on the outside of each tenderloin boosted browning significantly.

WHEN WE HAVE PLENTY OF TIME ON OUR HANDS, OUR go-to summer pork roast is a bone-in, well-marbled cut that we can throw on the grill for as long as it takes for the meat to become tender and juicy while picking up plenty of smoke flavor from the fire. But when a laid-back meal isn't possible, a fast-cooking alternative like pork tenderloin can come in handy. This readily available cut has the added advantages of being supremely tender and uniformly shaped for even cooking and slicing. But while it offers convenience, the lean, mild-mannered roast—basically the pork equivalent of boneless, skinless chicken breast—is sorely lacking in flavor and juiciness. Throw the unpredictable heat of the grill into the equation, and you're well on your way to producing a dry, bland log.

Most recipes tackle these issues by dressing the cooked roast with relishes or sauces, but those solutions are only skin-deep. For a flavor boost that would literally get at the interior of the tenderloin—arguably the blandest part—we wanted to try stuffing the roast with a rich-tasting filling.

We decided to work with two tenderloins, which would make enough to feed four to six people. The average pork tenderloin is only 2 inches in diameter, so we had to think carefully about the most effective way to butterfly it for stuffing. We had two options in mind. One was a simple hinge method, in which the meat is bisected lengthwise about half an inch shy of its back edge, opened up like a book and stuffed, and then closed and secured with twine. The other approach took this method further, pounding the butterflied meat until it was wide and thin, so that once stuffed, it could be rolled up. The first technique seemed less fussy, but we found that it allowed too much stuffing to ooze from the seams. Though it took a little more effort, pounding and rolling turned out to have two benefits. Pounding the meat created more surface area for the filling, and rolling the pork around the stuffing helped prevent leakage during cooking and carving.

But even with this wider plane to work with, we had to keep the filling's bulk to a minimum. That meant forgoing a traditional bread stuffing. What we needed was some sort of intense-tasting paste, so that a little would go a long way. We perused the test kitchen's pantry for flavor-packed ingredients that wouldn't require extensive prep or precooking. It didn't take us long to come up with three robustly flavored combinations that required nothing more than a whirl in the food processor. One balanced spicy roasted piquillo peppers with buttery Manchego cheese and smoked paprika. Another featured briny kalamata olives, sweet sun-dried tomatoes, and a few flavor-enhancing anchovies. The third brought together porcini with artichoke hearts and Parmesan. Layering raw baby spinach leaves over the fillings freshened their rich flavors and added bright color.

Now for the grilling method. Lean pork tenderloin needs a forgiving heat source that won't parch the meat's exterior before the interior has a chance to cook through. We opted for a modified two-level fire, where all the coals are spread evenly over one side of the grill, leaving the other side cooler. But when we grilled the roasts across from the coals for 25 minutes, we found that the indirect heat produced mixed results. While the roasts were quite tender with perfectly warmed-through fillings, they looked utterly pale.

Fortunately, this was a problem the test kitchen had tackled before. When we want to boost browning on

GRILLED STUFFED PORK TENDERLOIN

lean meat, we coat the exterior with a little sugar. Sure enough, when we mixed about 4 teaspoons of sugar with the salt and pepper we were rubbing on the roasts just before grilling, they came off the fire nicely browned with deeper flavor. The effect was even more profound when we traded granulated sugar for dark brown sugar.

When we have the time, we still like to take it slow with a fatty bone-in cut. But our buttery-tender, faintly smoky tenderloins with their robustly flavored fillings were on the table in less than an hour. Who could argue with that?

Grilled Stuffed Pork Tenderloin

SERVES 4 TO 6

You will need kitchen twine to tie the roast.

- **4 teaspoons packed dark brown sugar**
- **2¼ teaspoons kosher salt**
- **1¼ teaspoons pepper**
- **2 (1¼- to 1½-pound) pork tenderloins, trimmed**
- **1 recipe stuffing (recipes follow)**
- **1 cup baby spinach**
- **2 tablespoons olive oil**

1. Combine sugar, 2 teaspoons salt, and 1 teaspoon pepper in bowl. Cut each tenderloin in half horizontally, stopping ½ inch away from edge so halves remain attached. Open up tenderloins, cover with plastic wrap, and pound to ¼-inch thickness. Trim any ragged edges to create rough rectangle about 10 inches by 6 inches. Sprinkle interior of each tenderloin with ⅛ teaspoon salt and ⅛ teaspoon pepper.

2. With long side of pork facing you, spread half of stuffing mixture over bottom half of 1 tenderloin followed by ½ cup spinach. Roll away from you into tight cylinder, taking care not to squeeze stuffing out ends. Position tenderloin seam side down, evenly space 5 pieces kitchen twine underneath, and tie. Repeat with remaining tenderloin, stuffing, and spinach.

3A. FOR A CHARCOAL GRILL: Open bottom vent completely. Light large chimney starter filled with charcoal briquettes (6 quarts). When top coals are partially covered with ash, pour evenly over half of grill. Set cooking grate in place, cover, and open lid vent completely. Heat grill until hot, about 5 minutes.

3B. FOR A GAS GRILL: Turn all burners to high, cover, and heat grill until hot, about 15 minutes. Leave primary burner on high and turn off other burner(s).

4. Clean and oil cooking grate. Coat pork with oil, then rub entire surface with brown sugar mixture. Place pork on cooler side of grill, cover, and cook until center of stuffing registers 145 degrees 25 to 30 minutes, rotating pork once halfway through cooking.

5. Transfer pork to carving board, tent loosely with aluminum foil, and let rest for 5 to 10 minutes. Remove twine, slice pork into ½-inch-thick slices, and serve.

NOTES FROM THE TEST KITCHEN

THE RIGHT (AND WRONG) WAY TO STUFF PORK TENDERLOIN

The trick to keeping the stuffing intact depends on how you butcher and bind the roast.

COMING UNHINGED

Butterflying the roast and simply folding the hinged flaps of meat around the stuffing can lead to oozing filling.

POUNDED AND ROLLED

Pounding the butterflied roast before stuffing allows the meat to be tightly rolled, not folded, around the filling.

Piquillo Pepper and Manchego Stuffing

MAKES ABOUT 1 CUP; ENOUGH FOR 1 RECIPE GRILLED STUFFED PORK TENDERLOIN

Roasted red peppers may be substituted for the piquillo peppers.

- **1 slice hearty white sandwich bread, torn into ½-inch pieces**
- **¾ cup jarred piquillo peppers, rinsed and patted dry**
- **2 ounces Manchego cheese, shredded (½ cup)**
- **¼ cup pine nuts, toasted**
- **2 garlic cloves, minced**
- **1 teaspoon minced fresh thyme**
- **½ teaspoon smoked paprika**
- **Salt and pepper**

Pulse all ingredients except salt and pepper in food processor until coarsely chopped, 5 to 10 pulses; season with salt and pepper to taste.

Olive and Sun-Dried Tomato Stuffing

MAKES ABOUT 1 CUP; ENOUGH FOR 1 RECIPE GRILLED STUFFED PORK TENDERLOIN

- **½ cup pitted kalamata olives**
- **½ cup oil-packed sun-dried tomatoes, rinsed and chopped coarse**
- **4 anchovy fillets**
- **2 garlic cloves, minced**
- **1 teaspoon minced fresh thyme**
- **1 teaspoon grated lemon zest**
- **Salt and pepper**

Pulse all ingredients except salt and pepper in food processor until coarsely chopped, 5 to 10 pulses; season with salt and pepper to taste.

Porcini and Artichoke Stuffing

MAKES ABOUT 1 CUP; ENOUGH FOR 1 RECIPE GRILLED STUFFED PORK TENDERLOIN

- **½ ounce dried porcini mushrooms, rinsed**
- **3 ounces (¾ cup) frozen artichoke hearts, thawed and patted dry**
- **1 ounce Parmesan cheese, grated (½ cup)**
- **¼ cup oil-packed sun-dried tomatoes, rinsed and chopped coarse**
- **¼ cup fresh parsley leaves**
- **2 tablespoons pine nuts, toasted**
- **2 garlic cloves, minced**
- **1 teaspoon grated lemon zest plus 2 teaspoons juice**
- **Salt and pepper**

Microwave ½ cup water and porcini in covered bowl until steaming, about 1 minute. Let stand until softened, about 5 minutes. Use fork to remove porcini from liquid and pat dry with paper towels. Discard soaking liquid. Pulse porcini, artichokes, Parmesan, tomatoes, parsley, pine nuts, garlic, and lemon zest and juice in food processor until coarsely chopped, 5 to 10 pulses; season with salt and pepper to taste.

LIGHTER CORN CHOWDER

LIGHTER CORN CHOWDER

WHY THIS RECIPE WORKS: For this version of corn chowder, we were looking for a recipe that would pack lots of corn flavor in every spoonful while still maintaining a satisfying, yet not too thick, chowder texture. Inspired by a recipe we found that juiced corn kernels, a trick that delivered pronounced corn flavor, we strained the scrapings and pulp from several cobs through a kitchen towel to get unadulterated corn juice (when we added the unstrained pulp to the pot, the soup curdled). This delivered the intense corn flavor we were after. We lightened things up by using water as our primary liquid, which allowed the pure corn flavor to shine through, then added just 1 cup of half-and-half to give our chowder the right richness. A sprinkling of basil before serving lent a fresh finish.

WE'RE ALL FOR THE SIMPLICITY OF EATING SWEET summer corn straight from the cob, but sometimes we have a bumper crop of ears and need a good corn chowder recipe. We can't say we've ever made a really bad version, but we've never made a great one either. Usually, the results are excessively rich—and while we enjoy cream-based chowders as much as the next New Englander, too much dairy can muddle the bottom line: fresh corn flavor. Our ideal version? A simple but substantial soup that lets the kernels' crisp sweetness stand out against a creamy (not stodgy) backdrop seasoned with bits of pork, aromatic vegetables, and fresh herbs.

The most promising recipe we tried was pretty traditional: The cobs were stripped of their kernels and "milked" with the back of a knife to extract all their pulp and juices; chopped onion was sautéed in rendered salt pork fat to build a flavor base, followed by a touch of flour for thickening; liquid—a combination of chicken broth and milk—was added along with cubed red potatoes, herbs, and the corn pulp. Once the potatoes were tender, in went the kernels and a big glug of heavy cream just before serving. Our tasters decided that, besides the almost undetectable pork, the key flavor elements were generally there, but given the weakness of the corn flavor, the proportions were clearly way off.

The pork problem was easily fixed. Salt pork may have been the go-to for early chowder recipes, but over time it has evolved from a meaty slab often cut from portions other than the belly to the muscle-streaked pieces of fat available today. Instead, we used bacon for its subtle sweet smokiness, adding it to the pot along with the onion and a pat of butter to keep it from browning and overwhelming the other elements.

As for the corn, we looked over the ingredient list and pinpointed the one component we knew was dulling its flavor: the dairy. We started dialing back on both the milk and the heavy cream until we had traded them for water and a mere cup of half-and-half, respectively. The results? Still plenty rich with much clearer corn flavor—but not fresh and sweet enough for a soup made with peak-season produce. Plus, without the cream, the broth lacked body. Adding more flour would have thickened things up a little, but not without undoing our flavor-boosting efforts.

As we thought more about the consistency problem, we realized that adding extra starch wasn't necessary. We already had all the thickening power we needed right in the pot with the potatoes. The trick would be to treat this chowder like other hearty soups and puree a portion of it in a blender. Sure enough, this method worked beautifully; when we poured the pureed portion back into the pot and gave the contents a stir, we had exactly the fluid yet spoon-coating results we were hoping for. But the nutty, sweet corn flavor we were after was still a work in progress.

Looking for other opportunities to highlight the corn, we scanned our recipe again and stopped at the chicken broth. What if we swapped this for a homemade corn broth, as some recipes suggest? We tried—but with little success. Simmering the denuded cobs and husks in water didn't produce anything better than chowder made with plain water. There was only one outlier technique that looked intriguing: "juicing" the corn pulp and adding the flavorful liquid to a water base. We admit, we balked at the idea at first, but we couldn't ignore its potential. So we stripped the kernels and milked the cobs as we had been doing, but instead of adding the pulp (2 cups or so) straight to the pot, we wrapped it in a clean kitchen towel, squeezed out every last bit of liquid into a bowl, and discarded the solids. When we measured the output, we had about ⅔ cup of "jus," which we stirred into the chowder just before serving to preserve its fresh sweetness. That did it. When our tasters slurped up this batch and reached for seconds, we knew that shot of pure corn extract was worth the trouble. With one final flourish—a small handful of chopped basil leaves sprinkled over the top—we had a chowder every bit as fresh and sweet as corn straight from the cob.

Lighter Corn Chowder

SERVES 6

When removing the kernels from the cob make sure to remove only the part of the kernel sticking out of the cob. Cutting deeper will result in too much fibrous material coming off the corn. Yukon Gold potatoes can be substituted for the red potatoes. Minced chives can be used in place of the basil.

- **8 ears corn, husks and silk removed**
- **3 tablespoons unsalted butter**
- **1 onion, chopped fine**
- **4 slices bacon, halved lengthwise, then cut crosswise into ¼-inch pieces**
- **2 teaspoons minced fresh thyme**
- **Salt and pepper**
- **¼ cup all-purpose flour**
- **5 cups water**
- **12 ounces red potatoes, cut into ½-inch cubes**
- **1 cup half-and-half**
- **Sugar**
- **3 tablespoons chopped fresh basil**

1. Using chef's knife or corn stripper, stand cobs on end and cut kernels from corn; transfer to bowl and set aside (you should have 5 to 6 cups kernels). Holding cobs over second bowl, use back of butter knife or vegetable peeler to firmly scrape any pulp remaining on cobs into bowl (you should have 2 to 2½ cups of pulp). Transfer pulp to center of clean kitchen towel set in bowl. Wrap towel tightly around pulp and squeeze tightly until dry. Discard pulp in towel and set corn juice aside (you should have about ⅔ cup juice).

2. Melt butter in Dutch oven over medium heat. Add onion, bacon, thyme, 2 teaspoons salt, and 1 teaspoon pepper and cook, stirring frequently, until onion is softened and beginning to brown, 8 to 10 minutes. Stir in flour and cook, stirring constantly, for 2 minutes. Whisking constantly, gradually add water and then bring to boil. Add corn kernels and potatoes. Return to simmer, reduce heat to medium-low, and cook until potatoes have softened, 15 to 18 minutes.

3. Transfer 2 cups chowder to blender and process until smooth, 1 to 2 minutes. Return puree to pot, stir in half-and-half, and return to simmer. Remove pot from heat and stir in reserved corn juice. Season with salt, pepper, and up to 1 tablespoon sugar to taste. Sprinkle with basil and serve.

RATING LIQUID MEASURING CUPS

The liquid measuring cup is a basic kitchen tool, where accuracy matters more than looks, and form should follow function. But when we shopped recently, we were greeted by a variety of innovative new shapes and materials. We selected 15 models and began testing, quickly whittling the list to eight. The first ones cut simply weren't accurate. Additionally, some weren't sturdy or heatproof, an issue made worse when there was no handle. To test durability, we ran all cups through numerous dishwasher cycles and dropped them on the floor. Others lacked ¼- or ⅓-cup markings, which we consider essential. We downgraded cups that contained Bisphenol A, a controversial material that has been linked to health issues. Brands are listed in order of preference. See www.americastestkitchen.com for updates to this testing.

RECOMMENDED

GOOD COOK by Bradshaw International 2-Cup Measuring Cup (model #19864)
PRICE: $3.99 **MATERIAL:** Plastic **BPA:** None
DISHWASHER: Top rack **MICROWAVE:** Yes
ACCURACY: ★★★ **PERFORMANCE:** ★★★
DESIGN: ★★★ **DURABILITY:** ★★

COMMENTS: While we'd prefer a cup that feels more substantial, this lightweight, crisply marked model was accurate and easy to read and provided all the measurements we needed—and no more. Most testers found it "easy and basic." And it's cheap.

ARROW Cool Grip 2.5-Cup Measuring Cup (model #473812 (00031))
PRICE: $11.80 **MATERIAL:** Plastic **BPA:** None
DISHWASHER: Top rack **MICROWAVE:** Yes; 15-min limit
ACCURACY: ★★★ **PERFORMANCE:** ★★★
DESIGN: ★★★ **DURABILITY:** ★★
COMMENTS: We liked this simple cup with its easy-on-the-eyes markings and stay-cool handle. Rounded corners made it easy to scrape out sticky honey. One quibble: the manufacturer squeezed in markings right to the rim, where liquids can spill.

RECOMMENDED WITH RESERVATIONS

OXO Good Grips 2-Cup Angled Measuring Cup (model #70981)
PRICE: $9.99 **MATERIAL:** Plastic **BPA:** Yes
DISHWASHER: Yes **MICROWAVE:** Yes; 4-min limit; no fats or oils
ACCURACY: ★★★ **PERFORMANCE:** ★★★
DESIGN: ★★ **DURABILITY:** ★★
COMMENTS: Comfortable to pour, with an ergonomic handle, oval shape, and sharp, drip-free spout. Angled measurement panels inside the cup, readable from above, were clear to testers, who got accurate results, but they were a nuisance when scraping out honey.

WILTON 2-Cup Liquid Measure (model #2103-334)
PRICE: $10.78 **MATERIAL:** Plastic **BPA:** None
DISHWASHER: Top rack **MICROWAVE:** No
ACCURACY: ★★★ **PERFORMANCE:** ★★
DESIGN: ★★ **DURABILITY:** ★★
COMMENTS: Accurate, comfortable, and lightweight, its oval shape helped control pouring. We liked the "stepped" design, but some testers found the markings hard to read.

NOT RECOMMENDED

ISI Basics Flex-It 2-Cup Measuring Cup (model #B 6400)
PRICE: $8.99 **MATERIAL:** Silicone **BPA:** None
DISHWASHER: Yes **MICROWAVE:** Yes
ACCURACY: ★★★ **PERFORMANCE:** ★★
DESIGN: ★ **DURABILITY:** ★★★
COMMENTS: This simple silicone cylinder was soft and pliable—a fatal flaw when boiling liquid turned it overly squishy and too hot to hold. Still, scraping honey out of the smooth, tubular body was easy and testers were able to obtain accurate results.

ZYLISS Mix-n-Measure Measuring Cup Set with Lid (1, 2 & 4 Cup) (model #13850)
PRICE: $19.99 **MATERIAL:** Plastic **BPA:** Yes
DISHWASHER: Yes **MICROWAVE:** No
ACCURACY: ★★★ **PERFORMANCE:** ★★
DESIGN: ★ **DURABILITY:** ★★★

COMMENTS: We liked the idea of markings readable from the top or side, but these were printed in such small, busy type that the information was lost on several testers; many also disliked the handle's sharp edges.

EMSA Perfect Beaker with Seal by Frieling (model #2206990096)
PRICE: $12.46 **MATERIAL:** Plastic **BPA:** None
DISHWASHER: Yes **MICROWAVE:** Yes; 3-min limit
ACCURACY: ★ **PERFORMANCE:** ★★
DESIGN: ★★ **DURABILITY:** ★★

COMMENTS: The "perfect beaker" it isn't. The 1-cup marking was short by nearly 1 tablespoon. It was easy to pour from, except when full of boiling water, when the lack of a handle was a true disadvantage.

PYREX 2-Cup Measuring Cup with Read from Above Graphics (model #1085812)
PRICE: $6.49 **MATERIAL:** Glass **BPA:** None
DISHWASHER: Yes **MICROWAVE:** Yes
ACCURACY: ★ **PERFORMANCE:** ★★
DESIGN: ★ **DURABILITY:** ★★★
COMMENTS: This redesigned cup was a disaster. Testers struggled to tell if they'd hit the mark and couldn't double-check from the outside (for one thing, markings appear backward); their uncertainty showed up in poor measuring results. The big, conical shape is hard to pour from and eats up storage space. Accuracy was off by 2 teaspoons.

America's
TEST KITCHEN

Rise and Shine
BREAKFAST

CHAPTER 22

Adam, our equipment expert, discusses with Chris whether toaster ovens are worth the space they take up on your counter.

WE'RE NOT AFRAID TO ADMIT IT; BREAKFAST IS WHAT GETS US OUT of bed. And we don't mean a bowl of cereal—we want food that will fuel us through the morning. Scrambled eggs top our list of simple, satisfying fare. But despite the fact that they typically contain just a couple of ingredients, our ideal scrambled eggs can be infuriatingly elusive; we've turned out tough, dry eggs more times than we'd care to admit. We've come to realize that the classic low-heat approach will never give us tender scrambled eggs with big, pillowy curds. But we knew we'd have to do more than just turn up the heat.

Cranberry-nut muffins are another favorite treat—flavorful and hearty, with a satisfying texture, they make the ultimate grab-and-go breakfast. But most cranberry-nut muffin recipes call for loading sour berries and chopped nuts into any old batter. Could that be why they often seem so out of whack? The sour flavor of the cranberries can easily overwhelm that of the muffin, and nuts that started out as toasty and crunchy become soggy, flavorless bits randomly strewn throughout. We set out to remedy these problems and create a moist, flavorful muffin accented by tart berries and rich, crunchy nuts.

SCRAMBLED EGGS

WHY THIS RECIPE WORKS: Scrambled eggs should be a foolproof, go-to breakfast. Yet surprisingly, we've successfully created our ideal scrambled eggs only a handful of times. More often than not, they're tough and dry. For moist and fluffy eggs with soft, big curds, we found it necessary to cook them over high heat, which creates enough steam to properly puff the eggs. Salt helps produce tender curds while gentle beating avoids a tough scramble. The addition of half-and-half provided just enough richness without making the eggs dense and a couple extra yolks boosted egg flavor. Lowering the heat at the end of cooking ensured the eggs didn't overcook.

WE TAKE PAINS WITH JUST ABOUT EVERYTHING WE cook, but not scrambled eggs. Usually our goal is just to get them on the table, fast. Our method, such as it is, goes something like this: Whisk eggs, add a splash of milk, pour the mixture into a hot skillet, and stir over medium-high heat until the eggs puff up into large, moist curds. Trouble is, that's not what usually happens. All it takes is the merest distraction for our eggs to go from glossy, fluffy, and wobbly to tough, dry slabs. But even when we take our time and gently stir the eggs over lower heat, we still don't get the results we want. Instead, we end up with spoon food: curds so pebbly and fine that the mixture looks like oatmeal.

It was time to get serious, to stop leaving everything to chance and nail down an approach to foolproof, fluffy, tender scrambled eggs.

We did a little investigation into the science of cooking eggs, and the first thing we discovered was that to produce the ideal voluptuous curds, our slapdash approach over higher heat wasn't far off. Only relatively high heat will produce enough steam (from the dairy and the water in eggs) to puff up the scramble. As the proteins in the eggs continue to heat, they unfold and then bond together to form a latticed gel in a process known as coagulation. The texture of the eggs depends on exactly how much unfolding and bonding occurs. To create moist curds, we needed the egg proteins to bond enough to transform from a liquid into a semisolid, but not so much that they seized up into a tough mass. Fortunately, we could fall back on some lessons learned in the test kitchen over the years to address this problem.

Lesson one: Adding salt to the raw eggs makes for more-tender curds. In the same way that soaking a piece of pork in a brine solution tenderizes its protein network, salt dissolves egg proteins so that they are unable to bond as tightly when cooked.

Lesson two: Don't overbeat the eggs or you'll have a tough scramble. This may seem counterintuitive (since physical agitation usually destroys structure), but the principle is easily illustrated by what happens when you whip egg whites into peaks. Vigorous whisking unfolds proteins in much the same way that heat does; once unfolded, the protein strands readily bond together to form a tighter structure. Since the last thing you want to do is accelerate the unfolding process before the eggs hit the heat, beat them until just combined with the gentler action of a fork rather than a whisk.

We kept those points in mind as we assumed the role of short-order cook, whipping up batch after batch of scrambled eggs to see how the other major component in the mix—dairy—affected the texture. Some of the recipes we consulted called for milk, others for half-and-half or heavy cream, but all three options contain two important tenderizers: water and fat. What we needed to know was how the water-to-fat ratio in each would affect coagulation; we also needed to know exactly how dairy-rich our tasters liked their eggs.

To feed four people, we beat eight eggs with both salt and pepper and varying proportions of all three dairy options; poured the eggs into a medium-hot, butter-slicked 12-inch skillet; and dragged a heatproof rubber spatula around the pan for about two minutes, until the eggs appeared clumpy but still shiny and wet. Our tasters mulled over the pros and cons of each dairy ingredient. Milk produced slightly fluffier, cleaner-tasting curds, but they were particularly prone to weeping. Heavy cream, on the other hand, rendered the eggs very stable but dense, and some tasters found their flavor just too rich. One-quarter cup of half-and-half fared best: Though everyone agreed that these curds could stand to be fluffier, they were decently puffed and stable thanks to the tandem effects of the liquid's water and fat.

Dairy offers a threefold benefit: First, the water it contains (80 percent in half-and-half) interrupts the protein network and dilutes the molecules, thereby raising the temperature at which eggs coagulate and providing a greater safety net against overcooking (and disproving the classic French theory that adding the dairy at the end of cooking is best). Second, as the water in the dairy vaporizes, it provides lift (just as in a loaf of baking bread), which causes the eggs to puff up. And third, the fat in the dairy also raises the coagulation temperature by coating and insulating part of each protein molecule so that they cannot stick together as tightly.

Half-and-half wasn't a perfect solution, however: Some tasters still found the dairy flavor too prominent. Less dairy would only make the recipe less foolproof, so we researched ways to boost egg flavor. The best suggestion came from a colleague. She mentioned that when her grandmother makes fresh pasta, she adds an extra yolk or two to the dough to approximate the richer flavor of farm-fresh eggs. We followed suit, and sure enough, the more yolks we added to the mix, the richer the results. There was no need to overdo it, though: Two yolks per eight eggs balanced the flavor nicely. Even better, the high proportion of fat and emulsifiers in the egg yolks further raised the coagulation temperature, helping to stave off overcooking.

SCIENCE DESK

UNSCRAMBLING PERFECT SCRAMBLED EGGS

To get big, fluffy, tender, and rich-tasting curds, we experimented with every element of the process until we nailed the right formula.

8 EGGS PLUS 2 YOLKS
Adding yolks not only enriches the egg flavor, but the extra fat and emulsifiers raise the coagulation temperature to stave off overcooking.

HALF-AND-HALF
Half-and-half offers more rich-flavored fat than milk but also contains enough water to generate the steam necessary to make the eggs puff up.

10-INCH SKILLET
Trading the usual 12-inch pan for a smaller 10-inch one keeps the eggs in a thicker layer, thereby trapping more steam and producing heartier curds.

DUAL-HEAT METHOD
Starting the egg mixture over medium-high heat creates puffy curds; turning the heat to low once the eggs coagulate ensures that they won't overcook.

Before we moved on to fine-tune the cooking method, we tried a couple of unconventional stir-ins that promised either fluffier or more tender eggs: vinegar and baking powder. The acidity in the former tenderized the eggs in much the same way that salt did but far more drastically: Just a drop rendered the curds mushy. A dash of baking powder was also too much of a good thing, puffing the eggs like a diner-style omelet as well as imparting a chemical aftertaste.

We also experimented with the advice of old-school French cookbooks to start with room-temperature eggs. While we've proved that egg temperature can influence the structure of some delicate cakes, we found that cold eggs and room-temperature eggs produced virtually identical scrambles.

So much for "secret weapons." It was time to face the fire. The bottom line was that no matter how perfectly we balanced the ratios of protein, fat, and water, the scrambled eggs would still fail if they overcooked. Low heat would curb overcooking, but we needed higher heat to produce nicely puffed curds. Suddenly it hit us like a whack with a cast-iron skillet: What if we used both high and low heat?

We mixed up another batch of eggs, tossed a piece of cold butter into the pan, and turned the heat to medium-high. Once the butter was melted but not brown (a cue that a pan is too hot), we added the eggs, constantly scraping the bottom and sides of the skillet to form large curds and prevent any spots from overcooking. As soon as our spatula could just leave a trail in the pan with minimal raw egg filling in the gap (about two minutes in), we dropped the heat to low and switched to a gentle folding motion to keep from breaking up the large curds. When the eggs looked cooked through but still glossy (about 45 seconds later), we slid them onto a plate to stop the cooking process. To our delight, the results were almost perfect—fluffy and tender, for sure—and the method was far more fail-safe than our high-heat-only attempts.

Our tasters' only holdover request? Larger curds, please. We tried scraping a bit less frequently, but while the curds were certainly bigger, they were also overcooked in spots. Stymied, we looked over all the elements in our recipe and realized that there was one component we hadn't addressed: the size of the pan. In theory, our vessel choice mattered more here than in any other recipe, since a smaller skillet would keep the eggs in a thicker layer, thereby trapping more steam and producing heartier curds. Whisking together one more batch of eggs, we put aside our 12-inch skillet and grabbed a 10-inch pan instead, and then proceeded with our recipe. About three minutes later, we had the best batch of scrambled eggs yet: big billowy curds that were perfect with or without a last-minute sprinkle of fresh herbs.

We were finished with slapdash. A simple, foolproof version of our favorite breakfast was finally served.

NOTES FROM THE TEST KITCHEN

SCRAMBLED EGG EXTREMES

The best puffy scrambled eggs aren't hastily cooked over high heat. Nor are they gently cooked over low heat.

RUBBER
Blasting the eggs over higher heat gets breakfast on the table in a hurry—but produces dried-out, rubbery curds.

WET
Keeping the heat low might prevent the eggs from overcooking, but the result will be loose, tiny curds that look like lumpy custard.

TURN IT DOWN

When your spatula just leaves a trail through the eggs, that's your cue in our dual-heat method to turn the dial from medium-high to low.

Perfect Scrambled Eggs

SERVES 4

If using an electric stove, heat one burner on low heat and a second on medium-high heat; move the skillet between burners when it's time to adjust the heat. If you don't have half-and-half, substitute 8 teaspoons of whole milk and 4 teaspoons of heavy cream. To dress up the dish, add 2 tablespoons of chopped parsley, chives, basil, or cilantro or 1 tablespoon of dill or tarragon to the eggs after reducing the heat to low.

8 large eggs plus 2 large yolks
¼ cup half-and-half
Salt and pepper
1 tablespoon unsalted butter, chilled

1. Beat eggs, egg yolks, half-and-half, ⅜ teaspoon salt, and ¼ teaspoon pepper with fork until eggs are thoroughly combined and color is pure yellow; do not overbeat.

2. Heat butter in 10-inch nonstick skillet over medium-high heat until fully melted (butter should not brown), swirling to coat pan. Add egg mixture and, using rubber spatula, constantly and firmly scrape along bottom and sides of skillet until eggs begin to clump and spatula just leaves trail on bottom of pan, 1½ to 2½ minutes. Reduce heat to low and gently but constantly fold eggs until clumped and just slightly wet, 30 to 60 seconds. Immediately transfer eggs to warmed plates and season with salt to taste. Serve immediately.

VARIATIONS

Perfect Scrambled Eggs for Two

Reduce eggs to 4, yolks to 1, half-and-half to 2 tablespoons, and salt and pepper to ⅛ teaspoon each. In step 2, reduce butter to ½ tablespoon. Cook eggs in 8-inch skillet for 45 to 75 seconds over medium-high heat, then for 30 to 60 seconds over low heat.

Perfect Scrambled Eggs for One

Reduce eggs to 2, yolks to 1, half-and-half to 1 tablespoon, and salt and pepper to pinch each. In step 2, reduce butter to ¼ tablespoon. Cook eggs in 8-inch skillet for 30 to 60 seconds over medium-high heat, then for 30 to 60 seconds over low heat.

CRANBERRY-NUT MUFFINS

WHY THIS RECIPE WORKS: Cranberry-nut muffins can make a quick and hearty breakfast, but all too often they are dense and leaden, with an overwhelming sour berry flavor and soggy nuts distributed haphazardly throughout. We wanted a moist, substantial muffin accented—not overtaken—by tart cranberries and toasted, crunchy nuts. Mixing the batter by hand was quick and gave our muffin enough structure to accommodate the fruit and nuts. Grinding the nuts and using them in place of some of the flour added complexity; to compensate for the smaller amount of gluten, we let the batter rest. Chopping the berries and tossing them with a little sugar toned down their tartness. Finally, a streusel topping added back the crunch lost from grinding up the nuts.

MOST RECIPES FOR CRANBERRY-NUT MUFFINS FOLLOW the same course as those for any fruit-studded muffin: Just toss a few handfuls of fresh berries and coarsely chopped nuts into the batter and then bake. It's an approach that works well enough when using ripe, sweet blueberries or raspberries, but the method is never as successful with cranberries. We love tart fruit in baked goods, but we find that cranberries' ultra-sour burst can completely overwhelm the delicate flavor of the muffin. As for the nuts, after steaming in the moist batter, their rich, toasty flavor washes away. And then there's the usual problem of unevenly distributed mix-ins. Depending on where you bite, you might get a mouthful of sour berries, a cluster of nuts, or plain old cake.

Hankering for a not-so-sweet breakfast pastry, we decided to reinvent the concept. Our muffin would feature a moist crumb with plenty of its own flavor, punctuated by zingy but not harsh cranberries and rich-tasting, crunchy nuts.

First things first: creating a muffin that could stand up to the heft of two mix-ins. As with all cake recipes, we could choose either the creaming method or the hand-mixed "quick-bread" method. In this case, only the latter's coarser, sturdier crumb would do. (Not hauling out the stand mixer was also a plus.) We whisked eggs, melted butter, and milk in one bowl and flour, baking powder, and salt in another. Then we gently combined the two components with a generous 2 cups of whole cranberries and 1¼ cups of toasted chopped pecans (our preference over more-common walnuts for their richer, sweeter, more buttery flavor), before filling and loading the pan into a 425-degree oven. About 18 minutes later, we had a good-looking batch of muffins—nicely domed and sturdy enough to accommodate the fruit and nuts. But looks and structure were about the only things going for this batch, as the nuts offered nothing but a little crunch and the cake's ho-hum flavor was no match for the sour pop of the berries.

Brainstorming for ways to enliven the muffin base, we gave our spice pantry a quick glance—and then thought better of it. Hits of cinnamon, cloves, or allspice would not add the kind of complexity we had in mind. Our other idea was to trade some of the all-purpose flour for a heartier grain like cornmeal, oat flour, or whole wheat flour, but those batches baked up respectively gritty, gummy, and dense.

However, cutting the all-purpose flour with a heftier, more flavorful flour wasn't a bad idea. It then dawned on us that just the right kind of ingredient had been sitting under our noses the whole time: nuts. In fact, not long ago in a torte recipe, we swapped out some of the all-purpose flour for almond flour that we ground from whole nuts in the food processor. Taking the same approach with the pecans in this recipe, it seemed, might remedy both the blandness of the muffin and the washed-out flavor of the steamed chopped nuts. We knew the trade would mean losing some of the wheat's gluten-forming proteins and, in turn, some of the muffins' tall, sturdy structure, but we decided to worry about that later. We processed the toasted pecans into a coarse, sandlike meal, which we then substituted for the regular flour in varying amounts—from just ¼ cup all the way up to 1¼ cups.

The results bore out our suspicion: These batches of muffin batter looked looser and runnier than those made with regular flour and, rather than baking up tall and self contained, they spread out—particularly those with more nut flour rather than baking up tall and self-contained.

CRANBERRY-PECAN MUFFINS

But once our tasters took a bite we knew the tradeoff hadn't been for naught. Despite their now-disappointing structure, these nut-based muffins boasted a richer-tasting, heartier crumb that helped counter the cranberries' acidity. As for the proportion of nut flour in the batter, tasters were definitive: the more, the better.

Our next move was to compensate for the nut flour's inability to form gluten, so we did the most logical thing we could think of: We committed baker's treason by overmixing the batter—a surefire way to overdevelop the gluten strands and toughen up the final product, which we thought might be exactly what this batter needed. We even went for a second count by mixing up another batch and trading the remaining all-purpose flour for bread flour, hoping that the latter's protein boost would build up some structure. But both tests were a bust. Instead of the domed tops that we were looking for, we got squat, chewy muffins with stunted peaks—two classic signs of overworking. Apparently, we'd been wrong: More gluten was not the answer.

But if a lack of gluten wasn't the problem, what was? We were pondering this question while throwing together another batch of batter when we were called across the kitchen to a colleague's tasting. When we returned 30 minutes later, a curious thing had happened: The batter had thickened up considerably. Intrigued, we portioned and baked the muffins and were rewarded with the best batch yet. The batter hadn't spread across the pan and the muffins were symmetrical, with gently rounded tops. When we described the outcome to our science editor, he explained that, while the rest undoubtedly allowed a little more gluten to form, its main effect was to hydrate the batter. Because this batter contained relatively little flour, there were fewer starch granules to absorb the liquid and thicken the batter. Letting the batter rest allowed what starch granules that were available to more fully absorb the free water, which, in turn, resulted in batter with more body.

The mystery of the spreading batter solved, it was time to temper the berries' sour punch. Sugar was the obvious go-to, but further sweetening the batter wouldn't help once the whole berries burst and released their sharp juice. The more effective solution was chopping the berries to expose some of their inner flesh—a fix that also helped distribute the fruit more evenly throughout the batter—and tossing them with sugar. We were already using the food processor to grind the nuts, so we saved ourselves some knife work and pulsed the berries with a spoonful of confectioners' sugar (which dissolves more quickly than granulated sugar). Sugar took the edge off the fruit, but tasters complained that the rough-chopped berries were still too tart—even bitter. That latter description triggered an idea: In the past, we've used salt to tame bitterness in eggplant and coffee. Sure enough, adding ¼ teaspoon to the processor bowl along with the berries and sugar did the trick.

These muffins were in good shape, but our tasters wanted still more nut flavor in the crumb. They also wanted to get back the crunchy element that had been eliminated when we switched from chopped to ground pecans. To meet the first request, instead of grinding the nuts by themselves, we processed them with the granulated sugar. The sugar's abrasiveness helped the nuts break down further, releasing more of their flavorful oils and preventing any bits from clumping together.

Recovering some of the crunchy texture was as simple as creating a topping. A sweet streusel mixture of flour, sugar, butter, and chopped pecans worked perfectly. The nuts browned nicely during baking and lent a toasty, buttery touch along with satisfying crunch.

With its crunchy topping and the pleasant pop of tart berries against the backdrop of nutty-tasting crumb, here, finally, was a cranberry muffin we could go nuts for.

Cranberry-Pecan Muffins

MAKES 12 MUFFINS

If fresh cranberries aren't available, substitute frozen cranberries. Before using, place the cranberries in a bowl and microwave until the cranberries are partially thawed, 30 to 45 seconds.

STREUSEL TOPPING

- **3 tablespoons all-purpose flour**
- **1 tablespoon packed light brown sugar**
- **1 tablespoon plus 1 teaspoon granulated sugar**
- **Pinch salt**
- **2 tablespoons unsalted butter, cut into ½-inch pieces and softened**
- **½ cup pecans**

MUFFINS

- **1⅓ cups (6⅔ ounces) all-purpose flour**
- **1½ teaspoons baking powder**
- **1 teaspoon salt**
- **1¼ cups (5 ounces) pecans, toasted and cooled**
- **1 cup plus 1 tablespoon (7½ ounces) granulated sugar**
- **2 large eggs**
- **6 tablespoons unsalted butter, melted and cooled**
- **½ cup whole milk**
- **8 ounces (2 cups) fresh cranberries**
- **1 tablespoon confectioners' sugar**

1. Adjust oven rack to upper-middle position and heat oven to 425 degrees. Grease and flour 12-cup muffin tin.

2. FOR THE STREUSEL: Pulse flour, brown sugar, granulated sugar, salt, and butter in food processor until mixture resembles coarse sand, 4 to 5 pulses. Add pecans and pulse until pecans are chopped coarse, about 4 pulses. Transfer to bowl; set aside.

3. FOR THE MUFFINS: Whisk flour, baking powder, and ¾ teaspoon salt together in bowl; set aside.

4. Process toasted pecans and granulated sugar in now-empty food processor until mixture resembles coarse sand, 10 to 15 seconds. Transfer to large bowl and whisk in eggs, butter, and milk until combined. Whisk flour mixture into egg mixture until just moistened and no streaks of flour remain. Set batter aside for 30 minutes to thicken.

5. Pulse cranberries, remaining ¼ teaspoon salt, and confectioners' sugar in now-empty food processor until very coarsely chopped, 4 to 5 pulses. Using rubber spatula, fold cranberries into batter. Using ice cream scoop or large spoon, divide batter equally among prepared muffin cups (batter should completely fill cups and mound slightly). Evenly sprinkle streusel topping over muffins, gently pressing into batter to adhere. Bake until muffin tops are golden and just firm, 17 to 18 minutes, rotating muffin tin halfway through baking. Let muffins cool in tin on wire rack for 10 minutes. Remove muffins from tin and let cool for 10 minutes before serving.

SCIENCE DESK

TO THICKEN THIN BATTER, GIVE IT A REST

We thought a lack of gluten was causing our nut flour–based muffin batter to be thin and runny, and led to the muffins baking up flat. But after letting the batter rest briefly—a fluke occurrence during testing when we walked away for 30 minutes—the batter thickened and the muffins baked up tall and nicely domed. Why did resting the batter improve the muffins' structure?

EXPERIMENT

To double-check the results, we prepared two batches of our muffin batter, letting one batch rest for 30 minutes before baking, and baking the other right away.

RESULTS

The rested batter thickened considerably and baked up into muffins with nicely domed tops. The unrested batter was thin and produced predictably flat muffins that spread across the tin.

EXPLANATION

As batter rests, water binds to and hydrates the starch granules and gluten-forming proteins. This allows a small amount of gluten to develop, providing structure. But the main effect is that the starches swell as they soak up the free liquid. This swelling literally thickens the batter and helps prevent it from spreading during baking.

UNRESTED

RESTED

RATING PEANUT BUTTER

Scan the peanut butter aisle at your supermarket and you'll find dozens of different brands and options. But no option seems to be taking up space like the "natural" peanut butters (which sometimes are more than just peanuts and salt). We set out to find the best creamy peanut butters, and gathered a number of both conventional and natural butters, some of which mimic conventional peanut butter with naturally hydrogenated palm oil. Tasters sampled 10 brands plain, in peanut butter cookies, and in a spicy satay sauce. When it came to great peanut butter, tasters made it clear that texture was paramount. The peanut butters had to be smooth, creamy, and spreadable; they also had to have a good balance of sweet and salty flavors. Brands are listed in order of preference. See www.americastestkitchen.com for updates to this testing.

RECOMMENDED

SKIPPY Peanut Butter
PRICE: $2.39 for 16.3 oz (15 cents per oz)
TOTAL SUGAR: 10.7% **SALT:** 1.25%
INGREDIENTS: Roasted peanuts, sugar, hydrogenated vegetable oils (cottonseed, soybean, and rapeseed) to prevent separation, salt
COMMENTS: In a contest that hinged on texture, tasters thought this "smooth," "creamy" sample was "swell," both plain and baked into cookies. Its rave reviews even compensated for a slightly "weak" nut flavor that didn't come through as well as other brands in the pungent satay sauce.

JIF Natural Peanut Butter Spread
PRICE: $2.29 for 18 oz (13 cents per oz)
TOTAL SUGAR: 11.5% **SALT:** 0.61%
INGREDIENTS: Peanuts, sugar, palm oil, contains 2% or less of salt, molasses
COMMENTS: The big favorite in satay sauce, this peanut butter's "dark, roasted flavor"—helped by the molasses—stood out well against the other heady ingredients and made cookies with "nice sweet-salty balance." Plus, as the top-rated palm oil-based sample, it was "creamy," "thick," and better emulsified than other "natural" butters.

REESE'S Peanut Butter
PRICE: $2.59 for 18 oz (14 cents per oz)
TOTAL SUGAR: 9.9% **SALT:** 1.11%
INGREDIENTS: Roasted peanuts, sugar, peanut oil, hydrogenated vegetable oil (contains rapeseed, cottonseed, and soybean oils), salt, molasses, monoglycerides, and cornstarch
COMMENTS: "This is what peanut butter should be like," declared one happy taster, noting specifically this product's "good," "thick" texture and "powerful peanut flavor." In satay sauce, however, some tasters felt that the heavier body made for a "pasty" end.

JIF Peanut Butter

PRICE: $2.29 for 18 oz (13 cents per oz)
TOTAL SUGAR: 10.7% **SALT:** 1.26%
INGREDIENTS: Roasted peanuts, sugar, contains 2% or less of molasses, fully hydrogenated vegetable oils (rapeseed and soybean), mono- and diglycerides, salt
COMMENTS: This classic butter lived up to its "creamy, rich" reputation and turned out "nice, chewy" cookies. But some tasters felt the chiles and other ingredients in satay sauce overpowered its "sweet, mellow" flavor.

RECOMMENDED *(cont.)*

SKIPPY Natural Peanut Butter Spread

PRICE: $2.39 for 15 oz (16 cents per oz)
TOTAL SUGAR: 8.8% **SALT:** 1.26%
INGREDIENTS: Roasted peanuts, sugar, palm oil, salt
COMMENTS: The only other palm oil-based peanut butter to make the "recommended" cut, this contender had a "looser" texture than its winning sibling but still won fans for being "super-smooth." Tasters thought it made an especially "well-balanced," satay sauce.

RECOMMENDED WITH RESERVATIONS

PEANUT BUTTER & CO. No-Stir Natural Smooth Operator
PRICE: $4.49 for 18 oz (25 cents per oz)
TOTAL SUGAR: 8.7% **SALT:** 0.85%
INGREDIENTS: Peanuts, evaporated cane juice, palm fruit oil, salt
COMMENTS: Though it says "no-stir" on the label, this "stiff" palm oil-enriched peanut butter was "weeping oil" and came across as "greasy" to some tasters. However, it turned out a respectable batch of cookies—"chewy in the center, crisp and short at the edge"—and made "perfectly good" satay sauce.

MARANATHA Organic No Stir Peanut Butter
PRICE: $5.69 for 16 oz (36 cents per oz)
TOTAL SUGAR: 9.3% **SALT:** 0.51%
INGREDIENTS: Organic dry roasted peanuts, organic palm oil, organic unrefined cane sugar, sea salt
COMMENTS: On the one hand, this organic peanut butter produced cookies that were "soft and sturdy" yet "moist," with "knockout peanut flavor." On the other hand, eating it straight from the jar was nearly impossible; its "loose," "liquid-y," and "dribbly" consistency had one taster wonder if it was "peanut soup."

PETER PAN Peanut Butter

PRICE: $2.49 for 18 oz (14 cents per oz)
TOTAL SUGAR: 10.8% **SALT:** 1.11%
INGREDIENTS: Roasted peanuts, sugar, less than 2% of hydrogenated vegetable oils (cottonseed and rapeseed), salt, partially hydrogenated cottonseed oil
COMMENTS: Though this peanut butter offered an ideally "cushiony, smooth" texture, it also left an "off-putting," "waxy," "stale" aftertaste that, according to some tasters, also plagued the cookies.

RATING TOASTER OVENS

Toaster ovens have come a long way from the days of just making toast and warming up leftover pizza. Many now offer a slew of additional features and have the price tag to match. We tested 10 toaster ovens, ranging in price from $60 to a staggering $250, to find the best one. We made single slices of toast (using white bread) on medium and dark settings to evaluate their ability to make toast. We also toasted multiple batches of six slices to evaluate the heating patterns in the ovens. To test cooking performance, we baked lemon cookies, melted cheese on sandwiches, heated frozen pizzas and macaroni and cheese, and roasted chickens. To gauge accuracy, we used a thermocouple to judge how well empty ovens held the standard temperature of 350 degrees. Finally, we considered design and usability. Brands are listed in order of preference. See www.americastestkitchen.com for updates to this testing.

HIGHLY RECOMMENDED

BREVILLE The Smart Oven (model #BOV800 XL)
PRICE: $249.95
TOASTING: ★★★ **COOKING:** ★★★
USER-FRIENDLINESS: ★★★
ACCURACY: ★★★
COMMENTS: While the price makes us wince, this well-designed oven aced every test and was simple to use. Food browned and cooked uniformly, whether we were roasting chicken, toasting bread, or melting cheese. Five quartz elements consistently cooled and reheated, producing steady, controlled heat.

RECOMMENDED

HAMILTON BEACH Set and Forget Toaster Oven with Convection Cooking (model #31230)
PRICE: $99.99 BEST BUY
TOASTING: ★★★ **COOKING:** ★★
USER-FRIENDLINESS: ★★★
ACCURACY: ★★
COMMENTS: Clearly designed buttons, a helpful electronic display, and an easy-to-understand manual made using this oven a snap. Not as accurate as our winner, it still produced golden-brown toast.

RECOMMENDED WITH RESERVATIONS

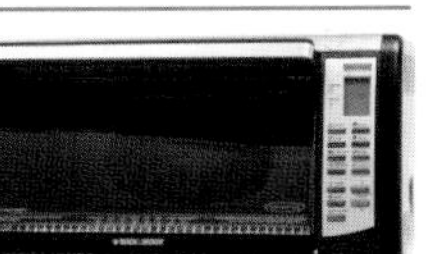

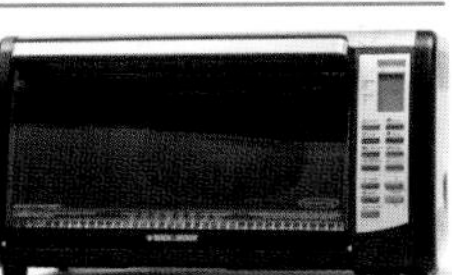

BLACK & DECKER Digital Convection Oven (model #CTO6305)
PRICE: $89.99
TOASTING: ★★★ **COOKING:** ★★
USER-FRIENDLINESS: ★★★
ACCURACY: ★
COMMENTS: This oven's performance was acceptable but a little uneven. Cookies and chicken browned unevenly, though mac and cheese and pizza were fine; toast was terrific with one slice but a little patchy in multiple batches.

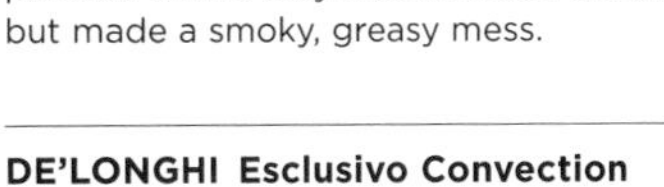

KRUPS 6-Slice Convection Toaster Oven (model #FBC2)
PRICE: $149.99
TOASTING: ★ **COOKING:** ★★
USER-FRIENDLINESS: ★★★
ACCURACY: ★★
COMMENTS: A pared-down version of our previous winner from Krups, which was discontinued, this oven just doesn't measure up. Ironically, the earlier Krups made decent toast. This time, single slices of toast colored too much or not at all.

RECOMMENDED WITH RESERVATIONS *(cont.)*

DUALIT Professional Mini Oven (model #89100)
PRICE: $249.95
TOASTING: ★★ **COOKING:** ★★★
USER-FRIENDLINESS: ★★
ACCURACY: ★
COMMENTS: Solidly built and simple to set, this pricey oven was well lit with a large window—a good thing, since testing confirmed that it ran so hot (cycling as high as 428 degrees when we wanted 350) that we usually had to pull out the food early before it overcooked. Still, it cooked evenly and well.

OSTER 6081 Channel 6-Slice Toaster Oven (model #6801)
PRICE: $58
TOASTING: ★★★ **COOKING:** ★★
USER-FRIENDLINESS: ★
ACCURACY: ★★
COMMENTS: This was the cheapest model in the lineup, and its slightly tinny feel and badly designed controls made that clear: Knobs are labeled underneath and hard to set without stooping; settings are printed in low-contrast color. But its heat was relatively accurate and the cooking, including toast, was above par.

NOT RECOMMENDED

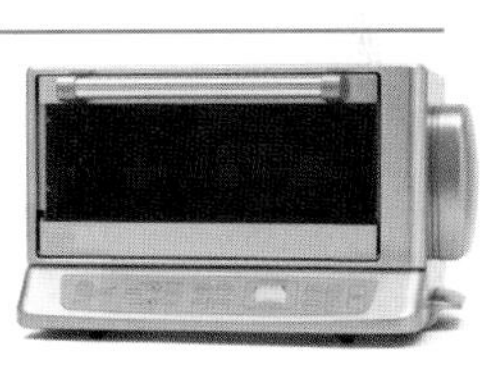

CUISINART Convection Toaster Oven (model #TOB-195)
PRICE: $179
TOASTING: ★★ **COOKING:** ★★
USER-FRIENDLINESS: ★★
ACCURACY: ★
COMMENTS: Toast turned out light when we wanted it medium or dark, plus it always colored unevenly. Cookies, pizza, and tuna melts also came out with darker patches where they'd been under the elements. Chicken cooked well but made a smoky, greasy mess.

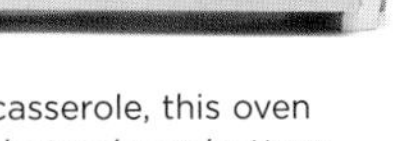

DE'LONGHI Esclusivo Convection Toaster Oven (model #DO1289)
PRICE: $149.95
TOASTING: ★ **COOKING:** ★★★
USER-FRIENDLINESS: ★
ACCURACY: ★★
COMMENTS: Though it was relatively accurate, baked perfect cookies, and heated a casserole, this oven took forever to cook. Toast was perfect on top, but pale on bottom.

CRÊPES AND *Croissants*

CHAPTER 23

THE RECIPES

Chris gets into character to discuss translating French classics for the home cook.

WHEN SOME PEOPLE THINK OF FRENCH CUISINE, RICH SAUCES, terrines, and other complex, savory foods come to mind. Not for us: we see crêpes and croissants. But French desserts and pastries are notoriously complicated to prepare, so most of the time we're resigned to getting our fix from the average versions found in restaurants and pastry shops. Crêpes are nothing more than thin pancakes, but they have a reputation for being temperamental divas, demanding pampered batter, a specialized pan, and supremely delicate handling. We set out to change that and create a foolproof batter and technique that would guarantee perfectly crisp, thin, delicate crêpes every time.

But while crêpes may be simple at heart, croissants are intrinsically elaborate. Preparing them involves multiple layers of fat and dough, repeated rolling and folding, and the challenge of dealing with the unpredictability of any baked good involving yeast. As a result, producing these flaky, multilayered beauties has always been the exclusive province of the pastry elite. But unless you have access to an authentic French pastry shop, store-bought versions usually disappoint. We wanted to make croissants accessible to the home cook, but they still had to deliver authentic flavor, structure, and texture. Join us as we start our own French revolution.

CRÊPES WITH SUGAR AND LEMON

CRÊPES

WHY THIS RECIPE WORKS: A crêpe is nothing but a thin pancake cooked quickly on each side and wrapped around a sweet or savory filling, but it has a reputation for being difficult. We wanted an easy method for crêpes that were thin and delicate yet rich and flavorfully browned in spots. Finding the perfect ratio of milk to flour and sugar gave us rich-tasting, lightly sweet pancakes. We were surprised to find that neither the type of flour nor the mixing method seemed to matter, and a plain old 12-inch nonstick skillet worked as well as a specialty crêpe pan. What does matter is heating the pan properly (over low heat for at least 10 minutes), using the right amount of batter (we settled on ¼ cup), and flipping the crêpe at precisely the right moment, when the edges appear dry, matte, and lacy.

MOST OF US HERE IN THE TEST KITCHEN HAVE AT LEAST a couple of unpleasant memories associated with cooking school, and for more than one of us, preparing crêpes stands out. A crêpe is nothing but a thin pancake cooked quickly on each side and wrapped around a sweet or savory filling, but despite its apparent simplicity, there are a number of conventions to learn. The classic steel crêpe pan can be too hot or too cool, you can use too much batter or not enough. Or you might flip too soon, producing crêpes that are limp and anemic, or let them linger too long so that they stick and tear. A few of us have firmly resolved to avoid crêpe-making forever.

Then there's the crêpe episode of Julia Child's vintage PBS series *The French Chef.* She made the process look so easy, throwing together the batter in a blender and—using an ordinary nonstick pan—blithely flipping crêpe after crêpe. Could making great crêpes—thin and delicate yet rich and flavorfully browned in spots—really be so painless, or did Child's expertise just make it look that way?

We were determined to face our bête noire, so we dug deep into the test kitchen's collection of French cookbooks to uncover a range of ingredients and techniques. But surprisingly, the 50-odd recipes we surveyed were remarkably similar: Flour and milk (and sometimes water) were either blended or hand-whisked with eggs, salt, and melted butter to form a creamy batter. Several recipes were spiked with brandy or lightly sweetened with sugar. The cooking instructions were universal: Spread the batter as thin as possible in the skillet, cook until the edges are golden and lacy, and then flip the crêpe to brown spottily on the other side. The only significant difference? About half of the recipes called for resting the batter for one to two hours after mixing, while the others skipped straight to cooking.

We didn't see much need for fiddling with the batter itself. A couple of quick tests determined that a 3:2 ratio of milk to flour touched with sugar produced the best pancakes: thin, rich tasting and lightly sweet. The type of flour in the mix and the mixing method, both of which we thought might affect the texture of the crêpes, didn't seem to matter. When we tested low-protein cake flour against higher-protein all-purpose and bread flours, our tasters deemed the results virtually indistinguishable. And batters simply whisked together by hand turned out crêpes every bit as good as those made from batters whirred by countertop or immersion blenders. Even the cooking vessel was nothing to fuss over: After making just a few crêpes, we followed Child's lead and ditched the specialty crêpe pan in favor of a plain old 12-inch nonstick skillet.

We were beginning to wonder if all that cooking-school hullabaloo about the fastidiousness of the recipe wasn't just a lot of hot air—but we also hadn't yet tackled the central controversy about whether or not to rest the batter. The traditional justification is twofold: First, resting allows the starch granules in the flour to hydrate more fully, which purportedly produces a more tender crêpe. Second, a rest means that there's time for any air incorporated into the batter during mixing to dissipate, so the crêpe will be as thin as possible.

Curious, we made a batch of crêpe batter and placed it in the fridge. Then, just to take the resting test to the extreme, we waited two hours and made two more batches—one with all-purpose flour and (though we were loath to introduce specialty ingredients) the other with Wondra flour. (Child used this instantly hydrating flour in place of a rest in a later edition of *The French Chef Cookbook*.) Tasters compared crêpes from all three batches. Once again, their votes indicated no clear winner. We repeated the test just to be certain, but it seemed that neither the rest nor the specialty flour intended to mimic the rest made any noticeable difference.

Save for a few ingredient tweaks here and there, our recipe hadn't changed much since we began developing it. But these later batches of crêpes were noticeably better—more tender and uniformly brown—than earlier attempts, and we realized that while the batter itself was relatively forgiving, there were some crucial crêpe-cooking tricks that we'd picked up along the way.

First, heat the pan properly. When we made it too hot, the batter set up before it evenly coated the surface, yielding a crêpe marred by thick, spongy patches and holes. When we made it too cool, the crêpe was pale (read: bland) and too flimsy to flip without tearing. To ensure steady, even cooking, we borrowed a technique that we have used in an omelet recipe: We slowly heated the oiled skillet over low heat for at least 10 minutes. We even found a quick test to determine when the pan was ready: Spoon a teaspoon of batter into the center of the preheated, lightly oil-slicked pan. If it turns perfectly golden brown in exactly 20 seconds, your skillet has hit that temperature "sweet spot."

Second, add just enough batter to coat the bottom of the pan. After trial and error, we settled on ¼ cup of batter as the ideal amount. The only glitch: The classic approach taught in culinary school—tilting the pan to swirl the batter around it—wasn't distributing the batter as evenly as we liked. Our minor adjustment? Tilting the pan and giving it a gentle shake at the same time.

Finally, pinpoint the precise moment to flip the crêpe. Our stopwatch tests showed that if the batter was added to a properly heated pan, it took about 25 seconds for it to go from wet to ready to flip—appearing dry, matte, and lacy around the edges. But to truly overcome all of our crêpe-cooking fears, we needed a way to flip the pancake without singeing our fingers. Opting for a blunt-edged tool to loosen the crêpe, we nudged it from underneath with a heatproof rubber spatula before grasping its edge, then nimbly turned it to the flip side to cook until spotty brown—about another 20 seconds.

Once we had these tactics down, we whipped up a few simple sweet fillings—banana-Nutella, chocolate-orange, honey-almond, utterly simple lemon-sugar, and dulce de leche–pecan were test kitchen favorites—and mused over how, with some careful testing and a few subtle tweaks, we'd turned a culinary school terror into an opportunity to create the simplest, friendliest of recipes.

NOTES FROM THE TEST KITCHEN

TROUBLESHOOTING CRÊPES

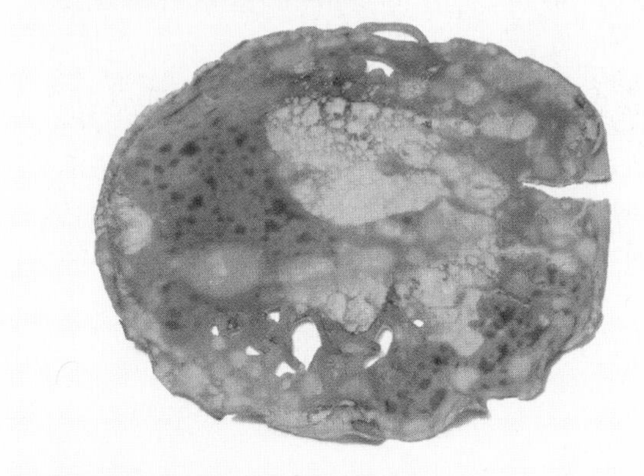

1. PROBLEM: Splotchy browning
SOLUTION: Exposing the skillet to too much heat too fast can yield unevenly browned crêpes. To ensure steady, even cooking, we warm the oiled pan over low heat for at least 10 minutes.

2. PROBLEM: Batter spreads unevenly
SOLUTION: To guarantee that the batter thinly but completely covers the cooking surface, we add just enough (¼ cup), then tilt and shake the skillet until the batter is evenly distributed.

3. PROBLEM: Crêpe tears when flipped
SOLUTION: If the crêpe begins to tear, the batter hasn't had a chance to fully set and isn't ready to be flipped. Wait a few seconds, until the edge of the crêpe turns light brown, and then gently slide a heatproof rubber spatula underneath, grasp it with your fingertips, and flip.

Crêpes with Sugar and Lemon

SERVES 4

Crêpes will give off steam as they cook, but if at any point the skillet begins to smoke, remove it from the heat immediately and turn down the heat. Stacking the crêpes on a wire rack allows excess steam to escape so they won't stick together. To allow for practice, the recipe yields 10 crêpes; only eight are needed for the filling.

- **½ teaspoon vegetable oil**
- **1 cup (5 ounces) all-purpose flour**
- **1 teaspoon sugar, plus 8 teaspoons for sprinkling**
- **¼ teaspoon salt**
- **1½ cups whole milk**
- **3 large eggs**
- **2 tablespoons unsalted butter, melted and cooled**
- **Lemon wedges**

1. Heat oil in 12-inch nonstick skillet over low heat for at least 10 minutes.

2. While skillet is heating, whisk flour, 1 teaspoon sugar, and salt together in bowl. In separate bowl, whisk together milk and eggs. Add half of milk mixture to dry ingredients and whisk until smooth. Add butter and whisk until incorporated. Whisk in remaining milk mixture until smooth.

3. Using paper towels, wipe out skillet, leaving thin film of oil on bottom and sides of pan. Increase heat to medium and let skillet heat for 1 minute. After 1 minute, test heat of skillet by placing 1 teaspoon batter in center and cook for 20 seconds. If mini crêpe is golden brown on bottom, skillet is properly heated; if it is too light or too dark, adjust heat accordingly and retest.

4. Pour ¼ cup batter into far side of pan and tilt and shake gently until batter evenly covers bottom of pan. Cook crêpe without moving until top surface is dry and edges are starting to brown, loosening crêpe from side of pan with heatproof rubber spatula, about 25 seconds. Gently slide spatula underneath edge of crêpe, grasp edge with fingertips, and flip crêpe. Cook until second side is lightly spotted, about 20 seconds. Transfer cooked crêpe to wire rack, inverting so spotted side is facing up. Return pan to heat and heat for 10 seconds before repeating with remaining batter. As crêpes are done, stack on wire rack.

NOTES FROM THE TEST KITCHEN

WHISK AWAY

Most recipes for traditional American pancakes caution against overmixing the batter; doing so activates the formation of gluten and will render the results tough and dense. In theory, the same logic would apply to crêpes, but our mixing tests showed that all that worry was for naught. Why? It all comes down to the liquid-to-flour ratio. The high proportion of liquid in crêpe batter makes it so diluted that the development of gluten—that is, the network of proteins that give baked goods their chew—is not actually a factor. This also means that you can use anything from low-protein cake flour to high-protein bread flour and get a similarly tender crêpe.

IS THE PAN READY?

Here's a test to make sure that the pan is hot enough: Drop a teaspoon of batter into its center. If this mini crêpe is golden brown on the bottom after 20 seconds, the pan is ready. If it's blond—or burned—adjust the heat accordingly.

5. Transfer stack of crêpes to large plate and invert second plate over crêpes. Microwave until crêpes are warm, 30 to 45 seconds (45 to 60 seconds if crêpes have cooled completely). Remove top plate and wipe dry with paper towel. Sprinkle half of top crêpe with 1 teaspoon sugar. Fold unsugared bottom half over sugared half, then fold in half again to make quarters. Transfer sugared crêpe to second plate. Continue with remaining crêpes. Serve immediately, passing lemon wedges separately.

VARIATIONS

Crêpes with Bananas and Nutella

Omit 8 teaspoons sprinkling sugar and lemon wedges. Spread 2 teaspoons Nutella over half of each crêpe followed by eight to ten ¼-inch-thick banana slices. Fold crêpes into quarters. Serve immediately.

Crêpes with Honey and Toasted Almonds

Omit 8 teaspoons sprinkling sugar and lemon wedges. Drizzle 1 teaspoon honey over half of each crêpe and sprinkle with 2 teaspoons finely chopped toasted sliced almonds and pinch salt. Fold crêpes into quarters. Serve immediately.

Crêpes with Chocolate and Orange

Omit 8 teaspoons sprinkling sugar and lemon wedges. Using fingertips, rub 1 teaspoon finely grated orange zest into ¼ cup sugar. Stir in 2 ounces finely grated bittersweet chocolate. Sprinkle 1½ tablespoons chocolate-orange mixture over half of each crêpe. Fold crêpes into quarters. Serve immediately.

Crêpes with Dulce de Leche and Toasted Pecans

Omit 8 teaspoons sprinkling sugar and lemon wedges. Drizzle 1 teaspoon dulce de leche over half of each crêpe and sprinkle with 2 teaspoons finely chopped toasted pecans and pinch salt. Fold crêpe into quarters. Serve immediately.

CROISSANTS

WHY THIS RECIPE WORKS: We wanted to create an approachable croissant recipe for home bakers—one that would deliver authentic flavor. The layered structure that characterizes croissants is formed through a process called lamination. First, a basic dough of flour, water, yeast, sugar, salt, and a small amount of butter is made. Then a larger amount of butter is formed into a block and encased in the relatively lean dough. This dough and butter package is rolled out and folded multiple times (each is called a "turn") to form paper-thin layers of dough separated by even thinner layers of butter. Once baked, it's these layers that make croissants so flaky and decadent. To start, we found that more turns didn't necessarily produce more layers—we stopped at three turns, as any more produced a homogeneous bready texture. As for the star ingredient, butter, we found that great croissants demanded higher-fat European-style butter. And one essential tip we discovered during our recipe development was to give the dough a 30-minute super-chill in the freezer to firm it to the consistency of the butter, thus ensuring perfectly distinct layers.

WE CAN THINK OF TWO REASONS WHY ALMOST NOBODY makes their own croissants. First, most folks buy them from a bakery, or even from a coffee shop or supermarket. Second, the process is long and daunting. It pairs the challenge of preparing a laminated pastry (that is, one composed of many alternating layers of fat and dough) with the potential unpredictability of a yeast-leavened item. Even if you follow a recipe to the letter, the results don't always bake up as they should: a deep golden-brown, shatteringly crisp surface that gives way to soft, delicate layers of buttery, rich-yet-light pastry within.

We can also think of two reasons why making your own croissants is absolutely worth the effort. For starters, a commercial croissant that lives up to that ideal is a rare find; many of the pastries out there are squat, dense, bready, or just plain bland. What's more, we know from

CROISSANTS

personal experience that there's nothing quite as satisfying as pulling off this feat yourself—from folding and shaping the dough, to filling your kitchen with the scent of warm pastry, to watching your brunch guests swoon.

That said, achieving consistent results is difficult. Sometimes the croissants collapse during baking and turn dense, losing their signature layers; other times the butter leaks out onto the baking sheet, yielding thick-crusted specimens that have essentially fried in their own fat. And then there's the sheer force required to muscle the gluten-heavy dough into submission. It would be a challenge, but we decided to get into the kitchen and learn where we were veering off course.

Before we homed in on specific problems, we reviewed the basics of laminated pastry. The process starts simply enough: Flour, milk, yeast, a bit of melted butter, sugar, and salt are mixed together, rested briefly, shaped into a rectangle, and then refrigerated to chill through. The dough is then rolled out into a bigger rectangle and wrapped around a large block of cold butter, and the dough-butter package (known as a plaque) is rolled out into a long rectangle. This is where the croissant's trademark layering happens: The plaque is folded into thirds, yielding layers of dough separated by layers of butter. This rolling and folding process (called a "turn") is repeated up to five times, depending on the recipe, tripling the number of layers formed with each turn. Finally, the plaque is rolled again, cut into triangles, shaped into crescents, left to rise, brushed with egg wash, and baked.

To get started, we rounded up several recipes and found that, while the ingredients and proportions were similar, the techniques—specifically the number of turns—varied widely: anywhere from two (which makes nine layers of dough) to a bicep-punishing five (which theoretically produces 243 layers). Figuring out the ideal number of turns would be an important first step, as the turning process has a twofold effect: It not only creates layers in the dough but also develops gluten (the elastic protein that is formed when the flour is moistened), which causes the dough to stubbornly bounce back and resist rolling. Strong dough is no problem for bakeshops, which use machines called sheeters (similar to huge pasta

machines) to roll out the plaque. But for our at-home recipe, we'd need a dough that could be managed with just your hands.

To our great relief, too many turns ended up being detrimental. As the layers of fat became thinner, they were more easily absorbed into the dough, eventually yielding a pastry more akin to brioche—rich and tender, but with a homogeneous, bready crumb. Three seemed to be the magic number of turns for producing the most distinct layers.

But rolling and folding the dough three times was still hard work. We thought that using a heftier piece of equipment might facilitate the process, so we switched from our favored tapered French-style rolling pin to a roller-style model. No luck: The dough still refused to cooperate, which made us realize that we needed to approach the problem—the gluten development—more directly. Knowing that the protein content of the flour was directly affecting the gluten development, we decided to experiment with the type (and brand) of flour we were using and made three new batches: one with moderate-protein (10.5 percent) Gold Medal all-purpose flour, another with relatively high-protein (11.7 percent) all-purpose flour from King Arthur, and a final sample with high-protein (14 percent) bread flour. As we expected, the higher the protein the more gluten developed, and the more difficult the plaque was to roll out. Still, the exercise was informative. The bread-flour croissants were the best we had ever made: majestically risen, crisp, and filled with airy spirals of buttery pastry.

It turns out that gluten doesn't just make a dough more elastic; it also makes it more resistant to breaking during rolling and as it expands during rising and baking. Stronger dough is also better at maintaining the thin sheets necessary for distinct layering. But our hands were blistered from rolling out this sturdy bread-flour dough. We decided to compromise with the higher-protein all-purpose flour, hoping that we could find another way to make the dough more compliant.

That left us with the other main ingredient: butter. From the start we'd defaulted to Land O'Lakes (about 81 percent butterfat), but some recipes called for European-style butter, the butterfat content of which typically starts at around 83 percent and goes up as high as 86 percent. Another point we noted: Recipes using standard butter called for kneading it with a couple of tablespoons of flour before shaping it into a block, while those that specified European-style butter added no flour to the block. Not sure what effect the flour or the extra fat might have on the final product, we made three batches of croissants using, respectively, European-style butter, standard butter mixed with flour, and unadulterated standard butter.

The differences in both the process and the final product were remarkable. When we tried to shape the cold, flourless standard butter, it broke into pieces, and the resulting dough baked up heavy and bready. The standard butter-and-flour block was more cooperative and the croissants were nicely layered, but the European-style-butter croissants were a revelation. Not only was this higher-fat dough easier to work with but it also boasted superior layering and stunningly rich butter flavor.

The results of this test had been more dramatic than we were expecting, so we did some homework and learned two reasons why the increased butterfat made such a difference. First, butter with less fat contains more water. A butter with 81 percent fat, for example, is made up of about 15 percent water while a butter with 83 percent fat is about 13 percent water. This variance may sound small, but it means that the lower-fat butter has about 15 percent more water than the higher-fat butter. The greater amount of water in the dough made with regular butter was gluing the layers together, leading to a dense crumb. It also explained the purpose of adding flour to the standard butter: It soaked up the extra moisture.

Second, higher-fat butter remains solid over a wider temperature range, meaning that it's more pliable when cold and also holds its shape better as it warms up. More specifically, the butter must be firm to function as a barrier between distinct layers of dough, and therefore must remain solid as the dough is handled.

We'd made great progress but had one more problem to iron out. For consistently tall, flaky results, we needed the butter and dough to be at exactly the same degree of malleability during rolling. We had been refrigerating the plaque between turns, but this often resulted in butter that was firmer than the dough and therefore prone to breaking (which caused the layers to stick together in spots where the butter was absent). Conversely, if we left the plaque at room temperature, the butter inevitably became softer than the dough and leaked out during rolling. The secret to perfectly laminated dough would be ensuring that these two markedly different components had the same puttylike texture. But how?

It wasn't until we contacted a talented local baker, Christy Timon of Clear Flour Bakery, in Brookline, Massachusetts, that we came upon the solution: freezing the dough. As Timon demonstrated, super-chilling the butter-dough square in the freezer for 30 minutes before rolling firmed the dough to the consistency of the butter without appreciably altering the texture of the butter. Together with the higher-protein all-purpose flour and the European-style butter, this freezer technique added up to a hat trick of discoveries that led to layering so distinct that it was visible even in the raw dough.

Confident that we had finally mastered the recipe, we shaped the croissants, let them rise until doubled in size, brushed them with egg wash to encourage deep browning, and baked them in a 425-degree oven. When we removed the bronzed beauties about 20 minutes later, the layering that had been subtly suggested in the raw dough had bloomed into crisp, delicate tiers. Colleagues (the fronts of their aprons covered with fine pastry flakes) declared the recipe a triumph, regretting only that the testing had come to an end.

Not to worry, we told them. Now that we have a recipe that guarantees success, we'll make croissants again and again.

NOTES FROM THE TEST KITCHEN

MAKING A BUTTER BLOCK FOR CROISSANTS

1. Fold 24-inch length of parchment in half to create 12-inch rectangle. Fold over 3 open sides of rectangle to form 8-inch square.

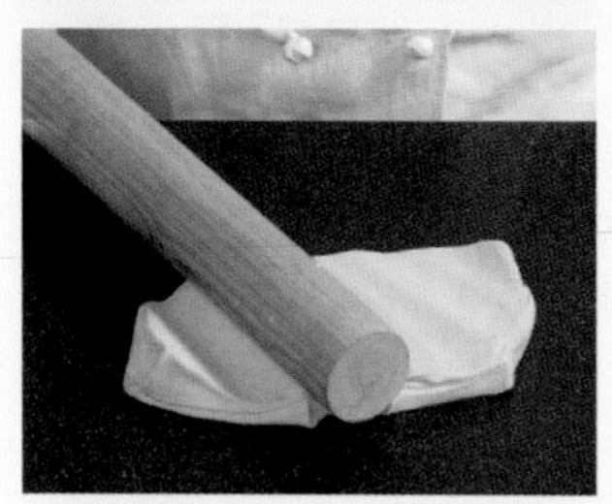

2. Using rolling pin, beat butter until it is just pliable, then fold butter in on itself using bench scraper. Beat butter into rough 6-inch square.

3. Unfold parchment envelope and, using bench scraper, transfer butter to parchment, refolding at creases to enclose. Turn packet over, and gently roll butter with rolling pin so butter block fills parchment square, taking care to achieve even thickness. Refrigerate.

LAMINATING THE DOUGH FOR CROISSANTS

1. Roll chilled dough into 17 by 8-inch rectangle. Unwrap butter and place in center of dough, aligning it so that edges of butter and dough are flush at top and bottom. Fold two sides of dough over butter so they meet in center of butter square.

2. Using fingertips, press seam together. Using rolling pin, press firmly on each open end of packet. Roll dough out lengthwise until it is 24 inches long and 8 inches wide.

3. Starting at bottom of dough, fold into thirds like business letter. Turn dough 90 degrees and roll and fold in thirds again. Place on baking sheet, wrap tightly with plastic wrap, and return to freezer for 30 minutes. Roll and fold in thirds one more time.

Croissants

MAKES 22 CROISSANTS

These croissants take at least 10 hours to make from start to finish, but the process can be spread over 2 days. European-style butters, like Lurpak, Kerrygold, and Plugra, have a higher butterfat content, which makes it easier to fold them into the dough. Any brand of all-purpose flour will produce acceptable croissants, but we recommend using King Arthur All-Purpose Flour, which has a slightly higher protein content. Do not attempt to make these croissants in a room that is warmer than 80 degrees. If at any time during rolling the dough retracts, dust it lightly with flour, fold it loosely, cover it, and return it to the freezer to rest for 10 to 15 minutes.

- **3 tablespoons unsalted butter plus 24 tablespoons (3 sticks) unsalted European-style butter, very cold**
- **1¾ cups whole milk**
- **4 teaspoons instant or rapid-rise yeast**
- **4¼ cups (21¼ ounces) all-purpose flour**
- **¼ cup (1¾ ounces) sugar**
- **Salt**
- **1 large egg**
- **1 teaspoon cold water**

1. Melt 3 tablespoons butter in medium saucepan over low heat. Remove from heat and immediately stir in milk (temperature should be lower than 90 degrees). Whisk in yeast; transfer milk mixture to bowl of stand mixer. Add flour, sugar, and 2 teaspoons salt. Using dough hook, knead on low speed until cohesive dough forms, 2 to 3 minutes. Increase speed to medium-low and knead for 1 minute. Remove bowl from mixer, remove dough hook, and cover bowl with plastic wrap. Let dough rest at room temperature for 30 minutes.

2. Transfer dough to parchment paper–lined baking sheet and shape into 10 by 7-inch rectangle about 1 inch thick. Wrap tightly with plastic and refrigerate for 2 hours.

3. FOR THE BUTTER BLOCK: While dough chills, fold 24-inch length of parchment in half to create 12-inch rectangle. Fold over 3 open sides of rectangle to form 8-inch square with enclosed sides. Crease folds firmly. Place 24 tablespoons cold butter directly on counter and beat with rolling pin for about 60 seconds until butter is just pliable, but not warm, folding butter in on itself using bench scraper. Beat into rough 6-inch square. Unfold parchment envelope. Using bench scraper, transfer butter to center of parchment square, refolding at creases to enclose. Turn packet over so that flaps are underneath and gently roll butter packet until butter fills parchment square, taking care to achieve even thickness. Refrigerate at least 45 minutes.

4. TO LAMINATE THE DOUGH: Transfer dough to freezer. After 30 minutes, transfer dough to lightly floured counter and roll into 17 by 8-inch rectangle with long side of rectangle parallel to edge of counter. Unwrap butter and place in center of dough so that butter and dough are flush at top and bottom. Fold 2 sides of dough over butter square so they meet in center. Press seam together with fingertips. With rolling pin, press firmly on each open end of packet. Roll out dough, perpendicular to

edge of counter, to rectangle 24 inches long and 8 inches wide. Bring bottom third of dough up, then fold upper third over it, folding like business letter into 8-inch square. Turn dough 90 degrees counterclockwise. Roll out dough again, perpendicular to edge of counter, into 24 by 8-inch rectangle and fold into thirds. Place dough on baking sheet, wrap tightly with plastic, and return to freezer for 30 minutes.

5. Transfer dough to lightly floured counter so that top flap of dough is facing right. Roll once more, perpendicular to edge of counter, into 24 by 8-inch rectangle and fold into thirds. Place dough on baking sheet, wrap tightly with plastic, and refrigerate for 2 hours.

6. Transfer dough to freezer. After 30 minutes, transfer to lightly floured counter and roll into 18 by 16-inch rectangle with long side of rectangle parallel to edge of counter. Fold upper half of dough over lower half. Using ruler, mark dough at 3-inch intervals along bottom edge with bench scraper (you should have 5 marks). Move ruler to top of dough, measure in 1½ inches from left, then use this mark to measure out 3-inch intervals (you should have 6 marks). Starting at lower left corner, use pizza wheel or knife to cut dough into triangles from mark to mark. You will have 12 single triangles and 5 double triangles; discard scraps. Unfold double triangles and cut into 10 single triangles (making 22 equal-size triangles in total). If dough begins to soften, return to freezer for 10 minutes.

7. TO SHAPE THE CROISSANTS: Position 1 triangle on counter. (Keep remaining triangles covered with plastic while shaping.) Cut ½-inch slit in center of short end of triangle. Grasp triangle by 2 corners on either side of slit, and stretch gently, then grasp bottom point and stretch. Fold 2 sides of slit down. Positioning palms on 2 outer points of top, begin to roll top partway toward point. Gently grasp point with one hand and stretch again. Continue to roll, tucking point underneath. Curve ends gently toward one another to create crescent shape. Repeat with remaining triangles.

8. Place 12 croissants on 2 parchment-lined baking sheets, leaving at least 2½ inches between croissants, 6 croissants per sheet. Lightly wrap baking sheets with plastic, leaving room for croissants to expand. Let stand at room temperature until nearly doubled in size, 2½ to 3 hours. (Shaped croissants can be refrigerated on trays for up to 18 hours. Remove from refrigerator to rise and add at least 30 minutes to rising time.)

9. After croissants have been rising for 2 hours, adjust oven racks to upper-middle and lower-middle positions and heat oven to 425 degrees. In small bowl, whisk together egg, water, and pinch of salt. Brush croissants with egg wash using pastry brush. Place croissants in oven and reduce temperature to 400 degrees. Bake for 12 minutes, then switch and rotate baking sheets. Continue to bake until deep golden brown, 8 to 12 minutes longer. Transfer croissants to wire rack and allow to cool until just warm, about 15 minutes. Serve warm or at room temperature.

TO MAKE AHEAD: After shaping, place croissants 1 inch apart on parchment-lined baking sheet. Wrap with plastic wrap and freeze until solid, about 2 hours. Transfer frozen croissants from baking sheet to zipper-lock bag and return to freezer for up to 2 months. Bake frozen croissants as directed from step 8, increasing rising time by 1 to 2 hours.

NOTES FROM THE TEST KITCHEN

SHAPING THE CROISSANTS

1. Transfer dough from freezer to lightly floured work surface and roll into 18 by 16-inch rectangle. (If dough begins to retract, fold it loosely in thirds, wrap it, and return it to freezer for 10–15 minutes.) Fold upper half of dough over lower half.

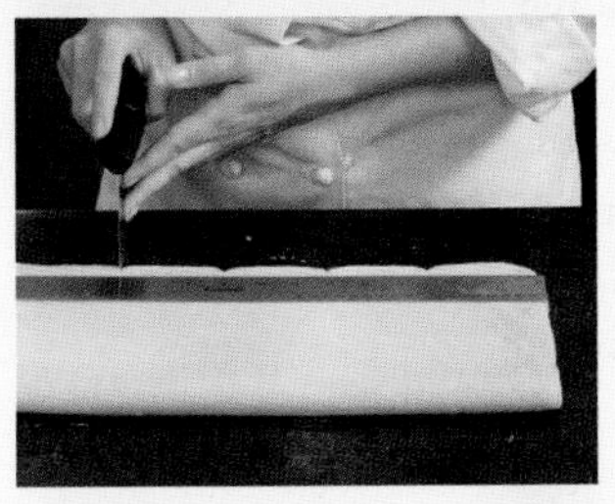

2. Using ruler, mark dough at 3-inch intervals along bottom edge. Move ruler to top of dough, measure in 1½ inches from left, then use this mark to measure out 3-inch intervals.

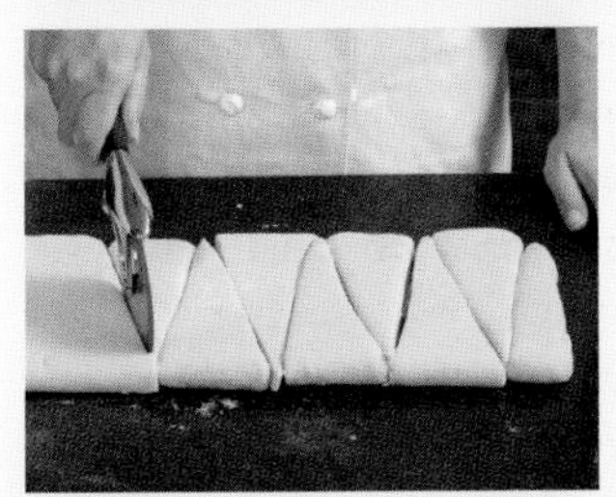

3. Using pizza wheel or knife, cut dough into triangles from mark to mark. You should have 12 single triangles and 5 double triangles; discard any scraps.

4. Unfold double triangle and cut in half to form 10 single triangles (making 22 triangles in all). If dough begins to soften, return to freezer for 10 minutes.

5. Cut ½-inch slit in center of short side of each triangle. If dough begins to soften, return to freezer for 10 minutes.

6. Grasp triangle by two corners, and stretch gently, then grasp point and stretch.

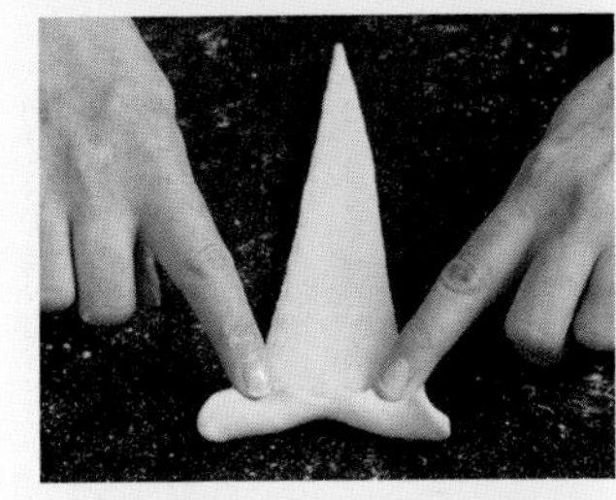

7. Place triangle on counter so point is facing toward you. Fold both sides of slit down.

8. Positioning palms on folds, roll partway toward point.

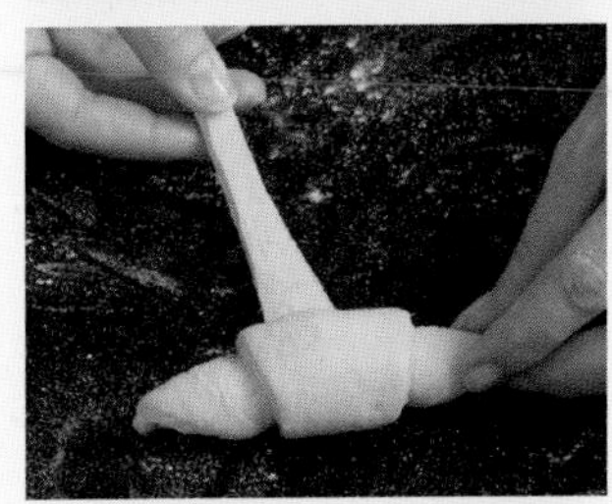

9. Gently grasp point with one hand and stretch again. Resume rolling, tucking point underneath.

10. Curve ends gently toward one another to form crescent shape.

PLATE
Dualit

COOL AND CREAMY *Desserts*

CHAPTER 24

THE RECIPES

Vanilla Ice Cream

Triple Ginger Ice Cream

Coffee Crunch Ice Cream

Creamy Chocolate Pudding

Creamy Mexican Chocolate Pudding

Creamy Mocha Pudding

SCIENCE DESK

Combating Iciness with Corn Syrup

TASTING LAB

Vanilla Beans

EQUIPMENT CORNER

Ice-Cream Makers

WE LOVE RICH, INTRICATE TARTS AND FANCY LAYER CAKES AS MUCH as anyone, but sometimes we yearn for the simpler desserts we enjoyed as kids. Cool, creamy treats such as vanilla ice cream and chocolate pudding come to mind; however, the simplest recipes are sometimes the most difficult to execute properly. The main reason more people don't make their own ice cream? It's never as creamy, smooth, or dense as the best stuff from the store. We set out to change that, and we knew that with relatively few ingredients—milk, cream, sugar, and eggs—finding the right technique would be the key to unlocking the secret to the best homemade ice cream.

Creamy chocolate pudding is another dessert we loved growing up, but nostalgia isn't enough to make a dessert worthwhile. Like ice cream, homemade pudding also suffers from textural issues, typically turning out grainy instead of smooth. And the chocolate flavor is usually underwhelming too; we wanted the chocolate to take center stage, not fade quietly into the background. To rescue chocolate pudding from obscurity, we'd have to ramp up the flavor while finding a way to preserve its silky texture. Join us we rediscover the simple joys of childhood.

Space gets tight in the test kitchen during filming, so we use every inch we have—even the pantry, where test cook Dan Souza checks on the progress of churning ice cream.

THE BEST HOMEMADE ICE CREAM

WHY THIS RECIPE WORKS: Homemade vanilla ice cream is never as creamy, smooth, or dense as the impossibly smooth "super-premium" ice cream found at gourmet markets or high-end ice cream shops. Instead of thick, dense, and velvety, ice cream made at home invariably turns out crumbly, fluffy, and icy. We wanted an incredibly creamy, dense custard-based vanilla ice cream that would rival any pricey artisanal batch. Creating smooth ice cream means reducing the size of the ice crystals; the smaller they are, the less perceptible they are. Our first move was to replace some of the sugar in our custard base with corn syrup, which interferes with crystal formation, making for a super-smooth texture. To speed up the freezing process, thereby ensuring small ice crystals, we froze a portion of the custard prior to churning, then mixed it with the remaining refrigerated custard. Finally, instead of freezing the churned ice cream in a tall container, we spread it into a thin layer in a cold metal baking pan and chilled it, which allowed the ice cream to firm up more quickly and delivered the smooth texture we were after.

IN THE TIME THAT WE'VE OWNED A CANISTER-STYLE ice-cream maker, we'd say that it has produced, optimistically, a mere couple of gallons of ice cream. It's not that we don't love the taste of homemade ice cream—believe us, we do. Rather, it's that the texture of our homemade creations never measures up to the ultra-dense, impossibly smooth "super-premium" ice cream at the grocery store. Instead of thick, dense, and velvety, our results invariably turn out crumbly, fluffy, and icy. But before we decided to get rid of our machine, we wanted to exhaust any lead that might allow us to make ice cream with a texture rivaling the highest quality commercial stuff.

We reviewed what we knew about custard-based ice cream, which typically calls for nothing more than milk, cream, sugar, eggs, and flavorings. Once the custard has frozen, the ice cream is composed of three basic elements: ice crystals of pure water; the proteins, sugars, and fats left behind as the water in the mix is crystallized; and air. The amount of air affects denseness, whereas both the makeup of the custard and how it is frozen contribute to smoothness. We decided to start with a standard custard base and focus first on finding the most effective way to freeze it.

Smooth ice cream isn't technically less icy than "icy" ice cream. Instead, its ice crystals are so small that our tongues can't detect them. One way to encourage the creation of small ice crystals is to freeze the ice-cream base as quickly as possible. Fast-freezing, along with agitation, causes the formation of thousands of tiny seed crystals, which in turn promote the formation of more tiny crystals. Speed is such an important factor in ice-cream making that commercial producers as well as restaurant kitchens spend tens of thousands of dollars on super-efficient "continuous batch" churners. The best of these can turn a 40-degree custard base (the coldest temperature it can typically achieve in a refrigerated environment) into soft-serve ice cream in 24 seconds, at which point roughly half of the freezable water has crystallized. Even the slowest commercial freezer will get the job done in 10 minutes. To maintain this superfine ice-crystal structure, the churned ice cream is then transferred to a blast freezer in smaller ice-cream shops or a hardening room in large commercial operations, where the temperature ranges from 20 to 50 degrees below zero. Under these arctic conditions, the remaining freezable water freezes in a matter of minutes.

We took stock of what we were working with: Our canister-style machine takes roughly 35 minutes to turn a chilled custard into soft-serve consistency—more than three times as long as the slowest commercial option. Even our favorite self-refrigerating model takes that long. Then, depending on how often the freezer door is opened, the partially frozen custard from either style of machine can take up to eight hours to fully freeze. No wonder our results are always icy.

Since the speed of freezing is critical, we wondered if we could improve our results by starting with a colder base. After letting our hot custard cool for a few minutes, we transferred a cup of it to a small bowl, which we popped into the freezer. We then put the rest of the custard in the fridge to cool overnight, per the usual method. The next day, we scraped the frozen custard into

VANILLA ICE CREAM

the refrigerated stuff and stirred it until the frozen custard dissolved, at which point the mixture registered around 30 degrees. Once in the canister, this base reached soft-serve consistency in just 18 minutes and, tasted straight from the machine, exhibited less iciness than previous batches had. Another bonus of this shortened churning time was that it allowed less air to be beaten into the mix; we needed some air, but too much only diluted the ice cream's flavor and lightened the texture. To our great disappointment, however, after four hours of hardening, this ice cream was almost as icy as before.

With no way to make our freezer colder, it would have seemed that we were out of luck. However, since the rate of cooling is a function of both temperature and surface area, there was still hope. For our next batch, instead of scraping our churned ice cream into a tall container before placing it in the freezer, we spread it into a thin layer in a chilled square metal baking pan (metal conducts heat faster than glass or plastic). In about an hour, our ice cream had firmed up significantly and could be easily scooped and transferred to an airtight container. Its hardening time had been cut drastically, and you could taste the difference—this was our smoothest batch yet.

However, as improved as the ice cream was, it still wasn't as smooth as store-bought. Could the ingredients themselves provide any help? Playing with the amounts of sugar and fat was out: Our tasters felt that the ice cream had optimal sweetness and richness with ¾ cup sugar, six egg yolks, and slightly more cream than milk. That left us with trying to manipulate the milk solids and water amounts. Milk solids interfere with the formation of crystals, so the more of them the better (up to a point—too much milk creates a sandy texture). And since crystals are created from water, the less of it the better (up to a point—too little water leads to gumminess).

A few of the recipes that we came across called for replacing a portion of the milk or cream with condensed or evaporated milk, which contain less water than fresh dairy does. While both products proved effective at reducing iciness, they contributed a "stale" and "cooked" flavor to the ice cream, even in relatively small doses. We also tried stirring in nonfat powdered milk to boost the milk solids. Unfortunately, in order to be effective, we needed at least ¼ cup, at which point tasters deemed the ice cream "cheesy" and "funky."

With these options exhausted, we began researching the ingredients in commercial ice cream. Many commercial producers use powerful stabilizer mixes to immobilize free water in a gel, preventing it from freezing into large ice crystals. We didn't have ready access to these magic powders, but we wondered if we couldn't approximate their effect with something else.

In the test kitchen, we often rely on cornstarch, gelatin, and pectin to provide body to recipes. Though each works slightly differently, we knew that they all thicken by trapping water in a weak gel. To test their effectiveness, we made three custards, adding cornstarch to one, bloomed gelatin to another, and pectin to the third. The ice crystals in all three batches were far less noticeable—in fact, the batch with gelatin was completely smooth. But this easy success came at a price: Each ice cream had an artificial texture and strange melting properties. The sample with gelatin refused to melt, even after 10 minutes at room temperature.

After racking up so many failures, we were tempted to throw in the towel and cede victory to the pros. Instead, we decided to call on a few of them for help.

We sought advice from two of the Boston area's best-known ice-cream makers: Gus Rancatore of Toscanini's, in nearby Cambridge, and Rick Katz, chef and owner of Pizza and Ice Cream Company, in Boston's South End. Each provided us with a different perspective on ice-cream theory (yes, ice-cream theory is a real thing). But each man circled back to an ingredient that we had all but glossed over in our testing: sugar. We'd stuck with granulated white sugar, without looking further. But ice-cream producers rely on a laundry list of different sweeteners to achieve particular textures and sweetness levels. One highly valued sweetener is invert sugar, a syrup made by cooking sugar water with an acid—a slow, finicky process that converts sucrose into glucose and fructose. With even more molecules than table sugar to interfere with ice formation, invert sugar dramatically lowers the freezing point of the ice-cream mixture so that more of the water remains liquid in the freezer. While a boon to an ice-cream shop that can hold its product at super-cold temperatures, a depressed freezing point spelled disaster in our home freezer. Even the smoothest ice cream eventually becomes coarse and icy in a home freezer due to inevitable shifts in temperature that cause thawing and refreezing. These temperature shifts have a more dramatic effect on ice creams with a depressed freezing point—they melt much more easily—than they have on ice creams that freeze harder at warmer temperatures. Furthermore, while professionals can buy ready-made invert syrup, we had to make our own—an activity that proved both time-consuming and unreliable. We crossed it off our list, along with two other unobtainable sweeteners: atomized glucose and dextrose powder.

We desperately rummaged through the pantry in search of neutral-tasting alternative sweeteners that we could use. The list was depressingly short: corn syrup. Containing about 25 percent water, corn syrup seemed like the last ingredient that might work in an effort to eliminate large ice crystals. But what did we have to lose?

We mixed up batches of our working recipe, replacing some of the sugar with increasing amounts of corn syrup. Right away, we could tell that something was different. The custard bases were more viscous than our all-sugar recipe straight out of the fridge, and they all churned to a thick, soft-serve consistency in record time. The real revelation, however, came when it was time to taste. The batch with ⅓ cup of corn syrup was the closest thing to super-premium perfection we had ever achieved. Not only was it dense, but, most important, it showed no trace of iciness. Though we were tempted to sit in the kitchen and finish off the rest of the quart, we were too eager to get back to work and figure out why this solution had worked so well.

After a few exchanges with our science editor, we had our answer. First, due to its viscosity, corn syrup prevents water molecules from grouping and freezing into large ice crystals. Second, corn syrup doesn't depress the freezing point as much as sugar does. Our corn-syrup ice cream froze faster in the canister and remained harder at home-freezer temperatures than did the all-sugar recipe. This stuff was virtually free of large ice crystals, and it stayed that way for nearly a week in the freezer.

After months of churning countless batches of ice cream, we had tasted sweet victory. Another thing we could count on: Our ice-cream machine wouldn't be showing up at a yard sale anytime soon.

NOTES FROM THE TEST KITCHEN

GETTING TO YES

Creating smooth ice cream means cutting back on ice crystals—or preventing them from forming in the first place. We tried a slew of ingredients promising to do just that, most with unfortunate side effects.

NO

Condensed and evaporated milk contribute less water to the mix, leading to fewer ice crystals, but ice cream made from each tasted "cooked."

NO

Cornstarch traps water so it can't form ice crystals, but it produced a "weird," "gummy" texture. Gelatin and pectin bombed, too.

NO

Nonfat dry milk ups the overall milk solids in the custard base, thus blocking ice crystal formation, but it left a "cheesy" flavor.

YES

Some granulated sugar plus corn syrup, which also interferes with crystal formation, made for a super-smooth texture—with no funky side effects.

Vanilla Ice Cream

MAKES ABOUT 1 QUART

Two teaspoons of vanilla extract can be substituted for the vanilla bean; stir the extract into the cold custard in step 3. An instant-read thermometer is critical for the best results. Using a prechilled metal baking pan and working quickly in step 4 will help prevent melting and refreezing of the ice cream and will speed the hardening process. If using a canister-style ice-cream machine, be sure to freeze the empty canister at least 24 hours and preferably 48 hours before churning. For self-refrigerating ice-cream machines, prechill the canister by running the machine for 5 to 10 minutes before pouring in the custard.

- **1 vanilla bean**
- **1¾ cups heavy cream**
- **1¼ cups whole milk**
- **½ cup plus 2 tablespoons (4⅓ ounces) sugar**
- **⅓ cup light corn syrup**
- **¼ teaspoon salt**
- **6 large egg yolks**

1. Place 8- or 9-inch square metal baking pan in freezer. Cut vanilla bean in half lengthwise. Using tip of paring knife, scrape out vanilla seeds. Combine vanilla bean, seeds, cream, milk, 6 tablespoons sugar, corn syrup, and salt in medium saucepan. Heat over medium-high heat, stirring occasionally, until mixture is steaming steadily and registers 175 degrees, 5 to 10 minutes. Remove saucepan from heat.

2. While cream mixture heats, whisk egg yolks and remaining ¼ cup sugar in bowl until smooth, about 30 seconds. Slowly whisk 1 cup heated cream mixture into egg yolk mixture. Return mixture to saucepan and cook over medium-low heat, stirring constantly, until mixture thickens and registers 180 degrees, 7 to 14 minutes. Immediately pour custard into large bowl and let cool until no longer steaming, 10 to 20 minutes. Transfer 1 cup custard to small bowl. Cover both bowls with plastic wrap. Place large bowl in refrigerator and small bowl in freezer and let cool completely, at least 4 hours or up to 24 hours. (Small bowl of custard will freeze solid.)

3. Remove custards from refrigerator and freezer. Scrape frozen custard from small bowl into large bowl of custard. Stir occasionally until frozen custard has fully dissolved. Strain custard through fine-mesh strainer and transfer to ice-cream machine. Churn until mixture resembles thick soft-serve ice cream and registers about 21 degrees, 15 to 25 minutes. Transfer ice cream to frozen baking pan and press plastic wrap on surface. Return to freezer until firm around edges, about 1 hour.

4. Transfer ice cream to airtight container, pressing firmly to remove any air pockets, and freeze until firm, at least 2 hours. Serve. (Ice cream can be stored for up to 5 days.)

VARIATIONS

Triple Ginger Ice Cream

Freeze the crystallized ginger for at least 15 minutes before adding it to the churning ice cream.

Omit vanilla bean. Add one 3-inch piece fresh ginger, peeled and sliced into thin rounds, and 2 teaspoons ground ginger to cream and milk mixture in step 1 and heat as directed. Add ½ cup chopped crystallized ginger to ice cream during last minute of churning.

Coffee Crunch Ice Cream

Freeze the cocoa nibs for at least 15 minutes before adding them to the churning ice cream.

Omit vanilla bean. Add ½ cup coarsely ground coffee to cream and milk mixture in step 1 and heat as directed. Add ¾ cup chocolate-covered cocoa nibs to ice cream during last minute of churning.

SCIENCE DESK

COMBATING ICINESS WITH CORN SYRUP

One key to our ice cream's smoothness was to replace some of the sugar with corn syrup. This sweetener has a twofold effect: First, it is made up of glucose molecules and large tangled chains of starch that interrupt the flow of water molecules in a custard base. Since the water molecules can't move freely, they are less likely to combine and form large crystals as the ice cream freezes. Second, corn syrup creates a higher freezing point in ice cream than granulated sugar does. This makes the ice cream less susceptible to the temperature shifts inevitable in a home freezer. These shifts cause constant thawing and refreezing, which creates crystallization even in the smoothest ice cream. Our ice cream stayed smooth for nearly a week—far longer than most homemade ice creams do.

NOTES FROM THE TEST KITCHEN

FOR SUPER-PREMIUM SMOOTHNESS, KEEP IT COLD

You don't need a commercial blast freezer to achieve super smooth ice cream—try our humble method:

1. CHILL HALF, FREEZE HALF: Transfer all but 1 cup cooled custard to large bowl and chill in refrigerator at least 4 hours, until it registers 40 degrees. Place remaining 1 cup custard in small bowl and freeze it for same amount of time.

2. COMBINE CUSTARDS: Scrape frozen custard into chilled custard and stir until fully dissolved; deeply chilled base now registers around 30 degrees.

3. CHURN BASE: Strain custard and churn until ice cream has soft-serve texture and registers about 21 degrees, 15 to 25 minutes.

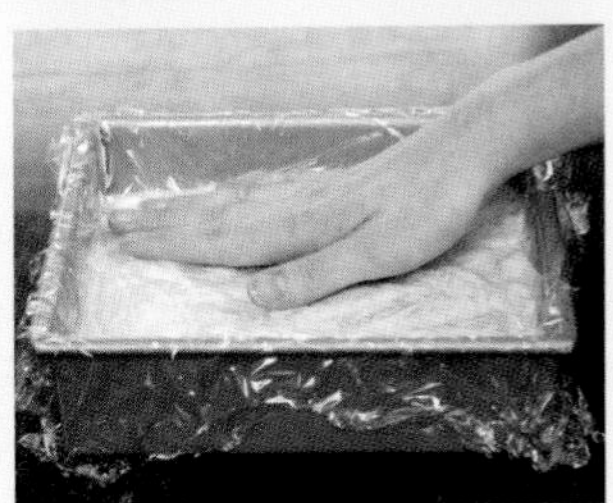

4. FAST-FREEZE: Freeze ice cream in chilled metal baking pan, where it will freeze faster than in usual tall containers, about 1 hour.

5. FULLY FREEZE: Transfer ice cream to airtight container, press out air pockets, and freeze until firm, at least 2 hours.

RATING ICE-CREAM MAKERS

Hand-cranked wooden barrels chilled with ice and rock salt offer old-fashioned charm, but modern ice-cream makers whip up frozen treats with the push of a button. The machines come in two styles: pricey self-refrigerating appliances that churn out continuous batches, and cheaper models with removable coolant-lined canisters. The latter must be frozen (usually overnight) before each use, requiring both precious freezer space and super-cold temperatures. To get the scoop on both styles, we churned vanilla ice cream and lime sorbet in six models (two self-refrigerating and four canister models ranging from $30 to $300), surveying texture, overrun percentage (the amount of air whipped into the ice cream, which can span from 0 to 100 percent), and noise, plus general user-friendliness. Brands are listed in order of preference. See www.americastestkitchen.com for updates to this testing.

HIGHLY RECOMMENDED

WHYNTER SNÖ Professional Ice Cream Maker (model #IC-2L)
PRICE: $305.99 **STYLE:** Self-Refrigerating **CAPACITY:** 2 qt
OVERRUN: 28% **TIME TO MAKE ONE BATCH:** 40 minutes
TEXTURE: ★★★ **NOISE LEVEL:** ★★
COMMENTS: This self-refrigerating model makes continuous batches of creamy, dense, smooth ice cream, without the need to freeze a canister. The ice cream was firm enough to eat right away, and the second batch came out faster and even smoother than the first. Simple and intuitive, the timer can be set for up to 60 minutes for walk-away convenience. Canister and blade are removable for easy cleaning. For the smoothest results, we recommend letting the machine run for 5 to 10 minutes to pre-chill it before adding the custard.

CUISINART Automatic Frozen Yogurt, Ice Cream & Sorbet Maker (model #ICE-21)
PRICE: $49.95 BEST BUY **STYLE:** Canister **CAPACITY:** 1.5 qt
OVERRUN: 29% **TIME TO MAKE ONE BATCH:** 25 minutes
TEXTURE: ★★★ **NOISE LEVEL:** ★★
COMMENTS: Our Best Buy made ice cream that rivaled the smooth texture of our top choice. Though a bit noisier than our winner, it was simple to use and one of the most compact models we tested. True, its canister must be frozen for 24 hours before each use for the best results—and new batches of ice cream refrozen for a few hours before serving for a densely packed texture—but given its modest price, you can hardly go wrong.

RECOMMENDED WITH RESERVATIONS

KITCHENAID Ice Cream Maker Attachment (model #KICA0WH)
PRICE: $99.99 **STYLE:** Canister **CAPACITY:** 2 qt
OVERRUN: 80% **TIME TO MAKE ONE BATCH:** 30 minutes
TEXTURE: ★★ **NOISE LEVEL:** ★★
COMMENTS: Producing ice cream with by far the highest overrun, this canister-style model attaches to any KitchenAid stand mixer manufactured within the past 20 years, and churned out ice cream so light and airy, testers equated it to whipped cream. For those who like their ice cream dense, this would not be a good option.

RECOMMENDED WITH RESERVATIONS *(cont.)*

CUISINART Pure Indulgence Frozen Yogurt, Ice Cream & Sorbet Maker (model #ICE-30BC)
PRICE: $79.95 **STYLE:** Canister **CAPACITY:** 2 qt
OVERRUN: 24% **TIME TO MAKE ONE BATCH:** 40 minutes
TEXTURE: ★★ **NOISE LEVEL:** ★
COMMENTS: We hoped this slightly larger, pricier Cuisinart model would yield even better ice cream than the brand's cheaper $49.95 model. Unfortunately, the differences were only negative: ear-piercing noise and more ice crystals. For an extra pint of ice cream, you sacrifice some quality—not to mention $30.

CUISINART Supreme Commercial Quality Ice Cream Maker (model #ICE-50BC)
PRICE: $299 **STYLE:** Self-refrigerating **CAPACITY:** 1.5 qt
OVERRUN: 23% **TIME TO MAKE ONE BATCH:** 43 minutes
TEXTURE: ★★ **NOISE LEVEL:** ★
COMMENTS: This self-refrigerating model was one of the loudest and bulkiest in the lineup. It made ice cream similar to the brand's mid-priced Pure Indulgence model, with noticeable ice crystals, which was not as good as the ice cream made in Cuisinart's least expensive model (our Best Buy). Plus it cost more than three times as much. Though you can make multiple batches of frozen treats without having to refreeze a canister, the less-than-perfect texture of the final product was unforgivable for the price.

NOT RECOMMENDED

BACK TO BASICS Freezer Fun Ice Cream Maker (model #SIT18091)
PRICE: $24.99 **STYLE:** Canister **CAPACITY:** 1.5 qt **OVERRUN:** 3%
TIME TO MAKE ONE BATCH: 55 minutes for an icy slush
TEXTURE: ★ **NOISE LEVEL:** ★★
COMMENTS: This machine does not beat enough air into the cream and failed to freeze the base further than a grainy slush, even after 55 minutes of churning. Despite a sojourn in the freezer, the finished product was flaky, gritty, and overly dense.

RATING VANILLA BEANS

For recipes in which vanilla is the star, we've always found that beans impart deeper flavor than extract. We tested five brands of vanilla beans, three mail order and two from the supermarket, wondering if the tides had changed since we rated them more than a decade ago. At that time, we couldn't recommend any supermarket samples, finding them dried out and hardened. We used the beans first in an uncooked cream cheese frosting, then cooked in the base of our Vanilla Ice Cream and in a simple crème anglaise. Turns out, times have changed: In a surprising reversal, we found the supermarket beans had not only improved but were better than the mail-order brands. Brands are listed in order of preference. See www.americastestkitchen.com for updates to this testing.

RECOMMENDED

MCCORMICK Madagascar Vanilla Beans
PRICE: $15.99 for two beans
COMMENTS: The maker of our favorite vanilla extract wins again, with a vanilla bean that offers "complex" flavor that suggests caramel with "a hint of butter and lemon."

SPICE ISLANDS Bourbon Vanilla Bean
PRICE: $9.49 for one bean
COMMENTS: Crème anglaise is where this supermarket brand was "clearly the star," offering "complex and lasting" flavor that tasters called "almost buttery," "nutty," and "bold."

NIELSEN-MASSEY Madagascar Bourbon Gourmet Vanilla Beans
PRICE: $7.99 for two beans
COMMENTS: This bean stood out particularly well in frosting, garnering compliments for its "warm," "refined and clean" flavor. Others noted its "toasty and buttery" undertones. In sum: "This is complex stuff."

PENZEYS Madagascar Vanilla Beans
PRICE: $7.25 for three beans
COMMENTS: This mail-order brand delivered a "burst" of vanilla flavor, though some tasters were disappointed when it "quickly dissipated." What they did catch was "clean," "rich," and "caramel-y" notes in both the ice cream and crème anglaise.

RECOMMENDED WITH RESERVATIONS

RODELLE Madagascar Vanilla Bourbon Beans
PRICE: $6.89 for two beans
COMMENTS: While some tasters praised this mail-order bean for its "nice balance" and "well-rounded" flavor, others found it understated at best. Complaints included "Tastes like yellow cake batter," "Just kind of flat," and "Where's the vanilla?"

CHOCOLATE PUDDING

WHY THIS RECIPE WORKS: Homemade chocolate pudding often suffers either from lackluster chocolate flavor, caused by a dearth of chocolate, or a grainy texture, caused by too much cocoa butter. We were after chocolate pudding that tasted deeply of chocolate, and was thickened to a perfectly silky, creamy texture. We found that using a moderate amount of bittersweet chocolate in combination with unsweetened cocoa and instant espresso powder helped us achieve maximum chocolate flavor. Cornstarch proved the right thickener for our pudding; using mostly milk and just half a cup of heavy cream, along with three egg yolks, ensured that our pudding had a silky smooth texture. Salt and vanilla enhanced the chocolate flavor even more.

IN THE 1980S, THE *NEW YORKER* RAN A CARTOON OF A woman and a child examining a dessert menu. The caption—"Chocolate pudding? Oh, you'll like that. It's like chocolate mousse"—suggests that even 25 years ago, chocolate pudding had fallen into obscurity. It had been pushed off the table by more glamorous, intensely flavored concoctions like truffle tarts and molten chocolate cakes. Today, diners' seemingly insatiable desire for increasingly darker, more bitter chocolate has ensured that this trend never reverses itself. (But feeble-tasting instant pudding, mystifyingly, lives on.)

Call us wimps, but we don't always want our chocolate in lethal doses or in ever-higher cacao percentages. We miss the simplicity—and the restraint—of a good homemade chocolate pudding: that wonderfully smooth, dense yet light marriage of chocolate with tempering dairy, thickened with cornstarch and maybe a few egg yolks. Usually we can manage only a few bites of dense, ganachelike pot de crème, but we can easily devour a generous serving of chocolate pudding.

Intent on bringing back this homey, satisfying dessert, we went into the test kitchen to gather recipes. We were happily reminded that making chocolate pudding from scratch couldn't be easier: Simmer dairy and sugar with

CREAMY CHOCOLATE PUDDING

cornstarch, whisk in chocolate and (typically) a few egg yolks, add vanilla, strain, chill, and serve.

That said, when we gave the recipes a closer look, the variety among them was startling for a dish with so few steps and ingredients. Some called for unsweetened chocolate, others bittersweet. Amounts ranged from a modest 1½ ounces to 10 times that amount. Still others ditched the solid chocolate for cocoa powder. We'd always thought that egg yolks were pretty much a given in pudding, but many recipes didn't include them, instead opting for a heftier dose of cornstarch. Then there was the question of dairy: Should it be milk, cream, half-and-half—or some combination? And was the inclusion of butter a good thing or overkill?

We decided to start conservatively, preparing a pudding from the 1975 edition of *Joy of Cooking* that called for 1 to 1½ ounces of unsweetened chocolate, milk, cornstarch, and no eggs. We went for the upper end of the chocolate range, but tasters still panned this pudding for its wan flavor and loose consistency reminiscent of the instant kind. Fast-forwarding to 1990, we tried the chocolate pudding in *Craig Claiborne's New York Times Cookbook*, which doubled the unsweetened chocolate to 3 ounces, swapped in some half-and-half, and added a few tablespoons of butter. The thicker consistency of this pudding was more to tasters' liking, but its chocolate flavor was still underwhelming.

Wondering if a switch to bittersweet would change things, we made a pudding that we'd read about on several food blogs that came from the Scharffen Berger website. This recipe called for 4 ounces of bittersweet chocolate, milk, and no eggs. Though 4 ounces of bittersweet chocolate is the equivalent of 3 ounces of unsweetened, tasters found that this pudding had richer, more complex chocolate flavor. This wasn't exactly surprising. Though there are many more options of unsweetened chocolate available in supermarkets these days, we find that their quality doesn't compare with a good brand of bittersweet (we prefer Callebaut Intense Dark Chocolate, L-60–40NV). In the test kitchen we tend to reserve unsweetened chocolate for recipes such as brownies, where nuance isn't as important and where we want strict control over the amount of sugar. But while the chocolate flavor had more dimension, tasters still clamored for more of it.

Leaving the past behind, we examined a pudding recipe from the food science cookbook *Ideas in Food* by former Boston chefs Aki Kamozawa and H. Alexander Talbot, released last year. It called for a whopping 12 ounces of bittersweet chocolate. It seemed as though this amount would take us into pot de crème territory, but it emboldened us to whip up a pudding made with 8 ounces. (For now, until we got the chocolate quantity settled, we were sticking with a base made with milk, cornstarch, and no eggs.) As we poured this newest batch into a bowl to chill, we admired its rich, dark color and sneaked a taste. The glossy pudding had a robust flavor that had been missing in the other puddings. But once set, it was marred by a distinctly chalky, grainy texture caused, we assumed, by too high a proportion of chocolate solids.

We began dialing back the chocolate to see how much we could incorporate while still keeping a velvety texture. To our great disappointment, we found that the 4 ounces we'd used in the Scharffen Berger recipe was as high as we could go before the pudding turned gritty.

Our only recourse was to attempt to highlight the modest chocolate flavor we had by cutting back on cornstarch and dairy, both of which dull flavor. We tried dropping the cornstarch from 3 tablespoons to 2 and adding some low-sugar pectin instead. This batch was marginally more chocolaty, but its consistency was considerably wetter and its texture was broken. Trading some of the cornstarch for gelatin produced results no better, turning out a pudding that was slick and springy.

Changing tactics, we tried swapping out a cup of the dairy for equal portions of water, coffee, and stout. Tasters panned all three samples as lean and noted that the latter two overwhelmed and muddied the chocolate flavor, respectively. As a last-ditch effort, we even tried a vegan chocolate pudding recipe from *New York Times* columnist Mark Bittman in which he replaces both the thickener and the dairy with silken tofu. But while tasters praised this pudding's rich chocolate punch, there was no denying that it lacked creaminess.

With no other leads to follow, we decided to test a recipe that we'd skipped for not sounding promising. The pudding, from *Betty Crocker's Big Red Cookbook* (1986 edition), calls for ⅓ cup of cocoa powder and no bar chocolate at all. We'd dismissed it on the assumption that the dry particles in the cocoa would contribute gritty texture and that it wouldn't have the well-rounded flavor of pudding made with solid chocolate, which contains significantly more cocoa butter. When we served this pudding to our colleagues, they deemed its flavor simply "OK." But they raved about its supremely silky texture—by far the smoothest pudding we'd turned out to date.

Why would cocoa powder—which is typically made up of 80 to 90 percent cocoa solids and 10 to 20 percent fat, while a typical bar of 60 percent cacao bittersweet chocolate averages about 25 percent cocoa solids and 35 percent cocoa butter—make for a smoother pudding? Could it actually be that cocoa butter—not cocoa solids—caused grittiness in pudding when used in overly high amounts?

As a test, we took our working recipe with 4 ounces of solid chocolate and began adding cocoa powder to it. We stopped at 3 tablespoons, which gave our pudding the depth of chocolate flavor it had been missing, and yet the texture was still perfectly smooth. It seemed certain that cocoa butter—not cocoa solids—was the culprit in causing graininess.

When we consulted our science editor, he had an explanation for this curious phenomenon: Solid chocolate is manufactured so that the cocoa butter it contains remains solid at room temperature but melts precisely at human body temperature. But when the same chocolate is melted for a recipe, the crystalline structure of the cocoa butter is reorganized; it becomes more stable and melts at higher temperatures. If present in high enough amounts, this more stable form of cocoa butter creates a grainy texture. Thus for a pudding with potent chocolate flavor but a supremely smooth texture, a combo of bittersweet chocolate and cocoa powder was the way to go.

With that mystery solved and the chocolate flavor of our pudding exactly where we wanted it to be, we moved on to address other aspects of the recipe—namely, that fact that it lacked a certain richness and body. To solve this, we added three egg yolks to the recipe and swapped ½ cup of the milk for ½ cup of heavy cream. These changes gave the pudding an even creamier taste and more luxurious texture, plus we were able to drop the cornstarch down to 2 tablespoons.

There was still something missing—some depth and roundness to the chocolate flavor. We thought back to our testing of nondairy liquids. While 8 ounces of coffee had overwhelmed the chocolate, a smaller amount might perfectly enhance its rich, roast-y undertones. We added just ½ teaspoon of instant espresso powder, and our pudding was finally complete.

With the help of two kinds of chocolate in a goodly—but not lethal—amount, we daresay we had engineered a new classic.

Creamy Chocolate Pudding

SERVES 6

We recommend using one of the test kitchen's favorite baking chocolates, Callebaut Intense Dark Chocolate or Ghirardelli Bittersweet Chocolate Baking Bar for this recipe, but any high-quality dark, bittersweet, or semisweet chocolate will work. This recipe was developed using a 60 percent cacao chocolate. Using a chocolate with a higher cacao percentage will result in a thicker pudding. Low-fat milk (1 percent or 2 percent) may be substituted for the whole milk with a small sacrifice in richness. Do not use skim milk as a substitute. Serve the pudding with lightly sweetened whipped cream and chocolate shavings.

- **2 teaspoons vanilla extract**
- **½ teaspoon instant espresso powder**
- **½ cup (3½ ounces) sugar**
- **3 tablespoons Dutch-processed cocoa**
- **2 tablespoons cornstarch**
- **¼ teaspoon salt**
- **3 large egg yolks**
- **½ cup heavy cream**
- **2½ cups whole milk**
- **5 tablespoons unsalted butter, cut into 8 pieces**
- **4 ounces bittersweet chocolate, chopped fine**

1. Stir vanilla extract and espresso powder together in bowl; set aside. Whisk sugar, cocoa, cornstarch, and salt together in large saucepan. Whisk in egg yolks and cream until fully incorporated, making sure to scrape corners of saucepan. Whisk in milk until incorporated.

2. Place saucepan over medium heat; cook, whisking constantly, until mixture is thickened and bubbling over entire surface, 5 to 8 minutes. Cook for 30 seconds longer, remove from heat, add butter and chocolate and whisk until melted and fully incorporated. Whisk in vanilla mixture.

3. Strain pudding through fine-mesh strainer into bowl. Place lightly greased parchment paper against surface of pudding and place in refrigerator to cool, at least 4 hours. Serve. (Pudding can be refrigerated for up to 2 days.)

VARIATIONS

Creamy Mexican Chocolate Pudding

Add ½ teaspoon ground cinnamon, ¼ teaspoon chipotle chile powder, and pinch cayenne pepper to saucepan along with cocoa.

Creamy Mocha Pudding

Increase instant espresso powder to 1 teaspoon. Add 1 tablespoon Kahlúa to vanilla mixture. Substitute ¼ cup brewed coffee for ¼ cup milk.

NOTES FROM THE TEST KITCHEN

PUDDING THROUGH THE AGES

Though the amount of chocolate in chocolate pudding has inched upward over the years, we found that most recipes still don't have much punch. But creating a pudding with robust chocolate flavor that doesn't also taste chalky and gritty turned out to be not so simple. The key was to start with the right kind of chocolate and use two kinds.

ERA	SOURCE	CHOCOLATE	COMMENTS
1970s	*Joy of Cooking*	1½ oz unsweetened chocolate	The minuscule amount of chocolate in this pudding gave it "wan" flavor. The choice of unsweetened chocolate also wasn't ideal, as tasters found it less complex than bittersweet.
1980s	*Betty Crocker's Big Red Cookbook*	⅓ cup cocoa powder	The cocoa powder in this pudding made for an extremely smooth texture, but cocoa powder can have a one-dimensional flavor, and tasters found that it didn't measure up.
1990	*Craig Claiborne's New York Times Cookbook*	3 oz unsweetened chocolate	Even with double the amount of unsweetened chocolate used in the *Joy of Cooking* recipe, this pudding's chocolaty taste was still underwhelming.
2011	*Cooks Illustrated*	4 oz bittersweet chocolate + 3 tbsp cocoa powder	When the cocoa butter in solid chocolate melts and then re-forms, it can give pudding a grainy texture. To get around this—and still create a dessert with rich chocolate flavor—we used a combo of bittersweet chocolate (which we find has better flavor than unsweetened chocolate) and cocoa powder, which has very little cocoa butter.

Chocolate TORTE

CHAPTER 25

THE RECIPES
Chocolate-Raspberry Torte

TASTING LAB
Unsweetened Chocolate

EQUIPMENT CORNER
Nut Choppers

The camera moves in for a close-up of our Chocolate-Raspberry Torte, which is so rich, just a small wedge will satisfy your deepest chocolate craving.

A CHOCOLATE TORTE IS A TRUE SHOWPIECE DESSERT, BUT IT NEEDS to taste as good as it looks. While we love the appearance of the Viennese classic Sacher torte—it features layers of chocolate sponge cake spread with apricot jam and covered with a chocolate glaze—the weak chocolate and one-dimensional fruit flavors often disappoint. We wanted to create a chocolate torte based on the basic structure of the Sacher torte, but with the richness and complexity that it usually lacks. We knew that to make this dessert more than a mere elegant centerpiece, we'd have to ditch the dull, dry cake and start with the fudgiest, most deeply chocolaty foundation we could find. Then we planned to substitute raspberries for the overly sweet apricot jam for bright fruit flavor that would contrast beautifully with the rich chocolate base. There's just no way we would settle for anything less than rich, chocolaty perfection.

CHOCOLATE-RASPBERRY TORTE

CHOCOLATE-RASPBERRY TORTE

WHY THIS RECIPE WORKS: Sacher torte, the classic Viennese dessert with layers of chocolate cake sandwiching apricot jam and enrobed in a creamy-rich chocolate glaze, always sounds more promising than it typically is in reality. We set out to create a rich, deeply chocolaty dessert using Sacher torte as the inspiration, giving it our own spin by pairing the chocolate with raspberries. For a rich, fudgy base, we started by baking a flourless chocolate cake in two 9-inch pans, so we could sandwich the two cakes together rather than deal with halving a single delicate cake. But when we tried to pick up the second layer and, later, eat it, the dense cake tore and fell apart. Adding ground nuts gave it the structure it needed, plus a good boost of flavor. The winning approach for our filling was to combine jam with lightly mashed fresh berries for a tangy-sweet mixture that clung to the cake. For the glaze, we kept things simple, melting bittersweet chocolate with heavy cream to create a rich-tasting, glossy ganache that poured smoothly over the cake. And to up the glamour quotient, we dotted fresh raspberries around the top perimeter of the torte and pressed sliced toasted almonds along its sides.

NINETEENTH-CENTURY ARISTOCRATS MAY HAVE considered Sacher torte an indulgent dessert, but the Viennese cake has never held the attention of chocoholics like us. Once you get past its alluring facade—a two-layer chocolate sponge cake sandwiching a spread of apricot jam and covered with a sleek-looking chocolate glaze—the confection's true colors reveal themselves. The cake is usually dry and anemic in flavor, as if the batter was merely tanned with cocoa rather than steeped in creamy bar chocolate. Meanwhile, the jam center adds only sweetness to each bite, not bright, complex fruit flavor. As for the glaze, it's typically nothing more than a thin, overly sugary coating. Perhaps our over-the-top American sensibilities have gotten the better of us, but we expect more from a dessert than good looks and historical precedent. Our mission: Create a rich, deeply chocolaty dessert, using the basic layered architecture of the Sacher torte as inspiration. While we were at it, we decided to put our own spin on the dessert and pair the chocolate with one of our favorite fruits: raspberries.

The cake's biggest problem—weak chocolate flavor—made sense once we started looking at recipes. The sponge cake (or genoise) used in most classic Sacher tortes relies on a modest amount of chocolate, typically about 4 ounces. Rather than fiddle with this model, we knew we would do better to start with an entirely different kind of cake. The obvious choice? A rich, fudgy flourless chocolate cake.

We started by baking our own flourless chocolate cake in two 9-inch pans instead of a springform pan. This way, we could sandwich the two cakes together rather than struggle to horizontally halve a single delicate cake.

NOTES FROM THE TEST KITCHEN

TORTE REFORM
Here's how we packed more chocolate flavor and fruitiness into our torte than in the classic European model.

1. REPLACE SPONGE WITH FLOURLESS
A flourless cake holds twice the chocolate of the usual sponge-cake base.

2. ADD GROUND ALMONDS
Ground toasted almonds lend complexity to the rich cake.

3. FILL WITH TWO KINDS OF RASPBERRIES
Fresh raspberries and raspberry jam make for a bright-tasting filling.

4. GLAZE WITH POTENT GANACHE
Use chocolate and cream only. Skip corn syrup and sugar, which dilute flavor.

We let the layers cool, then spread raspberry jam on one. So far, so good. But when we picked up the second layer to lay it on top of the first, the dense cake tore and fell apart. Undeterred, we patched the layers together, poured a simple chocolate glaze over the top, and then chilled the assembly. There was no denying the intense chocolate taste, but each forkful crumbled on its way to our mouths. Obviously our cake needed more structure.

We tried to remedy this problem by judiciously mixing flour into the batter, but when we added enough to sufficiently strengthen the cake (about ½ cup), we created a new problem: a heavy, pasty texture. Leaveners proved ineffective at lightening this heavy, chocolate-laden batter. Separating the eggs and folding in the beaten whites did no better.

At a dead end, we went back to the books and came across a technique that we'd initially ignored. Many classic tortes contain either bread crumbs or ground nuts in place of some of the flour. We had thought this was a little off base for modern cooks, but we figured it was worth a shot. In fact, the latter turned out to be a game-changing improvement. While bread crumbs merely created a spongy, mushy cake, substituting ground toasted almonds for half of the flour worked perfectly. The layers were still moist but had enough structure so that a filling could be added and the second layer placed on top of the first without any collateral damage. What's more, the flavor of the cake benefited from the depth provided by toasted nuts.

Our only gripe was that this cake—and the eventual cleanup—was turning into quite the project. All along, we had been using a stand mixer to whip the eggs, but now that we were using a food processor to grind the nuts, we wondered if we could consolidate appliances. We processed the almonds and flour, then transferred the mixture to a bowl. Next, we processed the eggs until they were almost doubled in volume, then added the sugar. After combining the eggs with the melted chocolate and butter, we folded in the almond-flour mixture and baked the cakes. This worked beautifully. The processor aerated the batter just as effectively as

the stand mixer, and we now had a recipe that dirtied only one piece of equipment.

As for the filling, the thin veneer of apricot jam in a traditional Sacher torte has always struck us as syrupy and dull, and the raspberry jam we'd been using as a stand-in was equally underwhelming. We needed something with as much complexity as the cake. Plain fresh raspberries lacked sweetness—and tended to tumble from the cut cake slices—while pulverizing them with sugar yielded a soupy mixture. Cooking the berries thickened them so they didn't ooze out of the cake but squelched their bright taste. Ultimately, the winning approach was to combine jam with lightly mashed fresh berries, for a tangy-sweet mixture that clung to the cake.

All we had left to do was apply a glaze. To keep things simple, we melted 5 ounces of bittersweet chocolate with ½ cup of heavy cream to create a rich-tasting, glossy ganache that poured smoothly over the cake. To up the glamour quotient, we dotted fresh raspberries around the top perimeter of the torte and pressed sliced toasted almonds along its sides. Our updated torte was a real beauty—inside and out.

Chocolate-Raspberry Torte

SERVES 12 TO 16

Be sure to use cake pans with at least 2-inch-tall sides.

CAKE

- **8 ounces bittersweet chocolate, chopped fine**
- **12 tablespoons unsalted butter, cut into ½-inch pieces**
- **2 teaspoons vanilla extract**
- **¼ teaspoon instant espresso powder**
- **1¾ cups (6⅛ ounces) sliced almonds, toasted**
- **¼ cup (1¼ ounces) all-purpose flour**
- **½ teaspoon salt**
- **5 large eggs, room temperature**
- **¾ cup (5¼ ounces) sugar**

FILLING

- **2½ ounces (½ cup) raspberries, plus 16 individual raspberries**
- **¼ cup seedless raspberry jam**

GLAZE

- **5 ounces bittersweet chocolate, chopped fine**
- **½ cup plus 1 tablespoon heavy cream**

NOTES FROM THE TEST KITCHEN

ASSEMBLING CHOCOLATE-RASPBERRY TORTE

This approach creates a torte with a perfectly flat bottom and top.

1. INVERT: Run paring knife around sides of cake and invert layers onto cardboard rounds.

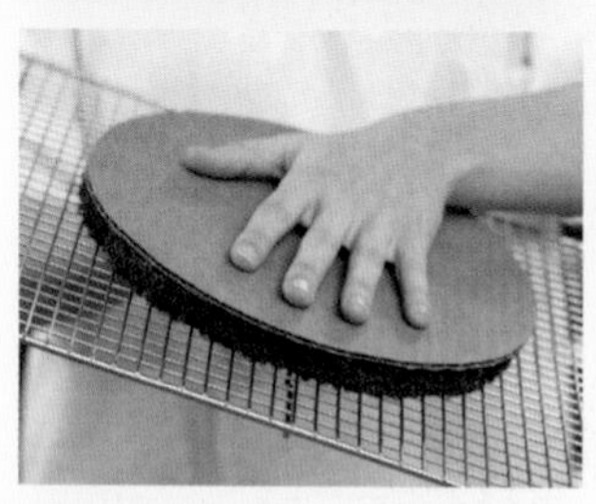

2. REINVERT ONE: Using wire rack, reinvert 1 cake so top faces up; slide back onto cardboard round.

3. TOP WITH FILLING: Spread raspberry filling over cake layer with its top side facing up.

4. TOP WITH CAKE: Top with second cake, leaving bottom facing up.

5. GLAZE: Use offset spatula to evenly spread ganache over top and sides.

1. FOR THE CAKE: Adjust oven rack to middle position and heat oven to 325 degrees. Grease two 9-inch round cake pans, line with parchment paper, grease parchment, then flour pans. Melt chocolate and butter in large heatproof bowl set over medium saucepan filled with 1 inch of simmering water, stirring occasionally until smooth. Remove from heat and let cool to room temperature, about 30 minutes. Stir in vanilla and espresso powder.

2. Pulse ¾ cup almonds in food processor until coarsely chopped, 6 to 8 pulses, and set aside. Process remaining 1 cup almonds until very finely ground, about 45 seconds. Add flour and salt and continue to process until combined, about 15 seconds. Transfer almond-flour mixture to bowl. Process eggs until lightened in color and almost doubled in volume, about 3 minutes. With processor running, slowly add sugar and process until thoroughly combined, about 15 seconds. Using whisk, gently fold egg mixture into chocolate mixture until some streaks of egg remain. Sprinkle half of almond-flour mixture over chocolate mixture and gently whisk until just combined. Sprinkle with remaining almond-flour mixture and gently whisk until just combined.

3. Divide batter evenly between prepared pans and smooth tops with rubber spatula. Bake until center is firm and toothpick inserted in centers comes out with few moist crumbs attached, 14 to 16 minutes. Transfer cakes to wire rack and let cool completely in pans, about 30 minutes.

4. Run paring knife around sides of cakes to loosen and invert cakes onto cardboard rounds cut same size as diameter of cake; discard parchment. Using wire rack, turn 1 cake right side up, then slide from rack back onto cardboard round.

5. FOR THE FILLING: Place ½ cup raspberries in medium bowl and coarsely mash with fork. Stir in raspberry jam until just combined.

6. TO ASSEMBLE THE TORTE: Spread raspberry mixture onto cake layer that is right side up. Top with second cake layer, leaving it upside down. Transfer assembled cake, still on cardboard round, to wire rack set in rimmed baking sheet.

7. FOR THE GLAZE: Melt chocolate and cream in heatproof bowl set over saucepan filled with 1 inch of simmering water, stirring occasionally until smooth. Remove from heat and gently whisk until very smooth. Pour glaze onto center of assembled cake. Using offset spatula, spread glaze evenly over top of cake, letting it drip down sides. Spread glaze along sides of cake to coat evenly.

8. Using fine-mesh strainer, sift reserved almonds to remove any fine bits. Holding bottom of cake on cardboard round with 1 hand, gently press sifted almonds onto cake sides with other hand. Arrange remaining 16 raspberries around circumference. Refrigerate cake on rack until glaze is set, at least 1 hour or up to 24 hours (if refrigerating cake for more than 1 hour, let sit at room temperature for about 30 minutes before serving). Transfer cake to platter and serve.

NOTES FROM THE TEST KITCHEN

DECORATING CHOCOLATE-RASPBERRY TORTE

1. Using cardboard round, lift and hold cake with one hand and gently press chopped nuts onto its sides with other hand.

2. Place 1 raspberry at top of cake at 12 o'clock, then another at 6 o'clock. Place third berry at 9 o'clock and fourth at 3 o'clock. Continue to place berries opposite each other until all are evenly spaced.

RATING UNSWEETENED CHOCOLATE

The purest form of chocolate, just cocoa solids and cocoa butter (no sugar added), unsweetened chocolate helps deepen chocolate flavor in desserts without adding sweetness. Baker's and Hershey's have been mainstays in the marketplace for more than a century, but, these days, there are more options on the shelves. To find out if any of the more expensive "premium" brands could outshine the basic brands, we gathered seven other chocolates and sampled all nine plain and in brownies and chocolate sauce. In the plain tasting, individual flavor nuances came to the forefront; chocolates were described as nutty, fruity, smoky, and coffeelike. Surprisingly, in the brownie and chocolate sauce tastings, some of the more exotic brands fell short, described as "bland" and "nothing special." After analyzing the percentages of cocoa solids and cocoa butter, it was clear that the winner contained more cocoa solids and less cocoa butter than its competitors, which explained why it was praised for its richer chocolate flavor. Brands are listed in order of preference. See www.americastestkitchen.com for updates to this testing.

RECOMMENDED

HERSHEY'S Unsweetened Baking Bar

PRICE: $1.99 for 4 oz (50 cents per oz)
FORM: Bar **FAT:** 50.30%
COMMENTS: "Straightforward and intense," "likable—like a firm handshake," this supermarket brand bolstered with cocoa was "well rounded and complex" and "rich" with "deep notes of cocoa" in both brownies and chocolate sauce. Tasters appreciated the complexity of its "caramel and coffee flavors," with a "hint of cinnamon."

VALRHONA Cacao Pate Extra 100%

PRICE: $21.95 for 2.2 lb (62 cents per oz) (mail order)
FORM: Block **FAT:** 54.64%
COMMENTS: Tasters praised this chocolate for "intense richness; full, almost coffeelike flavor," and a texture that was "nicely creamy," with a "pleasant balance of roasted beans and buttery richness" and "hints of honey." "Not overly bitter," it struck tasters as "very cocoa-y," with "good chocolate thunder, bass tones of chocolate."

SCHARFFEN BERGER Unsweetened Dark Chocolate

PRICE: $9.99 for 9.7 oz ($1.03 per oz)
FORM: Bar **FAT:** 55.03%
COMMENTS: This brand containing vanilla beans had "strong" chocolate flavor with "raspberry," "fruity," "raisiny," and "slightly smoky" notes, accenting its "rich," "dark chocolate profile." With one of the highest percentages of fat in the lineup, it was "crazy smooth," with a "lush, creamy" texture in chocolate sauce.

RECOMMENDED WITH RESERVATIONS

GHIRARDELLI Unsweetened Baking Bar

PRICE: $3.79 for 4 oz (95 cents per oz)
FORM: Bar **FAT:** 55.35%
COMMENTS: "Mild and a little bitter" with a "tropical" flavor like "banana" or "guava," this mid-ranked chocolate struck tasters overall as "pleasant," with "average chocolate intensity," "not terrible, not great," with "a little bit of chocolate punch at the end, but not enough."

RECOMMENDED WITH RESERVATIONS *(cont.)*

CALLEBAUT Unsweetened Chocolate Liquor Disks

PRICE: $16.50 for 2.2 lb (47 cents per oz) (mail order)
FORM: Disks **FAT:** 55.59%
COMMENTS: While it has "really chocolaty flavor," this chocolate had some "harsh," "slightly charred" notes that tasters detected in chocolate sauce; in brownies it was "pretty meek, mild," "sandy and sweet," and "way too one-dimensional." In short, an "average sample, a bit too sweet but not bad."

GUITTARD Unsweetened Baking Chocolate

PRICE: $9.95 for 1 lb (62 cents per oz) (mail order)
FORM: Disks **FAT:** 53.32%
COMMENTS: "Where's the chocolate?" tasters asked. They described brownies made with this brand as "more sugary than chocolaty," "plain and boring like the brownies I grew up eating from the school cafeteria." In sum: "not a showstopper" and "ho-hum."

BAKER'S Unsweetened Baking Chocolate Squares

PRICE: $3.39 for 8 oz (42 cents per oz)
FORM: Bar **FAT:** 52.19%
COMMENTS: Tasters noted that this brand has "some bitterness and complexity, but falls flat pretty quickly," though they did praise its "cinnamon-y" notes and "creamy" texture in sauce. In brownies, a few tasters liked the "cherry undertones," but many felt it suffered from being too sugary. "Tastes like low-end milk chocolate Easter candy," said one taster.

NOT RECOMMENDED

DAGOBA Organic Prima Materia Pure Unsweetened Chocolate

PRICE: $2.69 for 2 oz ($1.35 per oz)
FORM: Bar **FAT:** 53.90%
COMMENTS: With a "weird cardboard-y" taste and "flat," "unremarkable" chocolate flavor, a "sour aftertaste," and "sugar-forward" profile, this brand, containing small amounts of milk and soy lecithin, also lost points for a distinct "charcoal," "tobacco," and "smoky" taste, "like licking charred bark" or "an ashtray."

RATING NUT CHOPPERS

When you've got a lot of nuts to chop, is it worth purchasing a tool that's dedicated to this sole task? We wanted to find out if a simple manual nut chopper would work faster than a chef's knife or food processor, so we pitted five choppers, from $7 crank-style jars to almost $30 mills, against a food processor and timed ourselves chopping pecans, hazelnuts, almonds, and walnuts. The highest-priced chopper fared the worst, processing nuts into gritty, mushy bits, and only one chopper actually performed well. Its sharp stainless steel tines pushed the nuts through slats that gave us a coarse texture as we turned the handle in one direction, a slightly finer texture in the other. Faster than using a chef's knife and with results more consistent than that of a food processor, it is the only manual nut chopper worth buying. Brands are listed in order of preference. See www.americastestkitchen.com for updates to this testing.

HIGHLY RECOMMENDED

PROGRESSIVE International Heavy Duty Nut Chopper (model #Pri1018)
PRICE: $8.89 **CHOP QUALITY:** ★★★
EASE OF USE: ★★★ **DESIGN:** ★★★
CLEANUP: ★★★ **DISHWASHER-SAFE:** Yes
COMMENTS: With a clear plastic body and stainless steel chopping tines, it chopped a cup of pecans into mostly even-size pieces in 90 seconds—with minimal dust. Turning the handle in the "fine" direction gave us the best results, but tougher almonds and bulbous hazelnuts went through only with slower cranking. Just detach the base from the hopper and remove the lid to clean it by hand; it's also dishwasher-safe.

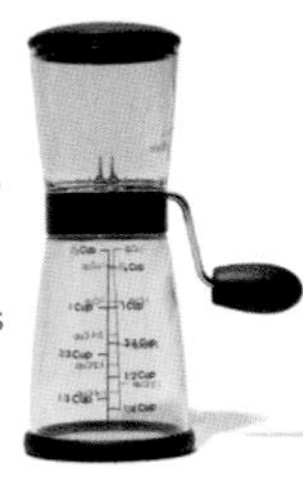

NOT RECOMMENDED

ZYLISS "Easy Chop" Food Chopper with Smart Base (model #10700)
PRICE: $19.95 **CHOP QUALITY:** ★
EASE OF USE: ★★★ **DESIGN:** ★★
CLEANUP: ★★★ **DISHWASHER-SAFE:** Yes
COMMENTS: This slap-chop model uses blades that descend guillotine-style to chop nuts and vegetables. Although it's easy to use and captures the nuts neatly in its base, the pieces ranged from large, almost unchopped to tiny bits. It also produced a fair amount of dust.

BLACK & DECKER Ergo 3-Cup Chopper (model #EHC650)
PRICE: $22 **CHOP QUALITY:** ★
EASE OF USE: ★★★ **DESIGN:** ★
CLEANUP: ★★★ **DISHWASHER-SAFE:** Yes
COMMENTS: This mini food processor, designed to chop nuts and vegetables, and "make salsa in seconds," easily accommodated 3 cups of pecans, but chopping even 1 cup gave us dust interspersed with whole pecans and every size in between. Chopping ½ cup at a time (using 30 pulses) solved some of the size variation, but too many large pieces were left. It was, though, easy to operate one-handed and easy to clean.

NOT RECOMMENDED *(cont.)*

NORPRO 576 Nut Chopper (model #NPW576)
PRICE: $6.99 **CHOP QUALITY:** ★★★
EASE OF USE: ★ **DESIGN:** ★
CLEANUP: ★★★ **DISHWASHER-SAFE:** Yes
COMMENTS: All went well with this crank-style chopper until it jammed on raw almonds and its tines twisted permanently out of alignment. Because the cranking radius is small, it balked at chopping hazelnuts. Plus its glass base felt fragile—we had to hold it as we cranked instead of resting it on the counter.

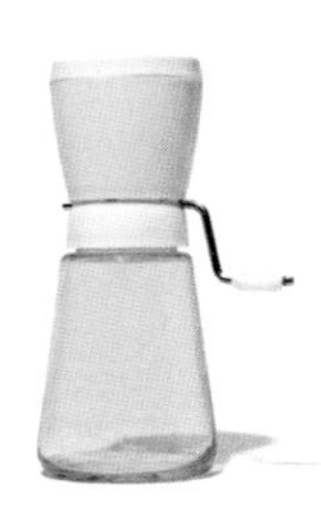

WESTON All-Purpose Seed, Nut, and Spice Grinder (model #7582)
PRICE: $29.99 **CHOP QUALITY:** ★
EASE OF USE: ★ **DESIGN:** ★
CLEANUP: ★ **DISHWASHER-SAFE:** No
COMMENTS: Even when we loosened the housing from the augur on this clamp-on crank-style grinder and fed it prechopped pecans and walnuts, the nuts simply bounced around the hopper. The few pieces that did pass through emerged as a mushy paste. Despite repeated cleaning, we found a lot of grayish machine grease in the processed bits.

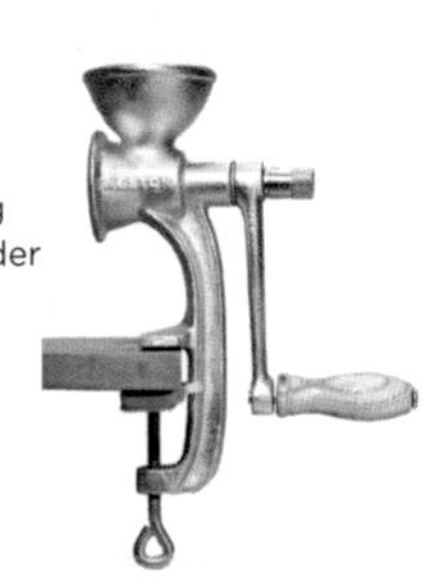

America's
TEST KITCHEN

Sweet SUMMER ENDINGS

CHAPTER 26

Yvonne takes a moment to savor the fruit of her labor—Summer Peach Cake.

WHEN FRESH SUMMER FRUIT IS AT ITS PEAK, NOTHING SATISFIES OUR collective sweet tooth more than a dessert bursting with the flavors of the season. Peach cake is one such favorite. But while loading a cake with fresh peaches sounds like a great idea, it can be a challenge to get right—the flavor often fizzles out and the crumb of the cake becomes drenched in juice. We wanted full fruit flavor—which would mean plenty of peaches—without the soggy cake. We knew this would mean finding a way to keep the peach juices from flooding the cake. For our ideal cake we would either fold the fruit right into the batter or arrange it on top just before baking.

Fresh strawberry pie is another summertime treat that's hard to beat. The best of the best feature perfectly ripe berries coated with a light, glossy glaze and held together by a flaky, buttery crust. But the key to this dessert's bright flavor—plump, uncooked berries—can also be its soupy downfall. We set out to find a way to firm up the filling without making it gluey and dull-tasting.

SUMMER PEACH CAKE

WHY THIS RECIPE WORKS: This dessert, which marries cake with fresh summer peaches, is a bakery favorite, but most versions are plagued by soggy cake and barely noticeable peach flavor. We wanted a buttery cake that was moist yet not at all soggy, with a golden-brown exterior and plenty of peach flavor. Roasting chunks of peaches, tossed in sugar and a little lemon juice, helped concentrate their flavor and expel moisture before we combined them with our cake batter. However, during roasting, the peach chunks became swathed in a flavorful but unpleasantly gooey film. Coating our roasted peaches in panko bread crumbs before combining them with the batter ensured the film was absorbed by the crumbs, which then dissolved into the cake during baking. To amplify the peach flavor we tossed the fruit with peach schnapps before roasting, and a little almond extract added to the batter lent a subtle complementary note. Fanning peach slices (macerated with a little more of the schnapps) over the top, then sprinkling some almond extract–enhanced sugar for a light glaze, ensured our cake looked as good as it tasted.

BAKERS HAVE BEEN ADDING FRESH PEACHES TO CAKE for ages, in as many forms as one can dream up. Peach upside-down cake, layer cake stacked with sweet peach filling, and yeasted dough topped with the fruit (known as Baltimore-style peach cake) are a few noteworthy approaches. But the version we like best is the most straightforward, taking its inspiration from the buckle, a classic American pairing of fruit folded into a cake batter or arranged on top of it before baking. The dessert we had in mind would adopt this humble construct and boast plenty of sweet peach flavor.

Little did we know that we'd end up re-engineering just about every aspect of the traditional approach to get full fruit flavor without soggy cake.

We ordered a couple of bushels of peaches and got down to business. We mixed together a basic cake batter: White and brown sugar (its caramel taste would pair nicely with peaches), flour, baking powder, and salt went in one bowl; eggs, melted butter, sour cream (for richness), and vanilla extract in another. We stirred the dry ingredients into the wet, folded in two peaches (cut into ½-inch chunks so that they would incorporate easily), scraped the batter into a springform pan for easy serving, and slid it into a 350-degree oven for 1 hour. Our colleagues offered nods of approval as they tucked into the golden-brown, moist, and buttery cake. And yet each bite offered only the mildest suggestion of peach flavor—and we wanted something really fruity.

Accordingly, we whipped up a second cake using four peaches. Our dessert was now chock-full of fruit, but it still didn't taste very peachy—and now it was a soggy mess. The peach chunks had settled to the bottom of the pan in a gummy pile, their juices flooding the cake. To achieve the right texture, we would have to remove some peaches.

Or would we? In a pie, juicy fruit is kept in check with a thickener, so why not dust the peaches with cornstarch before incorporating them? No go. A cake made with cornstarch-coated fruit still exhibited a horribly sodden crumb. It struck us that instead of trying to thicken the juices, we needed to eliminate them altogether.

Macerating is an effective way to draw juice from fruit, so for our next try we sprinkled the peaches with sugar and let them drain in a colander set over a bowl. After an hour, ¼ cup of juice had dripped out. We poured off the liquid, folded the peaches into the batter, and baked the cake. We took a taste, discovering that while we'd made a small step in the right direction, the cake was still soggy. Would heating the peach-sugar mixture in the microwave expel even more fluid?

We piled the peach chunks into a bowl and zapped them for two minutes. The fruit certainly exuded more juice, but it also turned mushy in spots. Next, we microwaved the chunks in a single layer on a plate, hoping that this would allow for more even cooking. Although this offered some improvement, the peaches still didn't dry out as much as we wanted them to.

Perhaps the oven would be a better option for dehydrating the peaches. We spread the chunks on a baking

SUMMER PEACH CAKE

sheet (lined with aluminum foil spritzed with vegetable oil spray to prevent sticking) and baked them in a 425-degree oven for 20 minutes. When a blast of steam whooshed out as we opened the oven door, we knew we were doing something right. The peaches had softened and shriveled a bit—a clear indication of moisture loss. Once they cooled, we assembled and baked a cake. Finally, the sludgy layer at the base of the dessert had been eliminated. What's more, the sweet flavor of the peaches concentrated during roasting.

There was just one more quandary to deal with: During roasting, the peach chunks became coated in a flavorful but unpleasantly gooey, viscous film. Cornstarch hadn't worked to eliminate watery peach juices, but perhaps a coarser ingredient would sop up this sticky covering. We gently tossed ⅓ cup of crushed panko bread crumbs with the roasted peaches, finding that they clung firmly to the syrup. Fearing that the batter would pull the crumbs off of the peaches if we folded them in, we spooned half of the batter into the pan, arranged the panko-coated peaches on the batter, and then spooned on the remaining batter. Presto. As the cake baked, the panko disappeared into the crumb, taking any trace of sticky, gloppy peach syrup with it.

The cake was now terrific when made with just-picked peaches, but we wanted to ensure intense peach flavor even when farm-fresh fruit wasn't available. To that end, we considered all of the peach-flavored ingredients we could get our hands on. Our first try—swapping peach-flavored yogurt for the sour cream—was ineffectual. We next contemplated adding peach jam, but we'd worked so hard to eliminate gooeyness that introducing a sticky ingredient seemed like a mistake. Chopped dried peaches, although intensely flavored, were too chewy. At last, we hit the jackpot when we spiked the macerating fruit with peach schnapps. The sweet, intense liqueur bolstered the flavor of not-so-perfect peaches. Finally, ¼ teaspoon of almond extract (a classic partner with stone fruit) stirred into the batter added a subtle complementary background note.

To make the cake look as good as it tasted, we decked out the top with fanned peach slices and a sprinkling of almond extract–enhanced sugar. As it baked, the sugary fruit caramelized, creating a glazed topping. Now that's one peach of a cake.

NOTES FROM THE TEST KITCHEN

PEACH CAKE RUN AMUCK

Things aren't peachy with most peach cakes, like this one.

1. PROBLEM: Fruit that isn't fruity

SOLUTION: Unless you're working with the best farm-stand fruit, peaches are notoriously bland. To boost fruity taste, we macerate the peach wedges we've reserved for shingling on top of the cake in peach schnapps and a little sugar and lemon juice.

2. PROBLEM: Soggy fruit sinks to bottom

SOLUTION: Roasting the peach chunks destined for the batter concentrates their flavor and drives off moisture, so there's not as much to weigh them down or to flood the cake.

3. PROBLEM: Wet, gummy crumb

SOLUTION: Tossing the roasted peach chunks with panko bread crumbs helps absorb any remaining sticky juices, ensuring a cake that's moist, not soggy.

KEEP YOUR PEACHES OUT OF THE COLD

Keeping peaches in the fridge might seem like a good way to prolong their shelf life, but unless the fruit is ripe, the cold temperatures can turn their flesh mealy. Storing the fruit at or below 40 degrees deactivates an enzyme that breaks down its pectin during ripening. If this happens before the flesh is ripe, the pectin will remain intact and the flesh texture will be mealy. The lesson: Store peaches on the counter.

Summer Peach Cake

SERVES 8

To crush the panko bread crumbs, place them in a zipper-lock bag and smash them with a rolling pin. If you can't find panko, ¼ cup of plain, unseasoned bread crumbs can be substituted. Orange liqueur can be substituted for the peach schnapps. If using peak-of-season, farm-fresh peaches, omit the peach schnapps.

2½ pounds peaches, halved, pitted, and cut into ½-inch wedges
5 tablespoons peach schnapps
4 teaspoons lemon juice
6 tablespoons plus ⅓ cup (5 ounces) granulated sugar
1 cup (5 ounces) all-purpose flour
1¼ teaspoons baking powder
¾ teaspoon salt
½ cup packed (3½ ounces) light brown sugar
2 large eggs, room temperature
8 tablespoons unsalted butter, melted and cooled
¼ cup sour cream
1½ teaspoons vanilla extract
¼ teaspoon plus ⅛ teaspoon almond extract
⅓ cup panko bread crumbs, crushed fine

1. Adjust oven rack to middle position and heat oven to 425 degrees. Line rimmed baking sheet with aluminum foil and spray with vegetable oil spray. Grease and flour 9-inch springform pan. Gently toss 24 peach wedges with 2 tablespoons schnapps, 2 teaspoons lemon juice, and 1 tablespoon granulated sugar in bowl; set aside.

2. Cut remaining peach wedges crosswise into 3 chunks. In bowl, gently toss chunks with remaining 3 tablespoons schnapps, remaining 2 teaspoons lemon juice, and 2 tablespoons granulated sugar. Spread peach chunks in single layer on prepared baking sheet and bake until exuded juices begin to thicken and caramelize at edges of pan, 20 to 25 minutes. Transfer pan to wire rack and let peaches cool to room temperature, about 30 minutes. Reduce oven temperature to 350 degrees.

3. Whisk flour, baking powder, and salt together in bowl. Whisk ⅓ cup granulated sugar, brown sugar, and eggs together in bowl until thick and thoroughly combined, about 45 seconds. Slowly whisk in butter until combined. Add sour cream, vanilla, and ¼ teaspoon almond extract; whisk until combined. Add flour mixture and whisk until just combined.

4. Pour half of batter into prepared pan. Using offset spatula, spread batter evenly to pan edges and smooth top. Sprinkle crushed panko evenly over cooled peach chunks and gently toss to coat. Arrange peach chunks on batter in pan in even layer, gently pressing peaches into batter. Gently spread remaining batter over peach chunks and smooth top. Arrange reserved peach wedges, slightly overlapped, in ring over surface of batter, placing smaller wedges in center. Stir remaining 3 tablespoons granulated sugar and remaining ⅛ teaspoon almond extract together in small bowl until sugar is moistened. Sprinkle sugar mixture evenly over top of cake.

5. Bake until center of cake is set and toothpick inserted in center comes out clean, 50 to 60 minutes. Transfer pan to wire rack and let cool for 5 minutes. Run thin knife between cake and sides of pan; remove sides of pan. Let cake cool completely, 2 to 3 hours, before serving.

FRESH STRAWBERRY PIE

STRAWBERRY PIE

WHY THIS RECIPE WORKS: Because uncooked berries shed so much liquid, the filling for strawberry pie is usually firmed up with some sort of thickener, which produces results that range from stiff and bouncy to runny and gloppy. We wanted a recipe for our ideal strawberry pie, featuring fresh berries lightly held together by a sheer, glossy glaze that would make their flavor pop in the buttery shell. We knew that the success of our strawberry pie hinged on getting the thickener just right. When none of the thickeners we tried worked on their own, we decided to use a combination of two: pectin (in the form of a homemade strawberry jam) and cornstarch. By themselves, pectin produced a filling that was too firm and cornstarch one that was too loose. But together they created just the right supple, lightly clingy glaze.

GROWING UP, WE COULD HARDLY WAIT FOR THE KICKoff of strawberry season—farm stands would overflow with baskets of ripe red berries, which local bakeries would pile whole into fresh strawberry pies. The best of these desserts trade on nothing more than fresh-picked berries, a sheer glaze that just barely holds the fruit together while making it sparkle, and a flaky, buttery crust. Serving neat slices is downright impossible—the pie inevitably splits into shards of pastry and a tumble of berries—but in a dessert so good, looks hardly matter. Besides, mounds of whipped cream always cover the mess.

Though strawberry pie is a treat we've indulged in on an annual basis, we've never really learned to make it ourselves. But this summer we were determined to nail down our own approach. We figured it couldn't be hard, since, with the best ripe berries, the pie would practically make itself. But to our dismay, most of the recipes we tried were flawed, and the fruit's sweet juice was the culprit. Because the uncooked berries shed so much liquid (even when they were left whole), the filling had to be firmed up with some sort of thickener, producing results that ranged from stiff and bouncy to runny and gloppy—hardly the dessert we remembered.

Clearly, re-creating our ideal—fresh berries lightly held together by a sheer, glossy glaze that would make their flavor pop in the buttery pastry shell—hinged on our getting the thickener just right.

Most recipes attacked the excess liquid problem with cornstarch; we also found a few that called for gelatin. The thickener of choice was simmered in a pan with liquid (often a juice like pineapple or grape, even water), sugar, and a dash of salt; mixed with the fresh whole berries; mounded in a prebaked pie shell; and chilled to set. Predictably, the gelatin produced a stiff and springy filling. And the cornstarch was no better, rendering the berry mixture cloudy, gummy, and not at all firm. Adjusting the amount of each type of thickener didn't improve matters. Ramping up the cornstarch simply led to an increasingly gloppy, dull-tasting filling that never actually firmed up. As for the gelatin, the line between lightly thickened and stiff proved impossible to nail down (⅓ teaspoon, anyone?).

Maybe we were just using the wrong type of thickener. We spent the next few days working through alternatives (flour, arrowroot, potato starch, tapioca), as well as strawberry jam and even a grated apple—a trick we had learned when developing a recipe for blueberry pie, in which the apple's natural pectin seamlessly gels up the juicy fruit filling. But nothing panned out, and we were left with pies that were off-flavored, unpredictable, or gluey. The jam offered a reasonably thick texture, but its flavor was dull and cloying, and in this (mostly) fresh-fruit filling, bits of grated apple were hardly a subtle fix.

Frustrated, we decided to try a recipe we'd found that didn't use any added liquid or thickener at all. Instead, half of the uncooked berries were turned into a smooth, thick puree in the food processor, mixed with sugar, simmered briefly in a saucepan to thicken, and then combined with the fresh berries. The puree tasted bright and sweet and added body to the cut-up fruit, but we weren't surprised when it didn't prove to be sufficient.

NOTES FROM THE TEST KITCHEN

THROUGH THICK AND THIN

Most fresh strawberry pies fail because they're overloaded with thickeners that either gum up the filling or never manage to thicken it at all.

TOO STIFF

Thicken strawberry pie filling with gelatin and the result resembles Jell-O.

TOO RUNNY

Thicken strawberry pie filling with cornstarch and the result typically turns out gloppy, dull-tasting, and still not firm enough.

Even after we assembled and chilled the pie for a couple of hours, the filling oozed from each cut slice.

The cooked puree was a keeper, but there was no getting around it: Some form of added thickener was a must. We circled back to our earlier tests. Of all the thickeners we'd tried, jam had been the most promising, at least texture-wise. The gelling agent in jam, of course, is pectin. What if we made our own jam by adding pectin to the cooked puree? That way we could control how much of it to add and how long to simmer it with the puree, ideally preserving as much fresh-fruit flavor as possible. Pectin comes in two varieties, regular and low-sugar, the latter engineered to set without a surplus of sugar or acid. Since we didn't want to overload our naturally sweet berries with excess sugar, we mixed some of the low-sugar product into the puree and proceeded with our recipe. But as soon as the knife hit the pie's stiff, springy surface, we knew that we still hadn't found the solution.

We were tempted to give up on strawberry pie altogether when our science editor suggested something so obvious we couldn't believe we hadn't thought of it before: If we couldn't get the effect we wanted from one thickener, why not try two? After all, combining thickeners to produce a particular effect is exactly what the processed food industry does. Pectin still seemed like our best bet, so we considered what we might use with it. Gelatin was out—it would only exacerbate pectin's springiness. The "alternative" starches we tried had too many issues, and we crossed them off the list as well. That left cornstarch. The more we thought about it, the better the idea seemed. Since cornstarch on its own produced a filling that was too loose and pectin produced a filling that was too firm, a combination of the two might actually do the trick. Excited, we headed back into the test kitchen. After some tinkering, we finally hit upon a formula that worked. With ¾ cup puree, 2 tablespoons cornstarch, and 1½ teaspoons pectin, we managed to produce just the right supple, lightly clingy glaze.

We knew the berry juices would leach out eventually (sugar extracts moisture), but that didn't worry us. A pie this irresistible would never sit around.

Fresh Strawberry Pie

SERVES 8

To account for any imperfect strawberries, the ingredient list calls for several more ounces of berries than will be used in the pie. If possible, seek out ripe, farmers' market–quality berries. Make sure to thoroughly dry the strawberries after washing. Make certain that you use Sure-Jell engineered for low- or no-sugar recipes (packaged in a pink box) and not regular Sure-Jell (in a yellow box); otherwise, the glaze will not set properly. The pie is at its best after two or three hours of chilling; as it continues to chill, the glaze becomes softer and wetter, though the pie will taste just as good.

PIE

- **3 pounds strawberries, hulled (9 cups)**
- **¾ cup (5¼ ounces) sugar**
- **2 tablespoons cornstarch**
- **1½ teaspoons Sure-Jell for low-sugar recipes**
- **Pinch salt**
- **1 tablespoon lemon juice**
- **1 Baked Pie Shell, cooled (recipe follows)**

WHIPPED CREAM

- **1 cup heavy cream, chilled**
- **1 tablespoon sugar**

1. FOR THE PIE: Select 6 ounces misshapen, underripe, or otherwise unattractive berries, halving those that are large; you should have about 1½ cups. Process berries in food processor to smooth puree, 20 to 30 seconds, scraping down bowl as necessary (you should have about ¾ cup puree).

2. Whisk sugar, cornstarch, Sure-Jell, and salt together in medium saucepan. Stir in berry puree, making sure to scrape corners of pan. Cook over medium-high heat, stirring constantly, and bring to boil. Boil, scraping bottom and sides of pan to prevent scorching, for 2 minutes to ensure that cornstarch is fully cooked (mixture will appear frothy when it first reaches boil, then will darken and thicken with further cooking). Transfer glaze to large bowl and stir in lemon juice; let cool to room temperature.

3. Meanwhile, pick over remaining berries and measure out 2 pounds of most attractive ones; halve only extra-large berries. Add berries to bowl with glaze and fold gently with rubber spatula until berries are evenly coated. Scoop berries into cooled prebaked pie shell, piling into mound. If any cut sides face up on top, turn them face down. If necessary, rearrange berries so that holes are filled and mound looks attractive. Refrigerate pie until filling is chilled and has set, about 2 hours. Serve within 5 hours of chilling.

4. FOR THE WHIPPED CREAM: Just before serving, use stand mixer fitted with whisk to whip cream and sugar on medium-low speed until foamy, about 1 minute. Increase speed to high and whip until soft peaks form, 1 to 3 minutes.

5. Cut pie into wedges. Serve with whipped cream.

SCIENCE DESK

DOUBLING UP TO THICKEN JUICY FRUIT

To create a filling with just enough sticking power to hold the berries together gently, we turned to a thickener more common in jam than in pie—low-sugar pectin—and used it in combination with cornstarch. Both products work similarly: When combined with liquid, then heated and cooled, some of their molecules bond together, trapping water and creating a solid, jellylike structure. But the strength and properties of the two structures differ. Amylose, one of two types of starch molecules in cornstarch, forms a weak structure that easily comes apart under the weight of heavy, juice-filled strawberries. Low-sugar pectin (which, unlike regular pectin, gels without added sugar and acid) contains bigger molecules that form a firmer structure held together more forcefully by calcium ions. Once created, this matrix resists coming apart.

When used independently, neither product resulted in a suitable pie filling, but together they yielded a glaze with just the right texture.

TOGETHER IS BETTER

Low-Sugar Pectin + Cornstarch = Great Texture

Baked Pie Shell

MAKES ONE 9-INCH PIE SHELL

Vodka is essential to the texture of the crust and imparts no flavor—do not substitute water. This dough is moister than most standard pie doughs and will require lots of flour to roll out (up to ¼ cup).

- **1¼ cups (6¼ ounces) all-purpose flour**
- **1 tablespoon sugar**
- **½ teaspoon salt**
- **6 tablespoons unsalted butter, chilled and cut into ¼-inch slices**
- **4 tablespoons vegetable shortening, chilled and cut into 4 pieces**
- **2 tablespoons cold vodka**
- **2 tablespoons cold water**

1. Pulse ¾ cup flour, sugar, and salt together in food processor until combined, about 2 pulses. Add butter and shortening and process until homogeneous dough just starts to collect in uneven clumps, about 10 seconds (dough will resemble cottage cheese curds with some very small pieces of butter remaining, but there should be no uncoated flour). Scrape down sides and bottom of bowl with rubber spatula and redistribute dough evenly around processor blade. Add remaining ½ cup flour and pulse until mixture is evenly distributed around bowl and mass of dough has been broken up, 4 to 6 quick pulses. Empty mixture into bowl.

2. Sprinkle vodka and water over mixture. With rubber spatula, use folding motion to mix, pressing down on dough until dough is slightly tacky and sticks together. Flatten dough into 4-inch disk. Wrap in plastic wrap and refrigerate at least 45 minutes or up to 2 days.

3. Adjust oven rack to lowest position, place rimmed baking sheet on rack, and heat oven to 425 degrees. Remove dough from refrigerator and roll out on generously floured (up to ¼ cup) work surface to 12-inch circle about ⅛ inch thick. Roll dough loosely around rolling pin and unroll into pie plate, leaving at least 1-inch overhang on each side. Working around circumference, ease dough into plate by gently lifting edge of dough with 1 hand while pressing into plate bottom with other hand. Leave overhanging dough in place; refrigerate until dough is firm, about 30 minutes.

4. Trim overhang to ½ inch beyond lip of pie plate. Fold overhang under itself; folded edge should be flush with edge of pie plate. Flute dough or press tines of fork against dough to flatten against rim of pie plate. Refrigerate dough-lined plate until firm, about 15 minutes.

5. Remove pie plate from refrigerator, line crust with aluminum foil, and fill with pie weights or pennies. Bake for 15 minutes. Remove foil and weights, rotate plate, and bake for 5 to 10 longer, until crust is golden brown and crisp. Let cool to room temperature.

RATING PARING KNIVES

Nothing can compare with a chef's knife when it comes to sawing through large cuts of meat, chopping chunky vegetables, or transforming herbs into mince. But for detail work—hulling strawberries, coring fruit, scraping out vanilla beans, or trimming away a tough patch of silverskin on a roast—smaller, more maneuverable paring knives are far better tools. To find the best one, we gathered 10 models and subjected them to a range of tasks to determine their precision; ability to peel around curves; cutting ability, blade strength, and sharpness; user-friendliness and comfort level; and edge retention. In the end, the best paring knives had well-shaped blades with sharply pointed tips and narrow edges, a compact length, a good handle-to-blade balance and weight, and a comfortable grip that felt secure. Brands are listed in order of preference. See www.americastestkitchen.com for updates to this testing.

HIGHLY RECOMMENDED

WÜSTHOF Classic with PEtec, 3½-inch (model #4066)
PRICE: $39.95 **WEIGHT:** 2⅛ oz
PRECISION: ★★★ **PEELING:** ★★★ **CUTTING:** ★★★
USER-FRIENDLINESS: ★★★ **EDGE RETENTION:** ★★½
COMMENTS: This razor-sharp knife with "Precision Edge Technology—PEtec" was comfortable and well proportioned. A recent redesign gave it a narrower blade angle of 14 degrees (previously 19 degrees) on each side and a new plastic handle that feels like hard, smooth wood.

HENCKELS Four Star Paring Knife, 3-inch (model #31070-080 (Note: -083 is same knife, packaged in box))
PRICE: $24.99 **WEIGHT:** 1⅝ oz
PRECISION: ★★★ **PEELING:** ★★★ **CUTTING:** ★★½
USER-FRIENDLINESS: ★★½ **EDGE RETENTION:** ★★★
COMMENTS: This knife with a super-sharp edge and 15-degree blade angle would have tied with the winning Wüsthof but for its slightly too short 3-inch blade. That said, most testers preferred its "grippier" handle, and our final paper-slicing test showed that it retained its edge a bit better than the Wüsthof.

VICTORINOX Fibrox Paring Knife, 3¼-inch (model #40600)
PRICE: $4.95 BEST BUY **WEIGHT:** ¾ oz
PRECISION: ★★★ **PEELING:** ★★★ **CUTTING:** ★★★
USER-FRIENDLINESS: ★★ **EDGE RETENTION:** ★★½
COMMENTS: At a fraction of the price of the top two knives, this sharp, precise blade is a real bargain—and feels more secure in the hand than its 4-inch sibling. Our only gripe? It's a featherweight compared with other models and feels a bit flimsy and plasticky.

RECOMMENDED

KUHN RIKON Paring Knife Colori I Nonstick, 3½-inch (model #2808)
PRICE: $10 **WEIGHT:** 1⅛ oz (without sheath)
PRECISION: ★★ **PEELING:** ★★½ **CUTTING:** ★★★
USER-FRIENDLINESS: ★★½ **EDGE RETENTION:** ★★½
COMMENTS: This inexpensive, lightweight knife was comfortable to hold and came with a snug sheath. Its stiff, nonstick-coated blade felt a bit unwieldy for intricate tasks—and the coating itself was generally superfluous—but the cutting edge was razor-sharp and slid through shallots with ease.

DEXTER-RUSSELL V-Lo Paring Knife, 3½-inch (model #V105-CP)
PRICE: $7.30 **WEIGHT:** ¾ oz
PRECISION: ★★ **PEELING:** ★★ **CUTTING:** ★★
USER-FRIENDLINESS: ★★½ **EDGE RETENTION:** ★★
COMMENTS: While we appreciated this knife's sharp blade, the ribbed, slim-waisted plastic handle and extreme lightweight design divided testers' votes: Those with small hands deemed it "a pleasure to hold," while those with large hands felt that it was "too insubstantial" and "like a toy."

VICTORINOX Fibrox Paring Knife, 4-inch (model #40501)
PRICE: $4.95 **WEIGHT:** ¾ oz
PRECISION: ★ **PEELING:** ★★½ **CUTTING:** ★★½
USER-FRIENDLINESS: ★★ **EDGE RETENTION:** ★★½
COMMENTS: "Nice, sharp" blade. But while the extra ¾ inch on this larger Victorinox twin came in handy for slicing fruit and cheese, it was too much metal for most testers, who complained that the elongated blade felt unwieldy during intricate tasks like hulling berries.

RECOMMENDED WITH RESERVATIONS

SHUN Classic Paring Knife, 3½-inch (model #DM0700)
PRICE: $70 **WEIGHT:** 2⅛ oz
PRECISION: ★½ **PEELING:** ★★½ **CUTTING:** ★★★
USER-FRIENDLINESS: ★ **EDGE RETENTION:** ★★½
COMMENTS: Though wonderfully sharp, this knife was handle-heavy and slick, making it awkward for cutting tasks like berry hulling. And at nearly twice the cost of our winner, we just couldn't bring ourselves to shell out for it.

CONVERSIONS & EQUIVALENCIES

SOME SAY COOKING IS A SCIENCE AND AN ART. WE would say that geography has a hand in it, too. Flour milled in the United Kingdom and elsewhere will feel and taste different from flour milled in the United States. So, while we cannot promise that the loaf of bread you bake in Canada or England will taste the same as a loaf baked in the States, we can offer guidelines for converting weights and measures. We also recommend that you rely on your instincts when making our recipes. Refer to the visual cues provided. If the bread dough hasn't "come together in a ball," as described, you may need to add more flour—even if the recipe doesn't tell you so. You be the judge.

The recipes in this book were developed using standard U.S. measures following U.S. government guidelines. The charts below offer equivalents for U.S., metric, and imperial (U.K.) measures. All conversions are approximate and have been rounded up or down to the nearest whole number. For example:

1 teaspoon = 4.929 milliliters, rounded up to 5 milliliters
1 ounce = 28.349 grams, rounded down to 28 grams

VOLUME CONVERSIONS

U.S.	METRIC
1 teaspoon	5 milliliters
2 teaspoons	10 milliliters
1 tablespoon	15 milliliters
2 tablespoons	30 milliliters
¼ cup	59 milliliters
⅓ cup	79 milliliters
½ cup	118 milliliters
¾ cup	177 milliliters
1 cup	237 milliliters
1¼ cups	296 milliliters
1½ cups	355 milliliters
2 cups	473 milliliters
2½ cups	591 milliliters
3 cups	710 milliliters
4 cups (1 quart)	0.946 liter
1.06 quarts	1 liter
4 quarts (1 gallon)	3.8 liters

WEIGHT CONVERSIONS

OUNCES	GRAMS
½	14
¾	21
1	28
1½	43
2	57
2½	71
3	85
3½	99
4	113
4½	128
5	142
6	170
7	198
8	227
9	255
10	283
12	340
16 (1 pound)	454

CONVERSIONS FOR INGREDIENTS COMMONLY USED IN BAKING

Baking is an exacting science. Because measuring by weight is far more accurate than measuring by volume, and thus more likely to achieve reliable results, in our recipes we provide ounce measures in addition to cup measures for many ingredients. Refer to the chart below to convert these measures into grams.

INGREDIENT	OUNCES	GRAMS
Flour		
1 cup all-purpose flour*	5	142
1 cup cake flour	4	113
1 cup whole wheat flour	5½	156
Sugar		
1 cup granulated (white) sugar	7	198
1 cup packed brown sugar (light or dark)	7	198
1 cup confectioners' sugar	4	113
Cocoa Powder		
1 cup cocoa powder	3	85
Butter†		
4 tablespoons (½ stick, or ¼ cup)	2	57
8 tablespoons (1 stick, or ½ cup)	4	113
16 tablespoons (2 sticks, or 1 cup)	8	227

* U.S. all-purpose flour, the most frequently used flour in this book, does not contain leaveners, as some European flours do. These leavened flours are called self-rising or self-raising. If you are using self-rising flour, take this into consideration before adding leavening to a recipe.

† In the United States, butter is sold both salted and unsalted. We generally recommend unsalted butter. If you are using salted butter, take this into consideration before adding salt to a recipe.

OVEN TEMPERATURES

FAHRENHEIT	CELSIUS	GAS MARK (imperial)
225	105	¼
250	120	½
275	135	1
300	150	2
325	165	3
350	180	4
375	190	5
400	200	6
425	220	7
450	230	8
475	245	9

CONVERTING TEMPERATURES FROM AN INSTANT-READ THERMOMETER

We include doneness temperatures in many of our recipes, such as those for poultry, meat, and bread. We recommend an instant-read thermometer for the job. Refer to the table above to convert Fahrenheit degrees to Celsius. Or, for temperatures not represented in the chart, use this simple formula:

Subtract 32 degrees from the Fahrenheit reading, then divide the result by 1.8 to find the Celsius reading.

EXAMPLE:

"Roast until the thickest part of a chicken thigh registers 175 degrees on an instant-read thermometer." To convert:

175° F - 32 = 143°
143° ÷ 1.8 = 79.44°C, rounded down to 79°C

INDEX

Note: Page references in *italics* indicate photographs.

C

E

F

G

H

I

J

K

L

M

N

O

P

Q

R

S

T

V

W

Y

Z